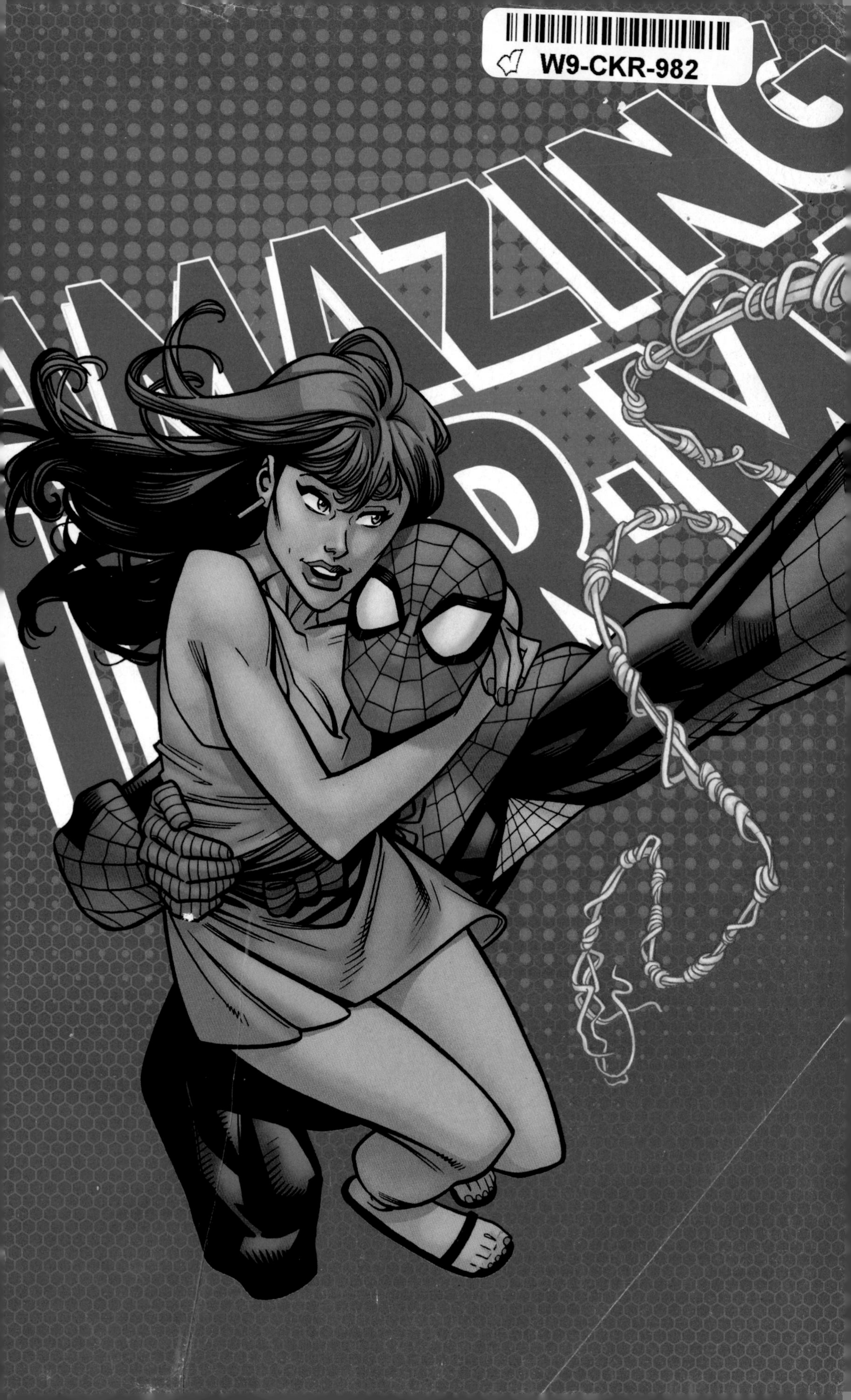

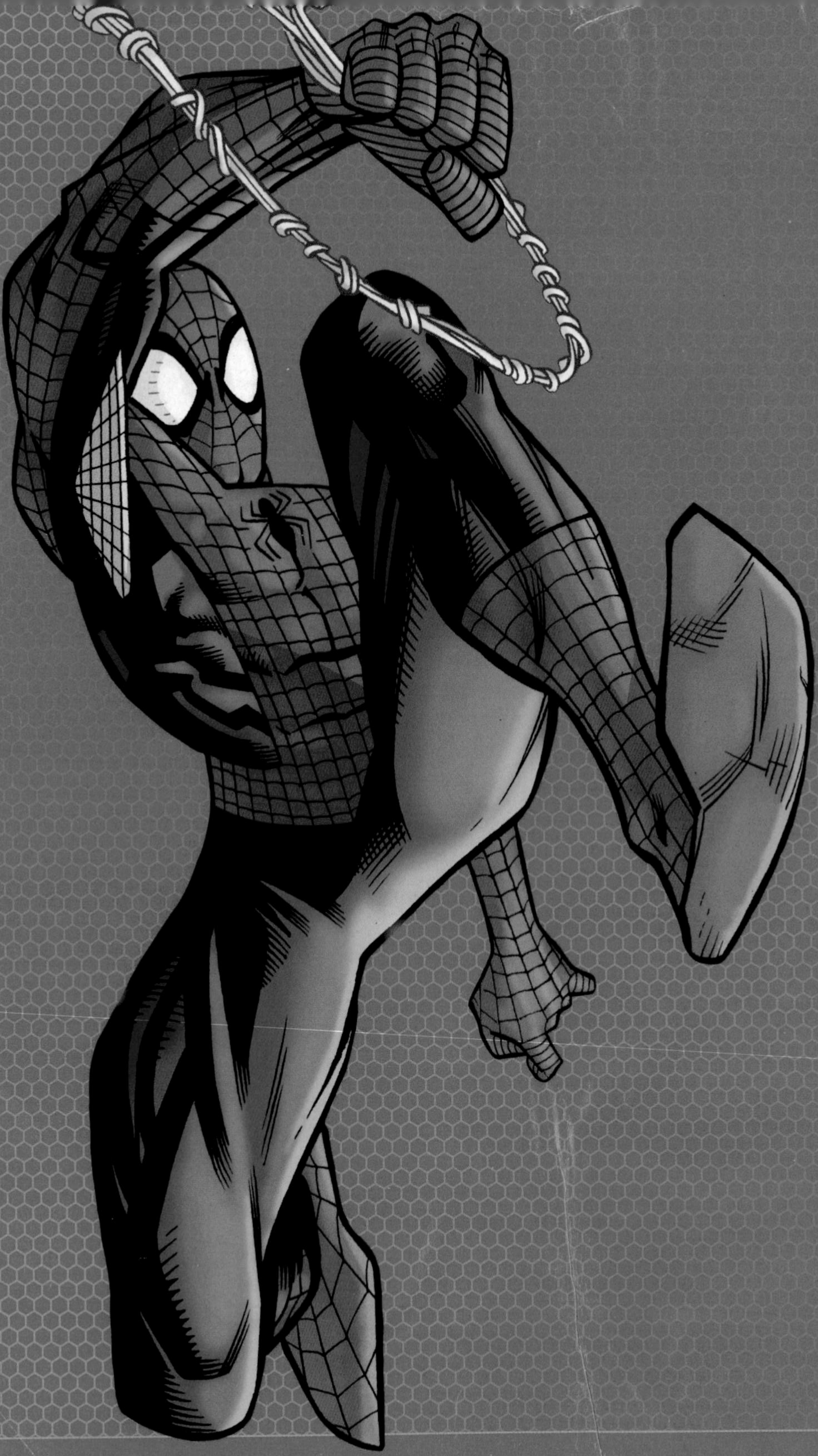

Between an alien invasion faked by Mysterio, the Robot-Master's Tri-Sentinel, the entire Bar With No Name, the entire Thieves Guild of New York, Scorpion and the son of Big Man, and then Kraven the Hunter plus Arcade, Kraven's son, and more animal-themed goons than you can name, you'd almost think Spider-Man hasn't had time to worry about any problem that's not literally beating him up. But there are a few things Pete always makes time for...

THE AMAZING SPIDER-MAN

BEHIND THE SCENES

WRITER **NICK SPENCER**

PENCILERS **RYAN OTTLEY** (#24-25), **HUMBERTO RAMOS** (#25),
PAT GLEASON (#25) & **KEV WALKER** (#25-28)

INKERS **MARK MORALES** (#24), **CLIFF RATHBURN** (#24-25),
VICTOR OLAZABA (#25), **DEXTER VINES** (#25),
PAT GLEASON (#25), **KEV WALKER** (#25-26) &
JOHN DELL (#27)

COLORISTS **NATHAN FAIRBAIRN** (#24-25), **EDGAR DELGADO** (#25),
DAVE STEWART (#25), **LAURA MARTIN** (#25-28) &
ANDREW CROSSLEY (#28)

"TEAM-UP"
WRITER **ZEB WELLS**
ARTIST **TODD NAUCK**
COLORIST **RACHELLE ROSENBERG**

"ROBO-HELPERS"
WRITER **KEATON PATTI**
ARTIST **DAN HIPP**

VC's JOE CARAMAGNA
LETTERER

RYAN OTTLEY &
NATHAN FAIRBAIRN
COVER ART

KATHLEEN WISNESKI
ASSISTANT EDITOR

NICK LOWE
EDITOR

SPIDER-MAN CREATED BY STAN LEE & STEVE DITKO

COLLECTION EDITOR MARK D. BEAZLEY
ASSISTANT EDITOR CAITLIN O'CONNELL ✦ ASSOCIATE MANAGING EDITOR KATERI WOODY
SENIOR EDITOR, SPECIAL PROJECTS JENNIFER GRÜNWALD ✦ VP PRODUCTION & SPECIAL PROJECTS JEFF YOUNGQUIST
BOOK DESIGNERS STACIE ZUCKER WITH JAY BOWEN

SVP PRINT, SALES & MARKETING DAVID GABRIEL ✦ DIRECTOR, LICENSED PUBLISHING SVEN LARSEN
EDITOR IN CHIEF C.B. CEBULSKI ✦ CHIEF CREATIVE OFFICER JOE QUESADA
PRESIDENT DAN BUCKLEY ✦ EXECUTIVE PRODUCER ALAN FINE

AMAZING SPIDER-MAN BY NICK SPENCER VOL. 5: BEHIND THE SCENES. Contains material originally published in magazine form as AMAZING SPIDER-MAN #24-28. First printing 2019. ISBN 978-1-302-91435-6. Published by MARVEL WORLDWIDE, INC., a subsidiary of MARVEL ENTERTAINMENT, LLC. OFFICE OF PUBLICATION: 135 West 50th Street, New York, NY 10020. © 2019 MARVEL No similarity between any of the names, characters, persons, and/or institutions in this magazine with those of any living or dead person or institution is intended, and any such similarity which may exist is purely coincidental. **Printed in the U.S.A.** DAN BUCKLEY, President, Marvel Entertainment; JOHN NEE, Publisher; JOE QUESADA, Chief Creative Officer; TOM BREVOORT, SVP of Publishing; DAVID BOGART, Associate Publisher & SVP of Talent Affairs; DAVID GABRIEL, SVP of Sales & Marketing, Publishing; JEFF YOUNGQUIST, VP of Production & Special Projects; DAN CARR, Executive Director of Publishing Technology; ALEX MORALES, Director of Publishing Operations; DAN EDINGTON, Managing Editor; SUSAN CRESPI, Production Manager; STAN LEE, Chairman Emeritus. For information regarding advertising in Marvel Comics or on Marvel.com, please contact Vit DeBellis, Custom Solutions & Integrated Advertising Manager, at vdebellis@marvel.com. For Marvel subscription inquiries, please call 888-511-5480. **Manufactured between 8/30/2019 and 10/1/2019 by LSC COMMUNICATIONS INC., KENDALLVILLE, IN, USA.**

10 9 8 7 6 5 4 3 2 1

24

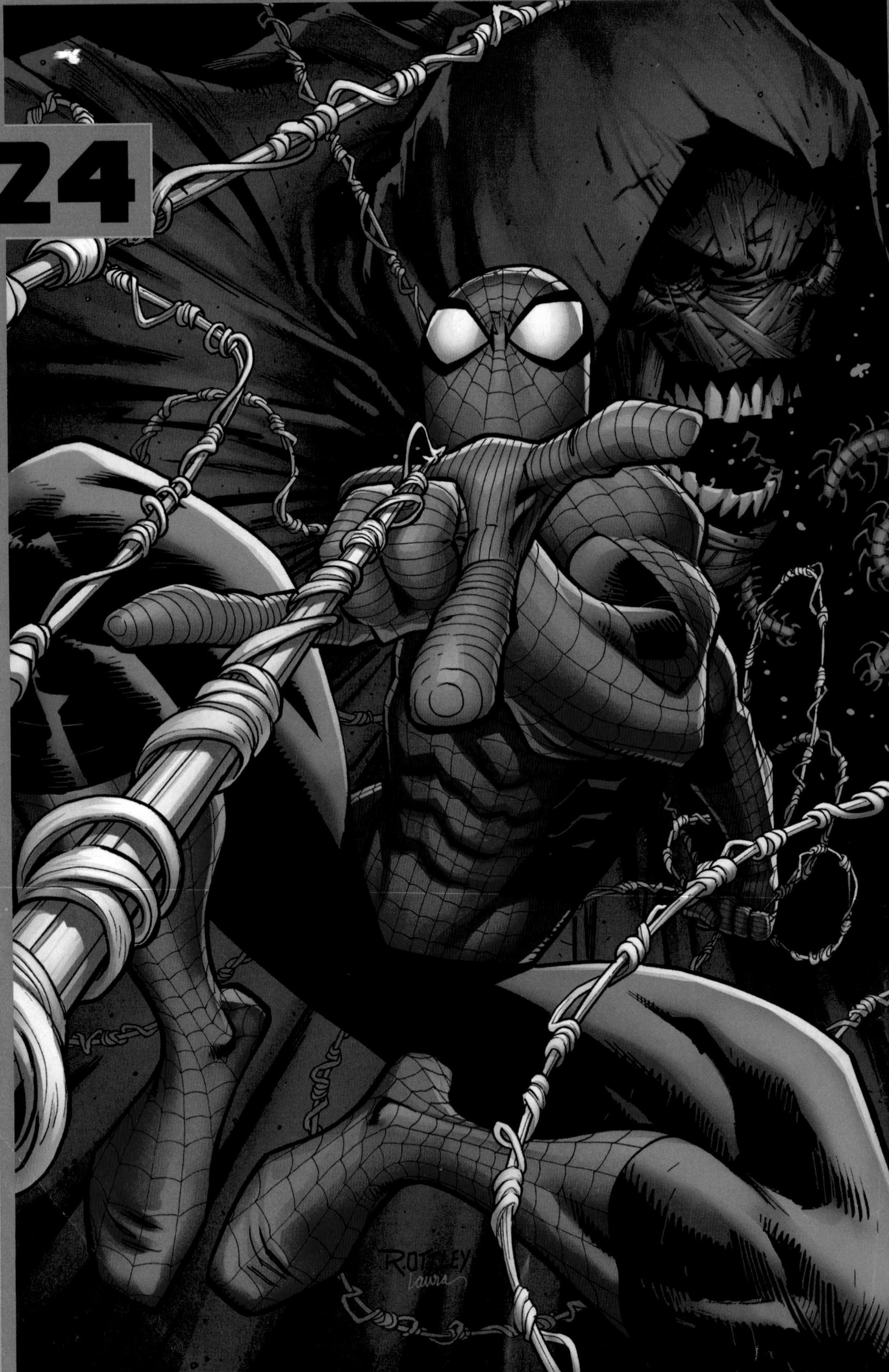

ONE-ON-ONE

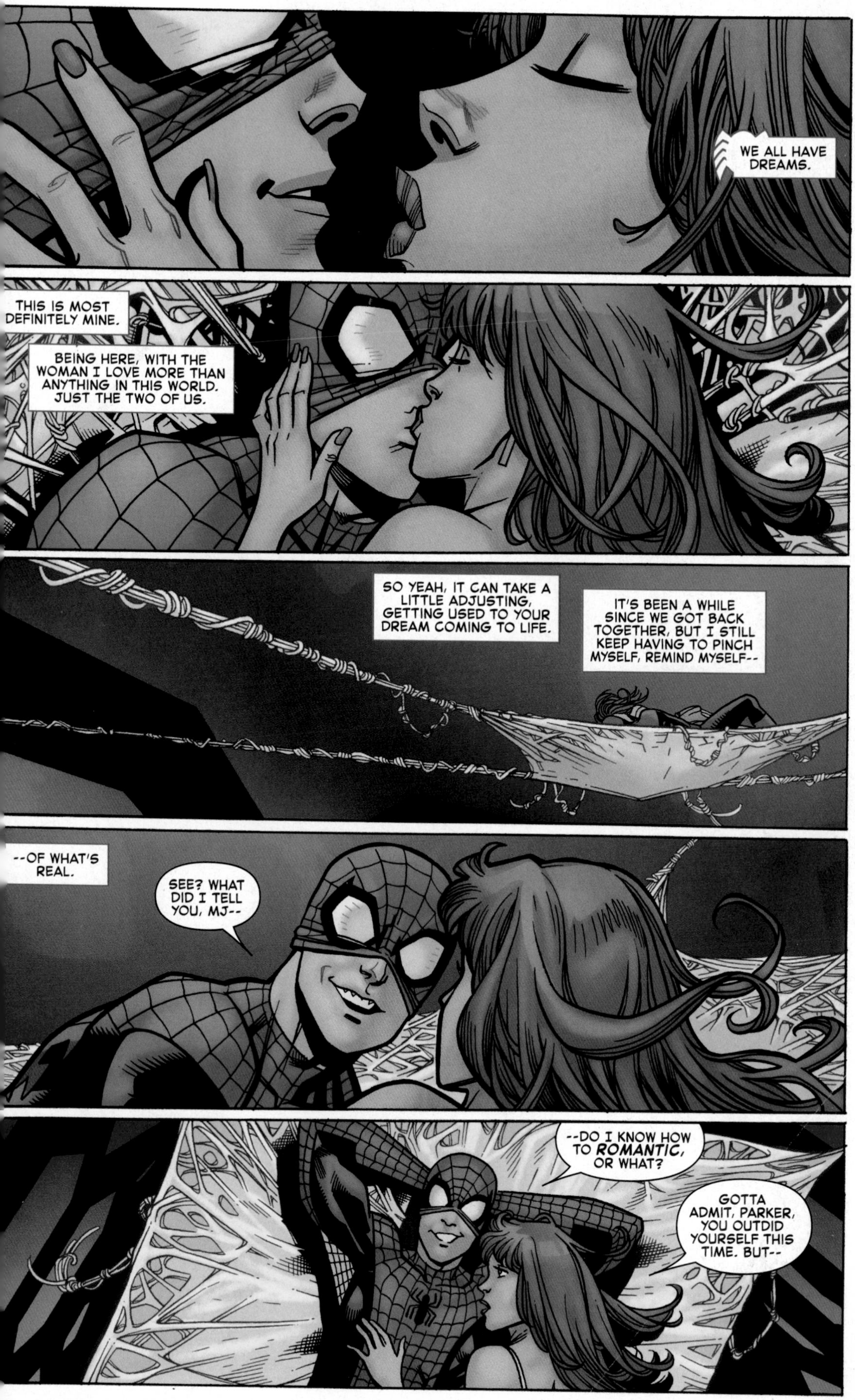
WE ALL HAVE DREAMS.
THIS IS MOST DEFINITELY MINE.
BEING HERE, WITH THE WOMAN I LOVE MORE THAN ANYTHING IN THIS WORLD. JUST THE TWO OF US.
SO YEAH, IT CAN TAKE A LITTLE ADJUSTING, GETTING USED TO YOUR DREAM COMING TO LIFE.
IT'S BEEN A WHILE SINCE WE GOT BACK TOGETHER, BUT I STILL KEEP HAVING TO PINCH MYSELF, REMIND MYSELF--
--OF WHAT'S REAL.
SEE? WHAT DID I TELL YOU, MJ--
--DO I KNOW HOW TO *ROMANTIC*, OR WHAT?
GOTTA ADMIT, PARKER, YOU OUTDID YOURSELF THIS TIME. BUT--

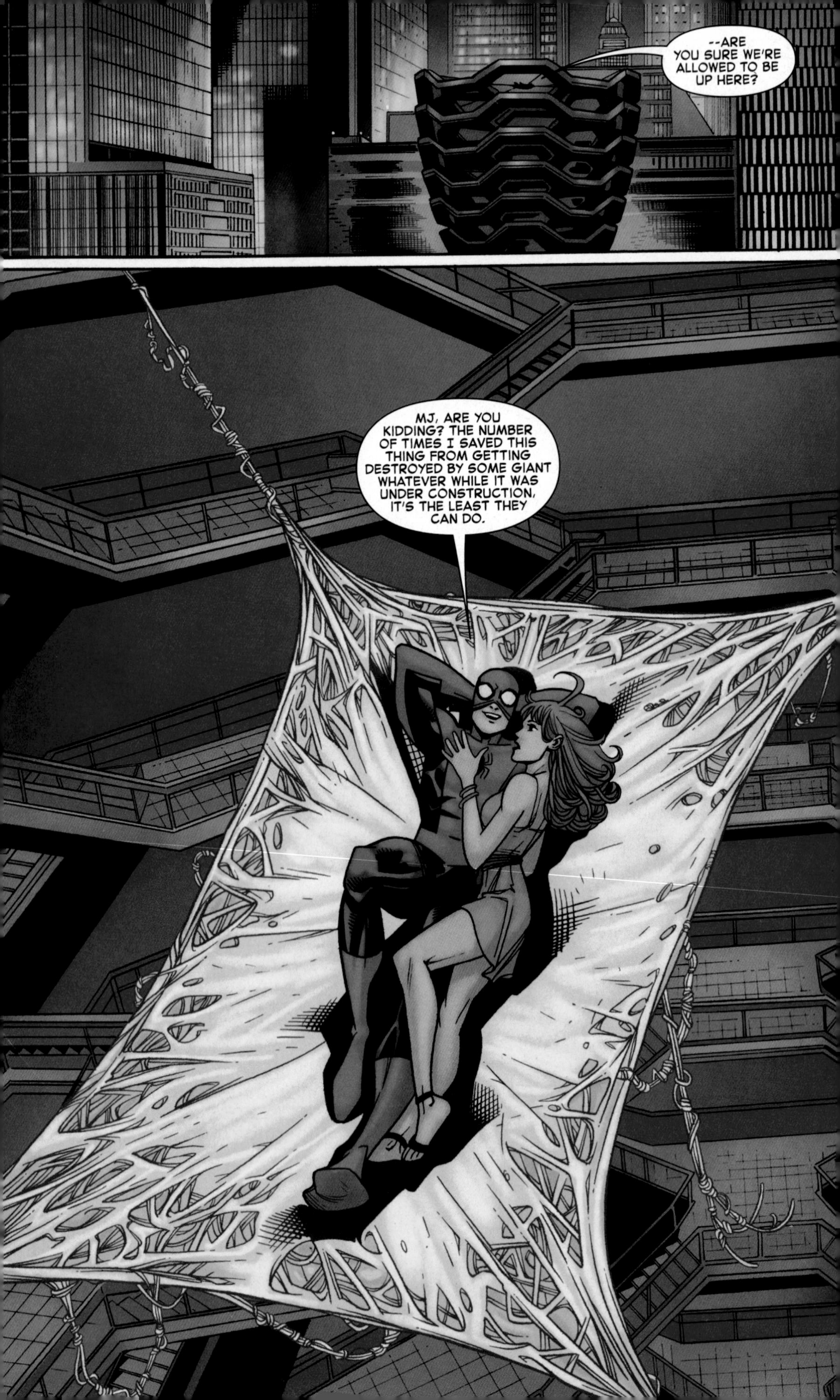
--ARE YOU SURE WE'RE ALLOWED TO BE UP HERE?
MJ, ARE YOU KIDDING? THE NUMBER OF TIMES I SAVED THIS THING FROM GETTING DESTROYED BY SOME GIANT WHATEVER WHILE IT WAS UNDER CONSTRUCTION, IT'S THE LEAST THEY CAN DO.

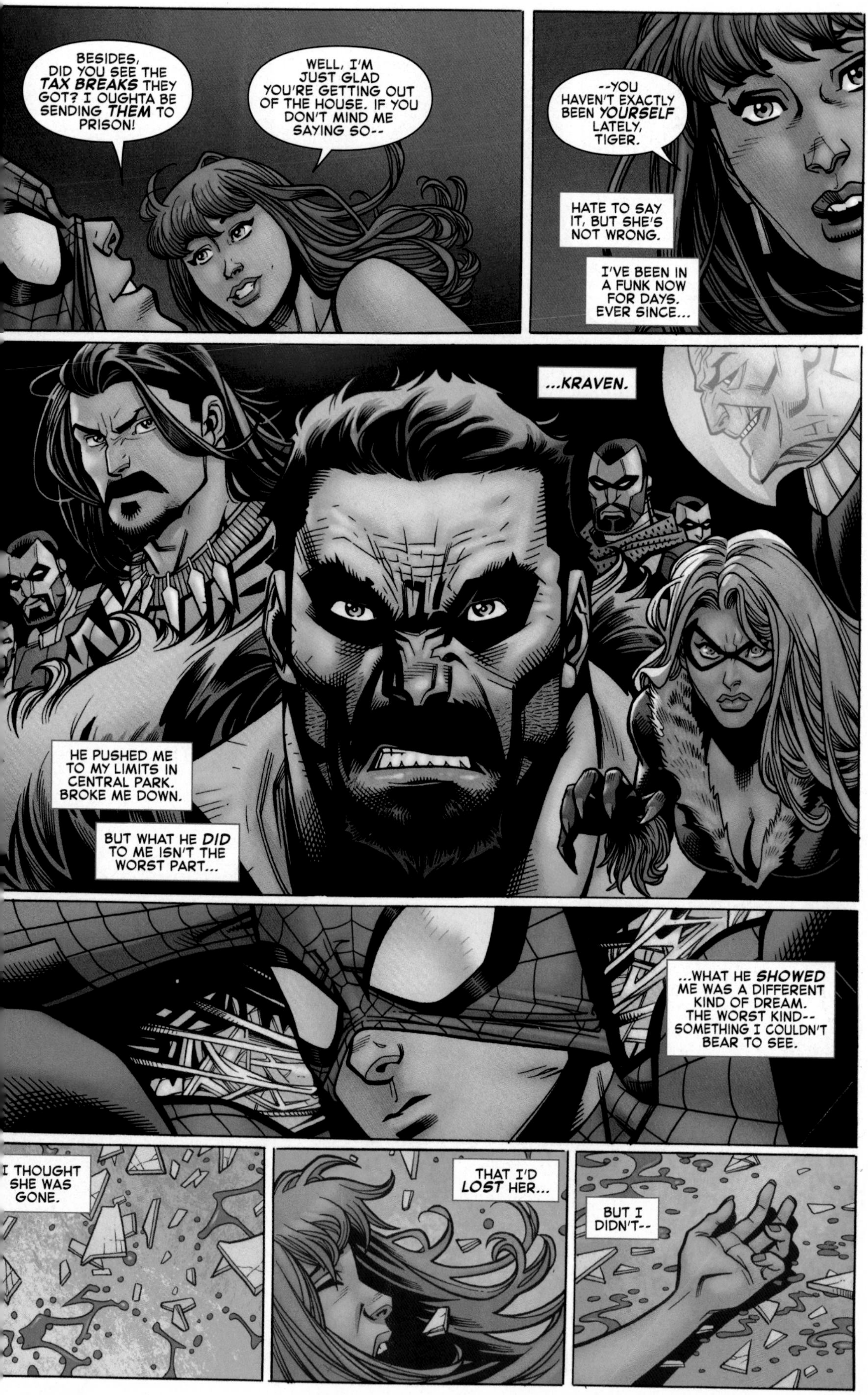
BESIDES, DID YOU SEE THE TAX BREAKS THEY GOT? I OUGHTA BE SENDING THEM TO PRISON!
WELL, I'M JUST GLAD YOU'RE GETTING OUT OF THE HOUSE. IF YOU DON'T MIND ME SAYING SO--
--YOU HAVEN'T EXACTLY BEEN YOURSELF LATELY, TIGER.
HATE TO SAY IT, BUT SHE'S NOT WRONG.
I'VE BEEN IN A FUNK NOW FOR DAYS. EVER SINCE...
...KRAVEN.
HE PUSHED ME TO MY LIMITS IN CENTRAL PARK. BROKE ME DOWN.
BUT WHAT HE DID TO ME ISN'T THE WORST PART...
...WHAT HE SHOWED ME WAS A DIFFERENT KIND OF DREAM. THE WORST KIND--SOMETHING I COULDN'T BEAR TO SEE.
I THOUGHT SHE WAS GONE.
THAT I'D LOST HER...
BUT I DIDN'T--

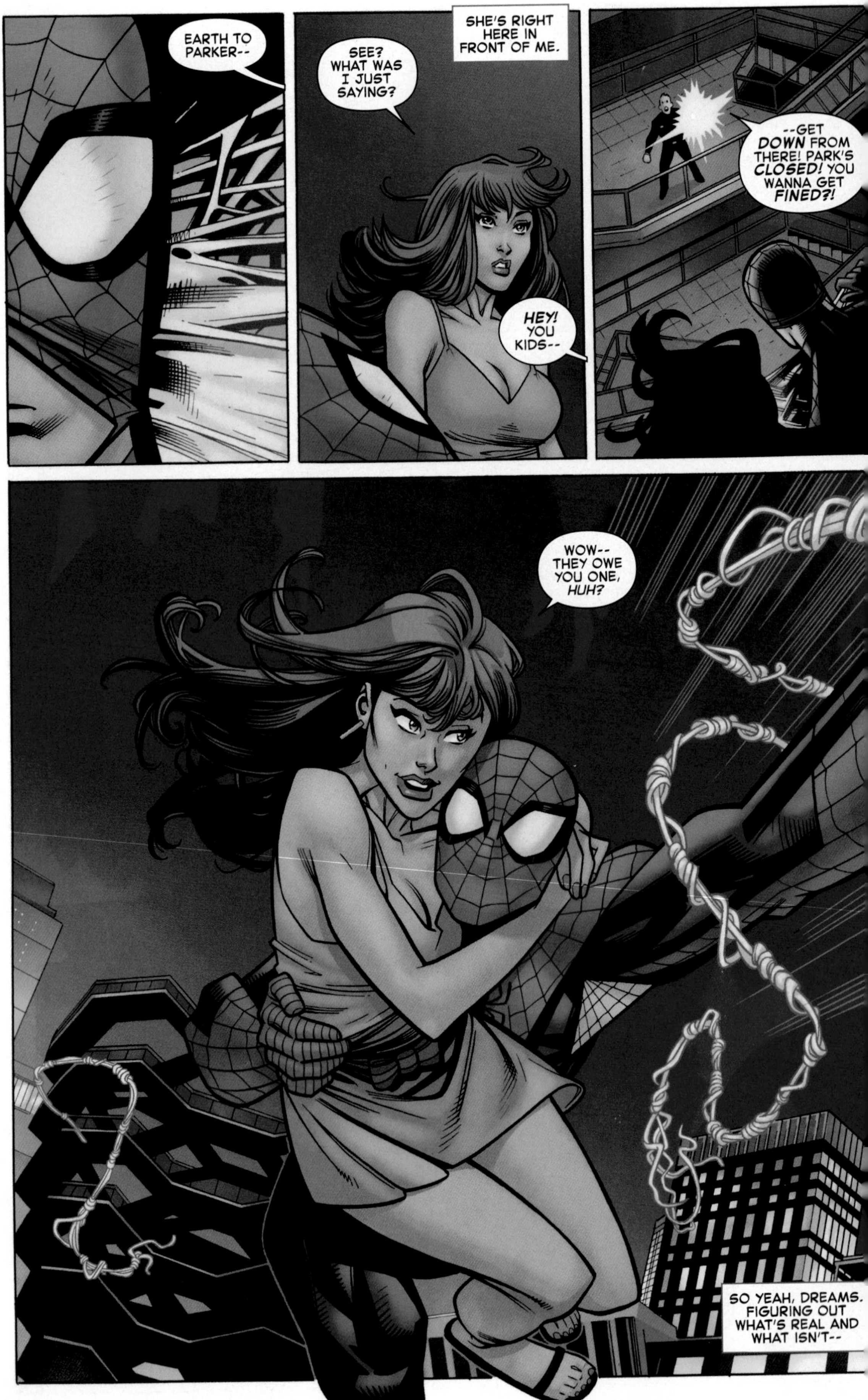
EARTH TO PARKER--
SEE? WHAT WAS I JUST SAYING?
SHE'S RIGHT HERE IN FRONT OF ME.
HEY! YOU KIDS--
--GET DOWN FROM THERE! PARK'S CLOSED! YOU WANNA GET FINED?!
WOW-- THEY OWE YOU ONE, HUH?
SO YEAH, DREAMS. FIGURING OUT WHAT'S REAL AND WHAT ISN'T--

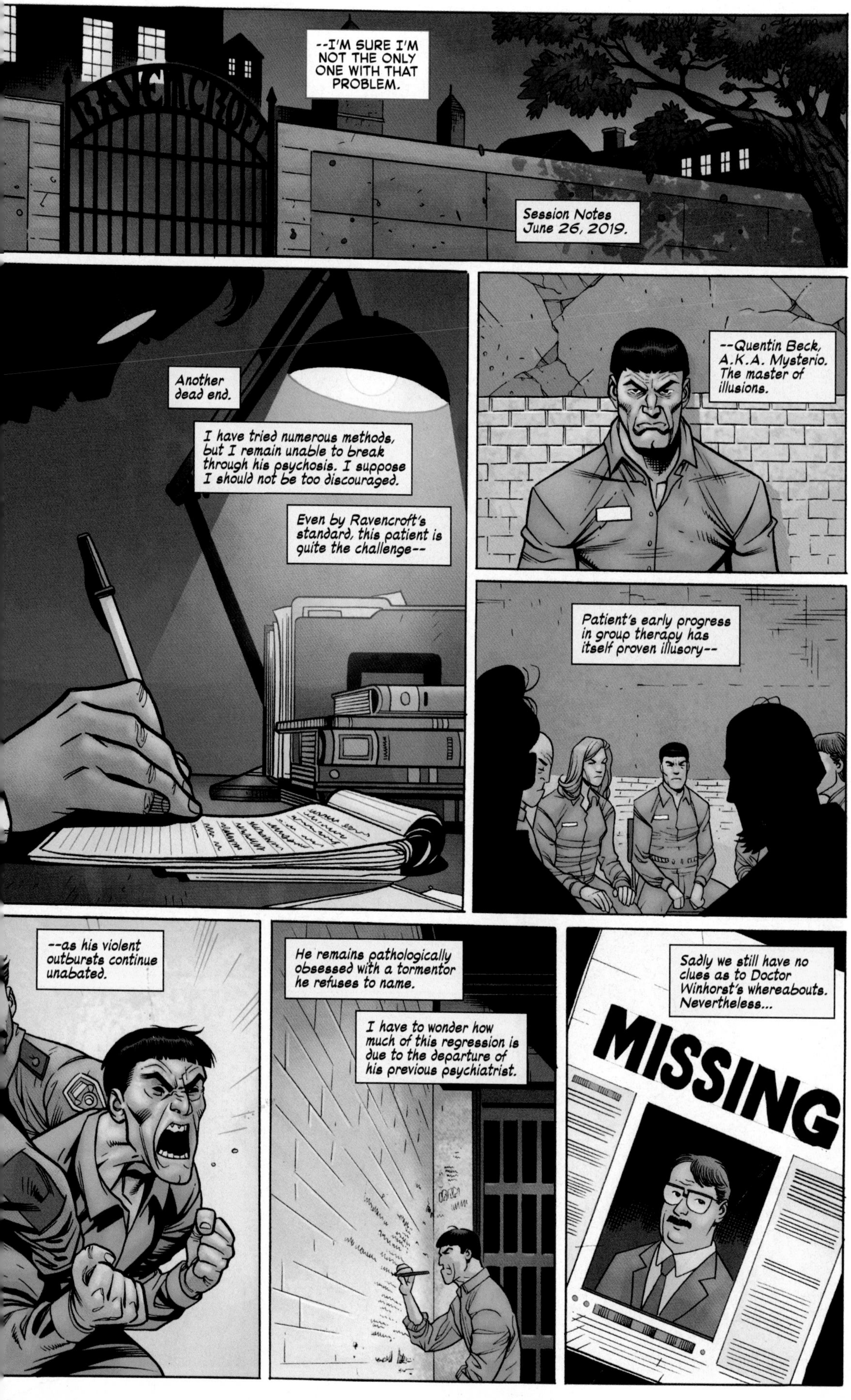
--I'M SURE I'M NOT THE ONLY ONE WITH THAT PROBLEM.
RAVENCROFT
Session Notes June 26, 2019.
Another dead end.
I have tried numerous methods, but I remain unable to break through his psychosis. I suppose I should not be too discouraged.
Even by Ravencroft's standard, this patient is quite the challenge--
--Quentin Beck, A.K.A. Mysterio. The master of illusions.
Patient's early progress in group therapy has itself proven illusory--
--as his violent outbursts continue unabated.
He remains pathologically obsessed with a tormentor he refuses to name.
I have to wonder how much of this regression is due to the departure of his previous psychiatrist.
Sadly we still have no clues as to Doctor Winhorst's whereabouts. Nevertheless...
MISSING

We must persevere in our treatment.

I SUPPOSE I JUST FEEL AS THOUGH THERE ARE NO MORE MOUNTAINS TO CLIMB, DOCTOR. THAT I'VE REACHED THE PINNACLE OF MY CAREER.

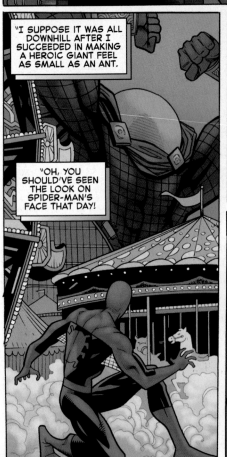

"I SUPPOSE IT WAS ALL DOWNHILL AFTER I SUCCEEDED IN MAKING A HEROIC GIANT FEEL AS SMALL AS AN ANT.

"OH, YOU SHOULD'VE SEEN THE LOOK ON SPIDER-MAN'S FACE THAT DAY!

"THAT'S NOT TO SAY THERE HAVEN'T BEEN REAL HIGH POINTS SINCE THEN. DID I EVER TELL YOU ABOUT MAKING J. JONAH JAMESON SEE THE DEVIL HIMSELF?"

"MR. BECK, PLEASE--"

--THIS IS NOT WHAT WE WERE SCHEDULED TO DISCUSS TODAY.

OH? FORGIVE ME, DOCTOR--THE CREATIVE MIND. ONE CAN NEVER TELL WHERE INSPIRATION LEADS...

WE'VE BEEN TRYING TO DISCUSS IT FOR SEVERAL SESSIONS, ACTUALLY...

I'D LIKE YOU TO TELL ME ABOUT THE TIME YOU DIED.

...

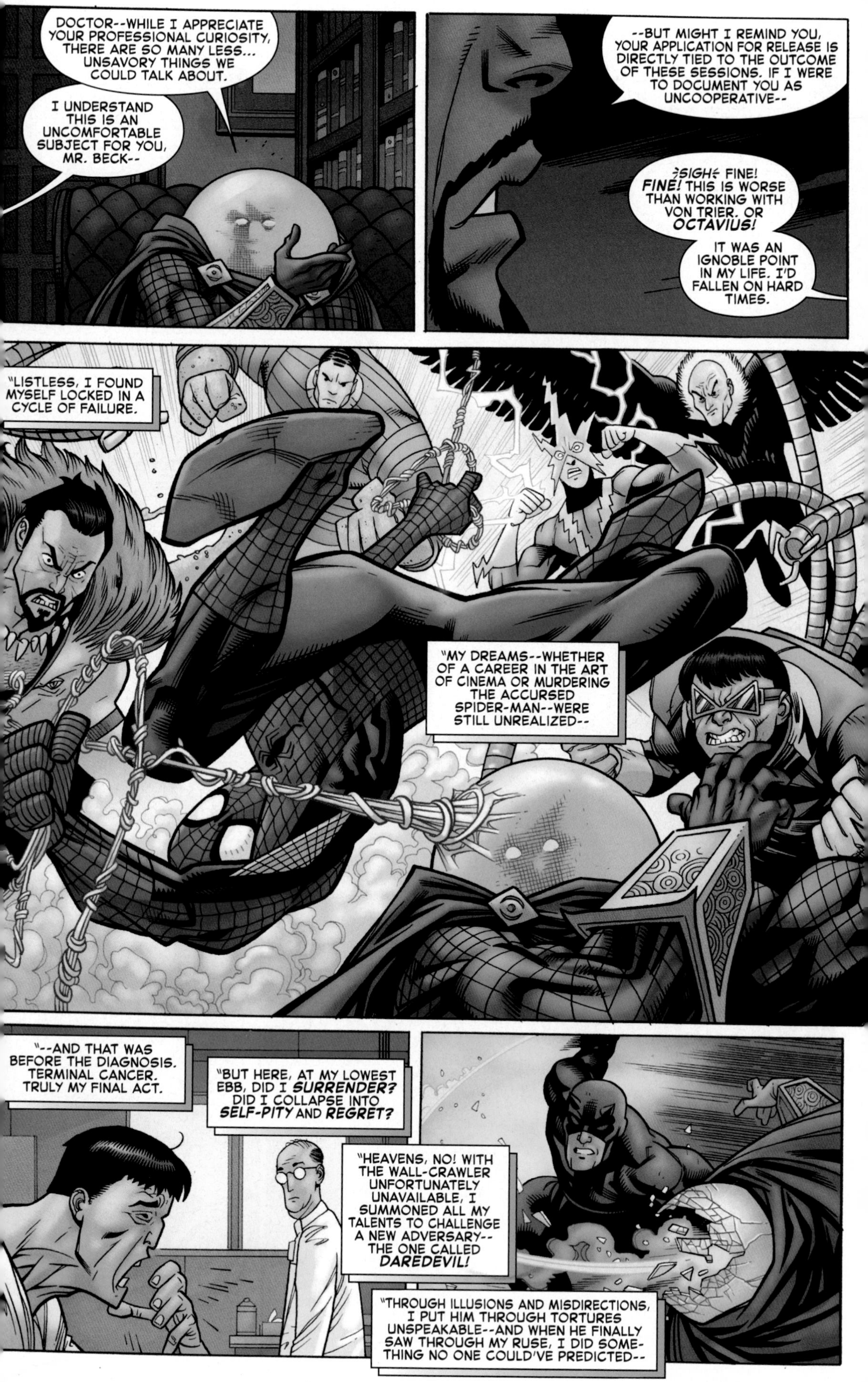
DOCTOR--WHILE I APPRECIATE YOUR PROFESSIONAL CURIOSITY, THERE ARE SO MANY LESS... UNSAVORY THINGS WE COULD TALK ABOUT.
I UNDERSTAND THIS IS AN UNCOMFORTABLE SUBJECT FOR YOU, MR. BECK--
--BUT MIGHT I REMIND YOU, YOUR APPLICATION FOR RELEASE IS DIRECTLY TIED TO THE OUTCOME OF THESE SESSIONS. IF I WERE TO DOCUMENT YOU AS UNCOOPERATIVE--
SIGH FINE! FINE! THIS IS WORSE THAN WORKING WITH VON TRIER. OR OCTAVIUS!
IT WAS AN IGNOBLE POINT IN MY LIFE. I'D FALLEN ON HARD TIMES.
"LISTLESS, I FOUND MYSELF LOCKED IN A CYCLE OF FAILURE.
"MY DREAMS--WHETHER OF A CAREER IN THE ART OF CINEMA OR MURDERING THE ACCURSED SPIDER-MAN--WERE STILL UNREALIZED--
"--AND THAT WAS BEFORE THE DIAGNOSIS. TERMINAL CANCER. TRULY MY FINAL ACT.
"BUT HERE, AT MY LOWEST EBB, DID I SURRENDER? DID I COLLAPSE INTO SELF-PITY AND REGRET?
"HEAVENS, NO! WITH THE WALL-CRAWLER UNFORTUNATELY UNAVAILABLE, I SUMMONED ALL MY TALENTS TO CHALLENGE A NEW ADVERSARY--THE ONE CALLED DAREDEVIL!
"THROUGH ILLUSIONS AND MISDIRECTIONS, I PUT HIM THROUGH TORTURES UNSPEAKABLE--AND WHEN HE FINALLY SAW THROUGH MY RUSE, I DID SOMETHING NO ONE COULD'VE PREDICTED--

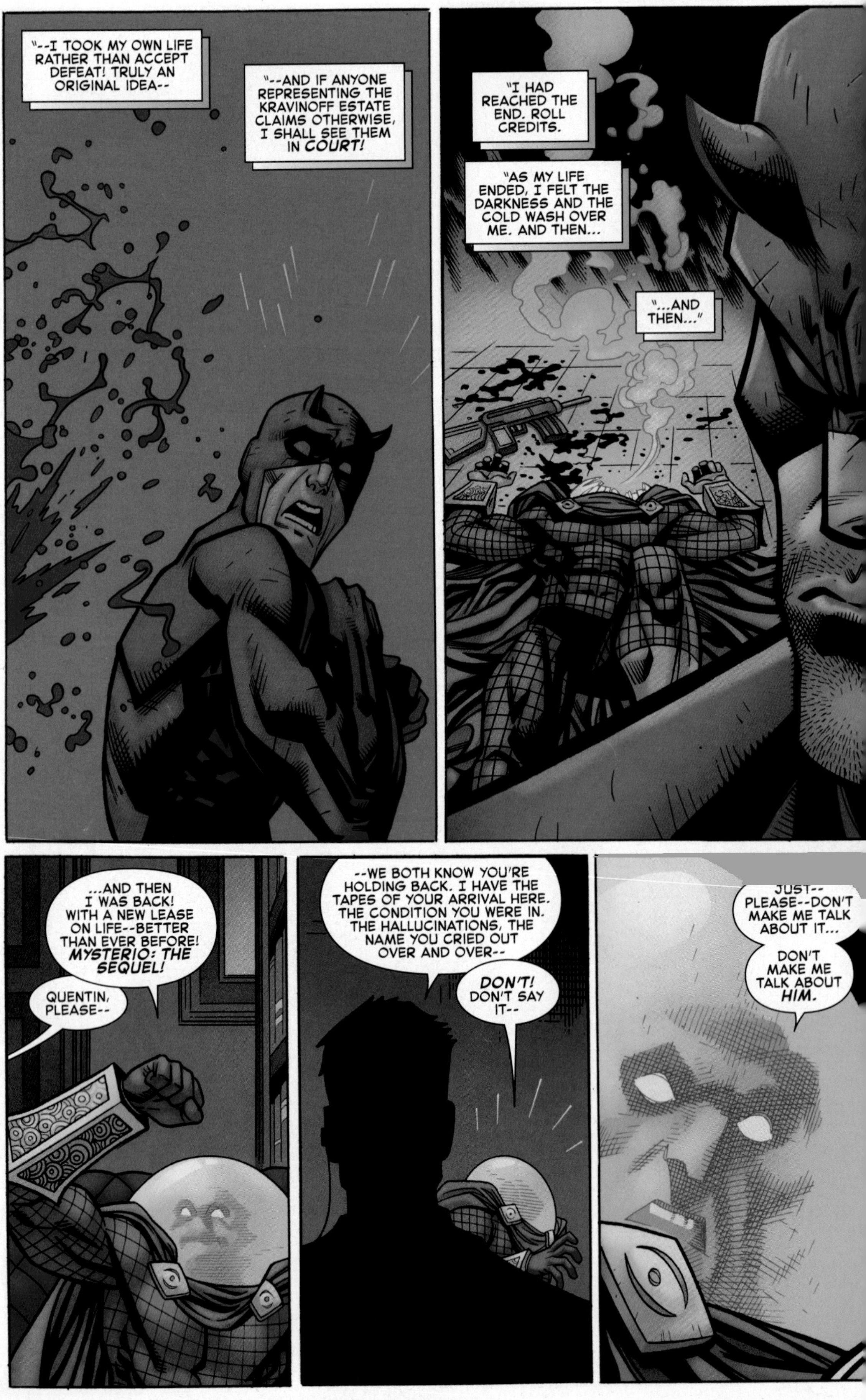
"--I TOOK MY OWN LIFE RATHER THAN ACCEPT DEFEAT! TRULY AN ORIGINAL IDEA--
"--AND IF ANYONE REPRESENTING THE KRAVINOFF ESTATE CLAIMS OTHERWISE, I SHALL SEE THEM IN COURT!
"I HAD REACHED THE END. ROLL CREDITS.
"AS MY LIFE ENDED, I FELT THE DARKNESS AND THE COLD WASH OVER ME. AND THEN...
"...AND THEN..."
...AND THEN I WAS BACK! WITH A NEW LEASE ON LIFE--BETTER THAN EVER BEFORE! MYSTERIO: THE SEQUEL!
QUENTIN, PLEASE--
--WE BOTH KNOW YOU'RE HOLDING BACK. I HAVE THE TAPES OF YOUR ARRIVAL HERE. THE CONDITION YOU WERE IN. THE HALLUCINATIONS, THE NAME YOU CRIED OUT OVER AND OVER--
DON'T! DON'T SAY IT--
JUST--PLEASE--DON'T MAKE ME TALK ABOUT IT...
DON'T MAKE ME TALK ABOUT HIM.

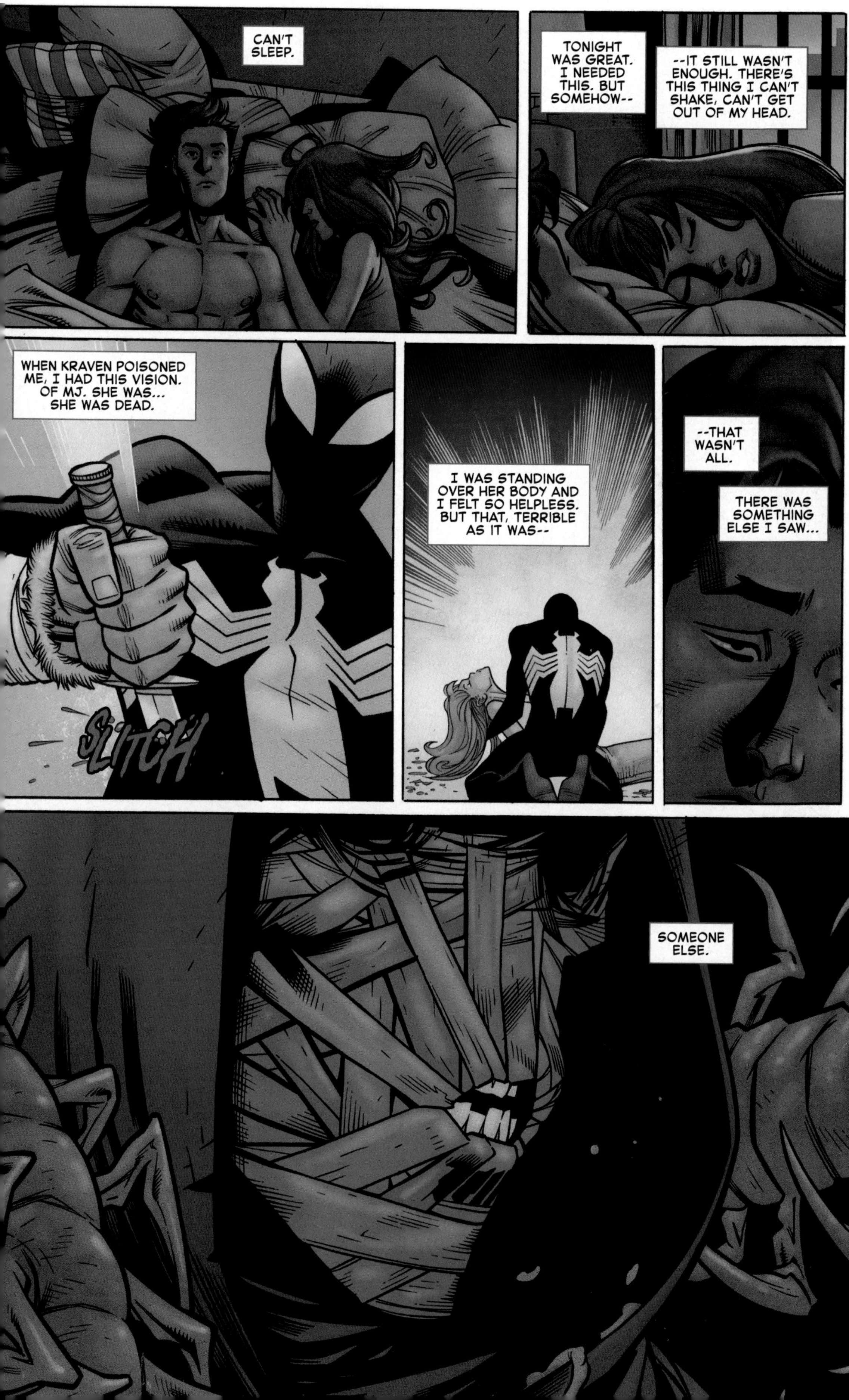
CAN'T SLEEP.
TONIGHT WAS GREAT. I NEEDED THIS. BUT SOMEHOW--
--IT STILL WASN'T ENOUGH. THERE'S THIS THING I CAN'T SHAKE, CAN'T GET OUT OF MY HEAD.
WHEN KRAVEN POISONED ME, I HAD THIS VISION. OF MJ. SHE WAS... SHE WAS DEAD.
SLITCH
I WAS STANDING OVER HER BODY AND I FELT SO HELPLESS. BUT THAT, TERRIBLE AS IT WAS--
--THAT WASN'T ALL.
THERE WAS SOMETHING ELSE I SAW...
SOMEONE ELSE.

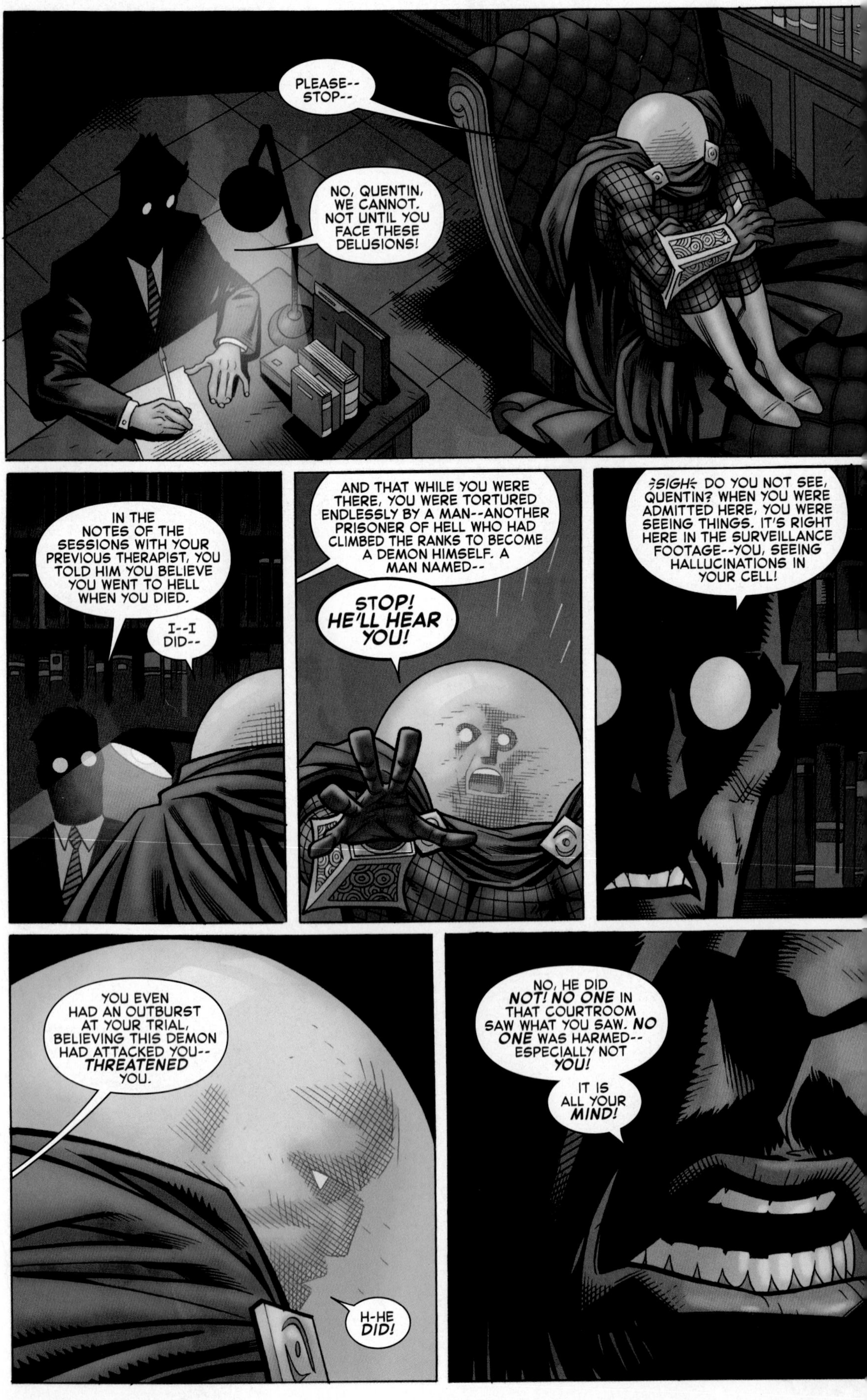
PLEASE--
STOP--
NO, QUENTIN, WE CANNOT. NOT UNTIL YOU FACE THESE DELUSIONS!
IN THE NOTES OF THE SESSIONS WITH YOUR PREVIOUS THERAPIST, YOU TOLD HIM YOU BELIEVE YOU WENT TO HELL WHEN YOU DIED.
I--I DID--
AND THAT WHILE YOU WERE THERE, YOU WERE TORTURED ENDLESSLY BY A MAN--ANOTHER PRISONER OF HELL WHO HAD CLIMBED THE RANKS TO BECOME A DEMON HIMSELF. A MAN NAMED--
STOP! HE'LL HEAR YOU!
SIGH DO YOU NOT SEE, QUENTIN? WHEN YOU WERE ADMITTED HERE, YOU WERE SEEING THINGS. IT'S RIGHT HERE IN THE SURVEILLANCE FOOTAGE--YOU, SEEING HALLUCINATIONS IN YOUR CELL!
YOU EVEN HAD AN OUTBURST AT YOUR TRIAL, BELIEVING THIS DEMON HAD ATTACKED YOU-- THREATENED YOU.
H-HE DID!
NO, HE DID NOT! NO ONE IN THAT COURTROOM SAW WHAT YOU SAW. NO ONE WAS HARMED-- ESPECIALLY NOT YOU!
IT IS ALL YOUR MIND!

NO...
NO, IT IS
REAL--

IS IT?
CONSIDER THIS--YOU
HAVE SPENT YEARS AS
A MASTER OF ILLUSION
AND HYPNOSIS--

--HOW MANY THOUSANDS OF
TIMES HAVE YOU BENT AND SHAPED
REALITY AROUND YOUR VICTIM? DID
YOU NEVER CONSIDER HOW THAT
MIGHT WARP YOUR *OWN*
PERCEPTIONS OF IT?

NO--THAT'S
IMPOSSIBLE--

I DISAGREE.
I THINK YOUR MIND CAN
NO LONGER DISTINGUISH
FACT FROM FICTION.
IN FACT--

--I DON'T
BELIEVE YOU
EVER TRULY *DIED*,
QUENTIN.

WHAT?

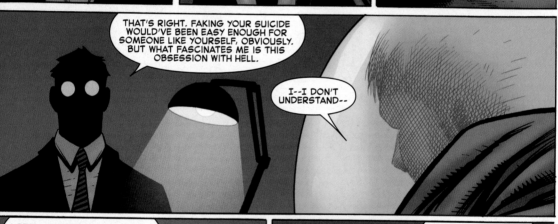

THAT'S RIGHT. FAKING YOUR SUICIDE
WOULD'VE BEEN EASY ENOUGH FOR
SOMEONE LIKE YOURSELF, OBVIOUSLY.
BUT WHAT FASCINATES ME IS THIS
OBSESSION WITH HELL.

I--I DON'T
UNDERSTAND--

REALLY? WEREN'T YOU JUST
TELLING ME HOW IN ORDER TO
TORTURE J. JONAH JAMESON
YOU MADE HIM BELIEVE *HE*
WAS IN HELL BEING PUNISHED
BY DEMONS?

YES,
BUT--

OR HOW IN
ORDER TO BREAK
DAREDEVIL YOU NEARLY
CONVINCED HIM A LITTLE
BABY WAS, IN FACT,
A DEMON AS WELL--
THE ANTICHRIST
ITSELF.

HOW MANY OF YOUR
ILLUSIONS RELY ON
THIS IMAGERY? IT IS AS
PLAIN AS DAY--YOU
HAVE A FIXATION
ON *HELL!*

SO TELL
ME, WHICH IS
MORE LIKELY,
THEN--

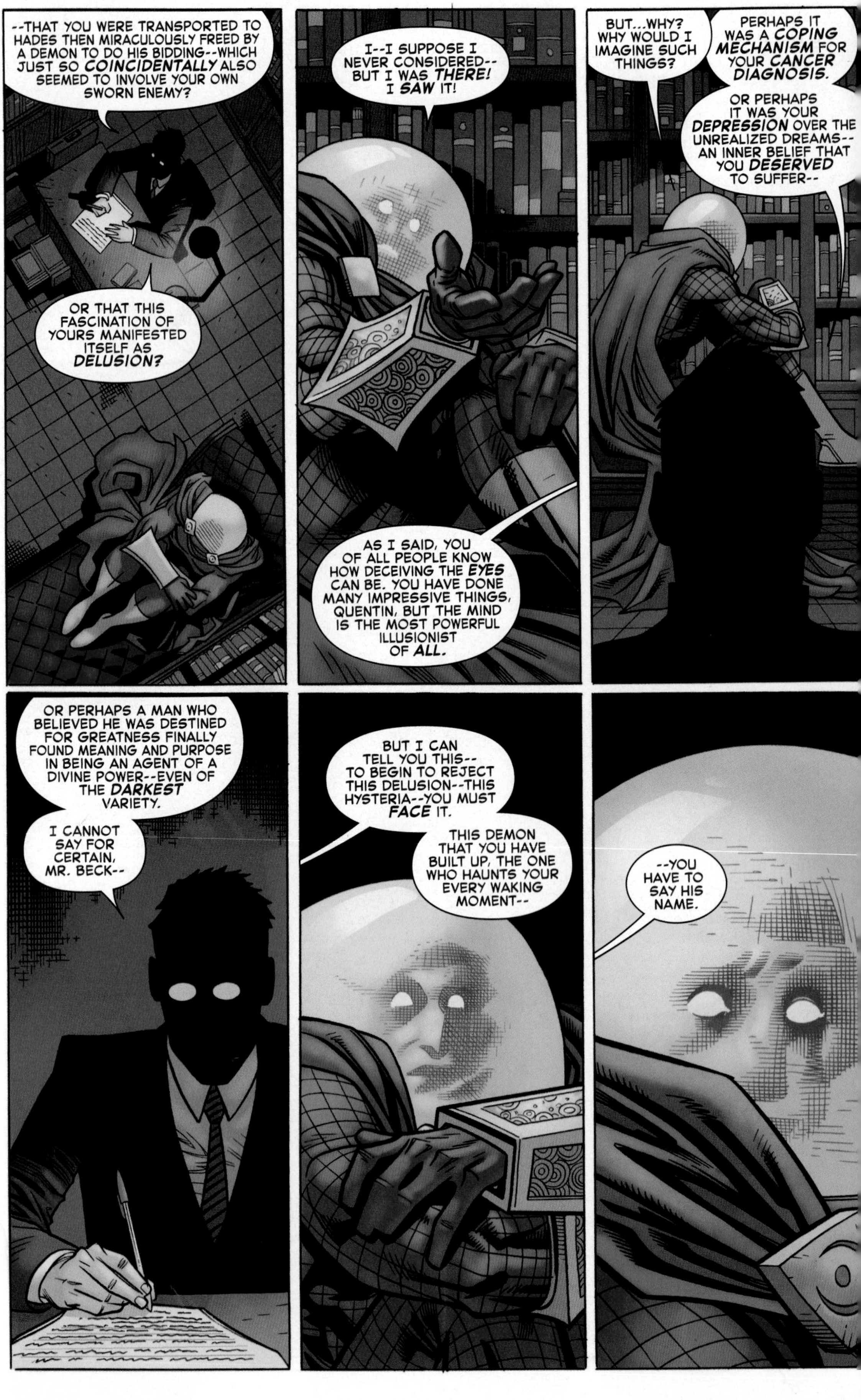
--THAT YOU WERE TRANSPORTED TO HADES THEN MIRACULOUSLY FREED BY A DEMON TO DO HIS BIDDING--WHICH JUST SO COINCIDENTALLY ALSO SEEMED TO INVOLVE YOUR OWN SWORN ENEMY?
OR THAT THIS FASCINATION OF YOURS MANIFESTED ITSELF AS DELUSION?
I--I SUPPOSE I NEVER CONSIDERED--BUT I WAS THERE! I SAW IT!
AS I SAID, YOU OF ALL PEOPLE KNOW HOW DECEIVING THE EYES CAN BE. YOU HAVE DONE MANY IMPRESSIVE THINGS, QUENTIN, BUT THE MIND IS THE MOST POWERFUL ILLUSIONIST OF ALL.
BUT...WHY? WHY WOULD I IMAGINE SUCH THINGS?
PERHAPS IT WAS A COPING MECHANISM FOR YOUR CANCER DIAGNOSIS.
OR PERHAPS IT WAS YOUR DEPRESSION OVER THE UNREALIZED DREAMS--AN INNER BELIEF THAT YOU DESERVED TO SUFFER--
OR PERHAPS A MAN WHO BELIEVED HE WAS DESTINED FOR GREATNESS FINALLY FOUND MEANING AND PURPOSE IN BEING AN AGENT OF A DIVINE POWER--EVEN OF THE DARKEST VARIETY.
I CANNOT SAY FOR CERTAIN, MR. BECK--
BUT I CAN TELL YOU THIS--TO BEGIN TO REJECT THIS DELUSION--THIS HYSTERIA--YOU MUST FACE IT.
THIS DEMON THAT YOU HAVE BUILT UP, THE ONE WHO HAUNTS YOUR EVERY WAKING MOMENT--
--YOU HAVE TO SAY HIS NAME.

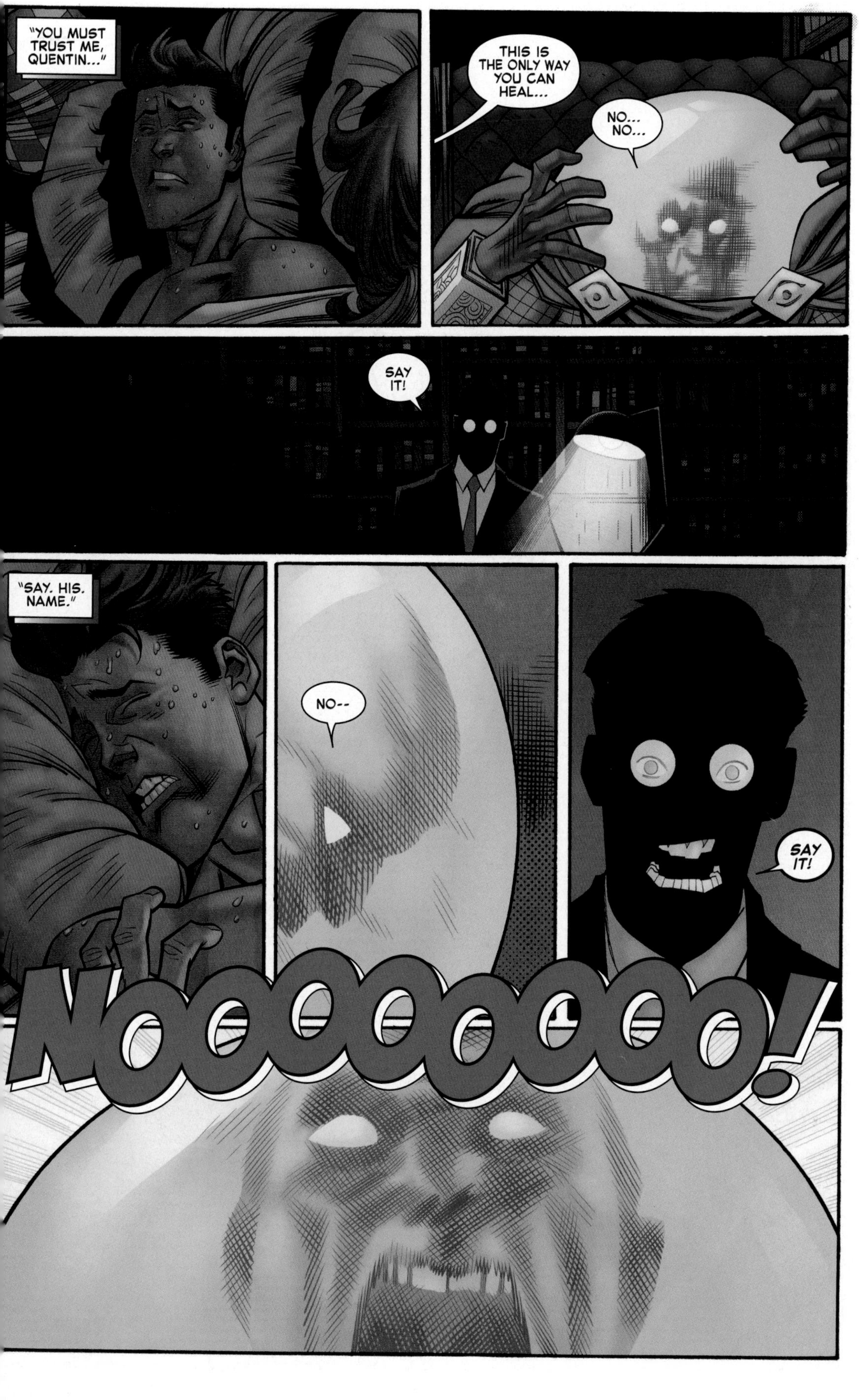
"YOU MUST TRUST ME, QUENTIN..."
THIS IS THE ONLY WAY YOU CAN HEAL...
NO... NO...
SAY IT!
"SAY. HIS. NAME."
NO--
SAY IT!
NOOOOOOOOO!

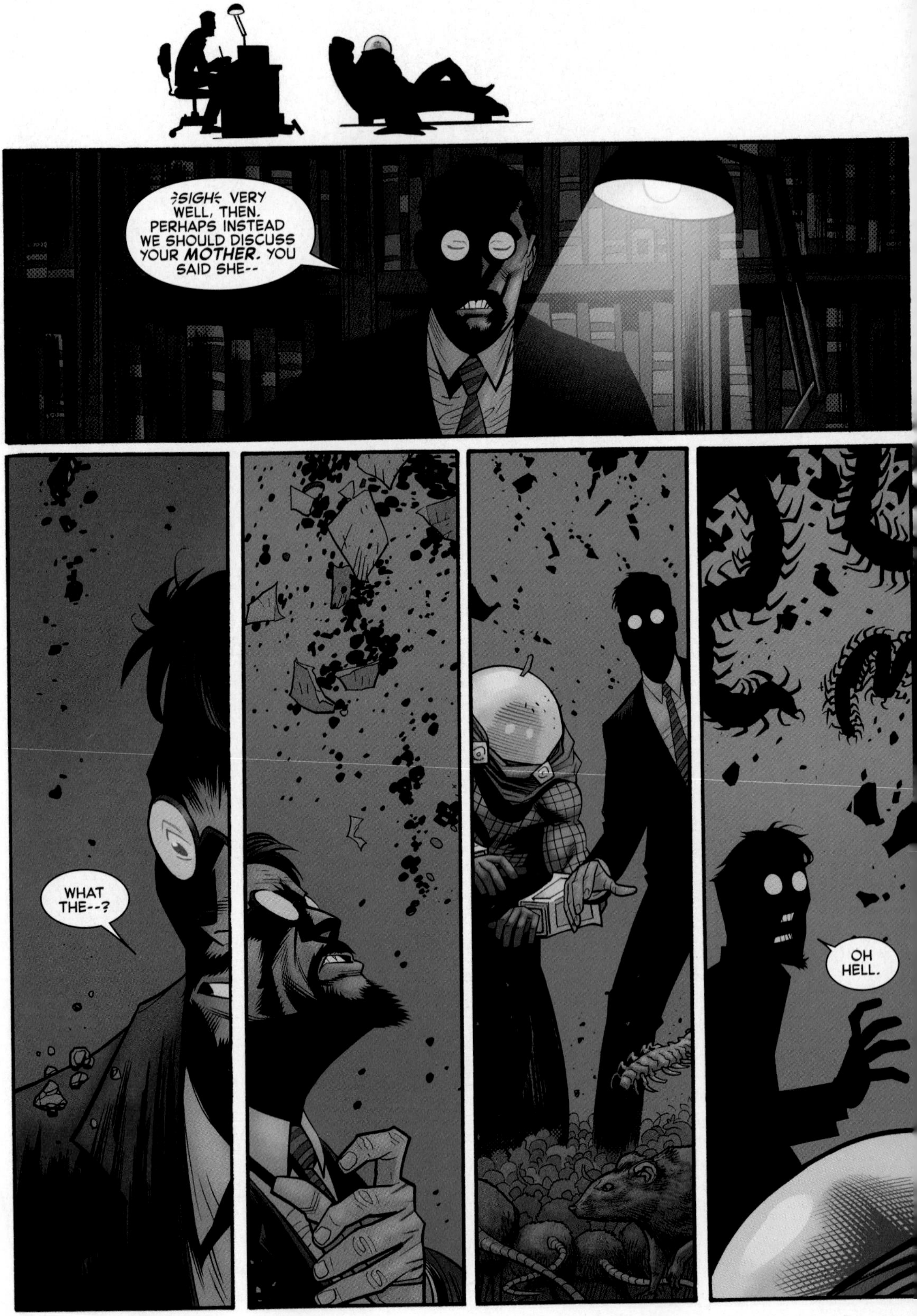

≠SIGH≠ VERY WELL, THEN. PERHAPS INSTEAD WE SHOULD DISCUSS YOUR MOTHER. YOU SAID SHE--
WHAT THE--?
OH HELL.

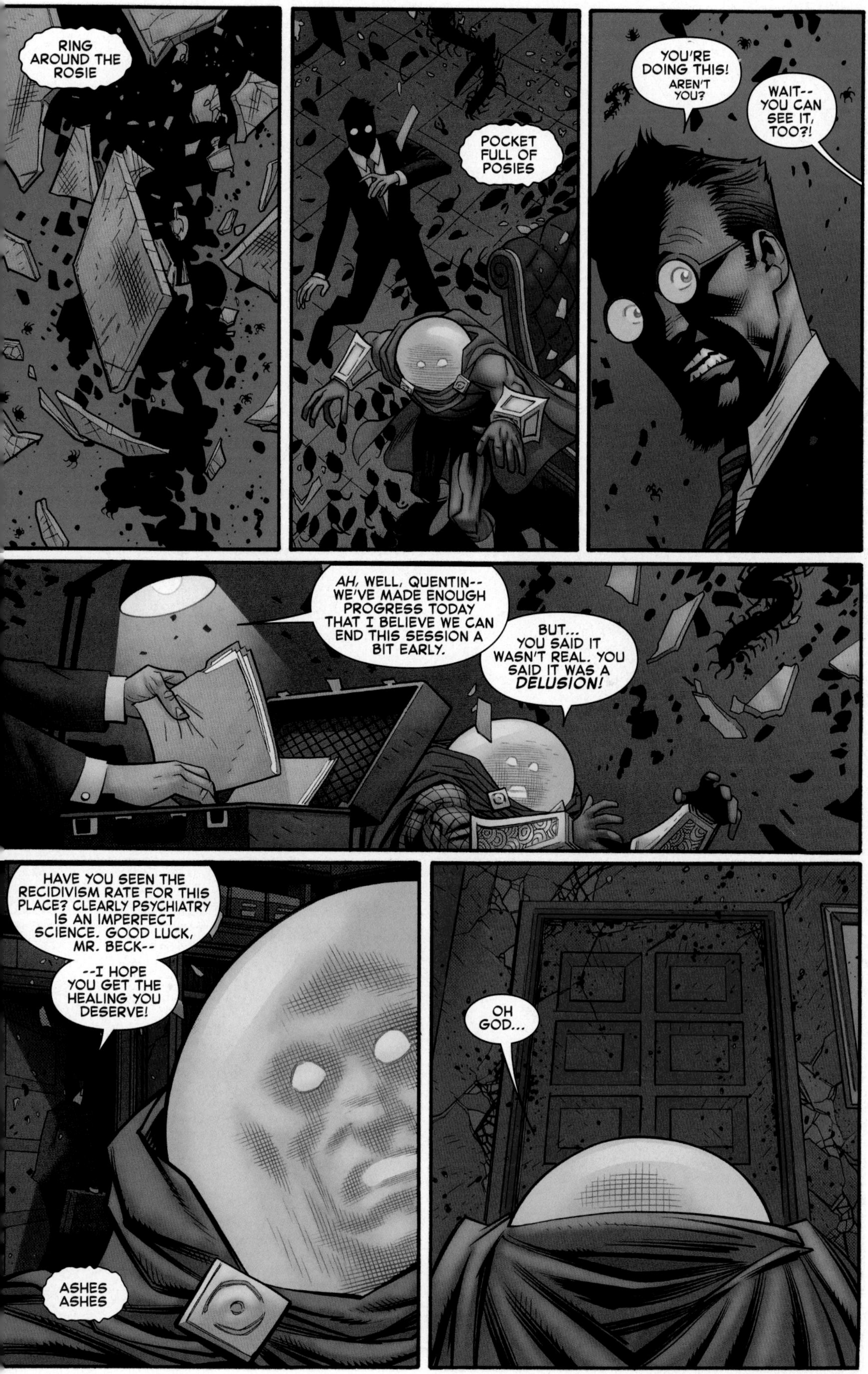
RING AROUND THE ROSIE
POCKET FULL OF POSIES
YOU'RE DOING THIS! AREN'T YOU?
WAIT-- YOU CAN SEE IT, TOO?!
AH, WELL, QUENTIN-- WE'VE MADE ENOUGH PROGRESS TODAY THAT I BELIEVE WE CAN END THIS SESSION A BIT EARLY.
BUT... YOU SAID IT WASN'T REAL. YOU SAID IT WAS A DELUSION!
HAVE YOU SEEN THE RECIDIVISM RATE FOR THIS PLACE? CLEARLY PSYCHIATRY IS AN IMPERFECT SCIENCE. GOOD LUCK, MR. BECK--
--I HOPE YOU GET THE HEALING YOU DESERVE!
ASHES ASHES
OH GOD...

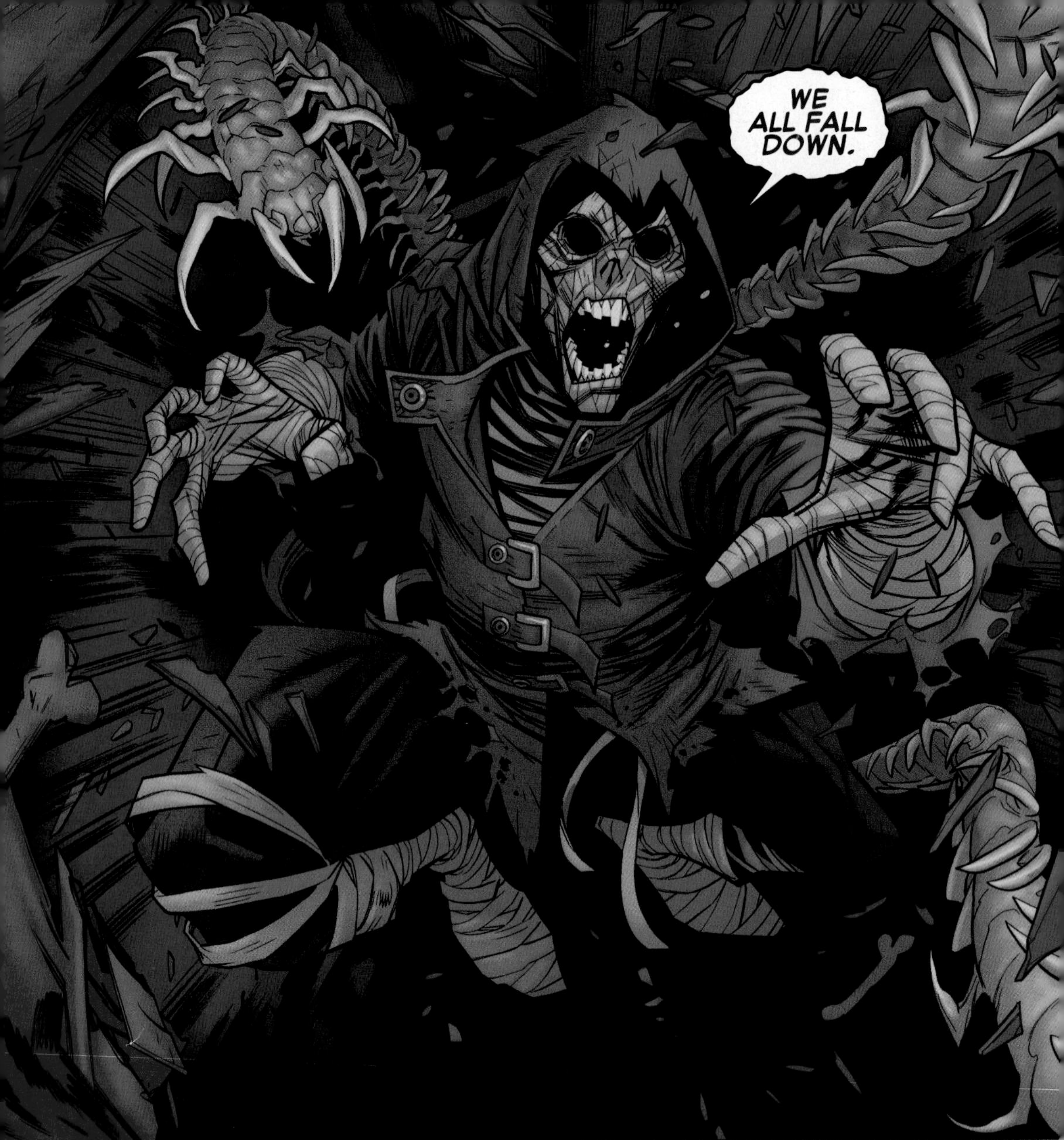
WE ALL FALL DOWN.

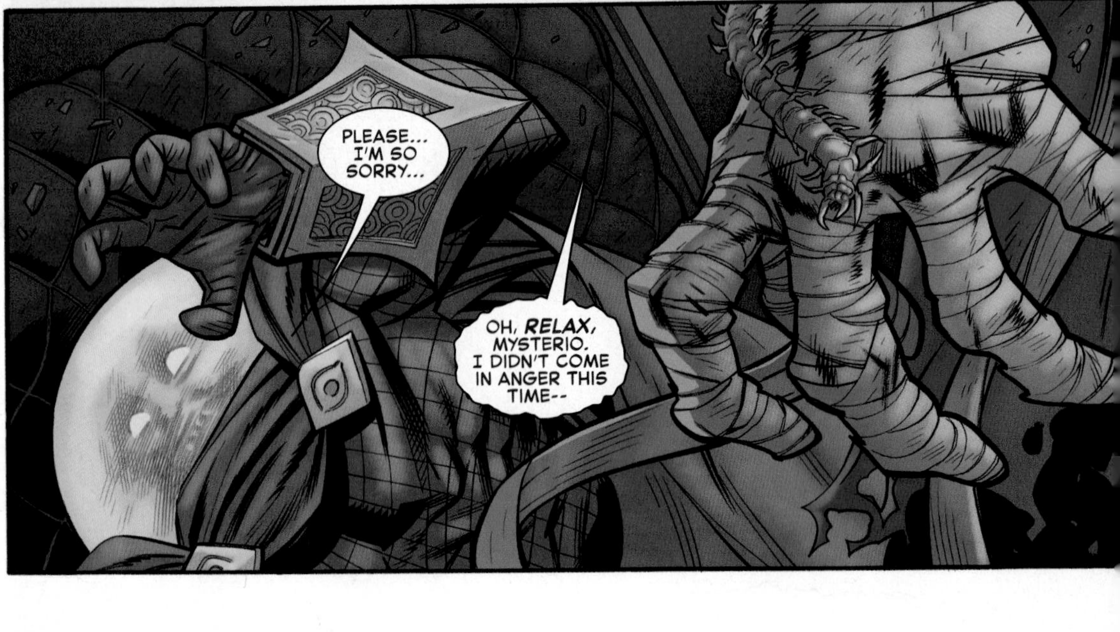
PLEASE... I'M SO SORRY...
OH, RELAX, MYSTERIO. I DIDN'T COME IN ANGER THIS TIME--

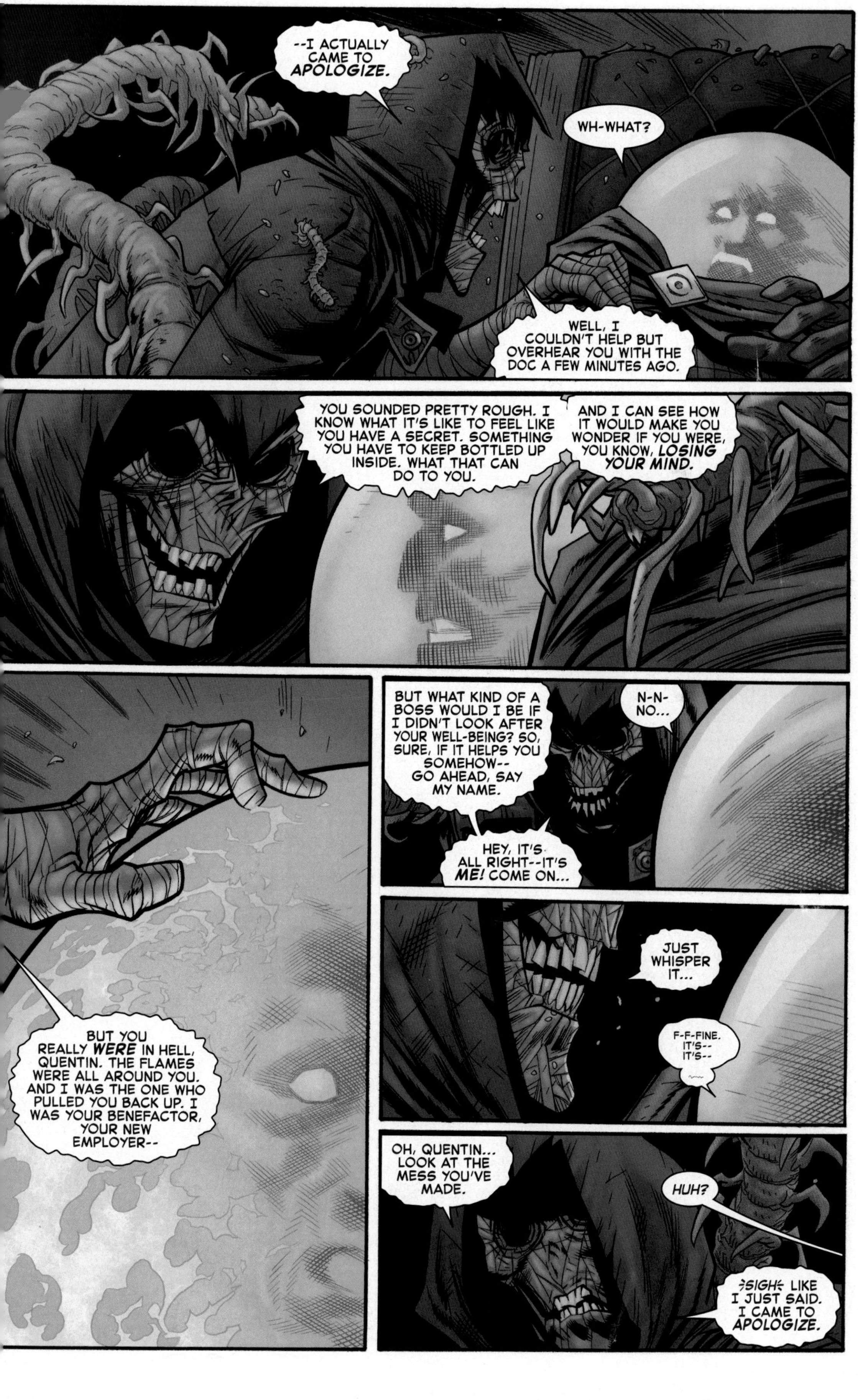
--I ACTUALLY CAME TO APOLOGIZE.
WH-WHAT?
WELL, I COULDN'T HELP BUT OVERHEAR YOU WITH THE DOC A FEW MINUTES AGO.
YOU SOUNDED PRETTY ROUGH. I KNOW WHAT IT'S LIKE TO FEEL LIKE YOU HAVE A SECRET. SOMETHING YOU HAVE TO KEEP BOTTLED UP INSIDE. WHAT THAT CAN DO TO YOU.
AND I CAN SEE HOW IT WOULD MAKE YOU WONDER IF YOU WERE, YOU KNOW, LOSING YOUR MIND.
BUT YOU REALLY WERE IN HELL, QUENTIN. THE FLAMES WERE ALL AROUND YOU. AND I WAS THE ONE WHO PULLED YOU BACK UP. I WAS YOUR BENEFACTOR, YOUR NEW EMPLOYER--
BUT WHAT KIND OF A BOSS WOULD I BE IF I DIDN'T LOOK AFTER YOUR WELL-BEING? SO, SURE, IF IT HELPS YOU SOMEHOW-- GO AHEAD, SAY MY NAME.
N-N-NO...
HEY, IT'S ALL RIGHT--IT'S ME! COME ON...
JUST WHISPER IT...
F-F-FINE. IT'S-- IT'S--
OH, QUENTIN... LOOK AT THE MESS YOU'VE MADE.
HUH?
SIGH LIKE I JUST SAID. I CAME TO APOLOGIZE.

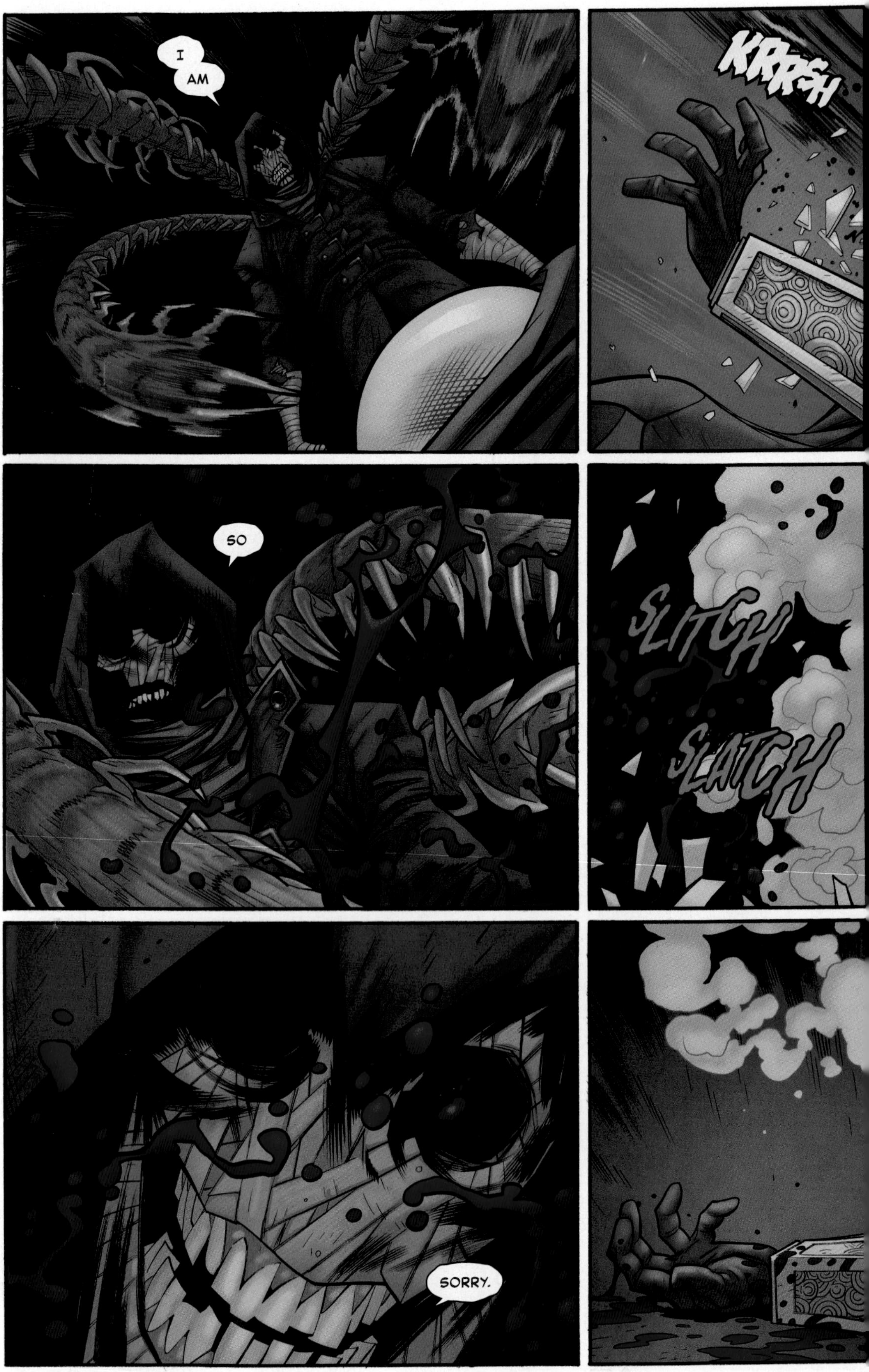
I
AM
KRRSH
SO
SLITCH
SLATCH
SORRY.

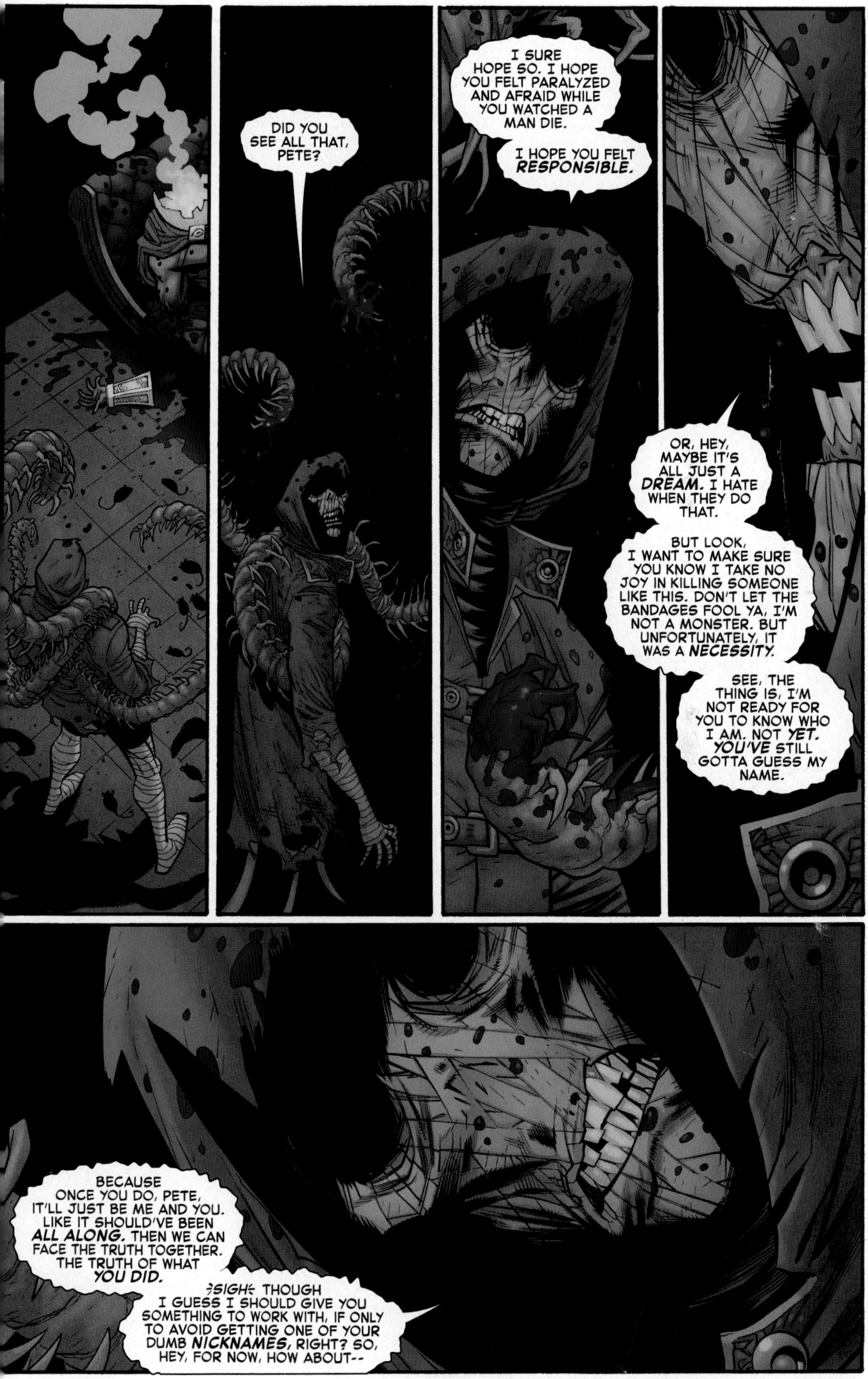

DID YOU SEE ALL THAT, PETE?
I SURE HOPE SO. I HOPE YOU FELT PARALYZED AND AFRAID WHILE YOU WATCHED A MAN DIE.
I HOPE YOU FELT **RESPONSIBLE.**
OR, HEY, MAYBE IT'S ALL JUST A **DREAM.** I HATE WHEN THEY DO THAT.
BUT LOOK, I WANT TO MAKE SURE YOU KNOW I TAKE NO JOY IN KILLING SOMEONE LIKE THIS. DON'T LET THE BANDAGES FOOL YA, I'M NOT A MONSTER. BUT UNFORTUNATELY, IT WAS A **NECESSITY.**
SEE, THE THING IS, I'M NOT READY FOR YOU TO KNOW WHO I AM. NOT **YET. YOU'VE** STILL GOTTA GUESS MY NAME.
BECAUSE ONCE YOU DO, PETE, IT'LL JUST BE ME AND YOU. LIKE IT SHOULD'VE BEEN **ALL ALONG.** THEN WE CAN FACE THE TRUTH TOGETHER. THE TRUTH OF WHAT **YOU DID.**
SIGH THOUGH I GUESS I SHOULD GIVE YOU SOMETHING TO WORK WITH, IF ONLY TO AVOID GETTING ONE OF YOUR DUMB **NICKNAMES,** RIGHT? SO, HEY, FOR NOW, HOW ABOUT--

AHHHHHHHH!

PETE?!

HEY! HEY, IT'S OKAY, JUST A *NIGHTMARE*--

NO...NO, IT *WASN'T*, MJ.

I SHOULD'VE TOLD YOU--

TOLD ME WHAT?

BACK IN THE PARK, WITH KRAVEN. I *SAW* SOMETHING. SOME KINDA, I DUNNO...A *VISION*. YOU WERE THERE. YOU WERE--

SOMETHING HAD HAPPENED TO YOU.

OKAY, WELL, WHATEVER IT WAS YOU SAW--I'M *FINE. NOTHING'S* HAPPENED TO ME.

I KNOW THAT. BUT-- THERE WAS *SOMEONE ELSE* THERE. AND I JUST SAW HIM AGAIN--

WHO WAS IT?

I DON'T KNOW. BUT HE JUST...SPOKE TO ME. HE TOLD ME TO CALL HIM--

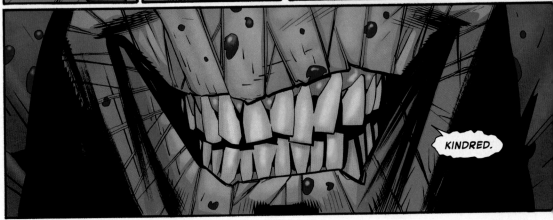

KINDRED.

25

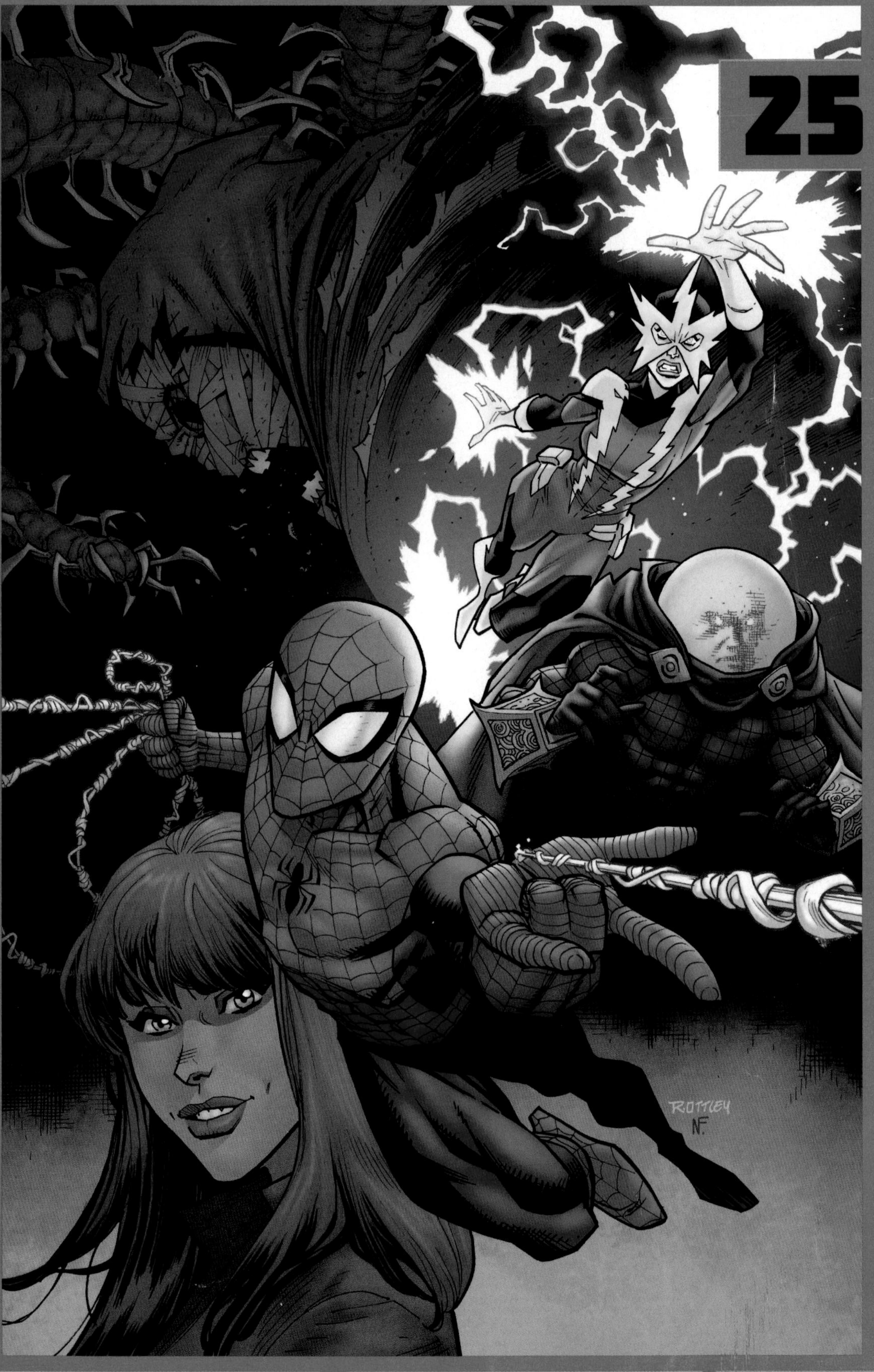

OPENING NIGHT

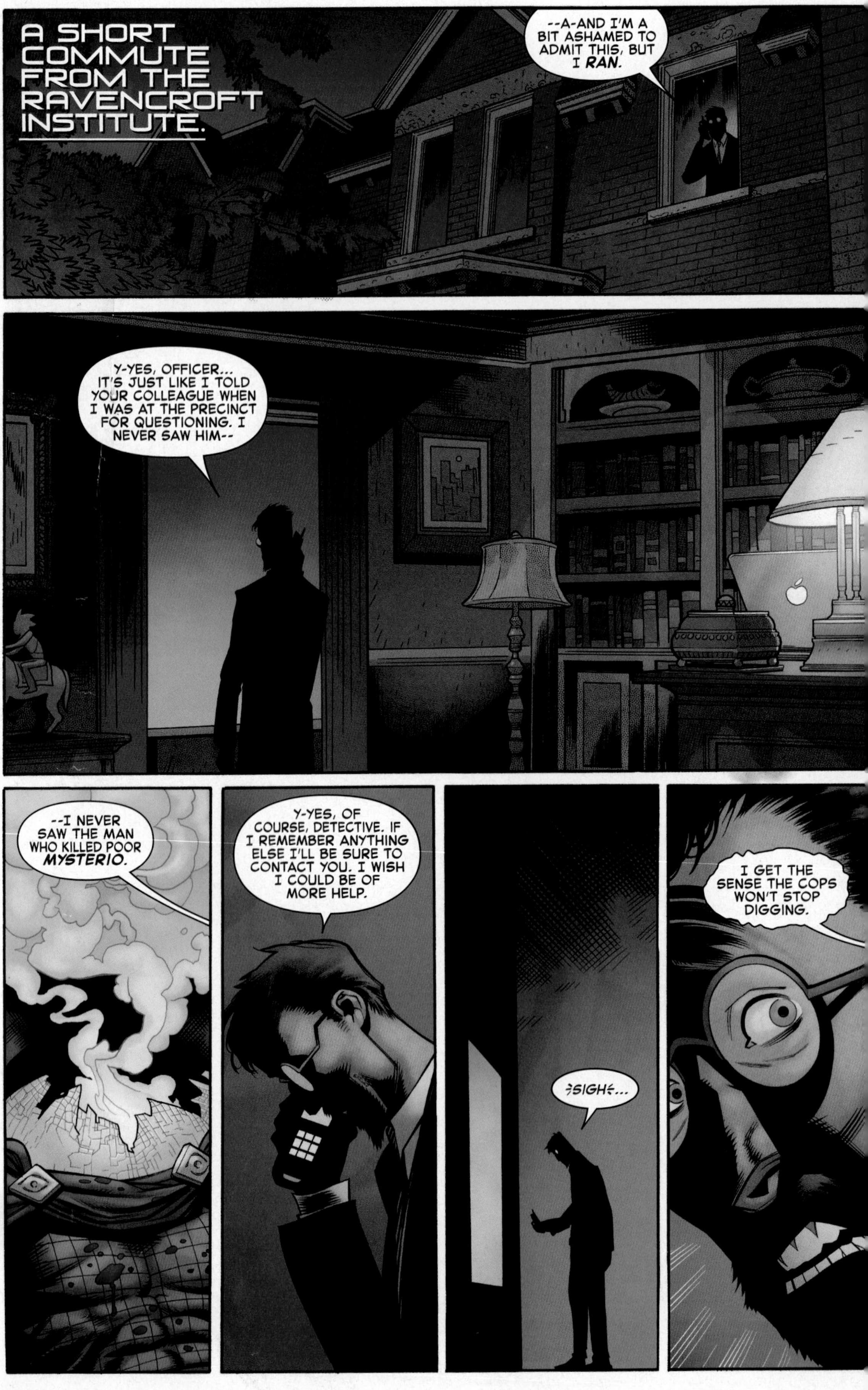

A SHORT COMMUTE FROM THE RAVENCROFT INSTITUTE.
--A-AND I'M A BIT ASHAMED TO ADMIT THIS, BUT I RAN.
Y-YES, OFFICER... IT'S JUST LIKE I TOLD YOUR COLLEAGUE WHEN I WAS AT THE PRECINCT FOR QUESTIONING. I NEVER SAW HIM--
--I NEVER SAW THE MAN WHO KILLED POOR MYSTERIO.
Y-YES, OF COURSE, DETECTIVE. IF I REMEMBER ANYTHING ELSE I'LL BE SURE TO CONTACT YOU. I WISH I COULD BE OF MORE HELP.
⇛SIGH⇚...
I GET THE SENSE THE COPS WON'T STOP DIGGING.

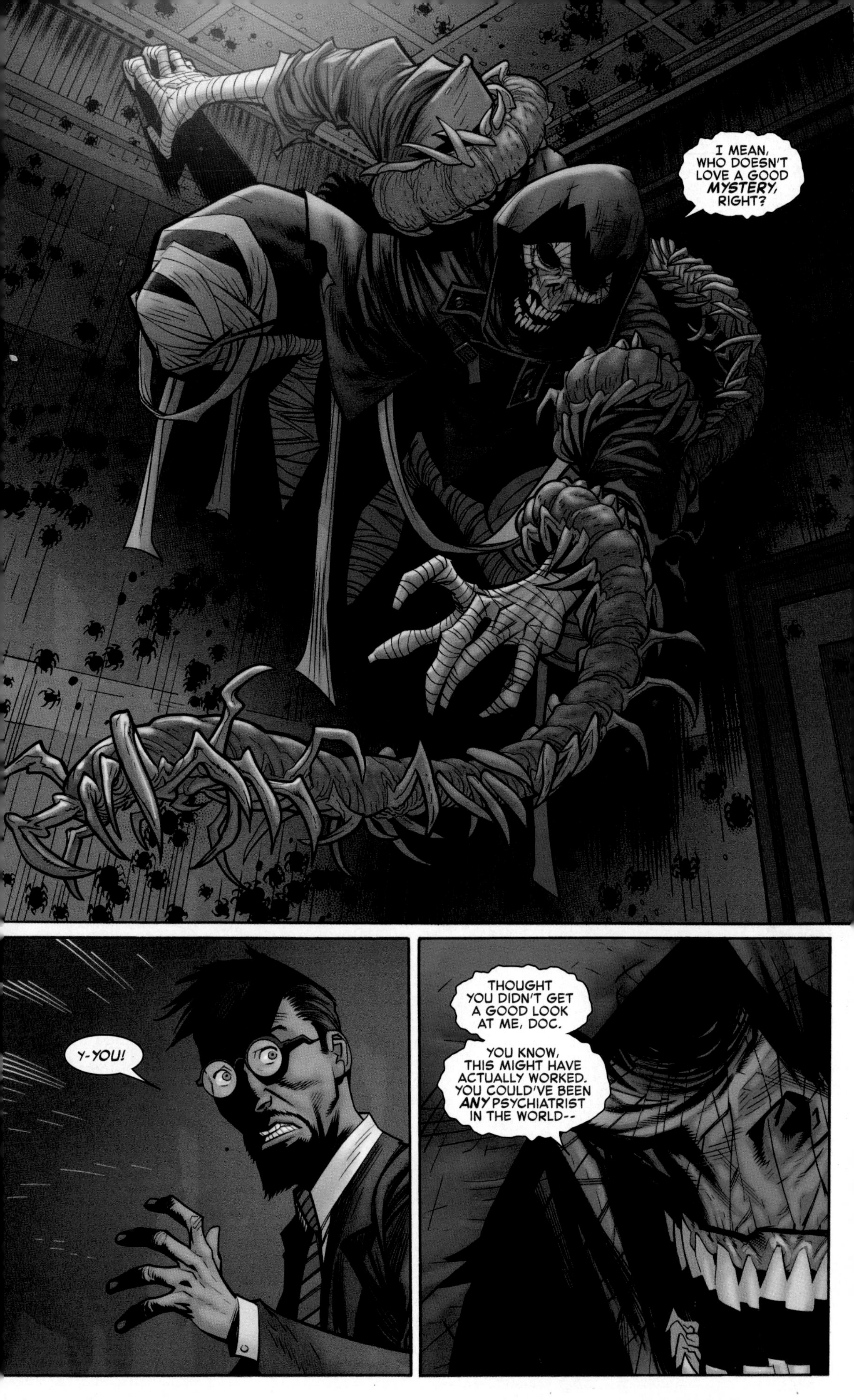
I MEAN, WHO DOESN'T LOVE A GOOD MYSTERY, RIGHT?
Y-YOU!
THOUGHT YOU DIDN'T GET A GOOD LOOK AT ME, DOC.
YOU KNOW, THIS MIGHT HAVE ACTUALLY WORKED. YOU COULD'VE BEEN ANY PSYCHIATRIST IN THE WORLD--

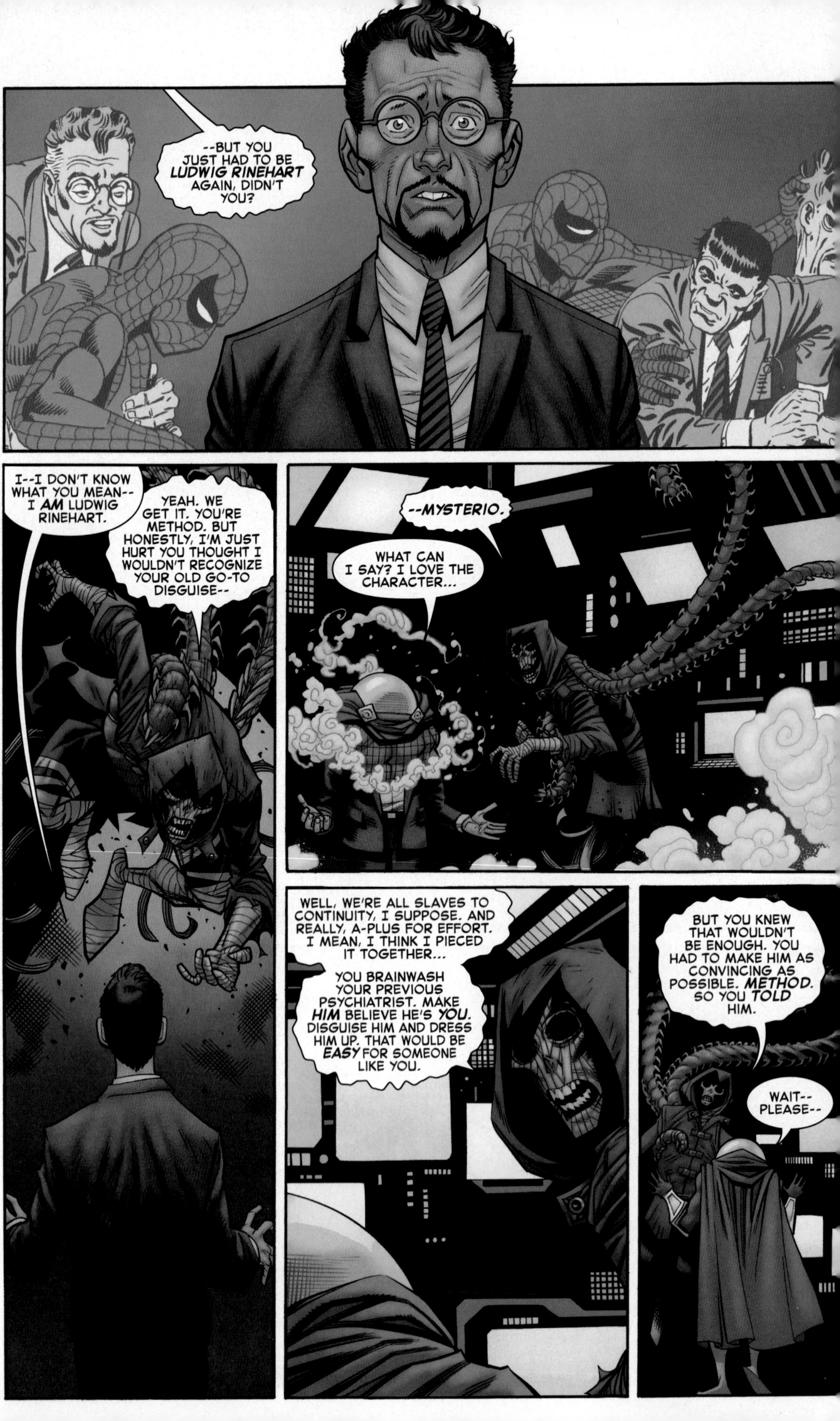
--BUT YOU JUST HAD TO BE LUDWIG RINEHART AGAIN, DIDN'T YOU?
I--I DON'T KNOW WHAT YOU MEAN-- I AM LUDWIG RINEHART.
YEAH. WE GET IT. YOU'RE METHOD. BUT HONESTLY, I'M JUST HURT YOU THOUGHT I WOULDN'T RECOGNIZE YOUR OLD GO-TO DISGUISE--
--MYSTERIO.
WHAT CAN I SAY? I LOVE THE CHARACTER...
WELL, WE'RE ALL SLAVES TO CONTINUITY, I SUPPOSE. AND REALLY, A-PLUS FOR EFFORT. I MEAN, I THINK I PIECED IT TOGETHER...
YOU BRAINWASH YOUR PREVIOUS PSYCHIATRIST. MAKE HIM BELIEVE HE'S YOU. DISGUISE HIM AND DRESS HIM UP. THAT WOULD BE EASY FOR SOMEONE LIKE YOU.
BUT YOU KNEW THAT WOULDN'T BE ENOUGH. YOU HAD TO MAKE HIM AS CONVINCING AS POSSIBLE. METHOD. SO YOU TOLD HIM.
WAIT-- PLEASE--

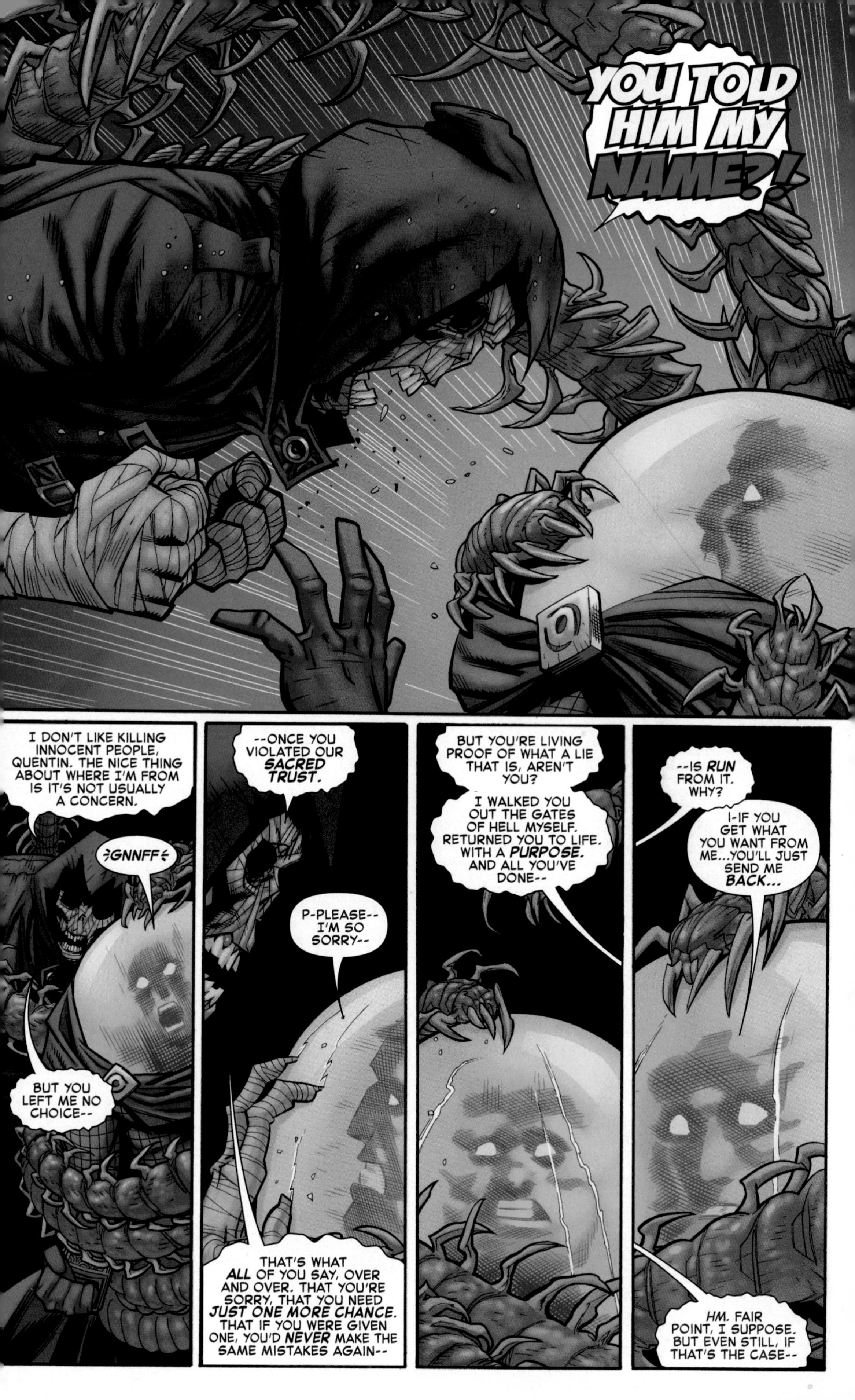
YOU TOLD HIM MY NAME?!
I DON'T LIKE KILLING INNOCENT PEOPLE, QUENTIN. THE NICE THING ABOUT WHERE I'M FROM IS IT'S NOT USUALLY A CONCERN.
GNNFF
BUT YOU LEFT ME NO CHOICE--
--ONCE YOU VIOLATED OUR SACRED TRUST.
P-PLEASE-- I'M SO SORRY--
THAT'S WHAT ALL OF YOU SAY, OVER AND OVER. THAT YOU'RE SORRY, THAT YOU NEED JUST ONE MORE CHANCE. THAT IF YOU WERE GIVEN ONE, YOU'D NEVER MAKE THE SAME MISTAKES AGAIN--
BUT YOU'RE LIVING PROOF OF WHAT A LIE THAT IS, AREN'T YOU?
I WALKED YOU OUT THE GATES OF HELL MYSELF. RETURNED YOU TO LIFE. WITH A PURPOSE. AND ALL YOU'VE DONE--
--IS RUN FROM IT. WHY?
I-IF YOU GET WHAT YOU WANT FROM ME...YOU'LL JUST SEND ME BACK...
HM. FAIR POINT, I SUPPOSE. BUT EVEN STILL, IF THAT'S THE CASE--

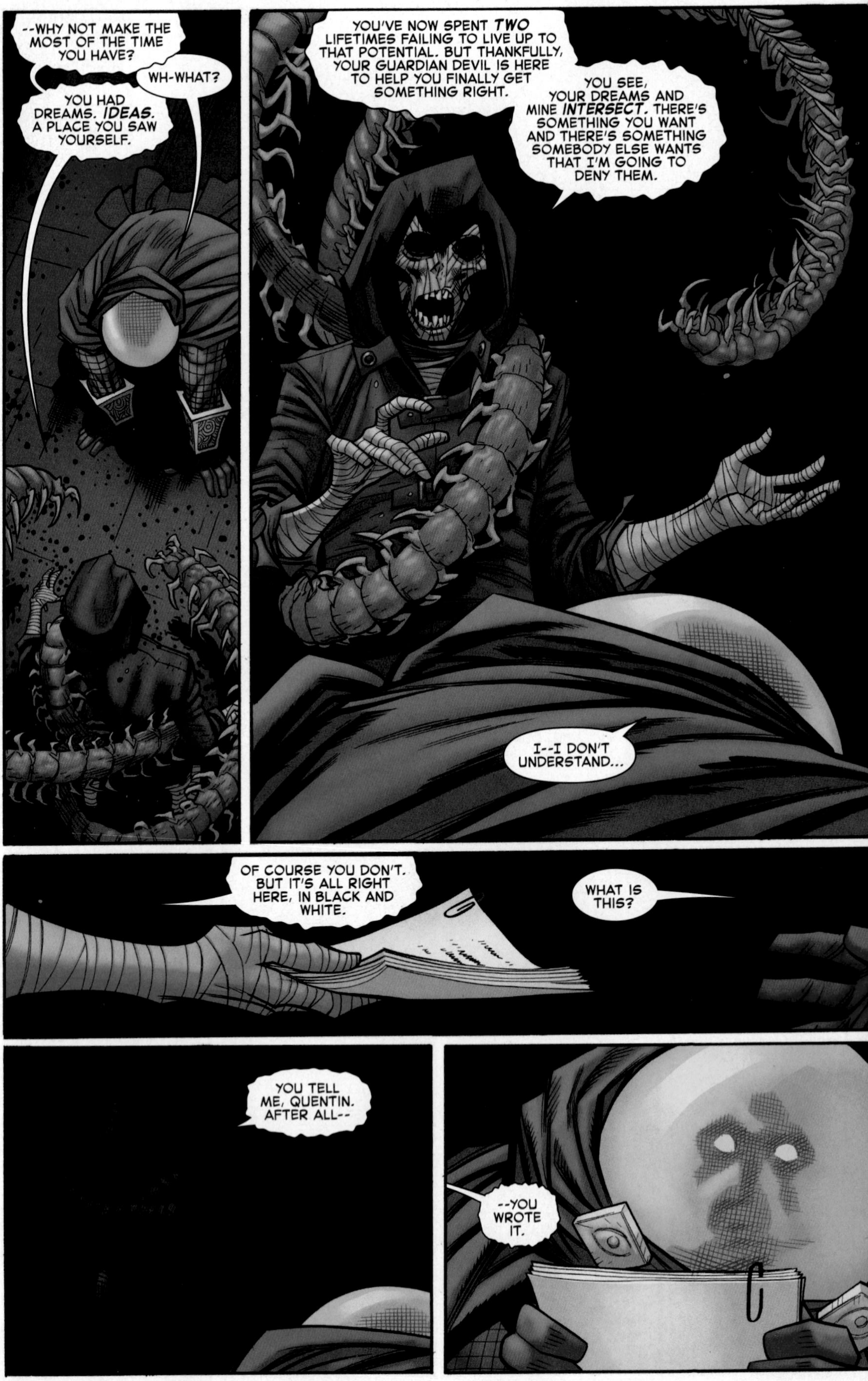
--WHY NOT MAKE THE MOST OF THE TIME YOU HAVE?
WH-WHAT?
YOU HAD DREAMS. IDEAS. A PLACE YOU SAW YOURSELF.
YOU'VE NOW SPENT TWO LIFETIMES FAILING TO LIVE UP TO THAT POTENTIAL. BUT THANKFULLY, YOUR GUARDIAN DEVIL IS HERE TO HELP YOU FINALLY GET SOMETHING RIGHT.
YOU SEE, YOUR DREAMS AND MINE INTERSECT. THERE'S SOMETHING YOU WANT AND THERE'S SOMETHING SOMEBODY ELSE WANTS THAT I'M GOING TO DENY THEM.
I--I DON'T UNDERSTAND...
OF COURSE YOU DON'T. BUT IT'S ALL RIGHT HERE, IN BLACK AND WHITE.
WHAT IS THIS?
YOU TELL ME, QUENTIN. AFTER ALL--
--YOU WROTE IT.

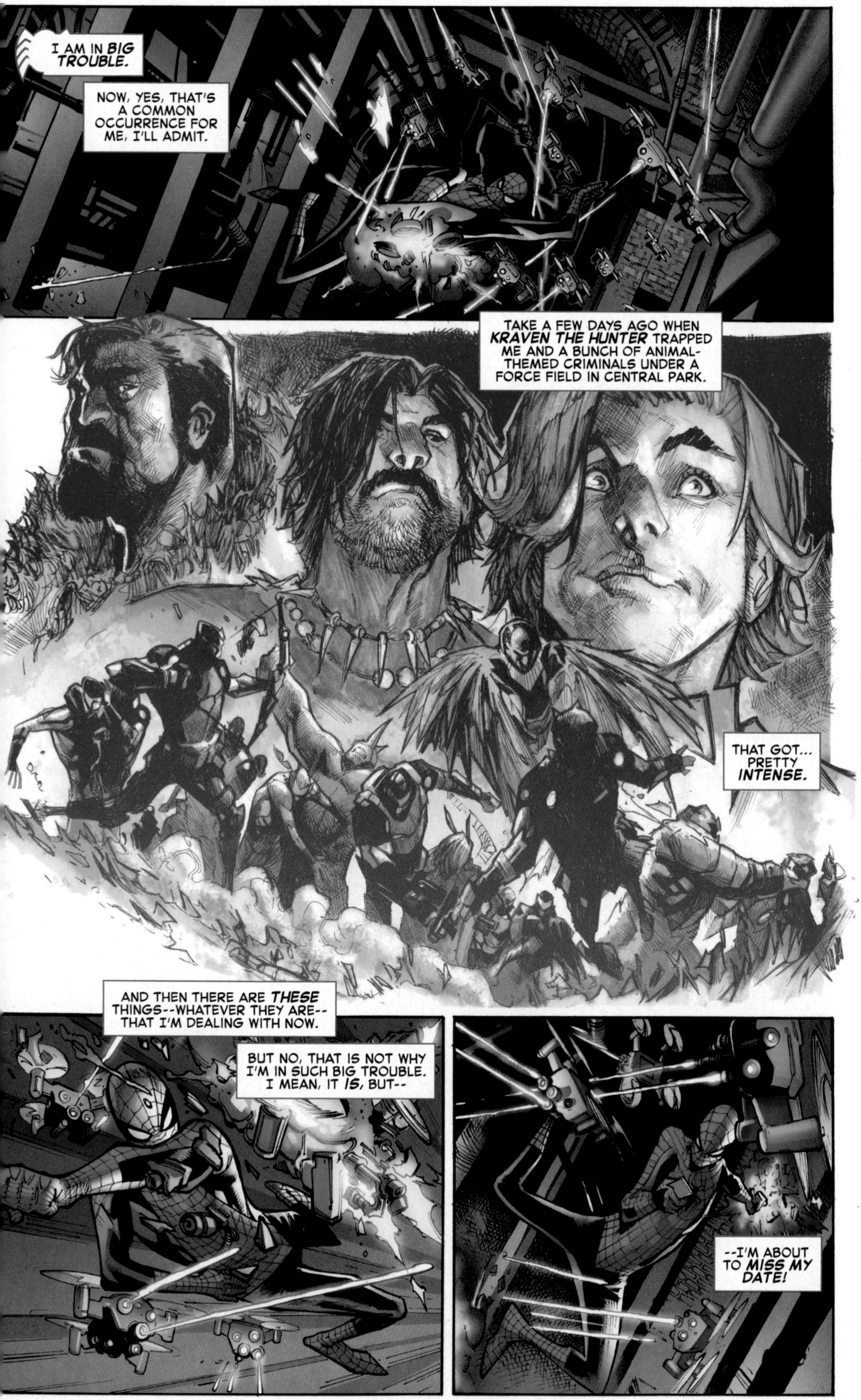
I AM IN BIG TROUBLE.
NOW, YES, THAT'S A COMMON OCCURRENCE FOR ME, I'LL ADMIT.
TAKE A FEW DAYS AGO WHEN KRAVEN THE HUNTER TRAPPED ME AND A BUNCH OF ANIMAL-THEMED CRIMINALS UNDER A FORCE FIELD IN CENTRAL PARK.
THAT GOT... PRETTY INTENSE.
AND THEN THERE ARE THESE THINGS--WHATEVER THEY ARE--THAT I'M DEALING WITH NOW.
BUT NO, THAT IS NOT WHY I'M IN SUCH BIG TROUBLE. I MEAN, IT IS, BUT--
--I'M ABOUT TO MISS MY DATE!

MJ IS GONNA KILL ME, BUT IT CAN'T BE HELPED.

SEE, THE INSANITY WITH KRAVEN AND COMPANY MIGHT BE OVER--

--BUT THERE WAS ONE *LOOSE END* I STILL NEEDED TO TRACK DOWN.

AH, WELL, AT LEAST I GOT *ONE THING* IN MY FAVOR HERE--

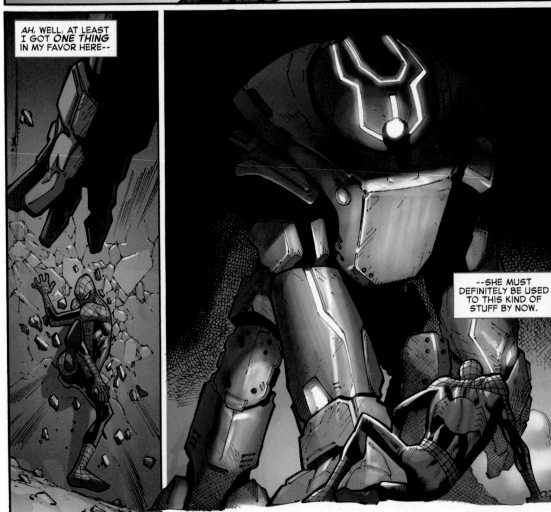

--SHE MUST DEFINITELY BE USED TO THIS KIND OF STUFF BY NOW.

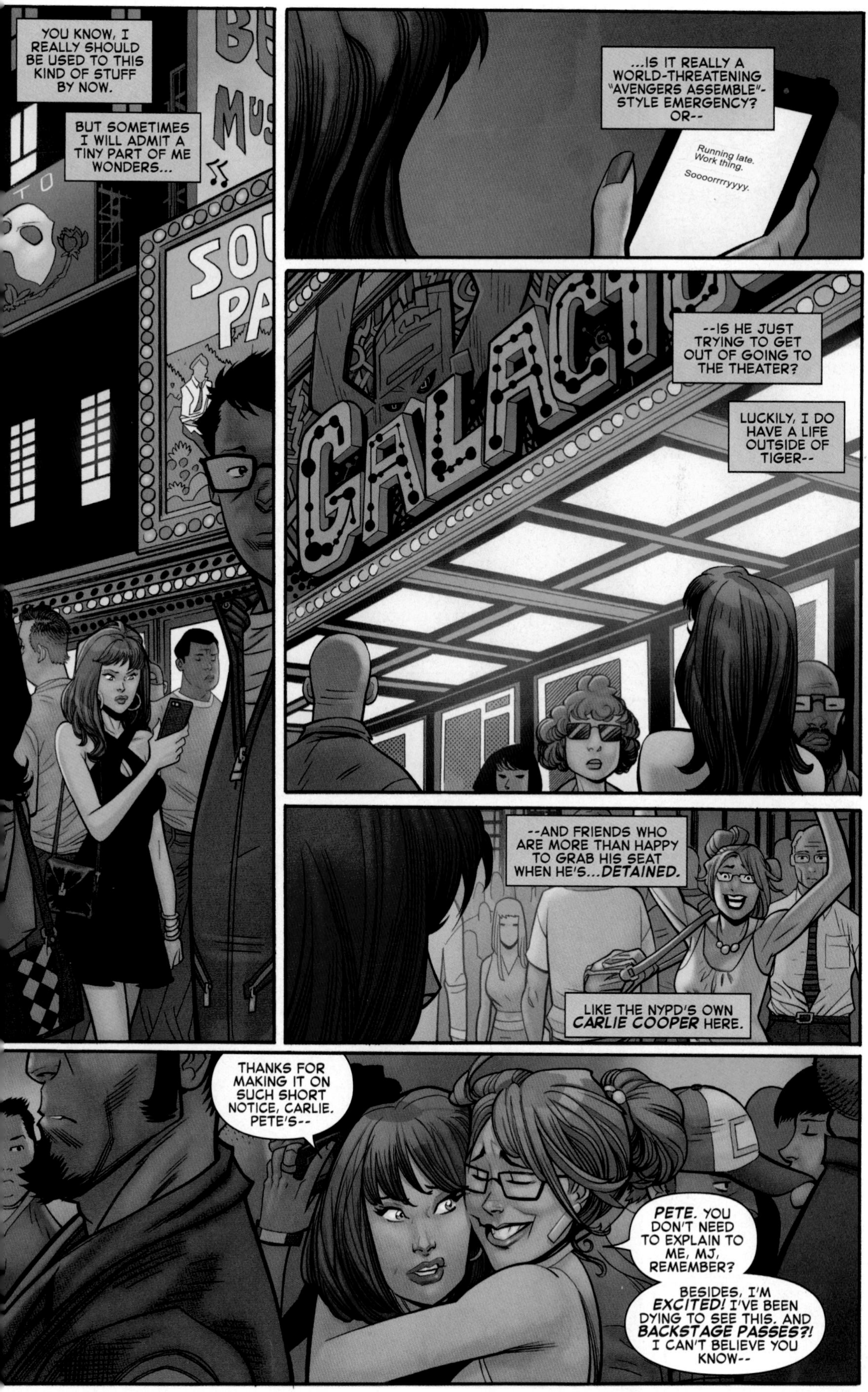
YOU KNOW, I REALLY SHOULD BE USED TO THIS KIND OF STUFF BY NOW.
BUT SOMETIMES I WILL ADMIT A TINY PART OF ME WONDERS...
...IS IT REALLY A WORLD-THREATENING "AVENGERS ASSEMBLE"-STYLE EMERGENCY? OR--
Running late. Work thing.
Soooorrrryyyy.
--IS HE JUST TRYING TO GET OUT OF GOING TO THE THEATER?
LUCKILY, I DO HAVE A LIFE OUTSIDE OF TIGER--
--AND FRIENDS WHO ARE MORE THAN HAPPY TO GRAB HIS SEAT WHEN HE'S...DETAINED.
LIKE THE NYPD'S OWN CARLIE COOPER HERE.
THANKS FOR MAKING IT ON SUCH SHORT NOTICE, CARLIE. PETE'S--
PETE. YOU DON'T NEED TO EXPLAIN TO ME, MJ, REMEMBER?
BESIDES, I'M EXCITED! I'VE BEEN DYING TO SEE THIS. AND BACKSTAGE PASSES?! I CAN'T BELIEVE YOU KNOW--

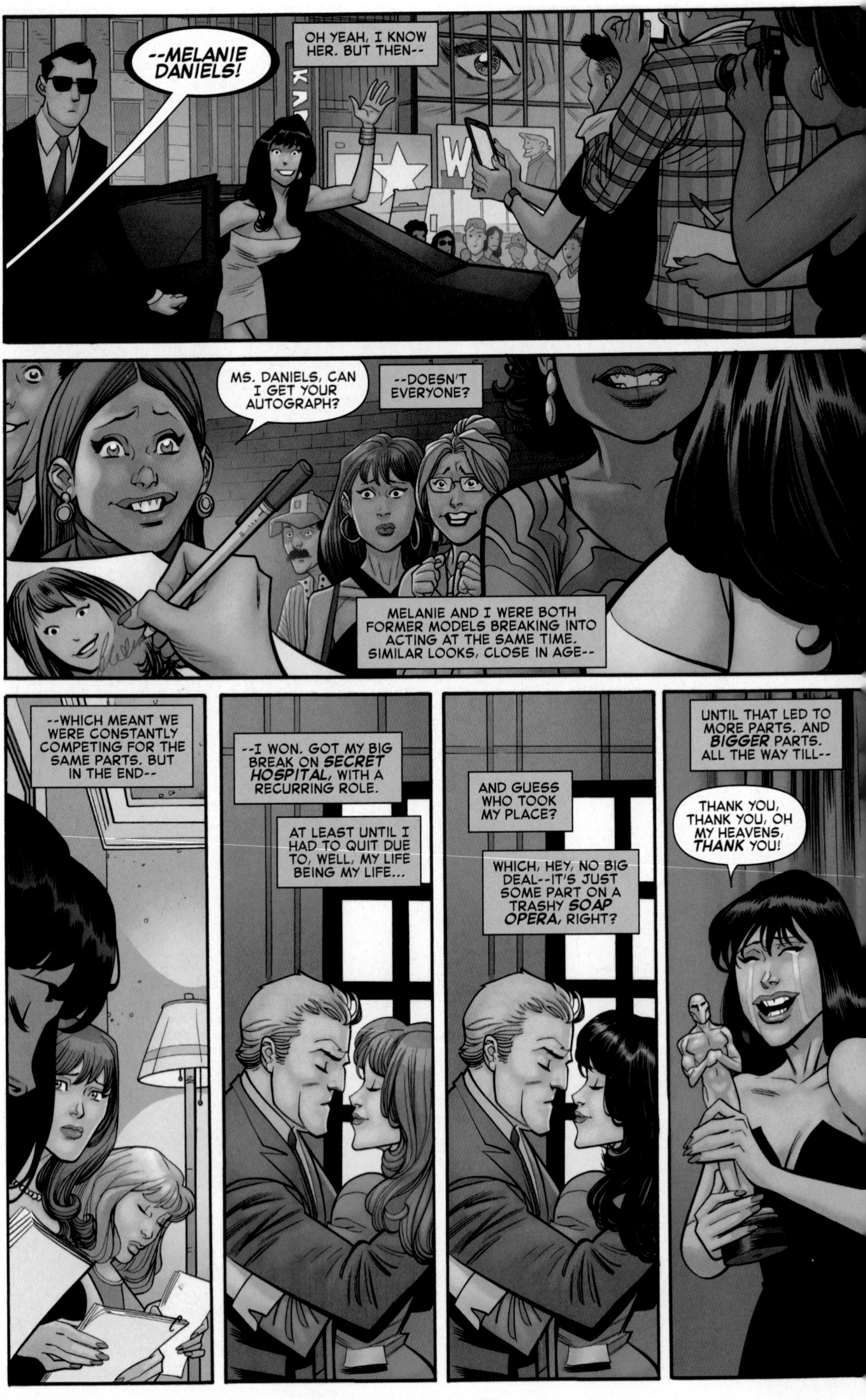

--MELANIE DANIELS!
OH YEAH, I KNOW HER. BUT THEN--
MS. DANIELS, CAN I GET YOUR AUTOGRAPH?
--DOESN'T EVERYONE?
MELANIE AND I WERE BOTH FORMER MODELS BREAKING INTO ACTING AT THE SAME TIME. SIMILAR LOOKS, CLOSE IN AGE--
--WHICH MEANT WE WERE CONSTANTLY COMPETING FOR THE SAME PARTS. BUT IN THE END--
--I WON. GOT MY BIG BREAK ON SECRET HOSPITAL, WITH A RECURRING ROLE.
AT LEAST UNTIL I HAD TO QUIT DUE TO, WELL, MY LIFE BEING MY LIFE...
AND GUESS WHO TOOK MY PLACE?
WHICH, HEY, NO BIG DEAL--IT'S JUST SOME PART ON A TRASHY SOAP OPERA, RIGHT?
UNTIL THAT LED TO MORE PARTS. AND BIGGER PARTS. ALL THE WAY TILL--
THANK YOU, THANK YOU, OH MY HEAVENS, THANK YOU!

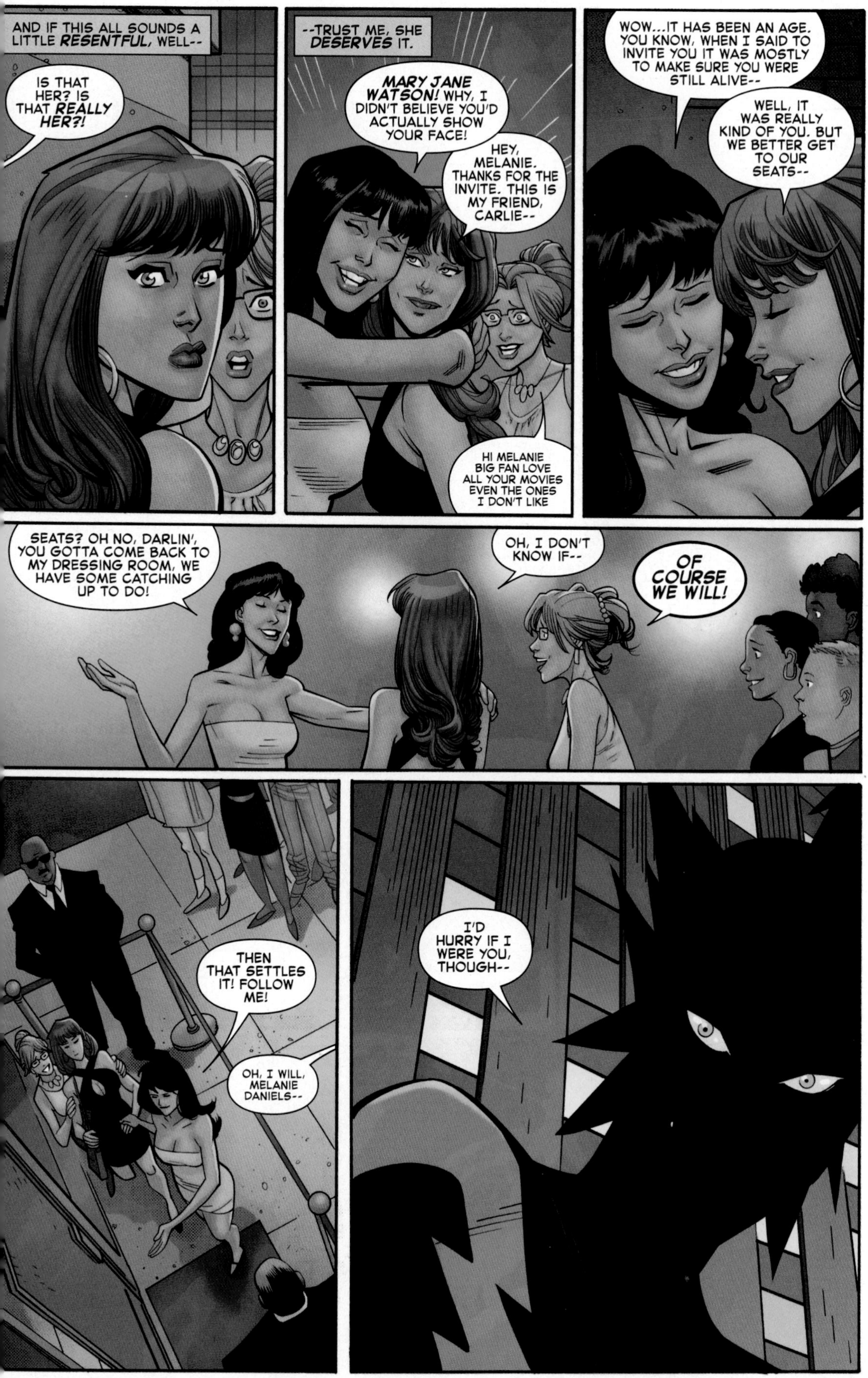

AND IF THIS ALL SOUNDS A LITTLE RESENTFUL, WELL--
IS THAT HER? IS THAT REALLY HER?!
--TRUST ME, SHE DESERVES IT.
MARY JANE WATSON! WHY, I DIDN'T BELIEVE YOU'D ACTUALLY SHOW YOUR FACE!
HEY, MELANIE. THANKS FOR THE INVITE. THIS IS MY FRIEND, CARLIE--
HI MELANIE BIG FAN LOVE ALL YOUR MOVIES EVEN THE ONES I DON'T LIKE
WOW...IT HAS BEEN AN AGE. YOU KNOW, WHEN I SAID TO INVITE YOU IT WAS MOSTLY TO MAKE SURE YOU WERE STILL ALIVE--
WELL, IT WAS REALLY KIND OF YOU. BUT WE BETTER GET TO OUR SEATS--
SEATS? OH NO, DARLIN', YOU GOTTA COME BACK TO MY DRESSING ROOM, WE HAVE SOME CATCHING UP TO DO!
OH, I DON'T KNOW IF--
OF COURSE WE WILL!
THEN THAT SETTLES IT! FOLLOW ME!
OH, I WILL, MELANIE DANIELS--
I'D HURRY IF I WERE YOU, THOUGH--

"--CURTAIN'S ALMOST UP."

HEY! THAT WAS MY FAVORITE FACE YOU ALMOST JUST BURNED OFF! WATCH THAT DEATH RAY--SOME OF US ARE JUST TRYING TO GET TO A SHOW.

THAT *WAS* A LITTLE TOO CLOSE.

THIS THING IS RELENTLESS. REALLY DOESN'T WANT ME TO GET FARTHER DOWN THIS HALL. WHICH IS A PROBLEM--

--SINCE I KNOW SOMEBODY'S *LIFE* IS ON THE LINE!

SORRY TO DO THIS, PAL--

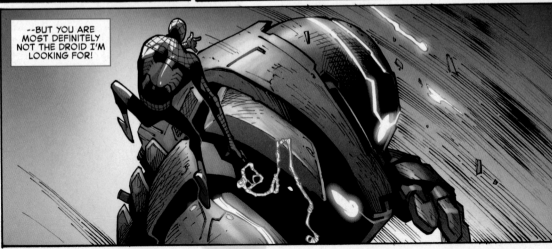

--BUT YOU ARE MOST DEFINITELY NOT THE DROID I'M LOOKING FOR!

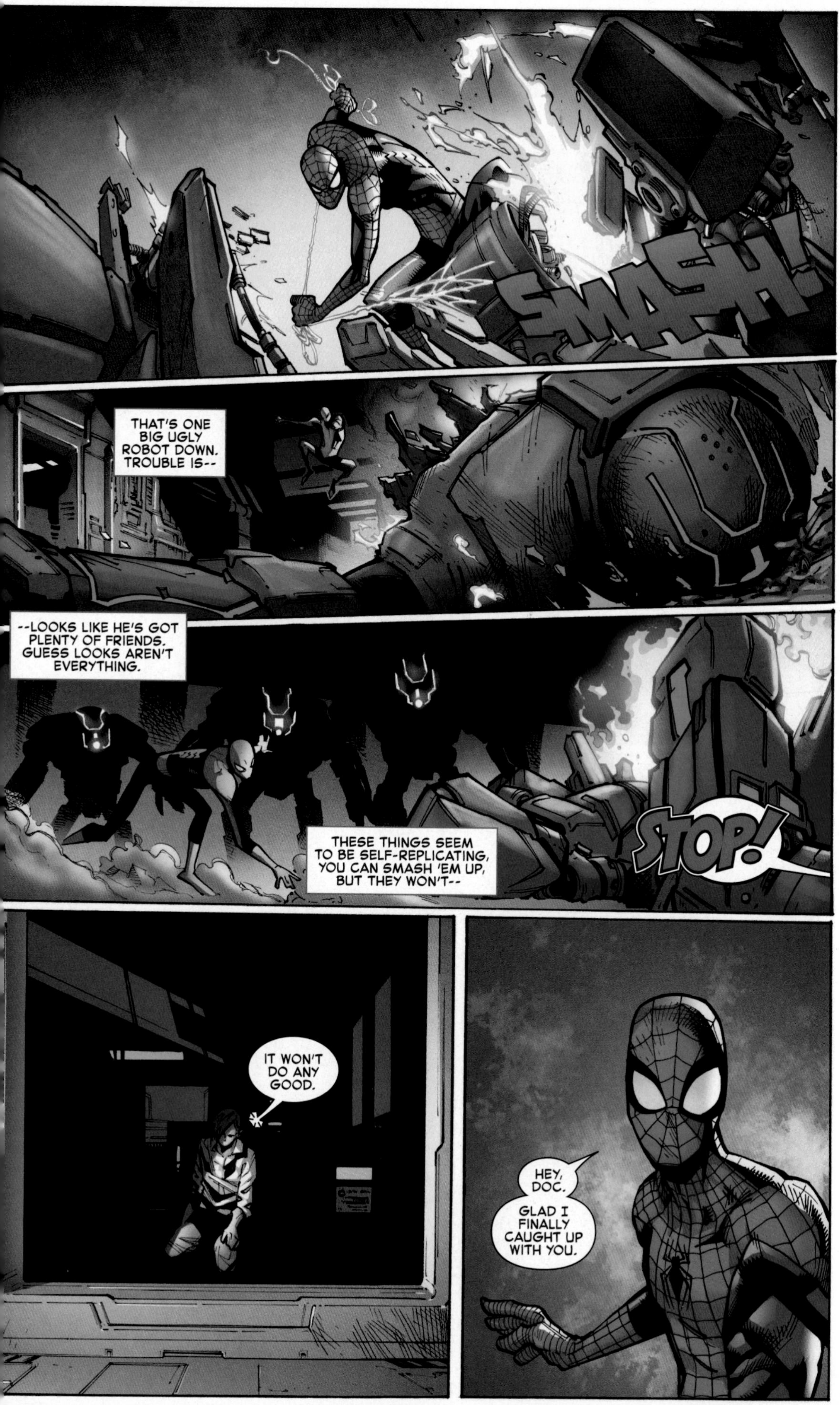
SMASH!
THAT'S ONE BIG UGLY ROBOT DOWN. TROUBLE IS--
--LOOKS LIKE HE'S GOT PLENTY OF FRIENDS. GUESS LOOKS AREN'T EVERYTHING.
THESE THINGS SEEM TO BE SELF-REPLICATING, YOU CAN SMASH 'EM UP, BUT THEY WON'T--
STOP!
IT WON'T DO ANY GOOD.
HEY, DOC.
GLAD I FINALLY CAUGHT UP WITH YOU.

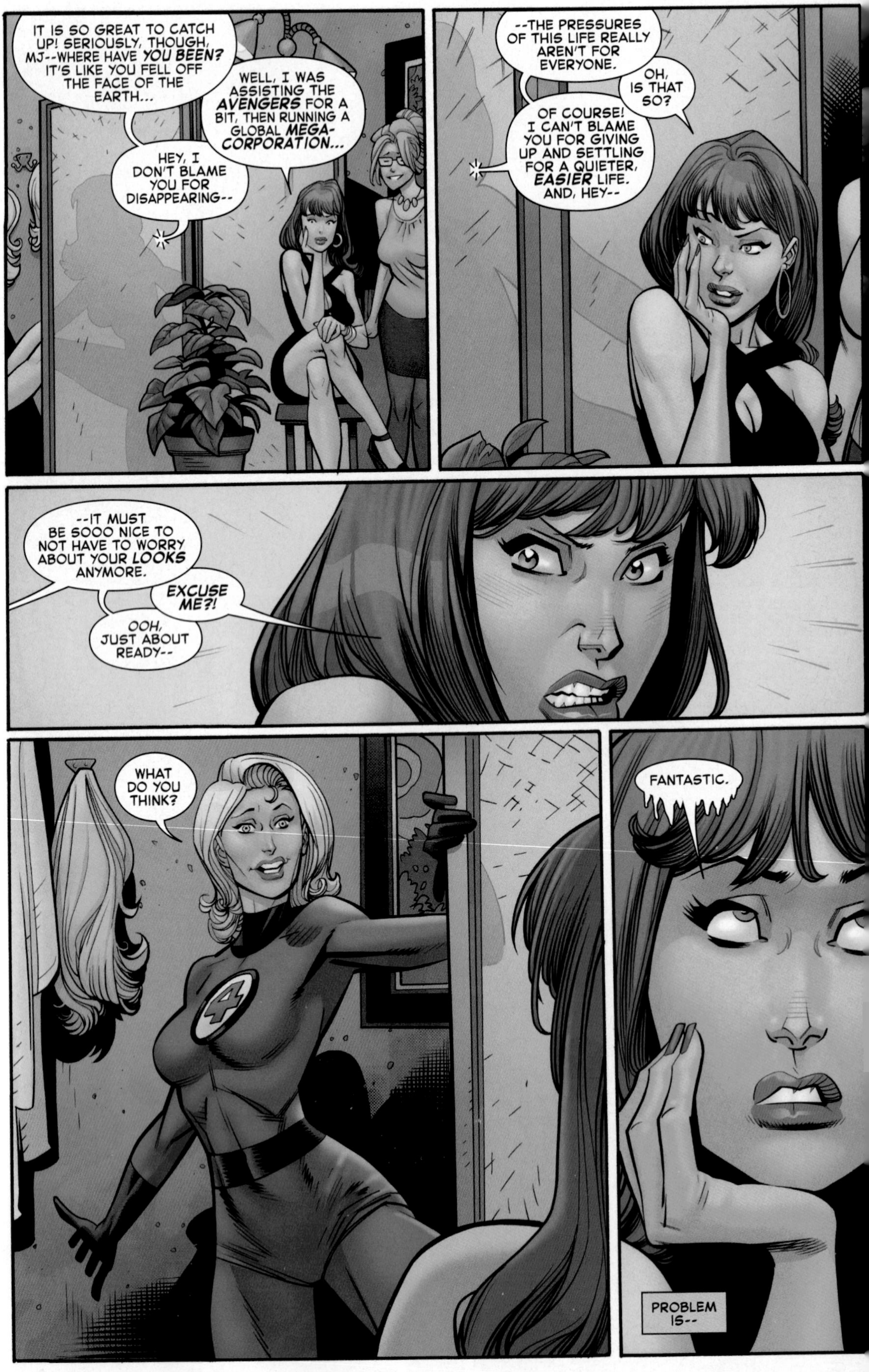
IT IS SO GREAT TO CATCH UP! SERIOUSLY, THOUGH, MJ--WHERE HAVE *YOU BEEN?* IT'S LIKE YOU FELL OFF THE FACE OF THE EARTH...
WELL, I WAS ASSISTING THE *AVENGERS* FOR A BIT, THEN RUNNING A GLOBAL *MEGA-CORPORATION...*
HEY, I DON'T BLAME YOU FOR DISAPPEARING--
--THE PRESSURES OF THIS LIFE REALLY AREN'T FOR EVERYONE.
OH, IS THAT SO?
OF COURSE! I CAN'T BLAME YOU FOR GIVING UP AND SETTLING FOR A QUIETER, *EASIER* LIFE. AND, HEY--
--IT MUST BE SOOO NICE TO NOT HAVE TO WORRY ABOUT YOUR *LOOKS* ANYMORE.
EXCUSE ME?!
OOH, JUST ABOUT READY--
WHAT DO YOU THINK?
FANTASTIC.
PROBLEM IS--

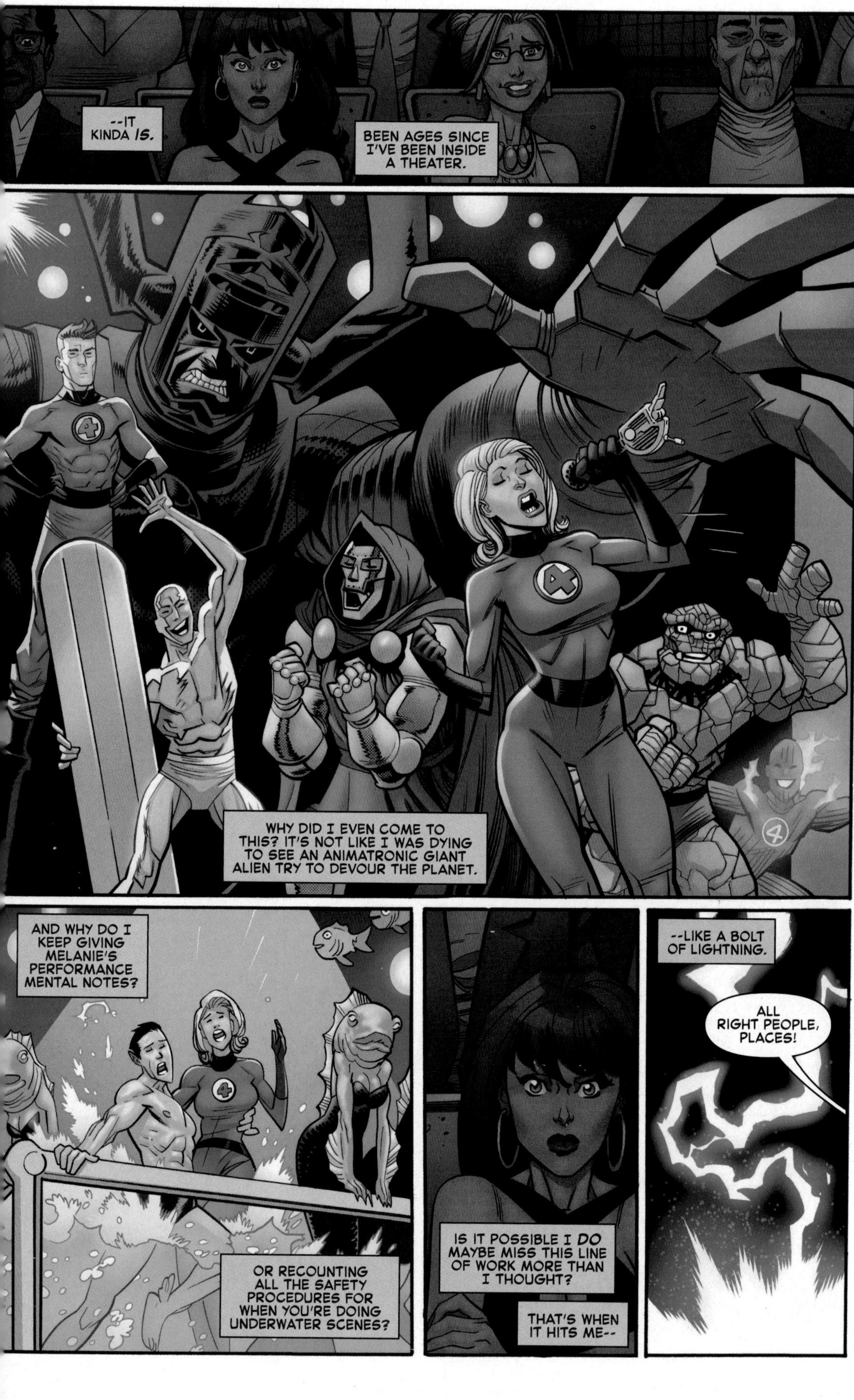
--IT KINDA IS.
BEEN AGES SINCE I'VE BEEN INSIDE A THEATER.
WHY DID I EVEN COME TO THIS? IT'S NOT LIKE I WAS DYING TO SEE AN ANIMATRONIC GIANT ALIEN TRY TO DEVOUR THE PLANET.
AND WHY DO I KEEP GIVING MELANIE'S PERFORMANCE MENTAL NOTES?
OR RECOUNTING ALL THE SAFETY PROCEDURES FOR WHEN YOU'RE DOING UNDERWATER SCENES?
IS IT POSSIBLE I DO MAYBE MISS THIS LINE OF WORK MORE THAN I THOUGHT?
THAT'S WHEN IT HITS ME--
--LIKE A BOLT OF LIGHTNING.
ALL RIGHT PEOPLE, PLACES!

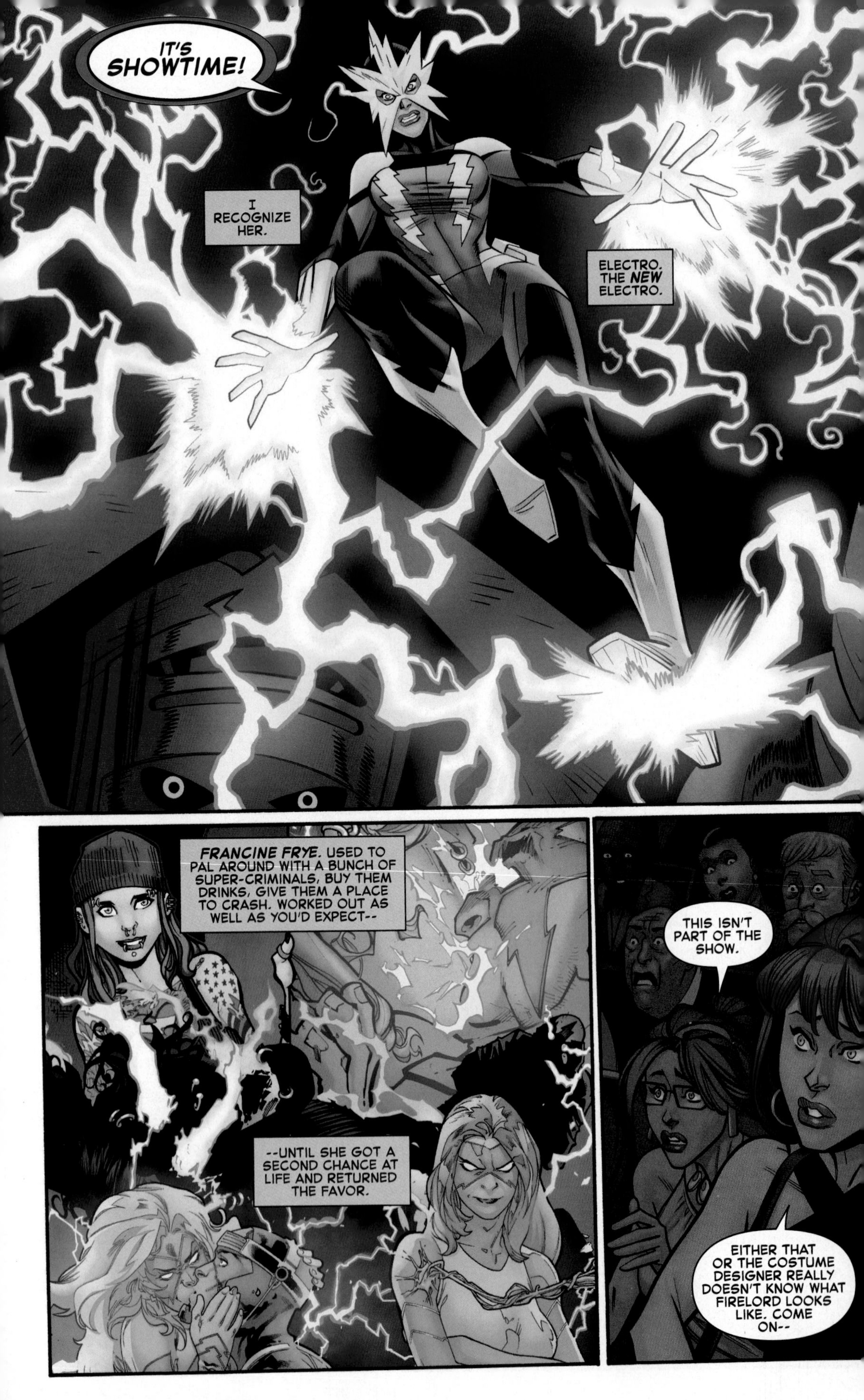
IT'S SHOWTIME!
I RECOGNIZE HER.
ELECTRO. THE NEW ELECTRO.
FRANCINE FRYE. USED TO PAL AROUND WITH A BUNCH OF SUPER-CRIMINALS, BUY THEM DRINKS, GIVE THEM A PLACE TO CRASH. WORKED OUT AS WELL AS YOU'D EXPECT--
--UNTIL SHE GOT A SECOND CHANCE AT LIFE AND RETURNED THE FAVOR.
THIS ISN'T PART OF THE SHOW.
EITHER THAT OR THE COSTUME DESIGNER REALLY DOESN'T KNOW WHAT FIRELORD LOOKS LIKE. COME ON--

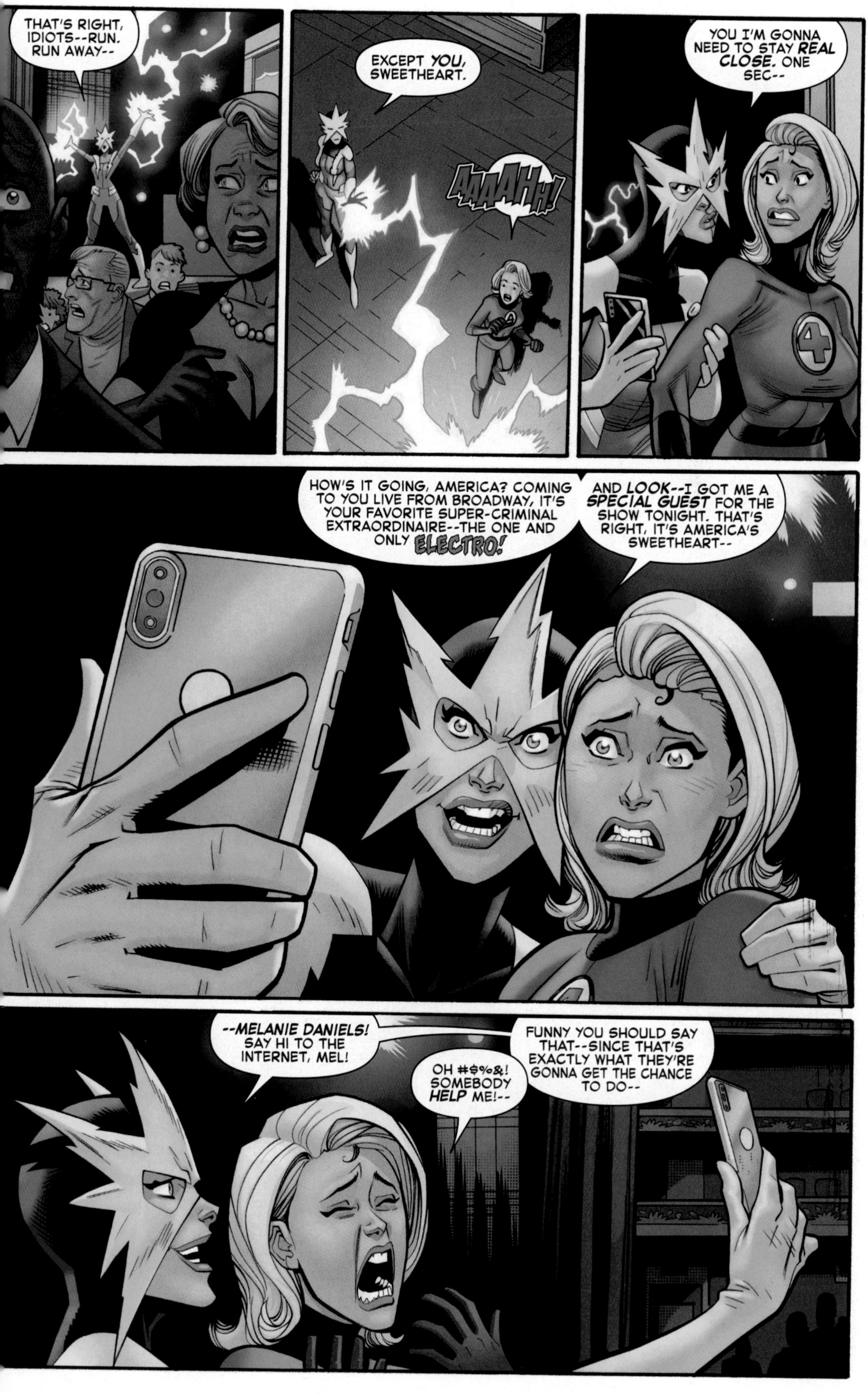
THAT'S RIGHT, IDIOTS--RUN. RUN AWAY--
EXCEPT YOU, SWEETHEART.
AAAAHH!
YOU I'M GONNA NEED TO STAY REAL CLOSE. ONE SEC--
HOW'S IT GOING, AMERICA? COMING TO YOU LIVE FROM BROADWAY, IT'S YOUR FAVORITE SUPER-CRIMINAL EXTRAORDINAIRE--THE ONE AND ONLY ELECTRO!
AND LOOK--I GOT ME A SPECIAL GUEST FOR THE SHOW TONIGHT. THAT'S RIGHT, IT'S AMERICA'S SWEETHEART--
--MELANIE DANIELS! SAY HI TO THE INTERNET, MEL!
OH #$%&! SOMEBODY HELP ME!--
FUNNY YOU SHOULD SAY THAT--SINCE THAT'S EXACTLY WHAT THEY'RE GONNA GET THE CHANCE TO DO--

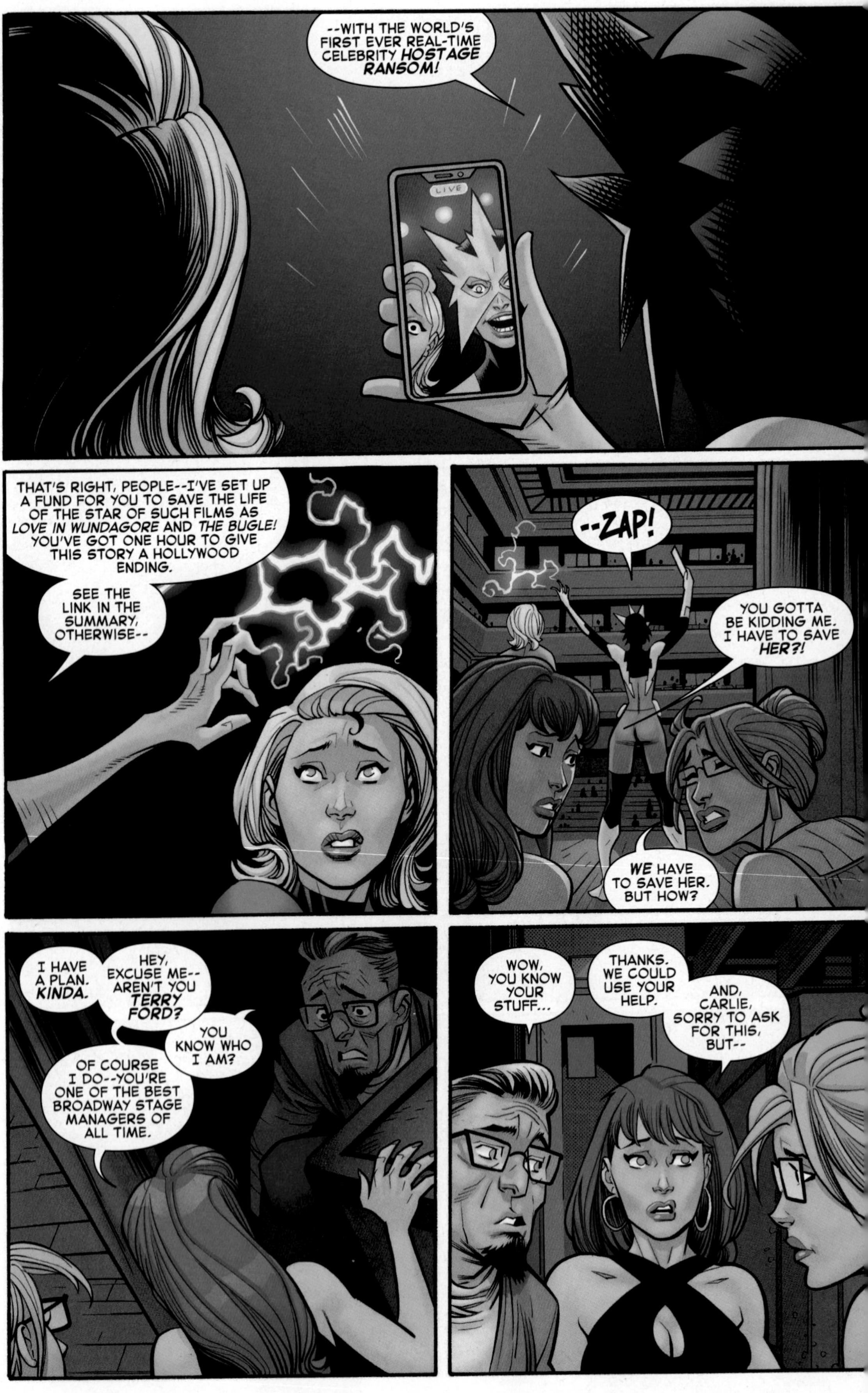
--WITH THE WORLD'S FIRST EVER REAL-TIME CELEBRITY HOSTAGE RANSOM!
LIVE
THAT'S RIGHT, PEOPLE--I'VE SET UP A FUND FOR YOU TO SAVE THE LIFE OF THE STAR OF SUCH FILMS AS LOVE IN WUNDAGORE AND THE BUGLE! YOU'VE GOT ONE HOUR TO GIVE THIS STORY A HOLLYWOOD ENDING.
SEE THE LINK IN THE SUMMARY, OTHERWISE--
--ZAP!
YOU GOTTA BE KIDDING ME. I HAVE TO SAVE HER?!
WE HAVE TO SAVE HER. BUT HOW?
I HAVE A PLAN. KINDA.
HEY, EXCUSE ME--AREN'T YOU TERRY FORD?
YOU KNOW WHO I AM?
OF COURSE I DO--YOU'RE ONE OF THE BEST BROADWAY STAGE MANAGERS OF ALL TIME.
WOW, YOU KNOW YOUR STUFF...
THANKS. WE COULD USE YOUR HELP.
AND, CARLIE, SORRY TO ASK FOR THIS, BUT--

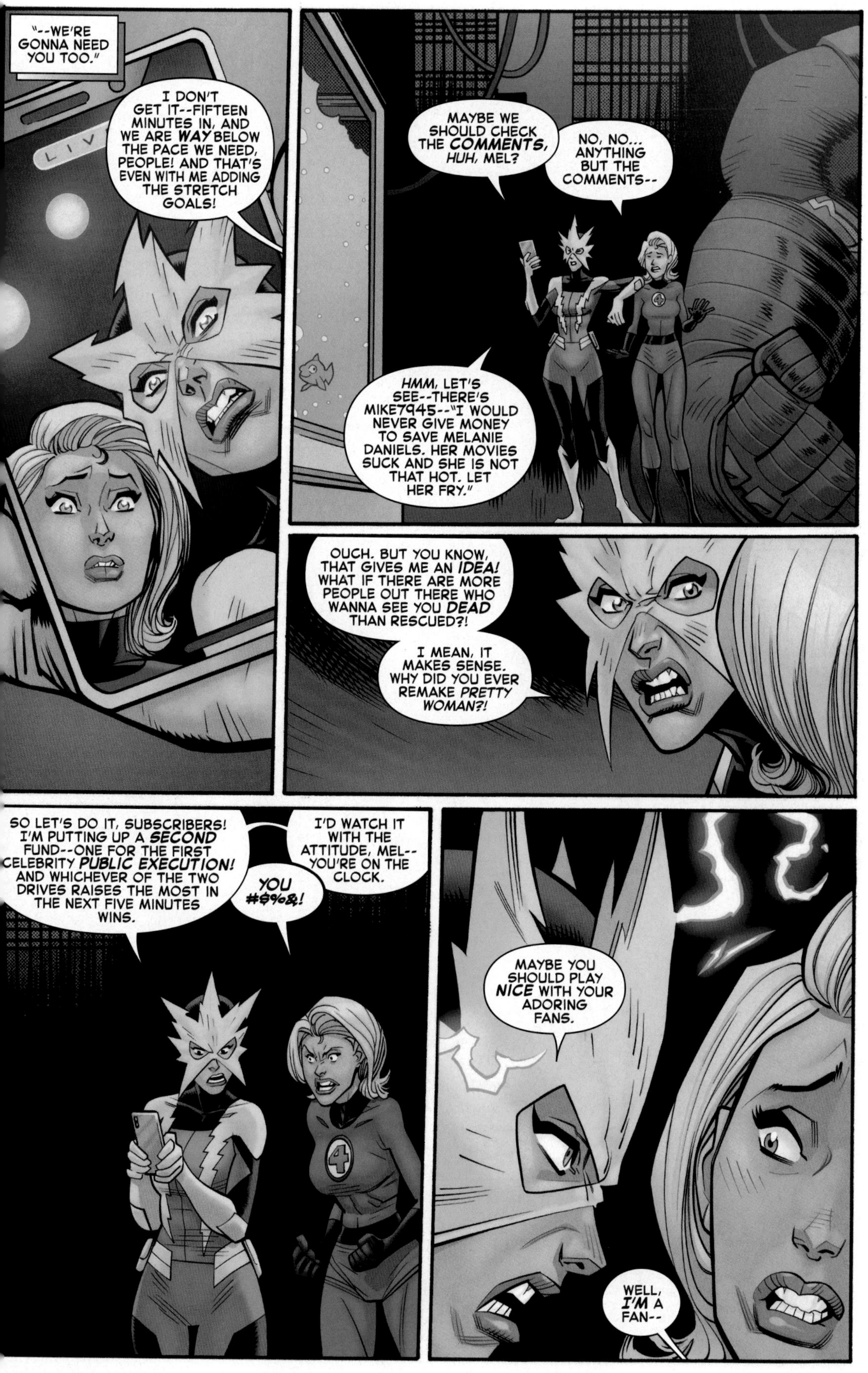
"--WE'RE GONNA NEED YOU TOO."
I DON'T GET IT--FIFTEEN MINUTES IN, AND WE ARE WAY BELOW THE PACE WE NEED, PEOPLE! AND THAT'S EVEN WITH ME ADDING THE STRETCH GOALS!
MAYBE WE SHOULD CHECK THE COMMENTS, HUH, MEL?
NO, NO... ANYTHING BUT THE COMMENTS--
HMM, LET'S SEE--THERE'S MIKE7945--"I WOULD NEVER GIVE MONEY TO SAVE MELANIE DANIELS. HER MOVIES SUCK AND SHE IS NOT THAT HOT. LET HER FRY."
OUCH. BUT YOU KNOW, THAT GIVES ME AN IDEA! WHAT IF THERE ARE MORE PEOPLE OUT THERE WHO WANNA SEE YOU DEAD THAN RESCUED?!
I MEAN, IT MAKES SENSE. WHY DID YOU EVER REMAKE PRETTY WOMAN?!
SO LET'S DO IT, SUBSCRIBERS! I'M PUTTING UP A SECOND FUND--ONE FOR THE FIRST CELEBRITY PUBLIC EXECUTION! AND WHICHEVER OF THE TWO DRIVES RAISES THE MOST IN THE NEXT FIVE MINUTES WINS.
YOU #$%&!
I'D WATCH IT WITH THE ATTITUDE, MEL--YOU'RE ON THE CLOCK.
MAYBE YOU SHOULD PLAY NICE WITH YOUR ADORING FANS.
WELL, I'M A FAN--

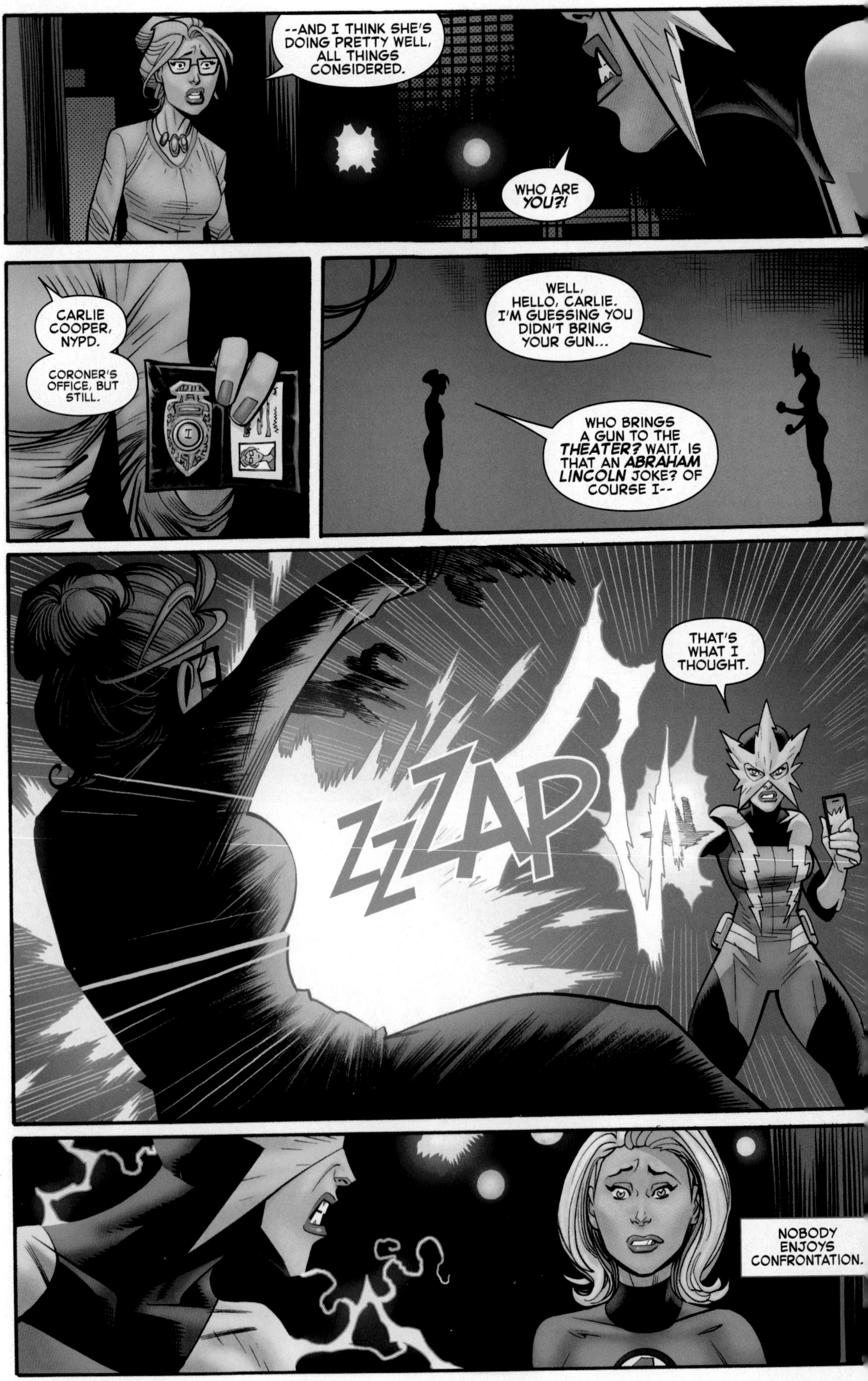
--AND I THINK SHE'S DOING PRETTY WELL, ALL THINGS CONSIDERED.
WHO ARE *YOU?!*
CARLIE COOPER, NYPD.
CORONER'S OFFICE, BUT STILL.
WELL, HELLO, CARLIE. I'M GUESSING YOU DIDN'T BRING YOUR GUN...
WHO BRINGS A GUN TO THE ***THEATER?*** WAIT, IS THAT AN ***ABRAHAM LINCOLN*** JOKE? OF COURSE I--
ZZZAP
THAT'S WHAT I THOUGHT.
NOBODY ENJOYS CONFRONTATION.

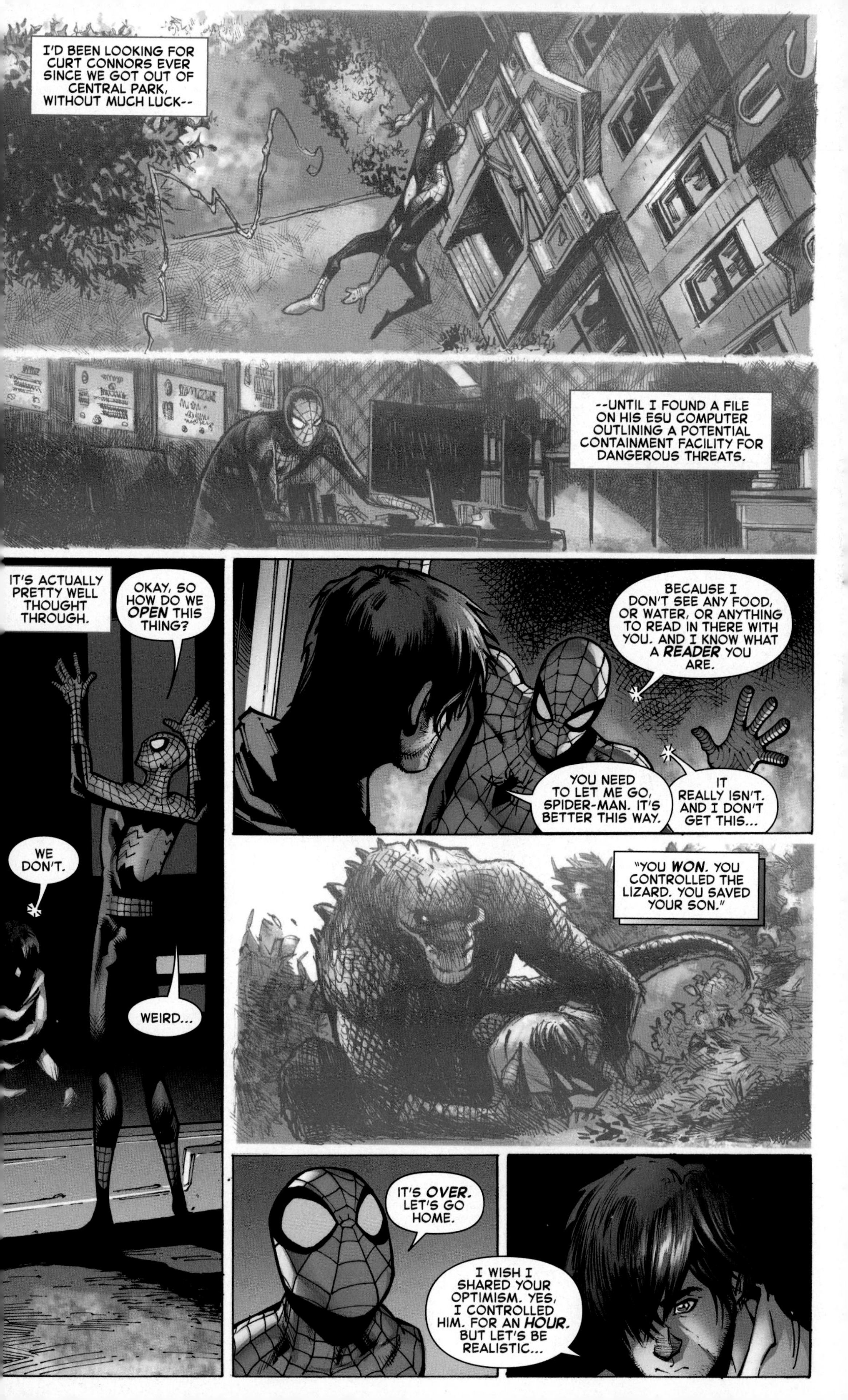

I'D BEEN LOOKING FOR CURT CONNORS EVER SINCE WE GOT OUT OF CENTRAL PARK, WITHOUT MUCH LUCK--
--UNTIL I FOUND A FILE ON HIS ESU COMPUTER OUTLINING A POTENTIAL CONTAINMENT FACILITY FOR DANGEROUS THREATS.
IT'S ACTUALLY PRETTY WELL THOUGHT THROUGH.
OKAY, SO HOW DO WE OPEN THIS THING?
WE DON'T.
WEIRD...
BECAUSE I DON'T SEE ANY FOOD, OR WATER, OR ANYTHING TO READ IN THERE WITH YOU. AND I KNOW WHAT A READER YOU ARE.
YOU NEED TO LET ME GO, SPIDER-MAN. IT'S BETTER THIS WAY.
IT REALLY ISN'T. AND I DON'T GET THIS...
"YOU WON. YOU CONTROLLED THE LIZARD. YOU SAVED YOUR SON."
IT'S OVER. LET'S GO HOME.
I WISH I SHARED YOUR OPTIMISM. YES, I CONTROLLED HIM. FOR AN HOUR. BUT LET'S BE REALISTIC...

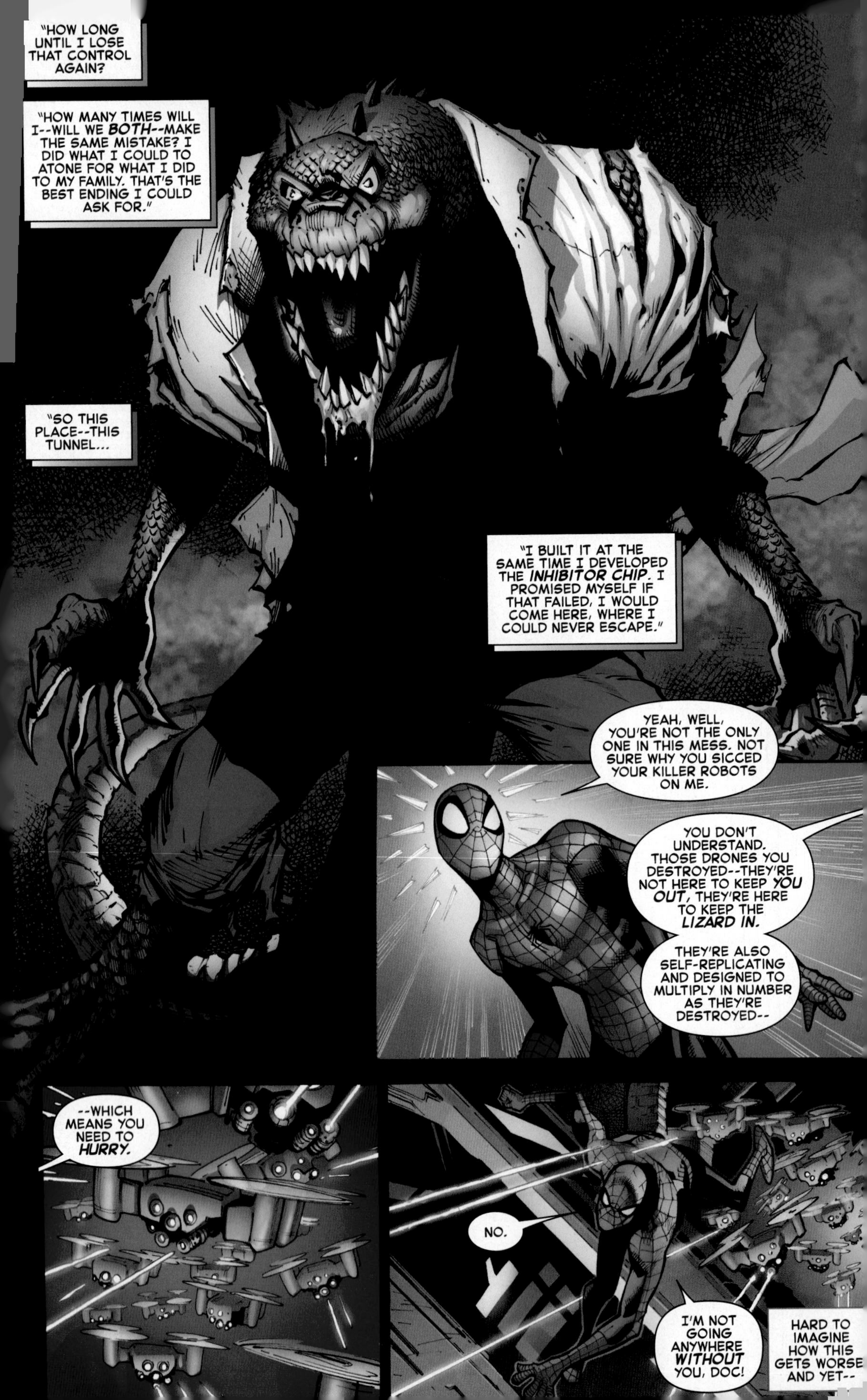
"HOW LONG UNTIL I LOSE THAT CONTROL AGAIN?
"HOW MANY TIMES WILL I--WILL WE BOTH--MAKE THE SAME MISTAKE? I DID WHAT I COULD TO ATONE FOR WHAT I DID TO MY FAMILY. THAT'S THE BEST ENDING I COULD ASK FOR."
"SO THIS PLACE--THIS TUNNEL...
"I BUILT IT AT THE SAME TIME I DEVELOPED THE INHIBITOR CHIP. I PROMISED MYSELF IF THAT FAILED, I WOULD COME HERE, WHERE I COULD NEVER ESCAPE."
YEAH, WELL, YOU'RE NOT THE ONLY ONE IN THIS MESS. NOT SURE WHY YOU SICCED YOUR KILLER ROBOTS ON ME.
YOU DON'T UNDERSTAND. THOSE DRONES YOU DESTROYED--THEY'RE NOT HERE TO KEEP YOU OUT, THEY'RE HERE TO KEEP THE LIZARD IN.
THEY'RE ALSO SELF-REPLICATING AND DESIGNED TO MULTIPLY IN NUMBER AS THEY'RE DESTROYED--
--WHICH MEANS YOU NEED TO HURRY.
NO.
I'M NOT GOING ANYWHERE WITHOUT YOU, DOC!
HARD TO IMAGINE HOW THIS GETS WORSE AND YET--

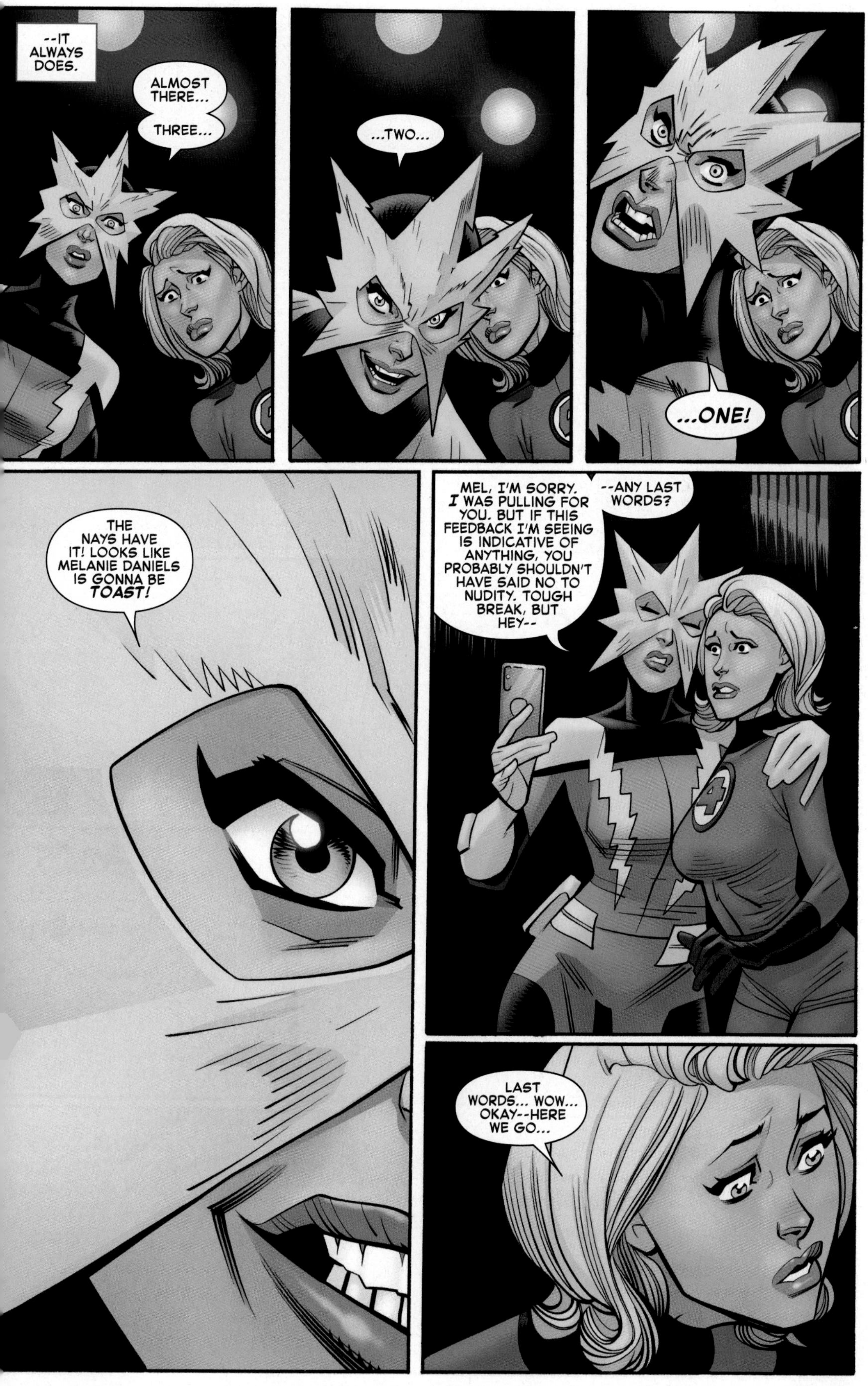
--IT ALWAYS DOES.
ALMOST THERE...
THREE...
...TWO...
...ONE!
THE NAYS HAVE IT! LOOKS LIKE MELANIE DANIELS IS GONNA BE TOAST!
MEL, I'M SORRY. I WAS PULLING FOR YOU. BUT IF THIS FEEDBACK I'M SEEING IS INDICATIVE OF ANYTHING, YOU PROBABLY SHOULDN'T HAVE SAID NO TO NUDITY. TOUGH BREAK, BUT HEY--
--ANY LAST WORDS?
LAST WORDS... WOW... OKAY--HERE WE GO...

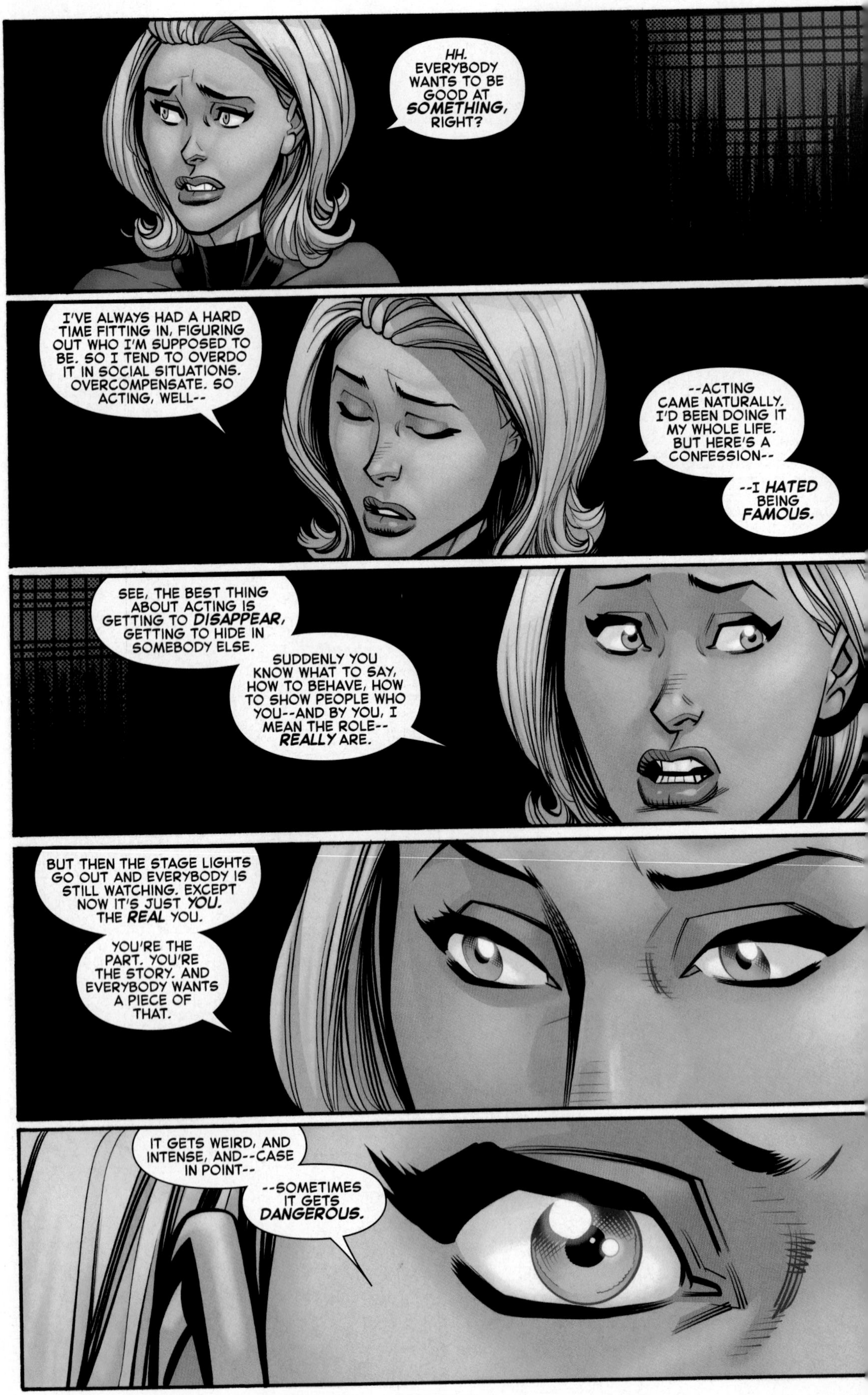

HH. EVERYBODY WANTS TO BE GOOD AT SOMETHING, RIGHT?
I'VE ALWAYS HAD A HARD TIME FITTING IN, FIGURING OUT WHO I'M SUPPOSED TO BE. SO I TEND TO OVERDO IT IN SOCIAL SITUATIONS. OVERCOMPENSATE. SO ACTING, WELL--
--ACTING CAME NATURALLY. I'D BEEN DOING IT MY WHOLE LIFE. BUT HERE'S A CONFESSION--
--I HATED BEING FAMOUS.
SEE, THE BEST THING ABOUT ACTING IS GETTING TO DISAPPEAR, GETTING TO HIDE IN SOMEBODY ELSE.
SUDDENLY YOU KNOW WHAT TO SAY, HOW TO BEHAVE, HOW TO SHOW PEOPLE WHO YOU--AND BY YOU, I MEAN THE ROLE--REALLY ARE.
BUT THEN THE STAGE LIGHTS GO OUT AND EVERYBODY IS STILL WATCHING. EXCEPT NOW IT'S JUST YOU. THE REAL YOU.
YOU'RE THE PART. YOU'RE THE STORY. AND EVERYBODY WANTS A PIECE OF THAT.
IT GETS WEIRD, AND INTENSE, AND--CASE IN POINT--
--SOMETIMES IT GETS DANGEROUS.

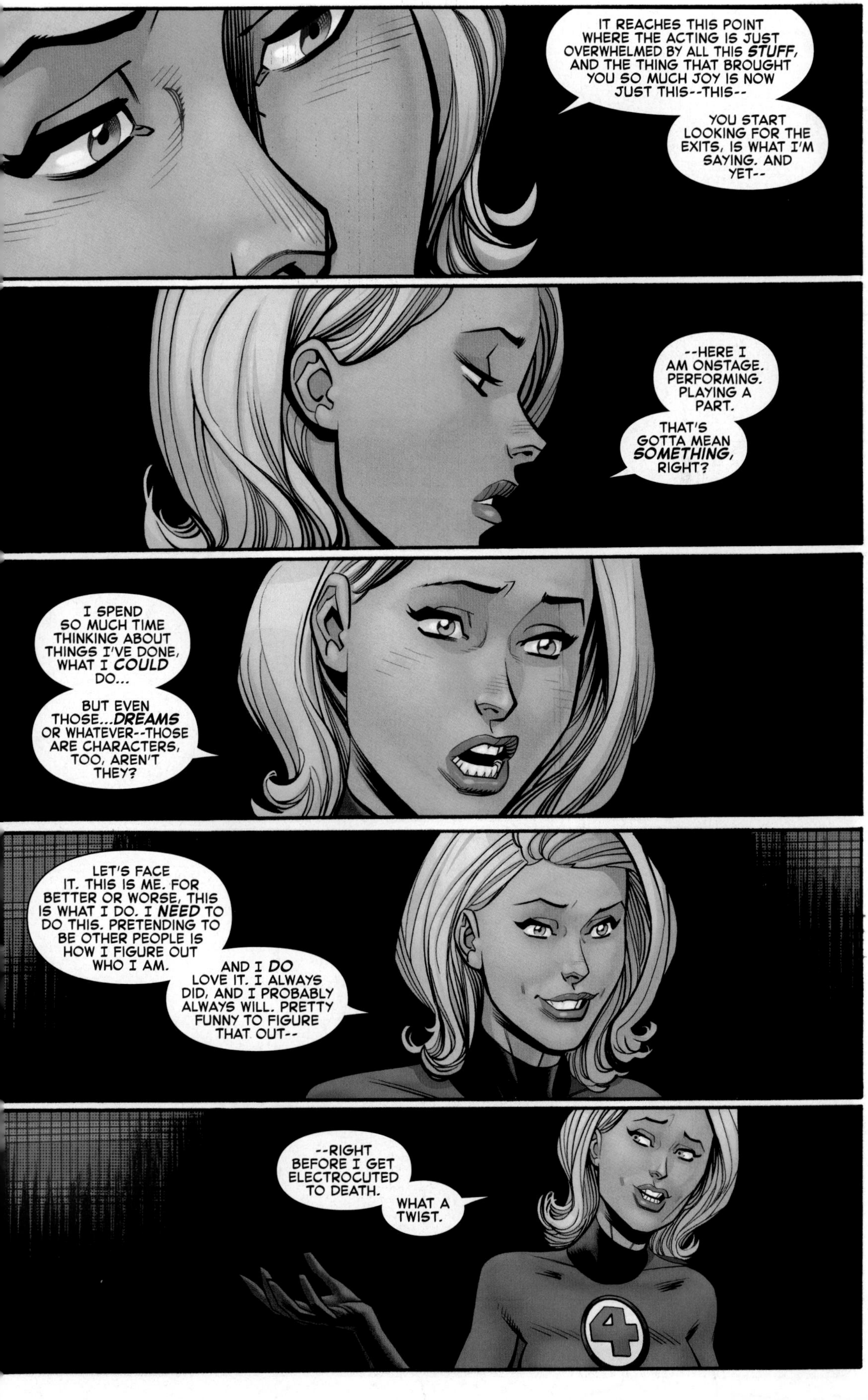
IT REACHES THIS POINT WHERE THE ACTING IS JUST OVERWHELMED BY ALL THIS *STUFF*, AND THE THING THAT BROUGHT YOU SO MUCH JOY IS NOW JUST THIS--THIS--
YOU START LOOKING FOR THE EXITS, IS WHAT I'M SAYING. AND YET--
--HERE I AM ONSTAGE. PERFORMING. PLAYING A PART.
THAT'S GOTTA MEAN *SOMETHING*, RIGHT?
I SPEND SO MUCH TIME THINKING ABOUT THINGS I'VE DONE, WHAT I *COULD* DO...
BUT EVEN THOSE...*DREAMS* OR WHATEVER--THOSE ARE CHARACTERS, TOO, AREN'T THEY?
LET'S FACE IT. THIS IS ME. FOR BETTER OR WORSE, THIS IS WHAT I DO. I *NEED* TO DO THIS. PRETENDING TO BE OTHER PEOPLE IS HOW I FIGURE OUT WHO I AM.
AND I *DO* LOVE IT. I ALWAYS DID, AND I PROBABLY ALWAYS WILL. PRETTY FUNNY TO FIGURE THAT OUT--
--RIGHT BEFORE I GET ELECTROCUTED TO DEATH.
WHAT A TWIST.

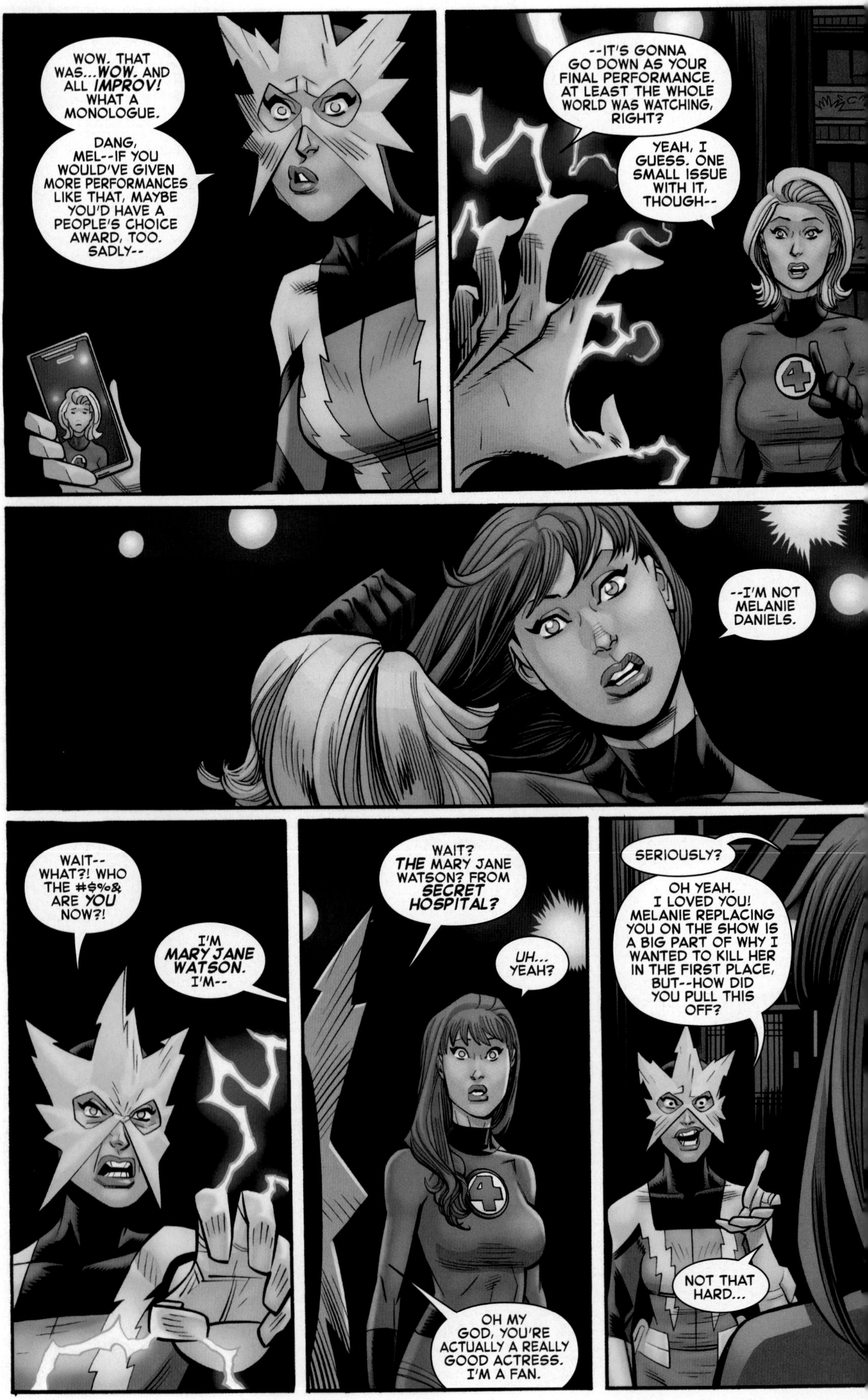
WOW. THAT WAS...WOW. AND ALL IMPROV! WHAT A MONOLOGUE.
DANG, MEL--IF YOU WOULD'VE GIVEN MORE PERFORMANCES LIKE THAT, MAYBE YOU'D HAVE A PEOPLE'S CHOICE AWARD, TOO. SADLY--
--IT'S GONNA GO DOWN AS YOUR FINAL PERFORMANCE. AT LEAST THE WHOLE WORLD WAS WATCHING, RIGHT?
YEAH, I GUESS. ONE SMALL ISSUE WITH IT, THOUGH--
--I'M NOT MELANIE DANIELS.
WAIT-- WHAT?! WHO THE #$%& ARE YOU NOW?!
I'M MARY JANE WATSON. I'M--
WAIT? THE MARY JANE WATSON? FROM SECRET HOSPITAL?
UH... YEAH?
OH MY GOD, YOU'RE ACTUALLY A REALLY GOOD ACTRESS. I'M A FAN.
SERIOUSLY?
OH YEAH. I LOVED YOU! MELANIE REPLACING YOU ON THE SHOW IS A BIG PART OF WHY I WANTED TO KILL HER IN THE FIRST PLACE, BUT--HOW DID YOU PULL THIS OFF?
NOT THAT HARD...

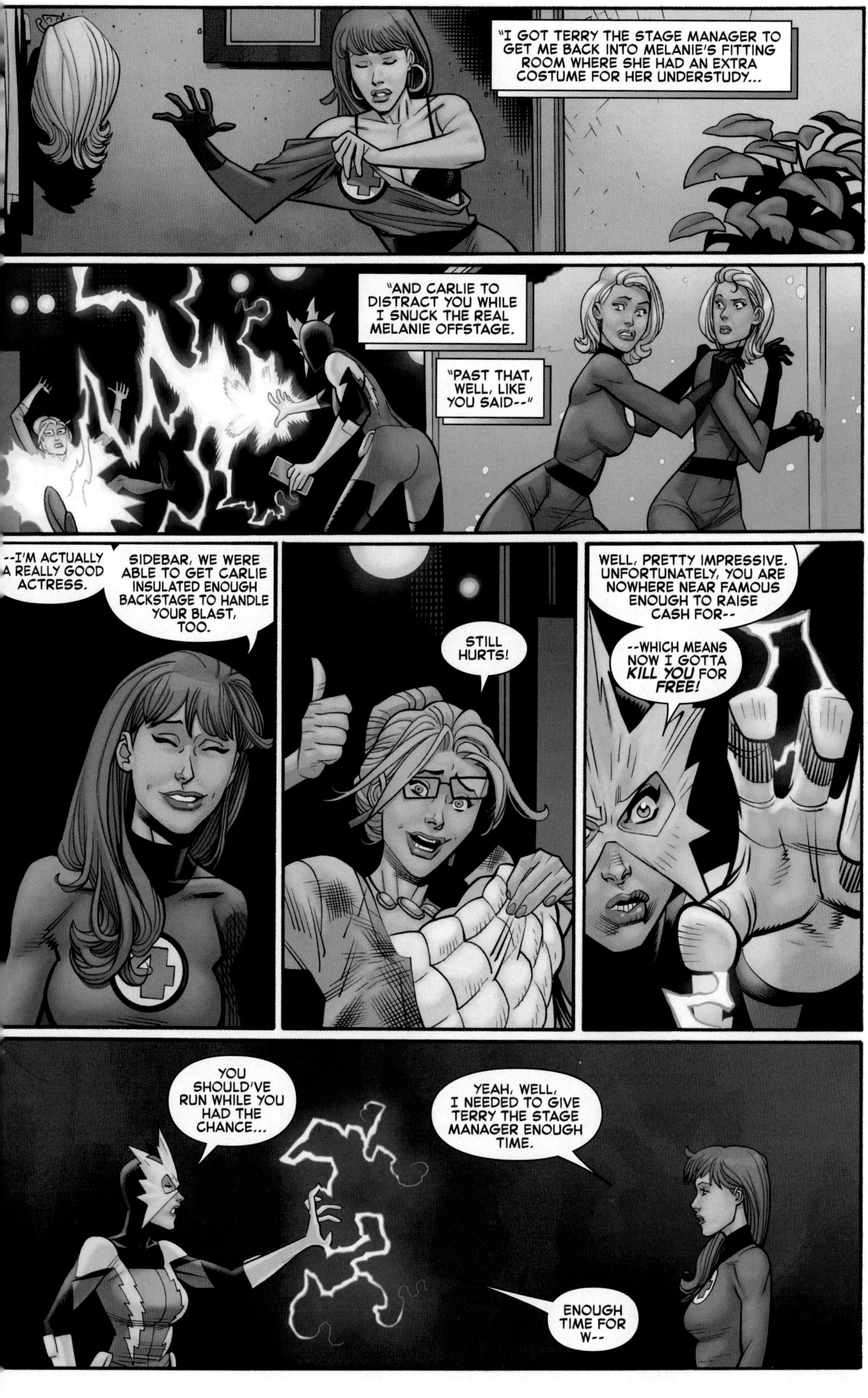
"I GOT TERRY THE STAGE MANAGER TO GET ME BACK INTO MELANIE'S FITTING ROOM WHERE SHE HAD AN EXTRA COSTUME FOR HER UNDERSTUDY...
"AND CARLIE TO DISTRACT YOU WHILE I SNUCK THE REAL MELANIE OFFSTAGE.
"PAST THAT, WELL, LIKE YOU SAID--"
--I'M ACTUALLY A REALLY GOOD ACTRESS.
SIDEBAR, WE WERE ABLE TO GET CARLIE INSULATED ENOUGH BACKSTAGE TO HANDLE YOUR BLAST, TOO.
STILL HURTS!
WELL, PRETTY IMPRESSIVE. UNFORTUNATELY, YOU ARE NOWHERE NEAR FAMOUS ENOUGH TO RAISE CASH FOR--
--WHICH MEANS NOW I GOTTA KILL YOU FOR FREE!
YOU SHOULD'VE RUN WHILE YOU HAD THE CHANCE...
YEAH, WELL, I NEEDED TO GIVE TERRY THE STAGE MANAGER ENOUGH TIME.
ENOUGH TIME FOR W--

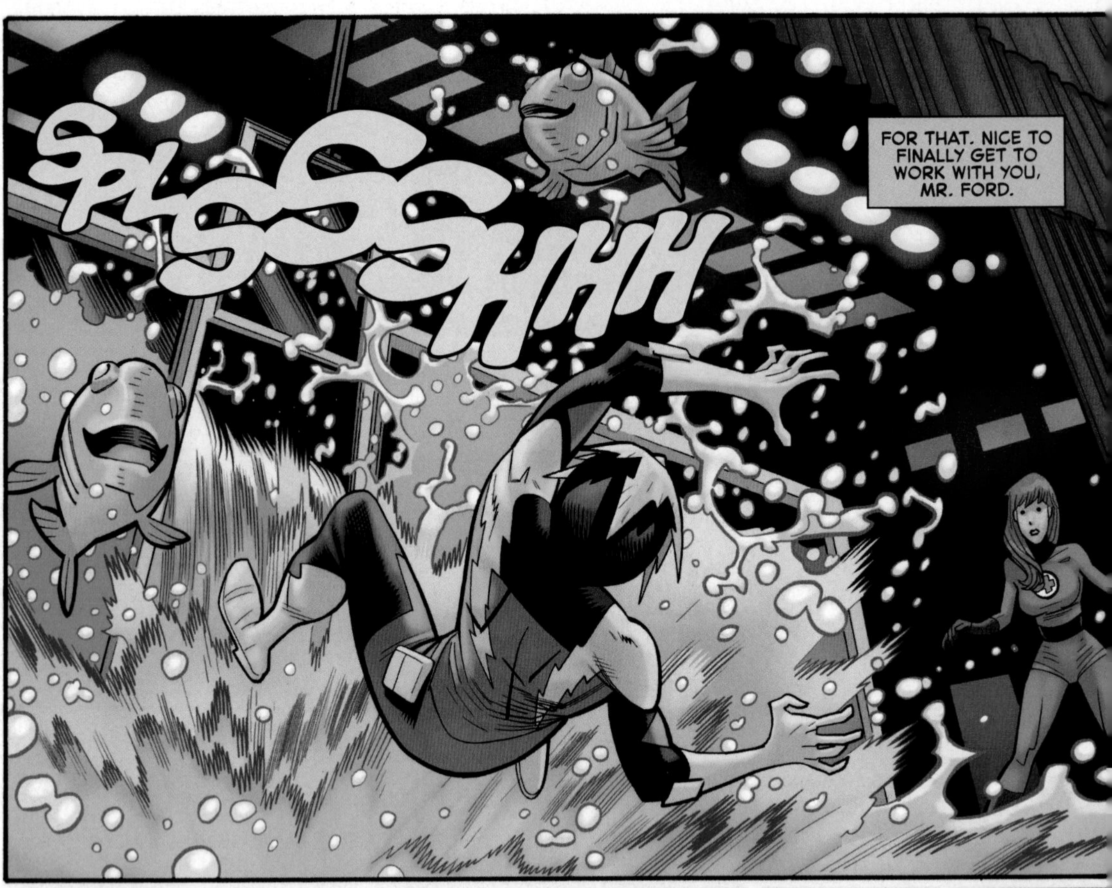
SPLSSSHHH
FOR THAT. NICE TO FINALLY GET TO WORK WITH YOU, MR. FORD.

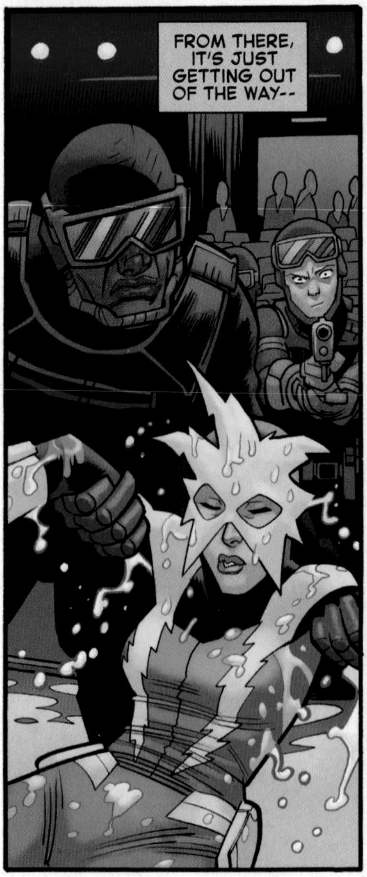
FROM THERE, IT'S JUST GETTING OUT OF THE WAY--

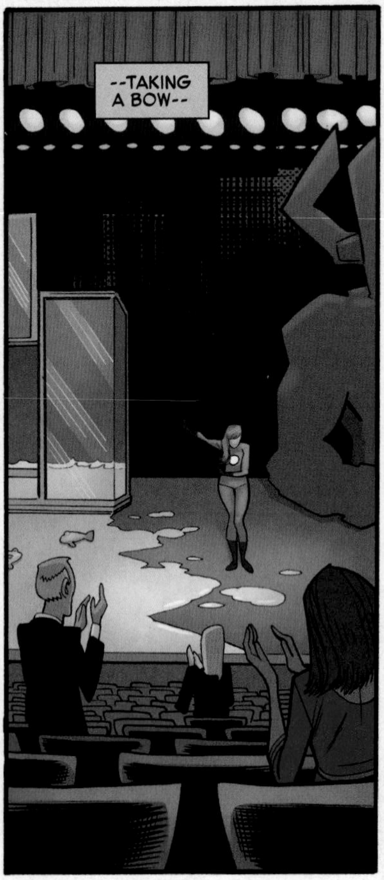
--TAKING A BOW--

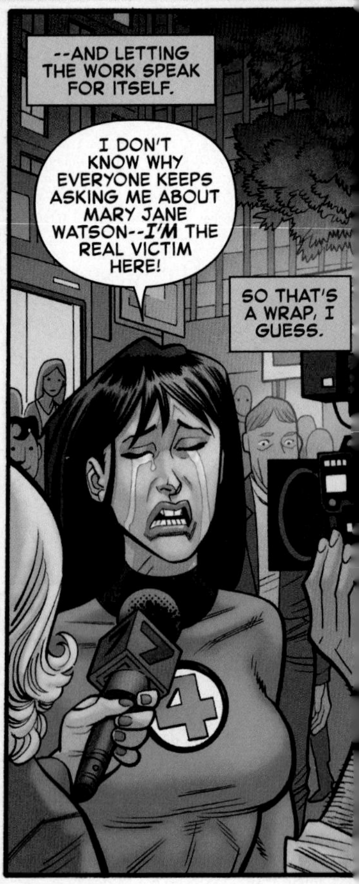
--AND LETTING THE WORK SPEAK FOR ITSELF.
I DON'T KNOW WHY EVERYONE KEEPS ASKING ME ABOUT MARY JANE WATSON--*I'M* THE REAL VICTIM HERE!
SO THAT'S A WRAP, I GUESS.

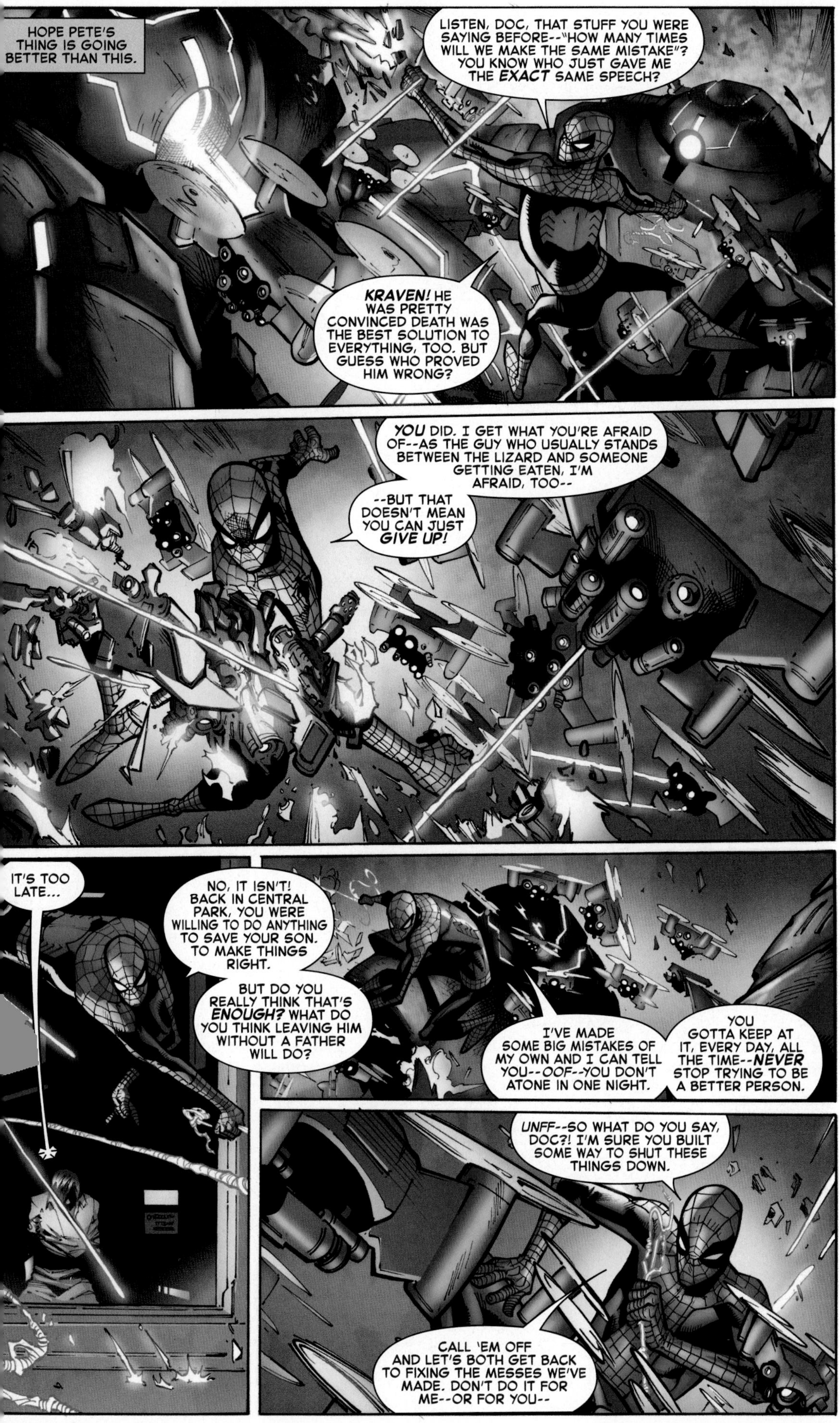
HOPE PETE'S THING IS GOING BETTER THAN THIS.
LISTEN, DOC, THAT STUFF YOU WERE SAYING BEFORE--"HOW MANY TIMES WILL WE MAKE THE SAME MISTAKE"? YOU KNOW WHO JUST GAVE ME THE EXACT SAME SPEECH?
KRAVEN! HE WAS PRETTY CONVINCED DEATH WAS THE BEST SOLUTION TO EVERYTHING, TOO. BUT GUESS WHO PROVED HIM WRONG?
YOU DID. I GET WHAT YOU'RE AFRAID OF--AS THE GUY WHO USUALLY STANDS BETWEEN THE LIZARD AND SOMEONE GETTING EATEN, I'M AFRAID, TOO--
--BUT THAT DOESN'T MEAN YOU CAN JUST GIVE UP!
IT'S TOO LATE...
NO, IT ISN'T! BACK IN CENTRAL PARK, YOU WERE WILLING TO DO ANYTHING TO SAVE YOUR SON. TO MAKE THINGS RIGHT.
BUT DO YOU REALLY THINK THAT'S ENOUGH? WHAT DO YOU THINK LEAVING HIM WITHOUT A FATHER WILL DO?
I'VE MADE SOME BIG MISTAKES OF MY OWN AND I CAN TELL YOU--OOF--YOU DON'T ATONE IN ONE NIGHT.
YOU GOTTA KEEP AT IT, EVERY DAY, ALL THE TIME--NEVER STOP TRYING TO BE A BETTER PERSON.
UNFF--SO WHAT DO YOU SAY, DOC?! I'M SURE YOU BUILT SOME WAY TO SHUT THESE THINGS DOWN.
CALL 'EM OFF AND LET'S BOTH GET BACK TO FIXING THE MESSES WE'VE MADE. DON'T DO IT FOR ME--OR FOR YOU--

--DO IT FOR *BILLY!*

BILLY.

AUGUST THIRTY-FIRST!

VOICE COMMAND CONFIRMED.

SELF-DESTRUCT SEQUENCE INITIATED.

SELF-DESTRUCT SEQUENCE INITIATED.

SELF-DESTRUCT SEQUENCE INITIATED.

SELF-DESTRUCT SEQUENCE INITIATED.

SELF-DESTRUCT SEQUENCE INITIATED.

SELF-DESTRUCT SEQUENCE INITIATED.

SELF-DESTRUCT SEQUENCE INITIATED.

SELF-DESTRUCT SEQUENCE INITIATED.

SELF-DESTRUCT SEQUENCE INITIATED.

IT'S HIS BIRTHDAY.

≶SIGH≷ GOOD JOB, DOC. LET'S GET YOU HOME.

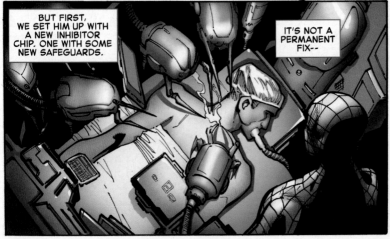

BUT FIRST, WE SET HIM UP WITH A NEW INHIBITOR CHIP. ONE WITH SOME NEW SAFEGUARDS.

IT'S NOT A PERMANENT FIX--

--BUT IT'S *SOMETHING.* WE SAY OUR GOODBYES--

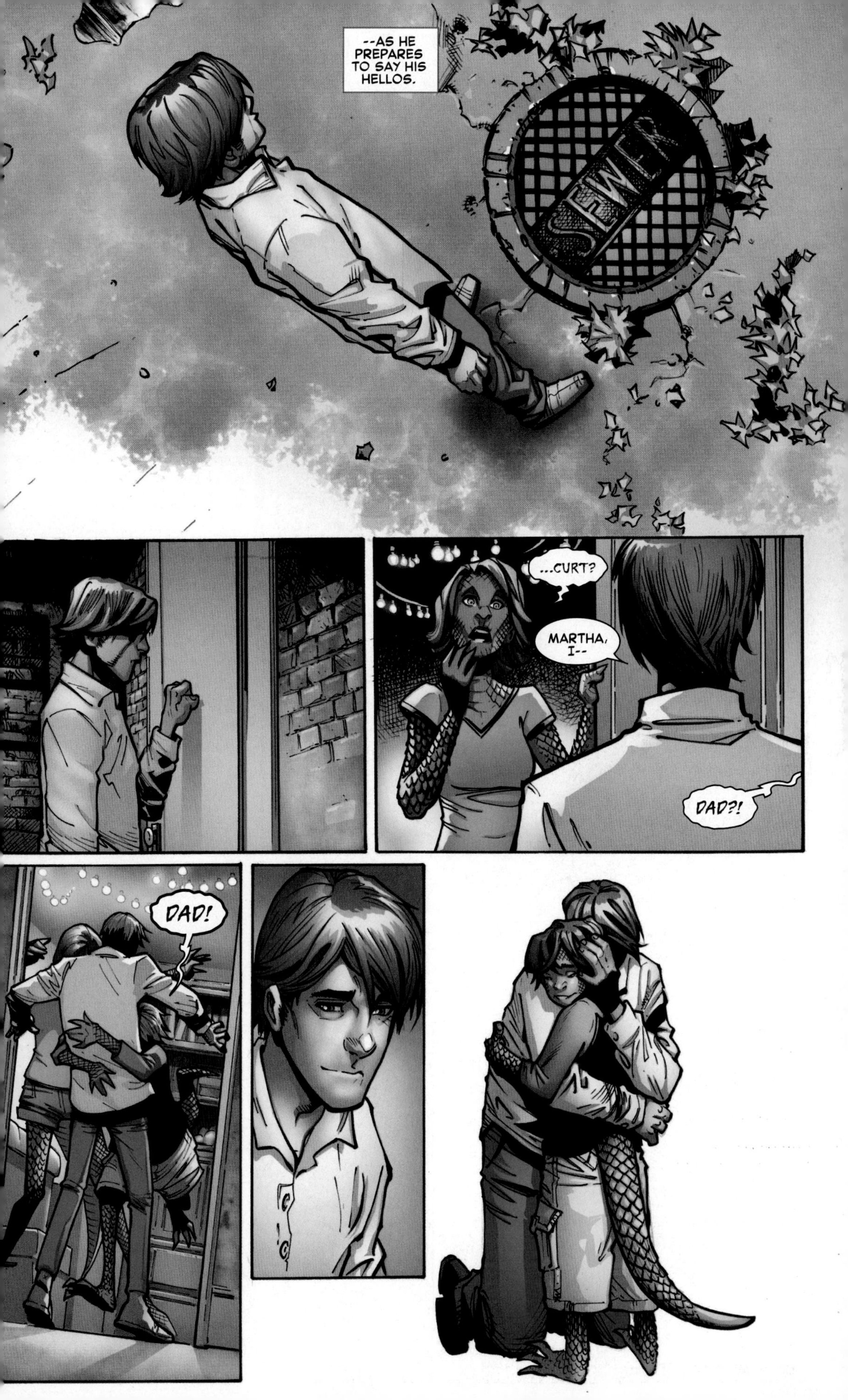
--AS HE PREPARES TO SAY HIS HELLOS.
SEWER
...CURT?
MARTHA, I--
DAD?!
DAD!

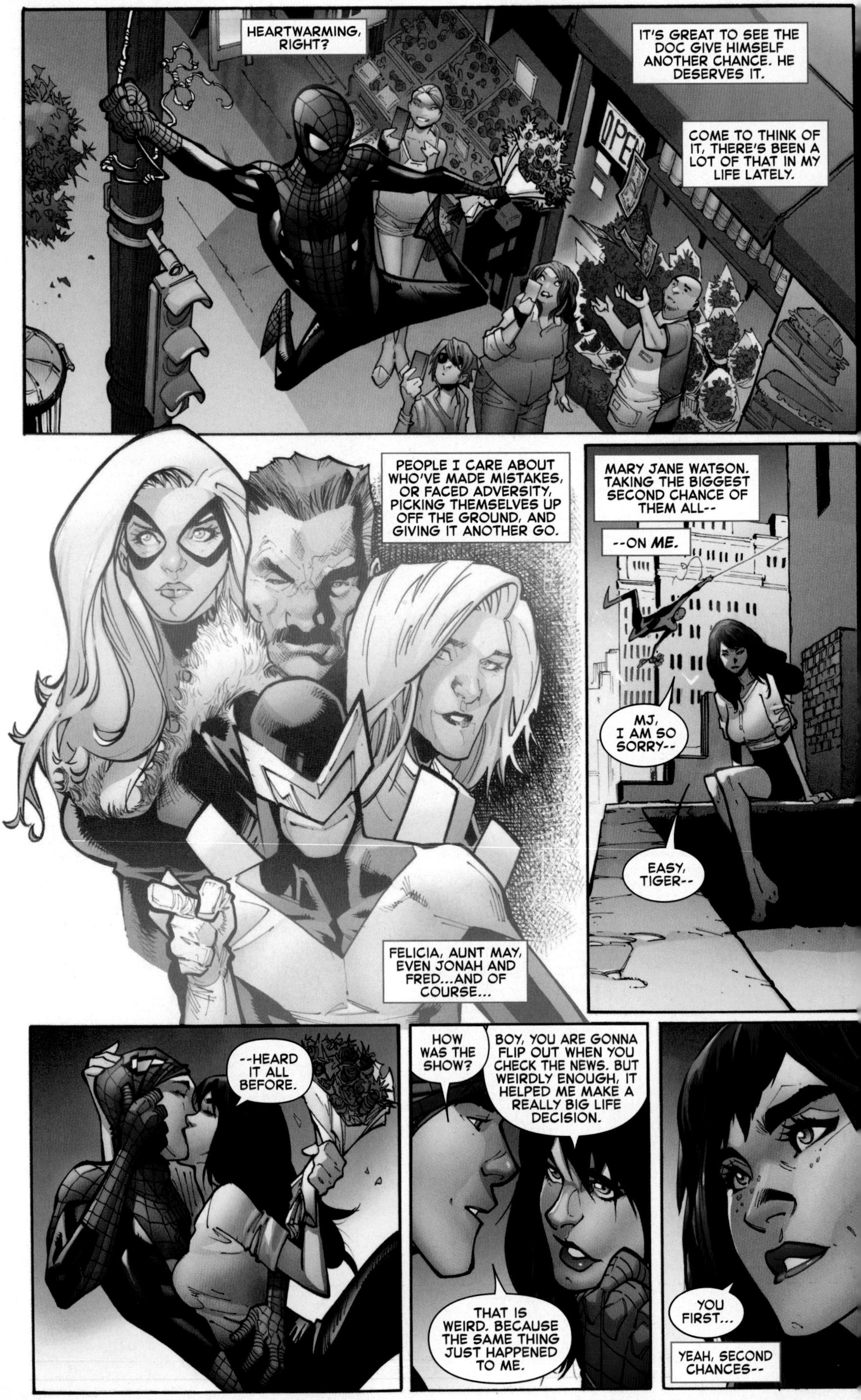
HEARTWARMING, RIGHT?
IT'S GREAT TO SEE THE DOC GIVE HIMSELF ANOTHER CHANCE. HE DESERVES IT.
COME TO THINK OF IT, THERE'S BEEN A LOT OF THAT IN MY LIFE LATELY.
OPEN
PEOPLE I CARE ABOUT WHO'VE MADE MISTAKES, OR FACED ADVERSITY, PICKING THEMSELVES UP OFF THE GROUND, AND GIVING IT ANOTHER GO.
FELICIA, AUNT MAY, EVEN JONAH AND FRED...AND OF COURSE...
MARY JANE WATSON. TAKING THE BIGGEST SECOND CHANCE OF THEM ALL--
--ON *ME.*
MJ, I AM SO SORRY--
EASY, TIGER--
--HEARD IT ALL BEFORE.
HOW WAS THE SHOW?
BOY, YOU ARE GONNA FLIP OUT WHEN YOU CHECK THE NEWS. BUT WEIRDLY ENOUGH, IT HELPED ME MAKE A REALLY BIG LIFE DECISION.
THAT IS WEIRD. BECAUSE THE SAME THING JUST HAPPENED TO ME.
YOU FIRST...
YEAH, SECOND CHANCES--

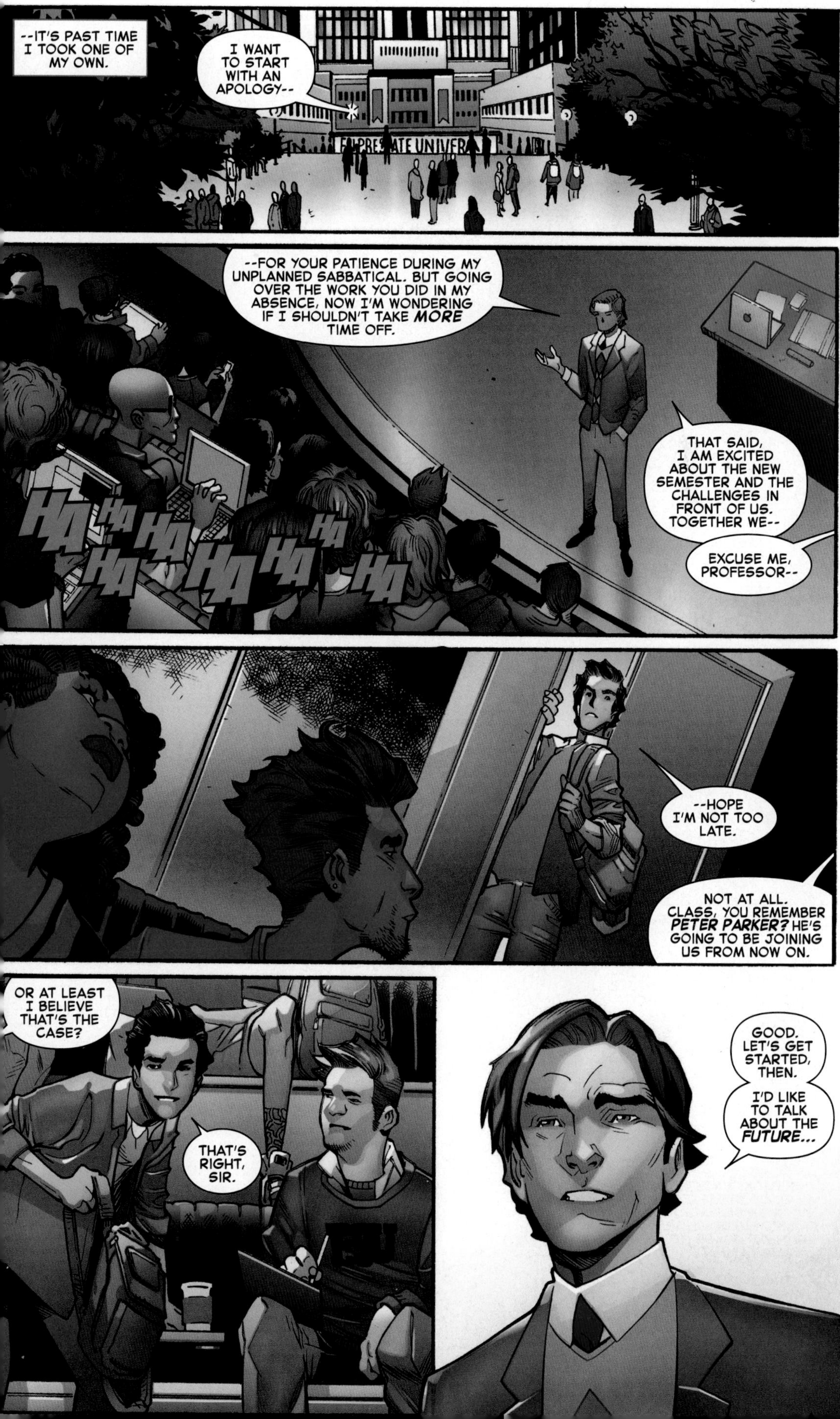
--IT'S PAST TIME I TOOK ONE OF MY OWN.
I WANT TO START WITH AN APOLOGY--
--FOR YOUR PATIENCE DURING MY UNPLANNED SABBATICAL. BUT GOING OVER THE WORK YOU DID IN MY ABSENCE, NOW I'M WONDERING IF I SHOULDN'T TAKE MORE TIME OFF.
HA HA HA HA HA HA HA HA HA
THAT SAID, I AM EXCITED ABOUT THE NEW SEMESTER AND THE CHALLENGES IN FRONT OF US. TOGETHER WE--
EXCUSE ME, PROFESSOR--
--HOPE I'M NOT TOO LATE.
NOT AT ALL. CLASS, YOU REMEMBER PETER PARKER? HE'S GOING TO BE JOINING US FROM NOW ON.
OR AT LEAST I BELIEVE THAT'S THE CASE?
THAT'S RIGHT, SIR.
GOOD. LET'S GET STARTED, THEN.
I'D LIKE TO TALK ABOUT THE FUTURE...

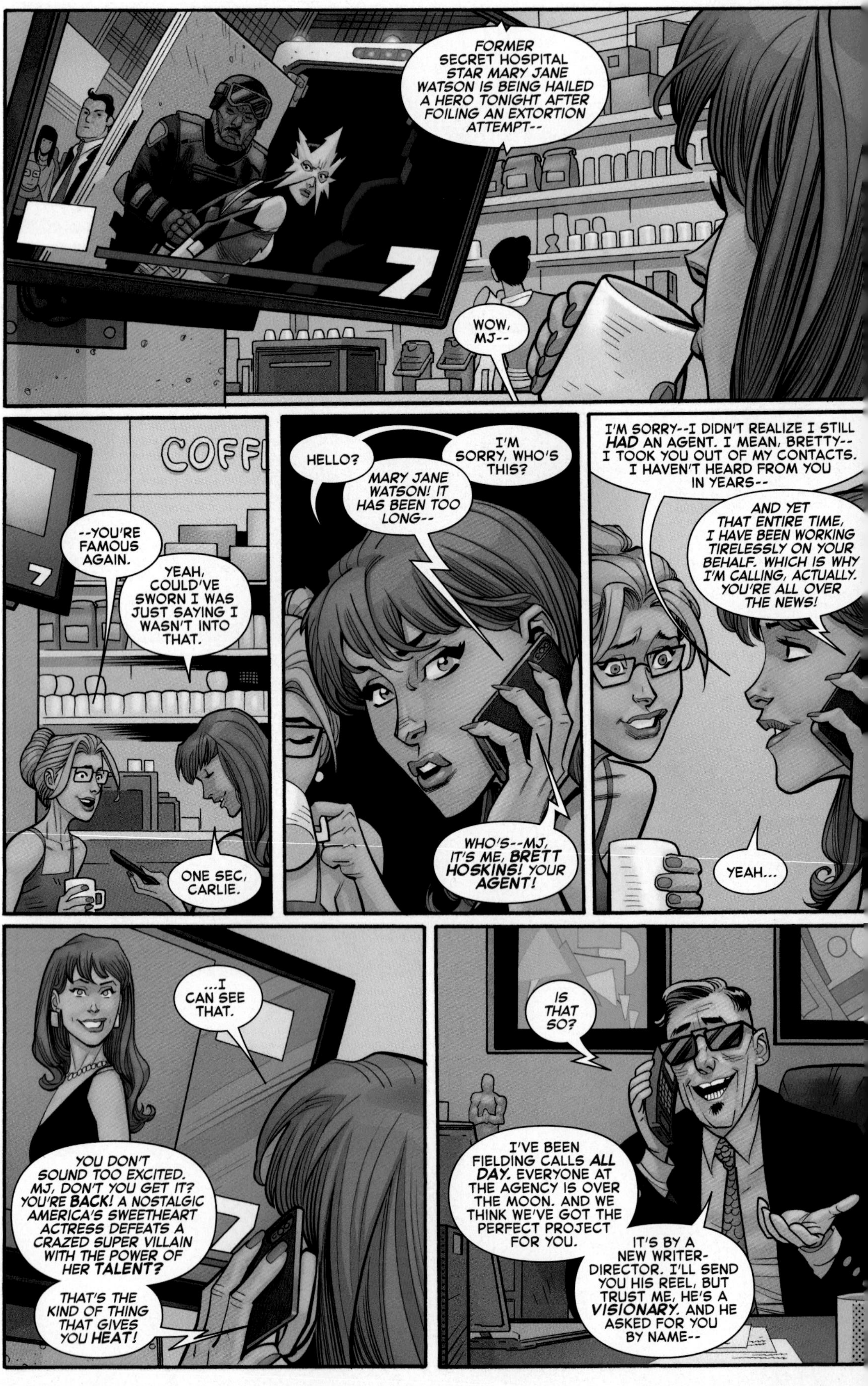
FORMER SECRET HOSPITAL STAR MARY JANE WATSON IS BEING HAILED A HERO TONIGHT AFTER FOILING AN EXTORTION ATTEMPT--
WOW, MJ--
COFF
--YOU'RE FAMOUS AGAIN.
YEAH, COULD'VE SWORN I WAS JUST SAYING I WASN'T INTO THAT.
ONE SEC, CARLIE.
HELLO?
MARY JANE WATSON! IT HAS BEEN TOO LONG--
I'M SORRY, WHO'S THIS?
WHO'S--MJ, IT'S ME, BRETT HOSKINS! YOUR AGENT!
I'M SORRY--I DIDN'T REALIZE I STILL HAD AN AGENT. I MEAN, BRETTY-- I TOOK YOU OUT OF MY CONTACTS. I HAVEN'T HEARD FROM YOU IN YEARS--
AND YET THAT ENTIRE TIME, I HAVE BEEN WORKING TIRELESSLY ON YOUR BEHALF. WHICH IS WHY I'M CALLING, ACTUALLY. YOU'RE ALL OVER THE NEWS!
YEAH...
...I CAN SEE THAT.
YOU DON'T SOUND TOO EXCITED. MJ, DON'T YOU GET IT? YOU'RE BACK! A NOSTALGIC AMERICA'S SWEETHEART ACTRESS DEFEATS A CRAZED SUPER VILLAIN WITH THE POWER OF HER TALENT?
THAT'S THE KIND OF THING THAT GIVES YOU HEAT!
IS THAT SO?
I'VE BEEN FIELDING CALLS ALL DAY. EVERYONE AT THE AGENCY IS OVER THE MOON. AND WE THINK WE'VE GOT THE PERFECT PROJECT FOR YOU.
IT'S BY A NEW WRITER-DIRECTOR. I'LL SEND YOU HIS REEL, BUT TRUST ME, HE'S A VISIONARY. AND HE ASKED FOR YOU BY NAME--

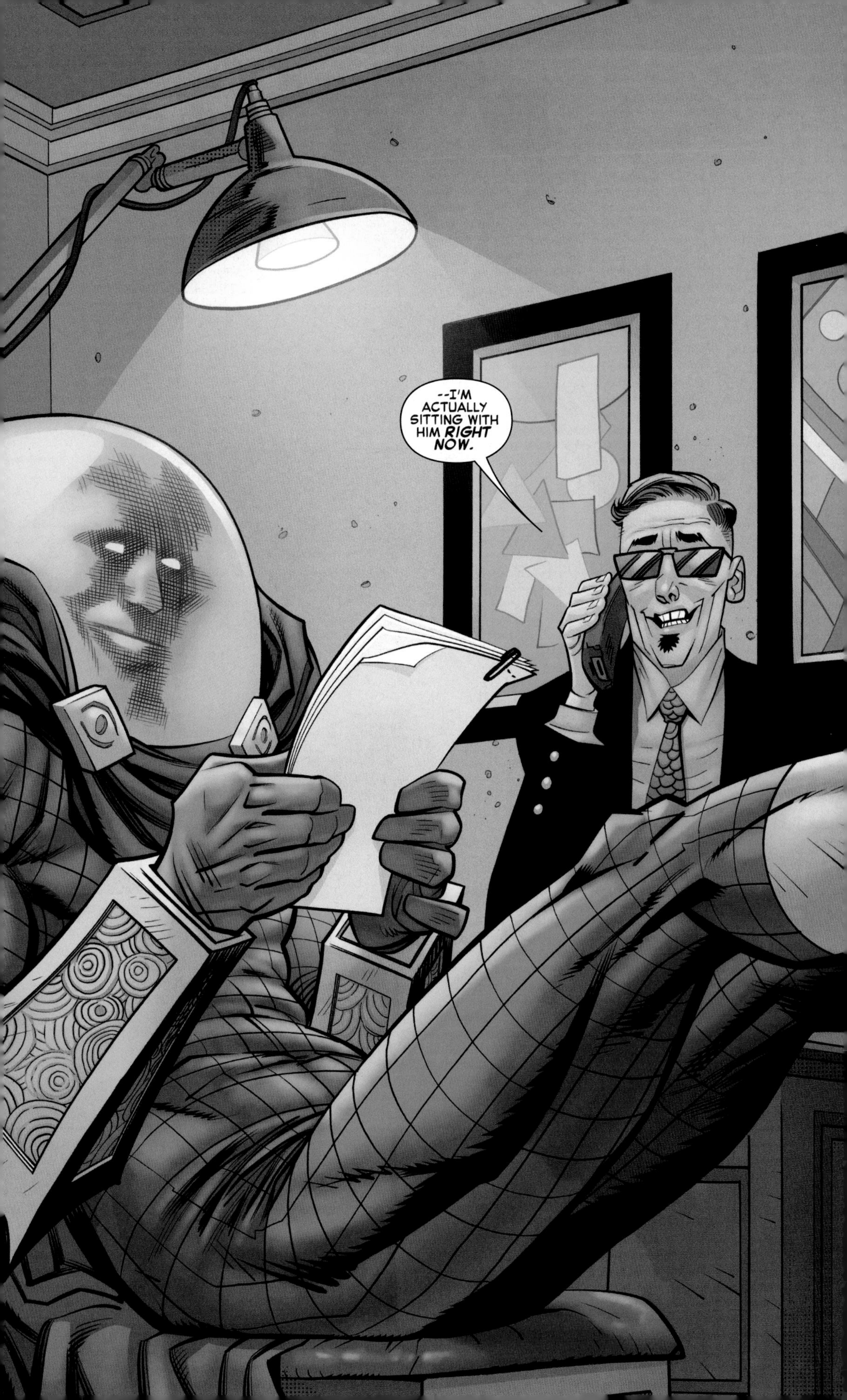
--I'M ACTUALLY SITTING WITH HIM RIGHT NOW.

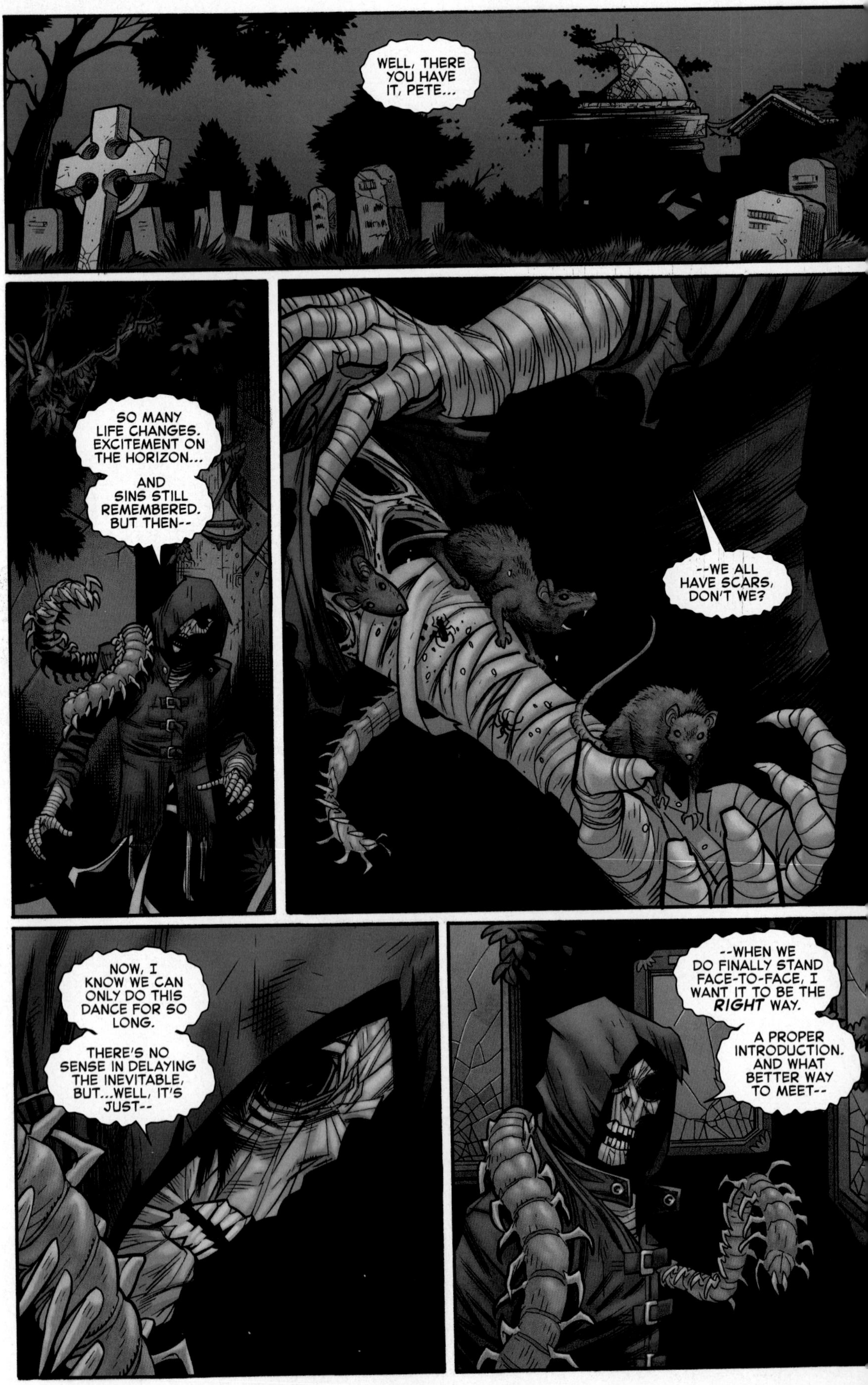
WELL, THERE YOU HAVE IT, PETE...
SO MANY LIFE CHANGES. EXCITEMENT ON THE HORIZON...
AND SINS STILL REMEMBERED. BUT THEN--
--WE ALL HAVE SCARS, DON'T WE?
NOW, I KNOW WE CAN ONLY DO THIS DANCE FOR SO LONG.
THERE'S NO SENSE IN DELAYING THE INEVITABLE, BUT...WELL, IT'S JUST--
--WHEN WE DO FINALLY STAND FACE-TO-FACE, I WANT IT TO BE THE *RIGHT* WAY.
A PROPER INTRODUCTION. AND WHAT BETTER WAY TO MEET--

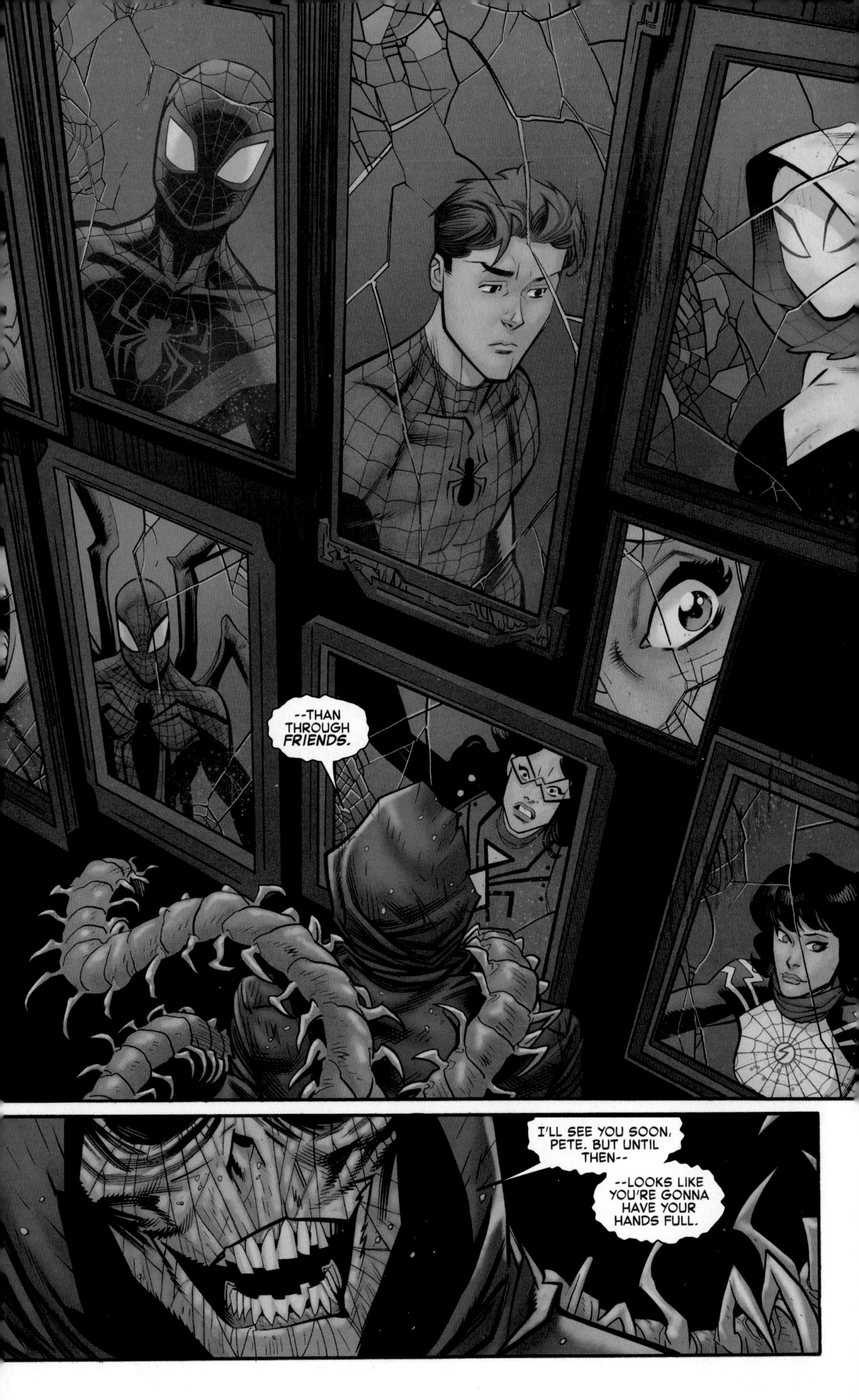
--THAN THROUGH *FRIENDS.*
I'LL SEE YOU SOON, PETE. BUT UNTIL THEN--
--LOOKS LIKE YOU'RE GONNA HAVE YOUR HANDS FULL.

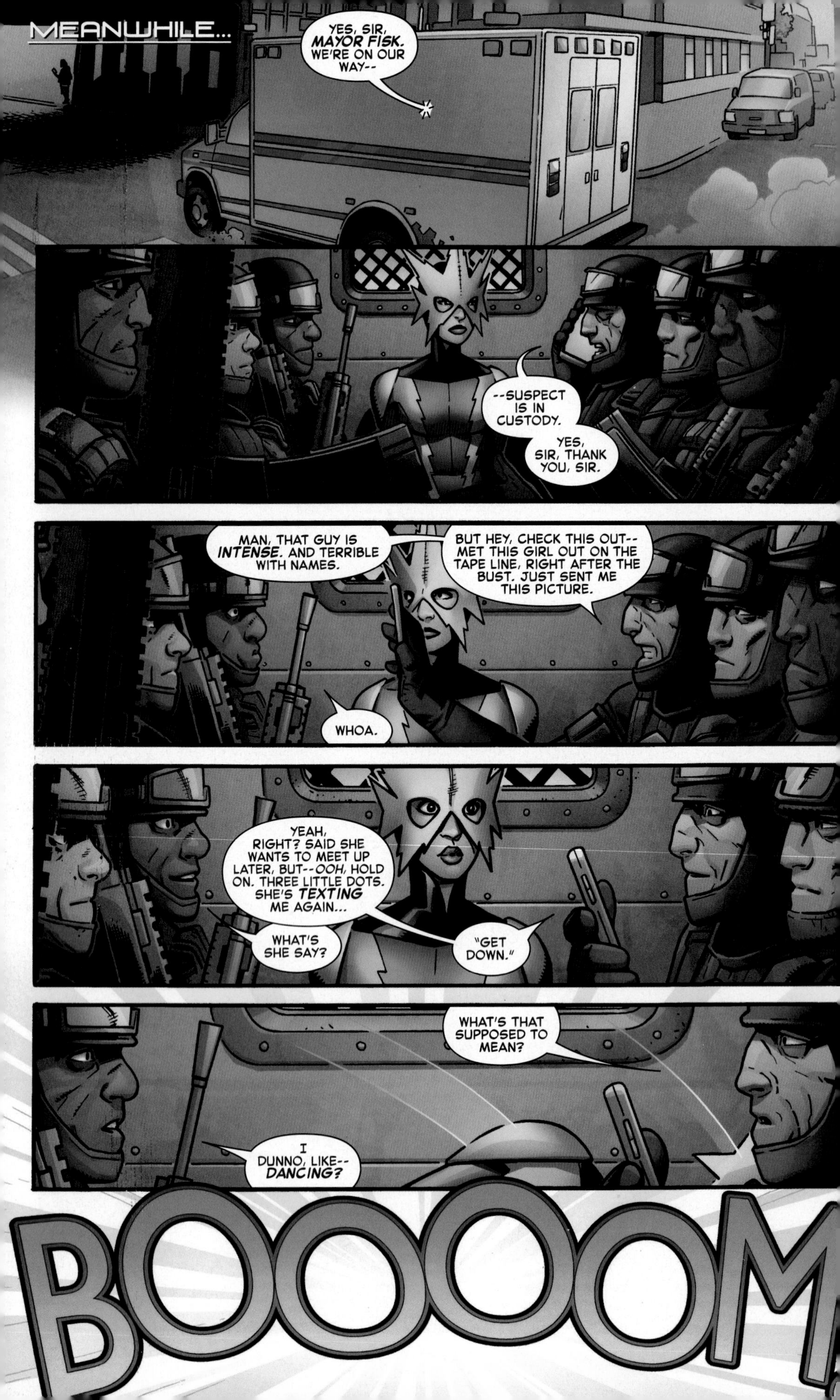
MEANWHILE...
YES, SIR, MAYOR FISK. WE'RE ON OUR WAY--
--SUSPECT IS IN CUSTODY.
YES, SIR, THANK YOU, SIR.
MAN, THAT GUY IS INTENSE. AND TERRIBLE WITH NAMES.
BUT HEY, CHECK THIS OUT-- MET THIS GIRL OUT ON THE TAPE LINE, RIGHT AFTER THE BUST. JUST SENT ME THIS PICTURE.
WHOA.
YEAH, RIGHT? SAID SHE WANTS TO MEET UP LATER, BUT--OOH, HOLD ON. THREE LITTLE DOTS. SHE'S TEXTING ME AGAIN...
WHAT'S SHE SAY?
"GET DOWN."
WHAT'S THAT SUPPOSED TO MEAN?
I DUNNO, LIKE-- DANCING?
BOOOOM

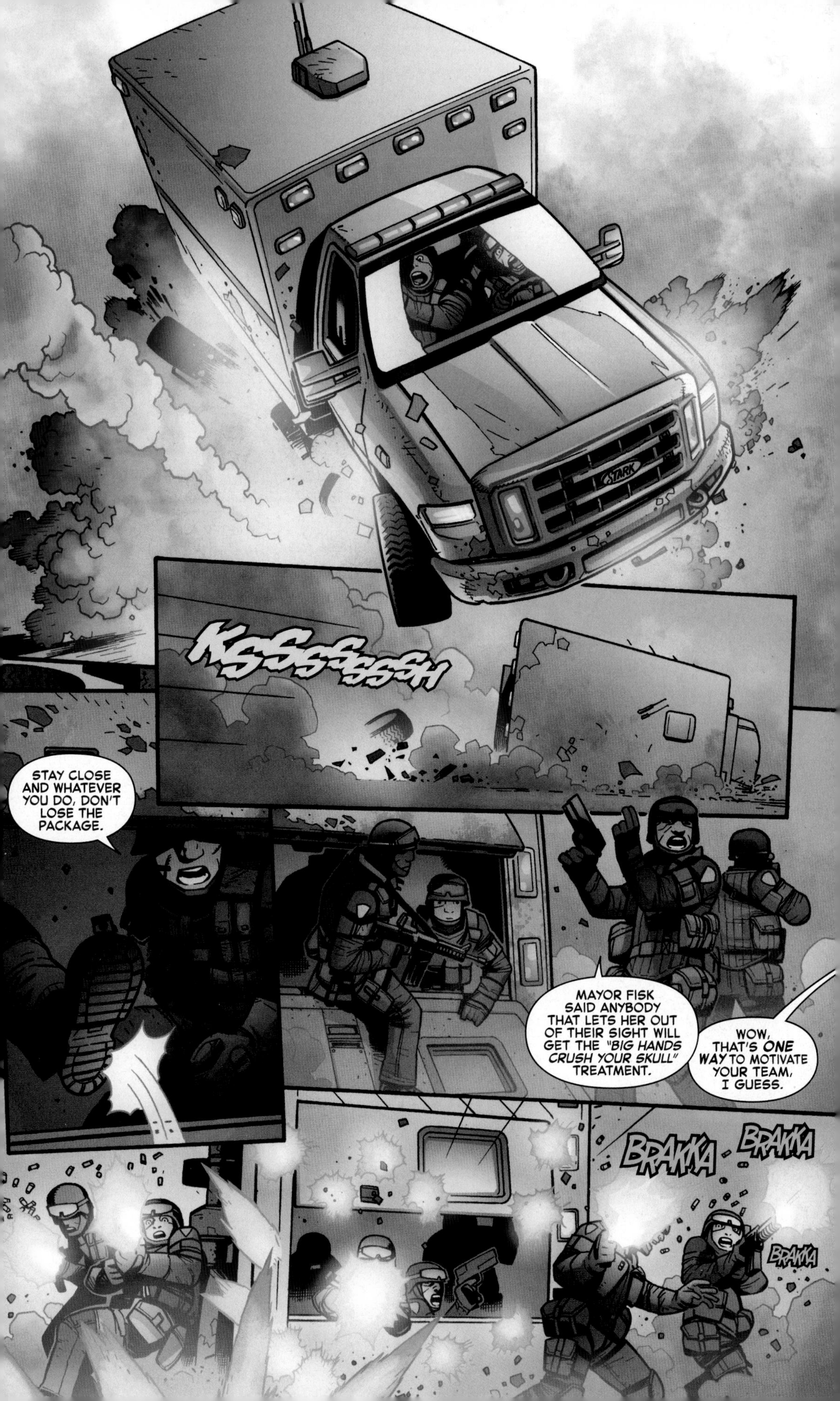
KSSSSSSSSH
STAY CLOSE AND WHATEVER YOU DO, DON'T LOSE THE PACKAGE.
MAYOR FISK SAID ANYBODY THAT LETS HER OUT OF THEIR SIGHT WILL GET THE "BIG HANDS CRUSH YOUR SKULL" TREATMENT.
WOW, THAT'S ONE WAY TO MOTIVATE YOUR TEAM, I GUESS.
BRAKKA BRAKKA
BRAKKA

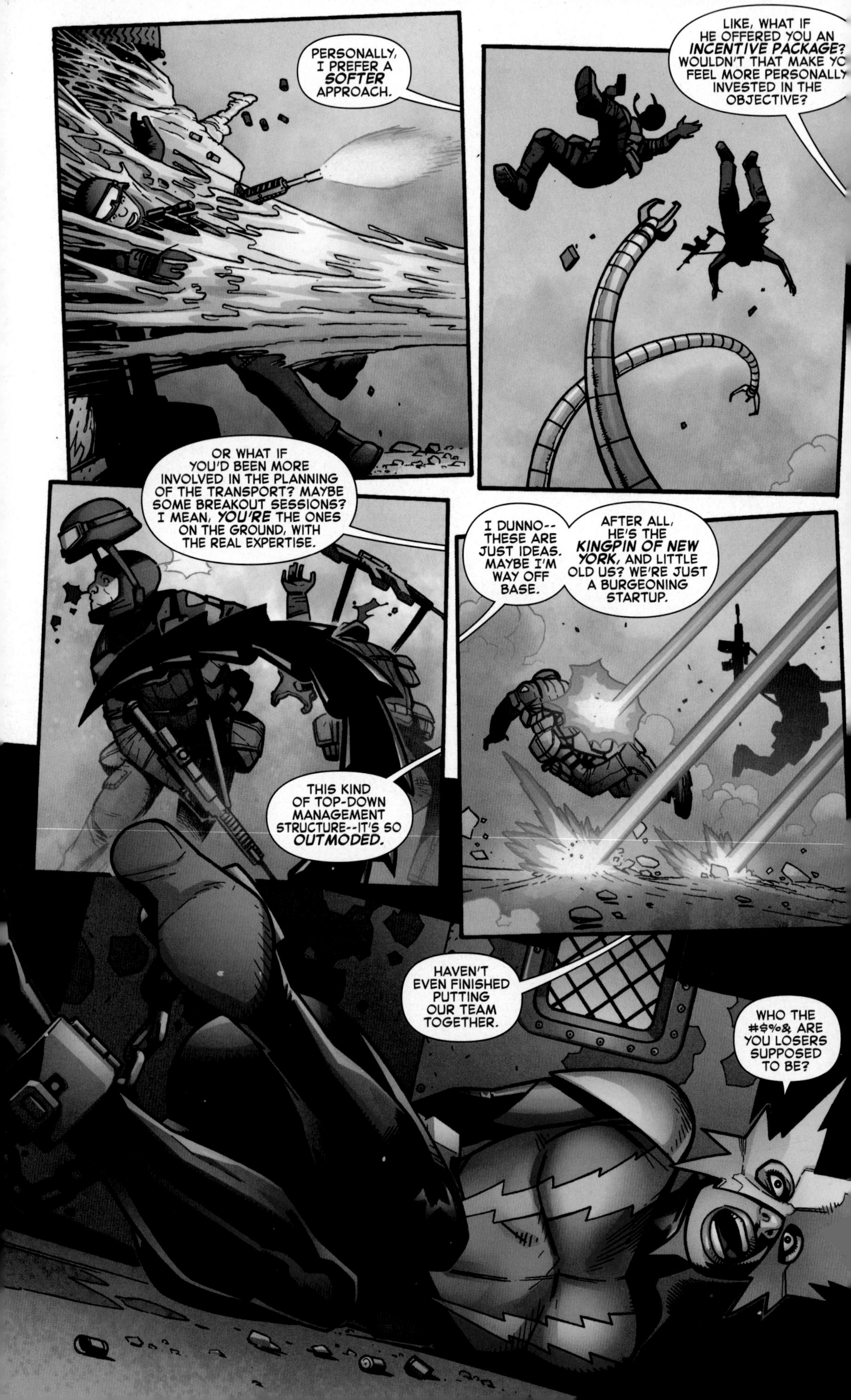
PERSONALLY, I PREFER A SOFTER APPROACH.
LIKE, WHAT IF HE OFFERED YOU AN INCENTIVE PACKAGE? WOULDN'T THAT MAKE YO FEEL MORE PERSONALLY INVESTED IN THE OBJECTIVE?
OR WHAT IF YOU'D BEEN MORE INVOLVED IN THE PLANNING OF THE TRANSPORT? MAYBE SOME BREAKOUT SESSIONS? I MEAN, YOU'RE THE ONES ON THE GROUND, WITH THE REAL EXPERTISE.
I DUNNO-- THESE ARE JUST IDEAS. MAYBE I'M WAY OFF BASE.
AFTER ALL, HE'S THE KINGPIN OF NEW YORK, AND LITTLE OLD US? WE'RE JUST A BURGEONING STARTUP.
THIS KIND OF TOP-DOWN MANAGEMENT STRUCTURE--IT'S SO OUTMODED.
HAVEN'T EVEN FINISHED PUTTING OUR TEAM TOGETHER.
WHO THE #$%& ARE YOU LOSERS SUPPOSED TO BE?

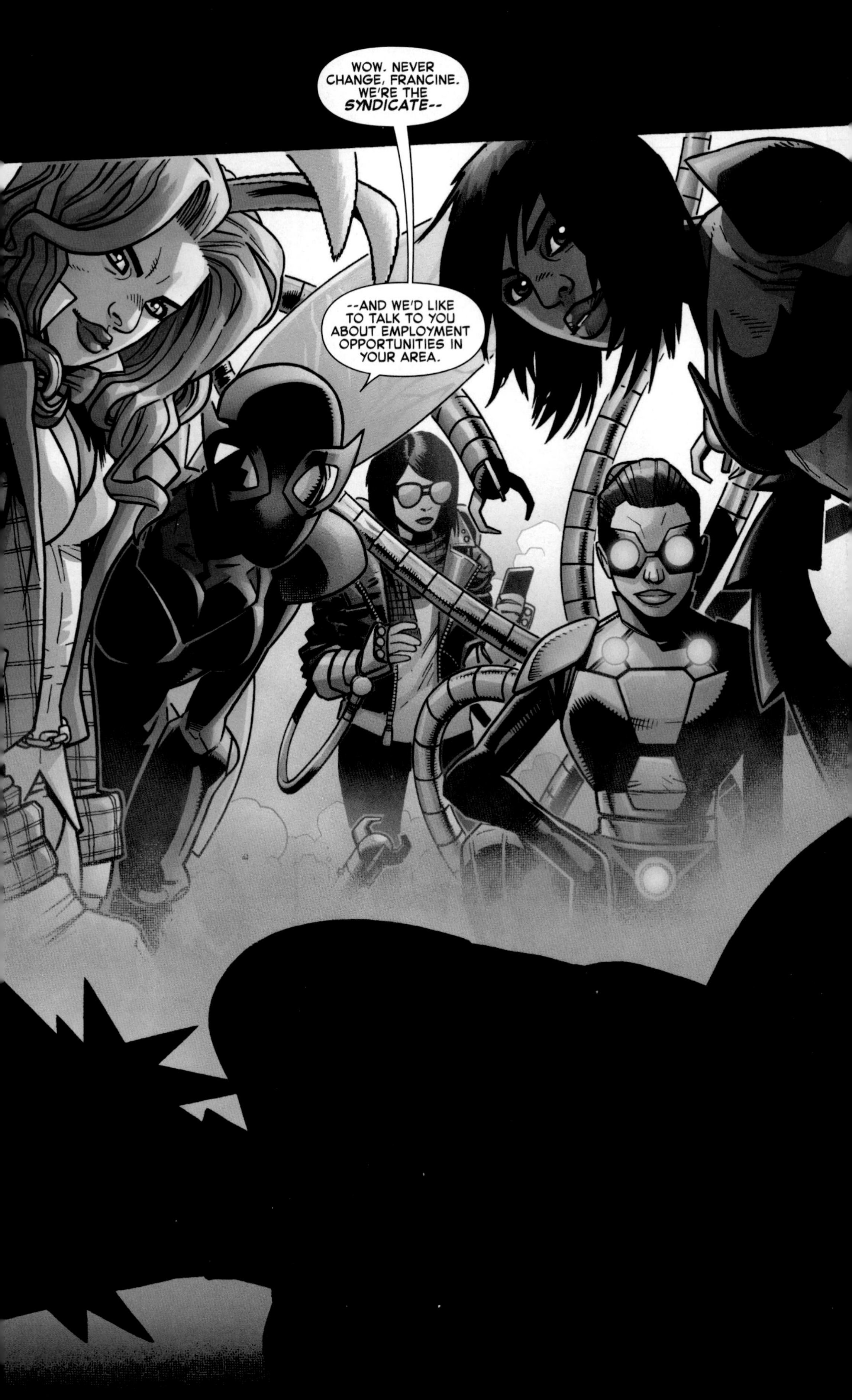
WOW. NEVER CHANGE, FRANCINE. WE'RE THE SYNDICATE--
--AND WE'D LIKE TO TALK TO YOU ABOUT EMPLOYMENT OPPORTUNITIES IN YOUR AREA.

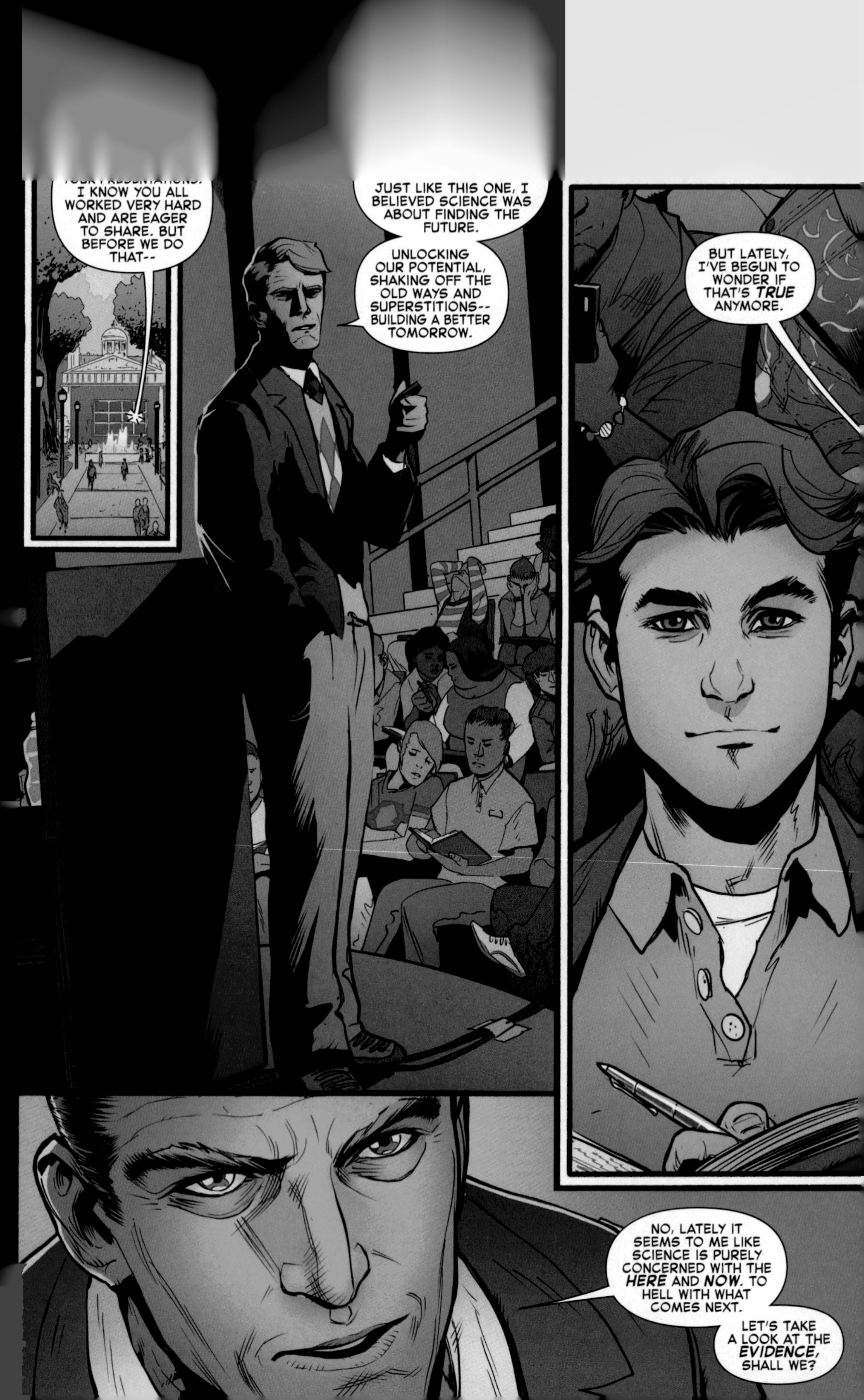
I KNOW YOU ALL WORKED VERY HARD AND ARE EAGER TO SHARE. BUT BEFORE WE DO THAT--
JUST LIKE THIS ONE, I BELIEVED SCIENCE WAS ABOUT FINDING THE FUTURE.
UNLOCKING OUR POTENTIAL, SHAKING OFF THE OLD WAYS AND SUPERSTITIONS-- BUILDING A BETTER TOMORROW.
BUT LATELY, I'VE BEGUN TO WONDER IF THAT'S TRUE ANYMORE.
NO, LATELY IT SEEMS TO ME LIKE SCIENCE IS PURELY CONCERNED WITH THE HERE AND NOW. TO HELL WITH WHAT COMES NEXT.
LET'S TAKE A LOOK AT THE EVIDENCE, SHALL WE?

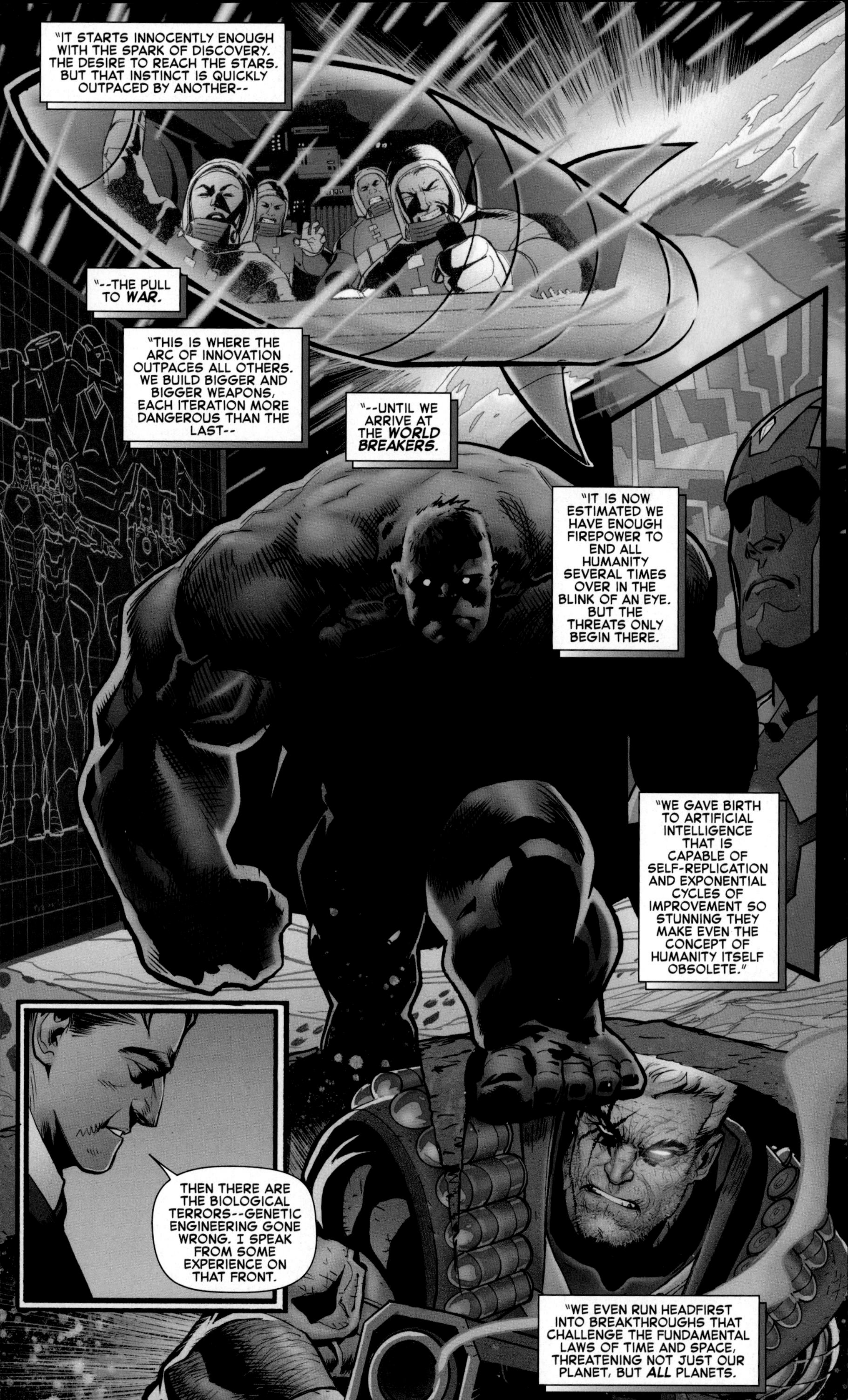
"IT STARTS INNOCENTLY ENOUGH WITH THE SPARK OF DISCOVERY. THE DESIRE TO REACH THE STARS. BUT THAT INSTINCT IS QUICKLY OUTPACED BY ANOTHER--
"--THE PULL TO WAR.
"THIS IS WHERE THE ARC OF INNOVATION OUTPACES ALL OTHERS. WE BUILD BIGGER AND BIGGER WEAPONS, EACH ITERATION MORE DANGEROUS THAN THE LAST--
"--UNTIL WE ARRIVE AT THE WORLD BREAKERS.
"IT IS NOW ESTIMATED WE HAVE ENOUGH FIREPOWER TO END ALL HUMANITY SEVERAL TIMES OVER IN THE BLINK OF AN EYE. BUT THE THREATS ONLY BEGIN THERE.
"WE GAVE BIRTH TO ARTIFICIAL INTELLIGENCE THAT IS CAPABLE OF SELF-REPLICATION AND EXPONENTIAL CYCLES OF IMPROVEMENT SO STUNNING THEY MAKE EVEN THE CONCEPT OF HUMANITY ITSELF OBSOLETE."
THEN THERE ARE THE BIOLOGICAL TERRORS--GENETIC ENGINEERING GONE WRONG. I SPEAK FROM SOME EXPERIENCE ON THAT FRONT.
"WE EVEN RUN HEADFIRST INTO BREAKTHROUGHS THAT CHALLENGE THE FUNDAMENTAL LAWS OF TIME AND SPACE, THREATENING NOT JUST OUR PLANET, BUT ALL PLANETS.

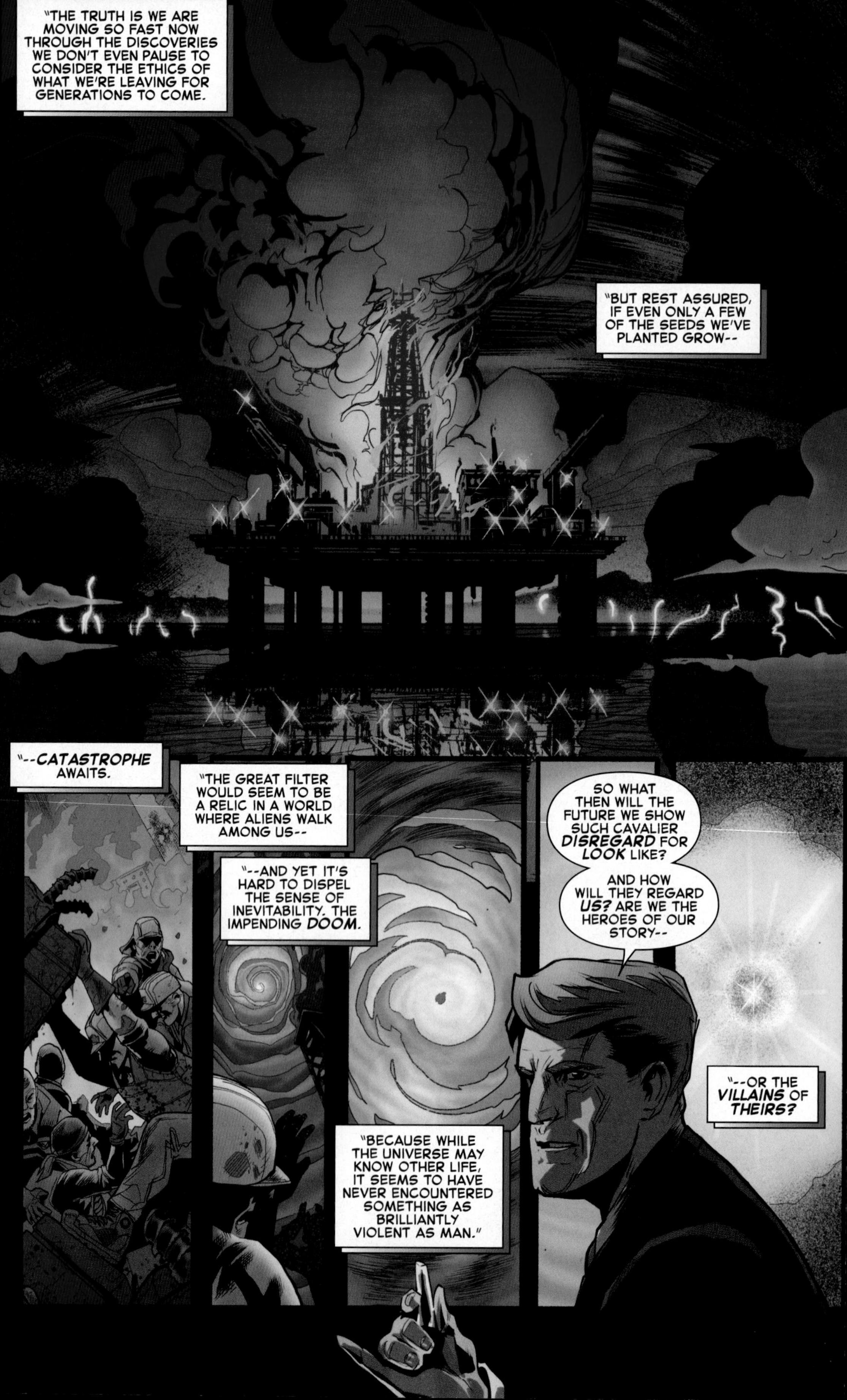
"THE TRUTH IS WE ARE MOVING SO FAST NOW THROUGH THE DISCOVERIES WE DON'T EVEN PAUSE TO CONSIDER THE ETHICS OF WHAT WE'RE LEAVING FOR GENERATIONS TO COME.
"BUT REST ASSURED, IF EVEN ONLY A FEW OF THE SEEDS WE'VE PLANTED GROW--
"--CATASTROPHE AWAITS.
"THE GREAT FILTER WOULD SEEM TO BE A RELIC IN A WORLD WHERE ALIENS WALK AMONG US--
"--AND YET IT'S HARD TO DISPEL THE SENSE OF INEVITABILITY. THE IMPENDING DOOM.
"BECAUSE WHILE THE UNIVERSE MAY KNOW OTHER LIFE, IT SEEMS TO HAVE NEVER ENCOUNTERED SOMETHING AS BRILLIANTLY VIOLENT AS MAN."
SO WHAT THEN WILL THE FUTURE WE SHOW SUCH CAVALIER DISREGARD FOR LOOK LIKE?
AND HOW WILL THEY REGARD US? ARE WE THE HEROES OF OUR STORY--
"--OR THE VILLAINS OF THEIRS?

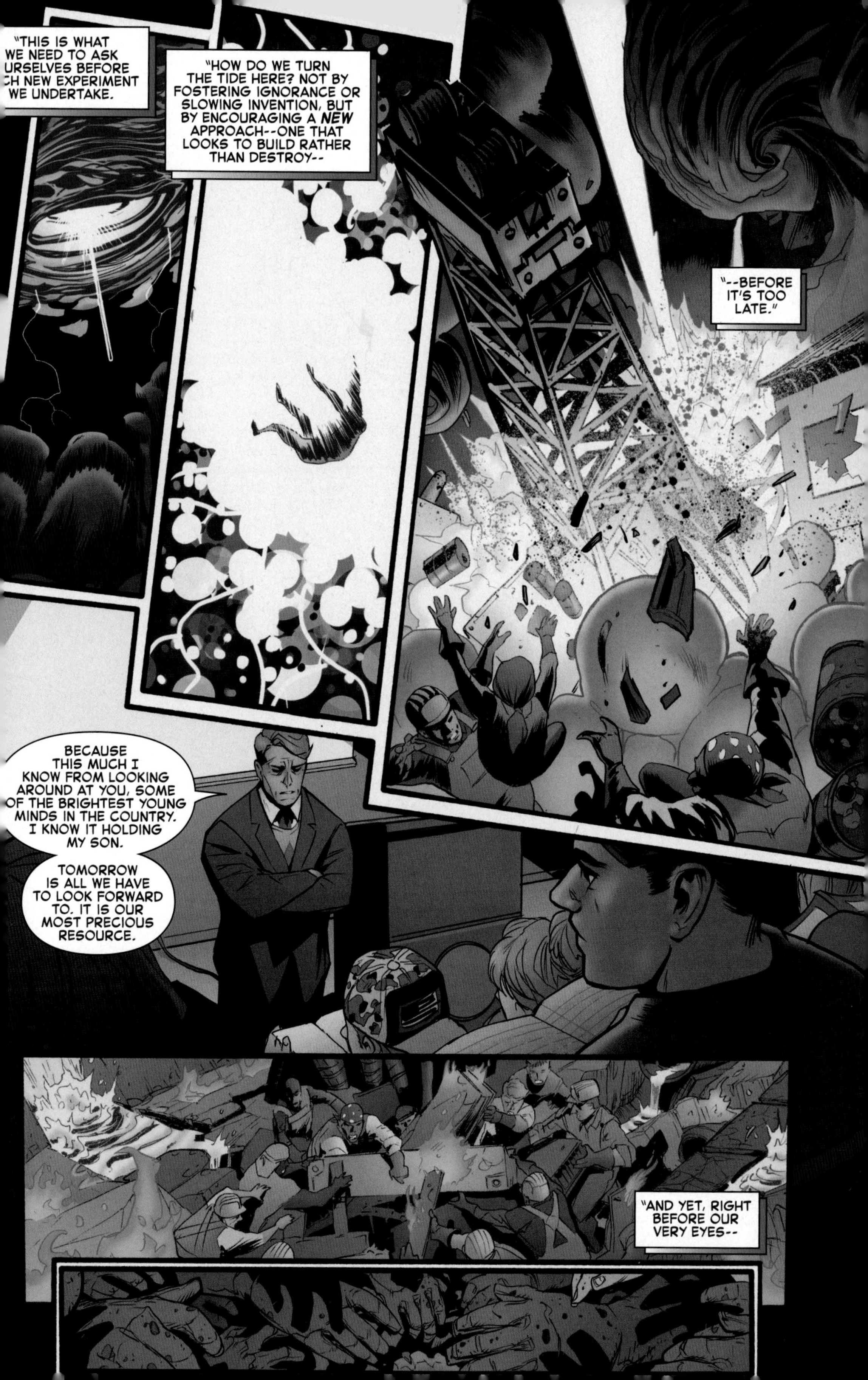
"THIS IS WHAT
WE NEED TO ASK
URSELVES BEFORE
CH NEW EXPERIMENT
WE UNDERTAKE.
"HOW DO WE TURN THE TIDE HERE? NOT BY FOSTERING IGNORANCE OR SLOWING INVENTION, BUT BY ENCOURAGING A NEW APPROACH--ONE THAT LOOKS TO BUILD RATHER THAN DESTROY--
"--BEFORE IT'S TOO LATE."
BECAUSE THIS MUCH I KNOW FROM LOOKING AROUND AT YOU, SOME OF THE BRIGHTEST YOUNG MINDS IN THE COUNTRY. I KNOW IT HOLDING MY SON.
TOMORROW IS ALL WE HAVE TO LOOK FORWARD TO. IT IS OUR MOST PRECIOUS RESOURCE.
"AND YET, RIGHT BEFORE OUR VERY EYES--

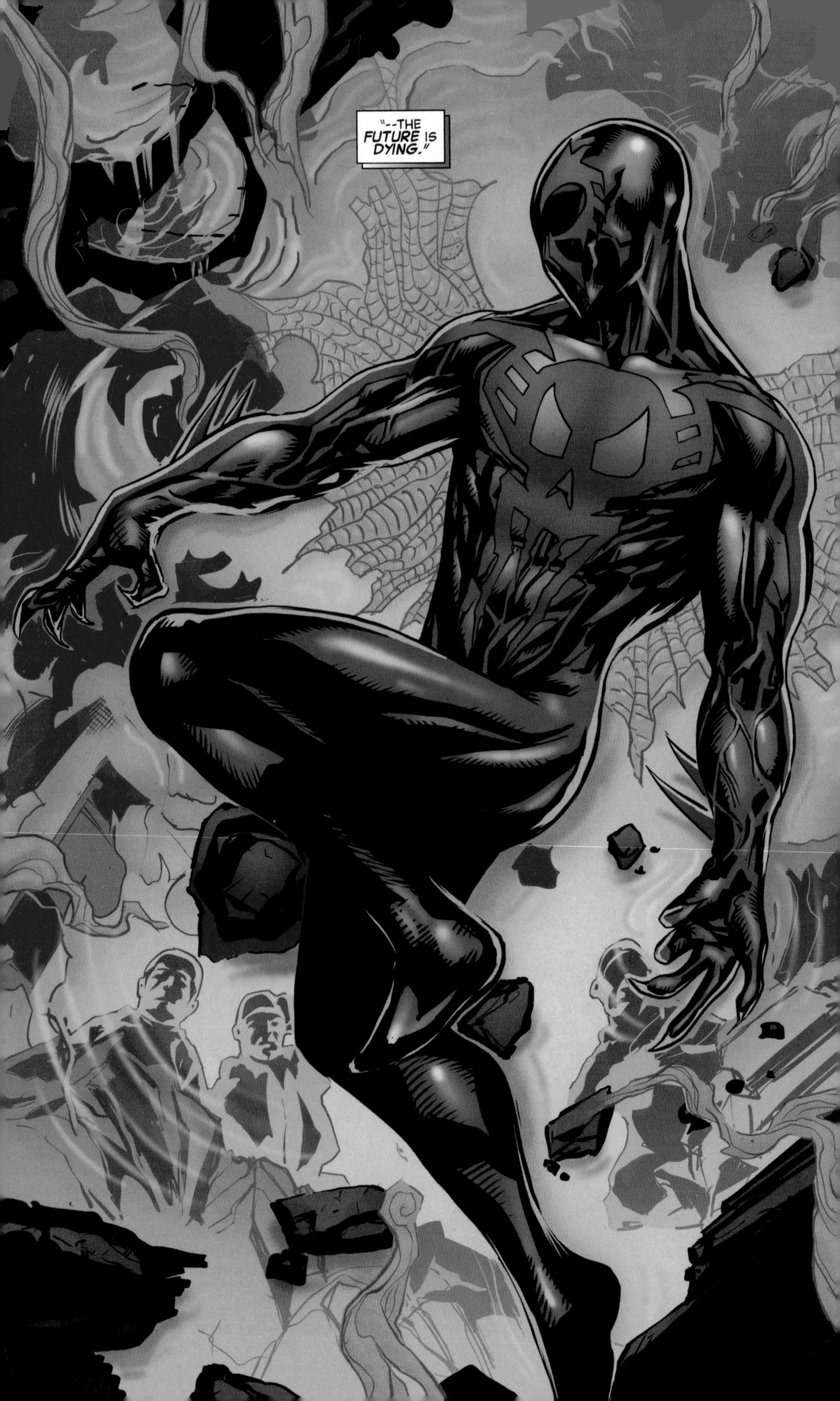
"--THE FUTURE IS DYING."

26

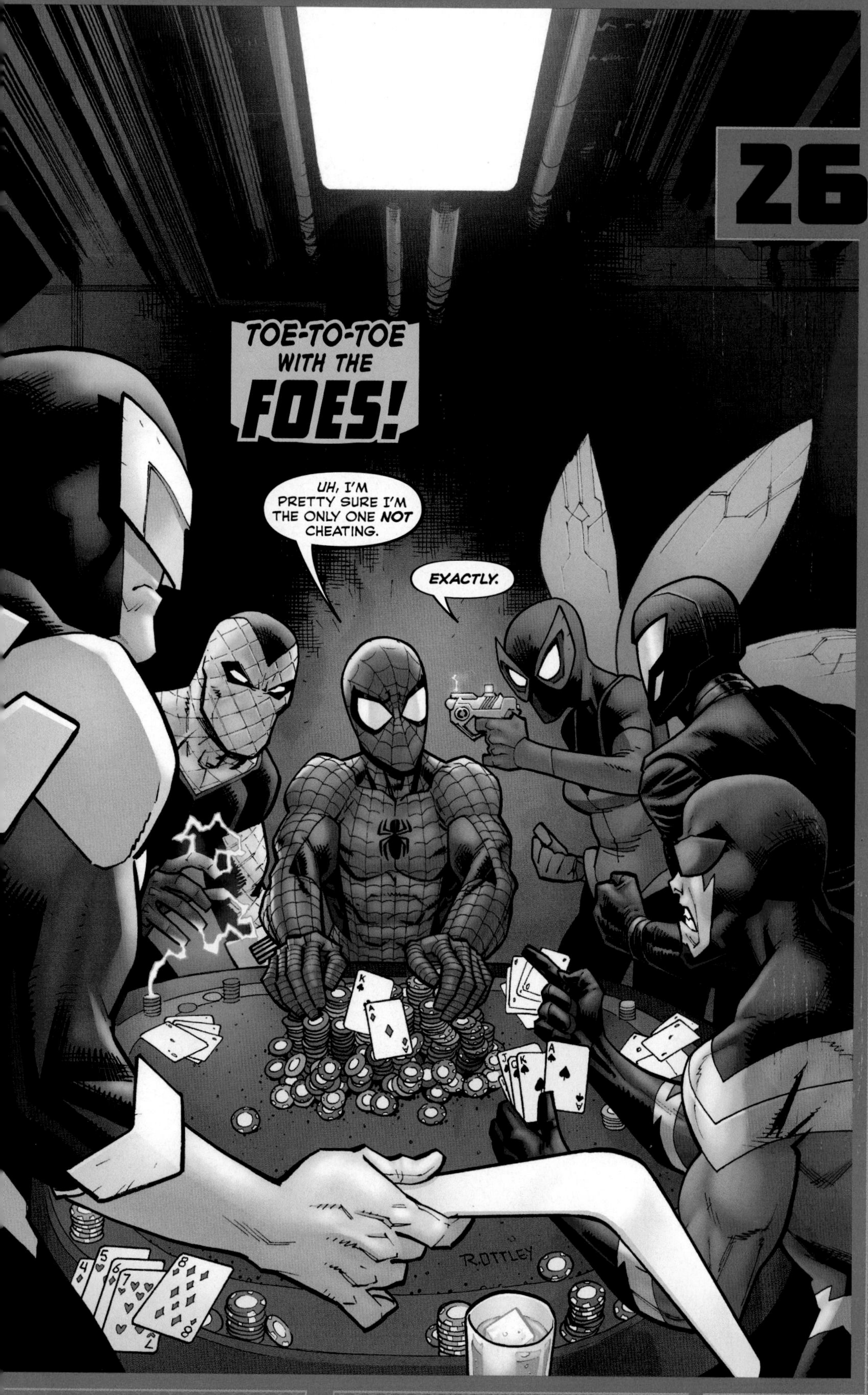

WHO RUN THE WORLD? PART 1

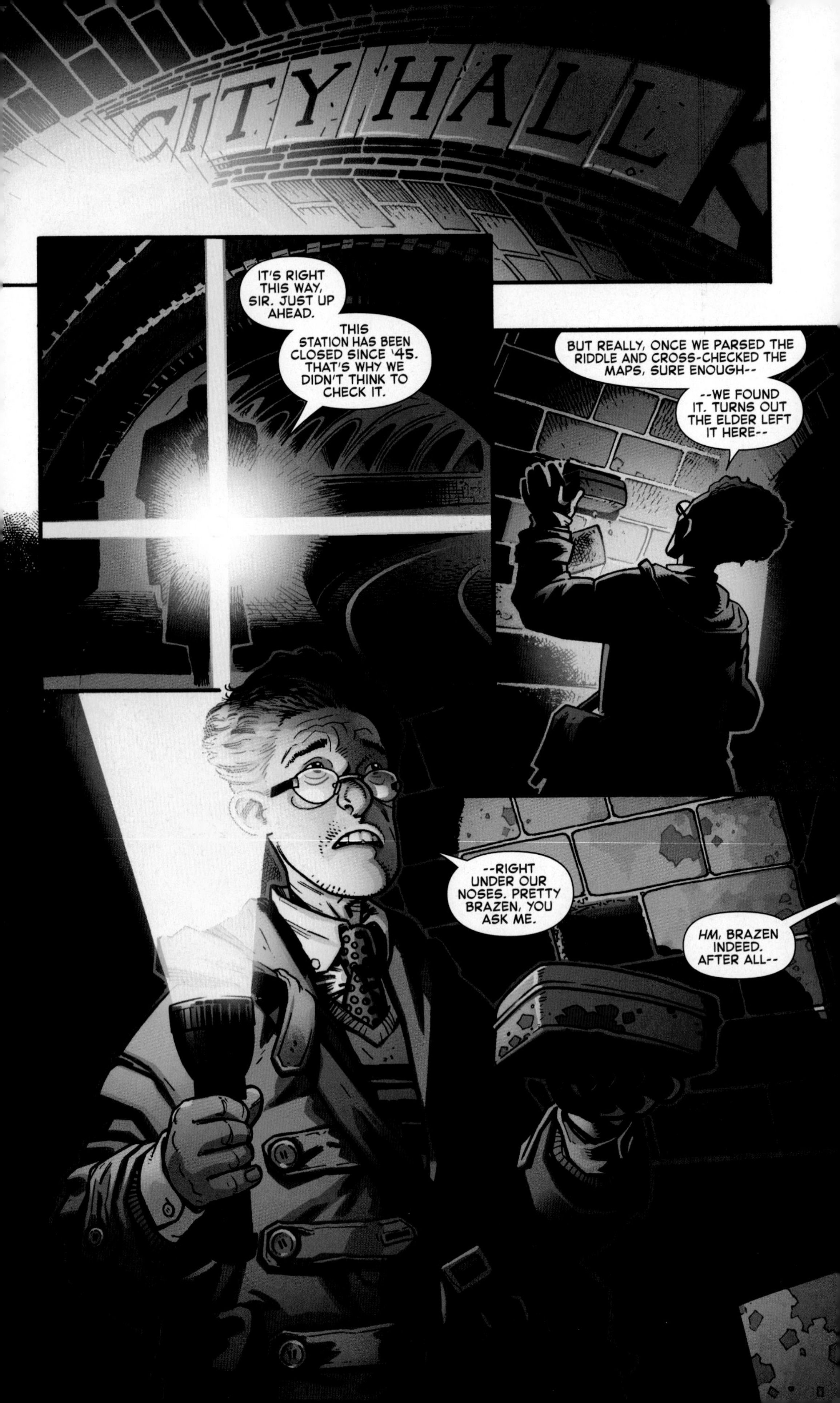
CITY HALL
IT'S RIGHT THIS WAY, SIR. JUST UP AHEAD.
THIS STATION HAS BEEN CLOSED SINCE '45. THAT'S WHY WE DIDN'T THINK TO CHECK IT.
BUT REALLY, ONCE WE PARSED THE RIDDLE AND CROSS-CHECKED THE MAPS, SURE ENOUGH--
--WE FOUND IT. TURNS OUT THE ELDER LEFT IT HERE--
--RIGHT UNDER OUR NOSES. PRETTY BRAZEN, YOU ASK ME.
HM, BRAZEN INDEED. AFTER ALL--

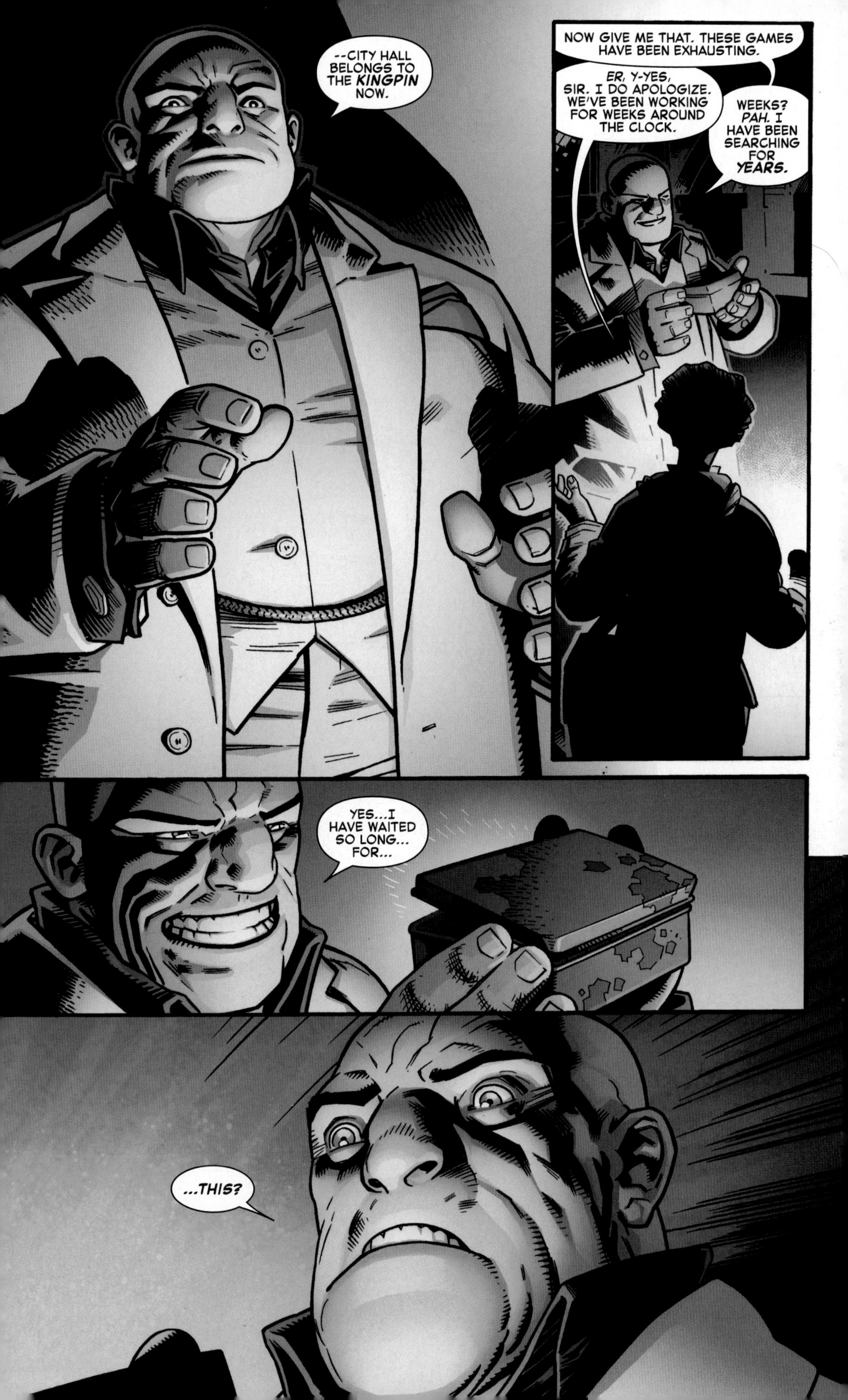
--CITY HALL BELONGS TO THE KINGPIN NOW.
NOW GIVE ME THAT. THESE GAMES HAVE BEEN EXHAUSTING.
ER, Y-YES, SIR. I DO APOLOGIZE. WE'VE BEEN WORKING FOR WEEKS AROUND THE CLOCK.
WEEKS? PAH. I HAVE BEEN SEARCHING FOR YEARS.
YES...I HAVE WAITED SO LONG... FOR...
...THIS?

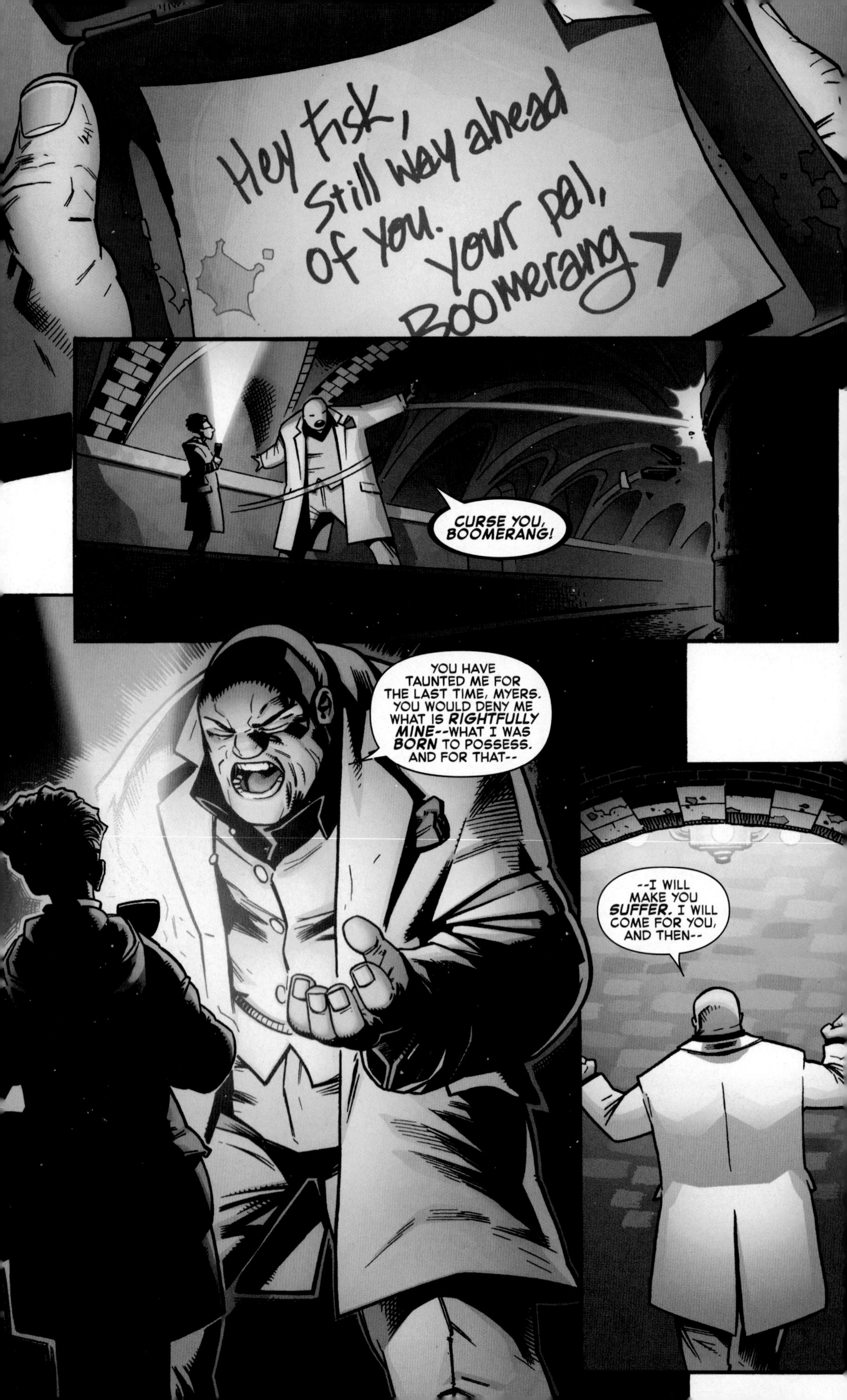
Hey Fisk, Still way ahead of you. Your pal, Boomerang
CURSE YOU, BOOMERANG!
YOU HAVE TAUNTED ME FOR THE LAST TIME, MYERS. YOU WOULD DENY ME WHAT IS RIGHTFULLY MINE--WHAT I WAS BORN TO POSSESS. AND FOR THAT--
--I WILL MAKE YOU SUFFER. I WILL COME FOR YOU, AND THEN--

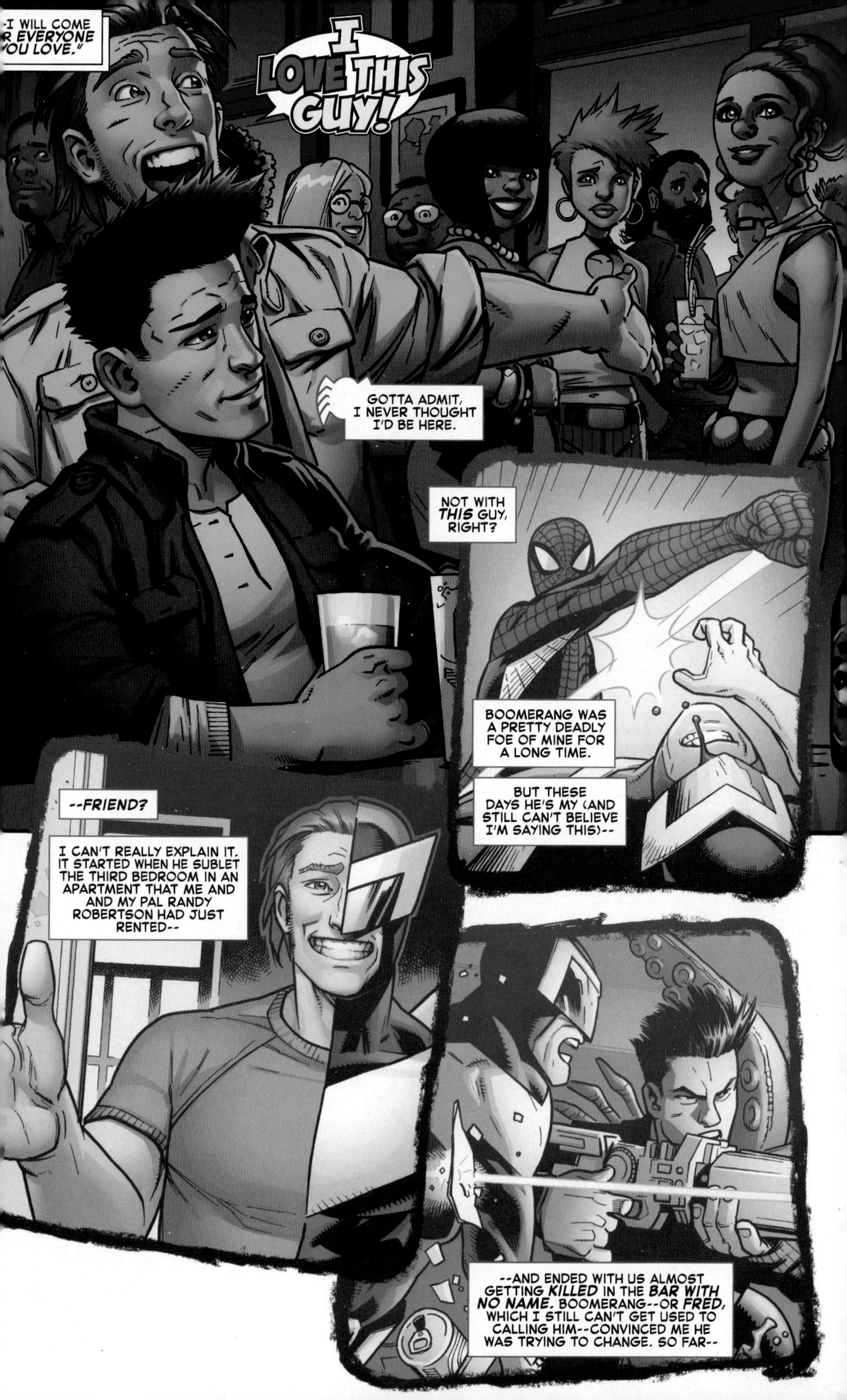
-I WILL COME
R EVERYONE
YOU LOVE."
I LOVE THIS GUY!
GOTTA ADMIT, I NEVER THOUGHT I'D BE HERE.
NOT WITH THIS GUY, RIGHT?
BOOMERANG WAS A PRETTY DEADLY FOE OF MINE FOR A LONG TIME.
BUT THESE DAYS HE'S MY (AND STILL CAN'T BELIEVE I'M SAYING THIS)--
--FRIEND?
I CAN'T REALLY EXPLAIN IT. IT STARTED WHEN HE SUBLET THE THIRD BEDROOM IN AN APARTMENT THAT ME AND AND MY PAL RANDY ROBERTSON HAD JUST RENTED--
--AND ENDED WITH US ALMOST GETTING KILLED IN THE BAR WITH NO NAME. BOOMERANG--OR FRED, WHICH I STILL CAN'T GET USED TO CALLING HIM--CONVINCED ME HE WAS TRYING TO CHANGE. SO FAR--

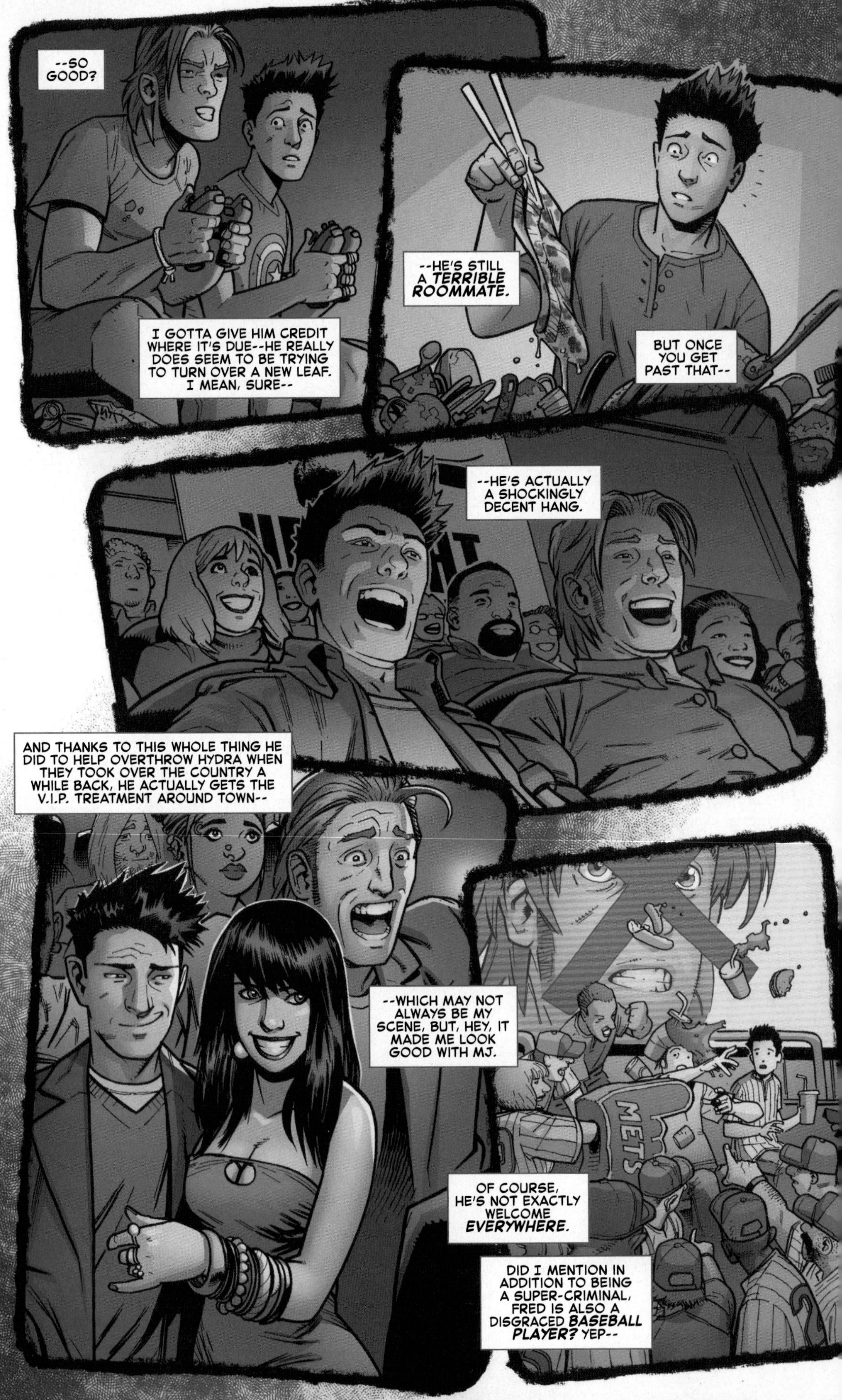
--SO GOOD?
I GOTTA GIVE HIM CREDIT WHERE IT'S DUE--HE REALLY DOES SEEM TO BE TRYING TO TURN OVER A NEW LEAF. I MEAN, SURE--
--HE'S STILL A TERRIBLE ROOMMATE.
BUT ONCE YOU GET PAST THAT--
--HE'S ACTUALLY A SHOCKINGLY DECENT HANG.
AND THANKS TO THIS WHOLE THING HE DID TO HELP OVERTHROW HYDRA WHEN THEY TOOK OVER THE COUNTRY A WHILE BACK, HE ACTUALLY GETS THE V.I.P. TREATMENT AROUND TOWN--
--WHICH MAY NOT ALWAYS BE MY SCENE, BUT, HEY, IT MADE ME LOOK GOOD WITH MJ.
OF COURSE, HE'S NOT EXACTLY WELCOME EVERYWHERE.
DID I MENTION IN ADDITION TO BEING A SUPER-CRIMINAL, FRED IS ALSO A DISGRACED BASEBALL PLAYER? YEP--
METS

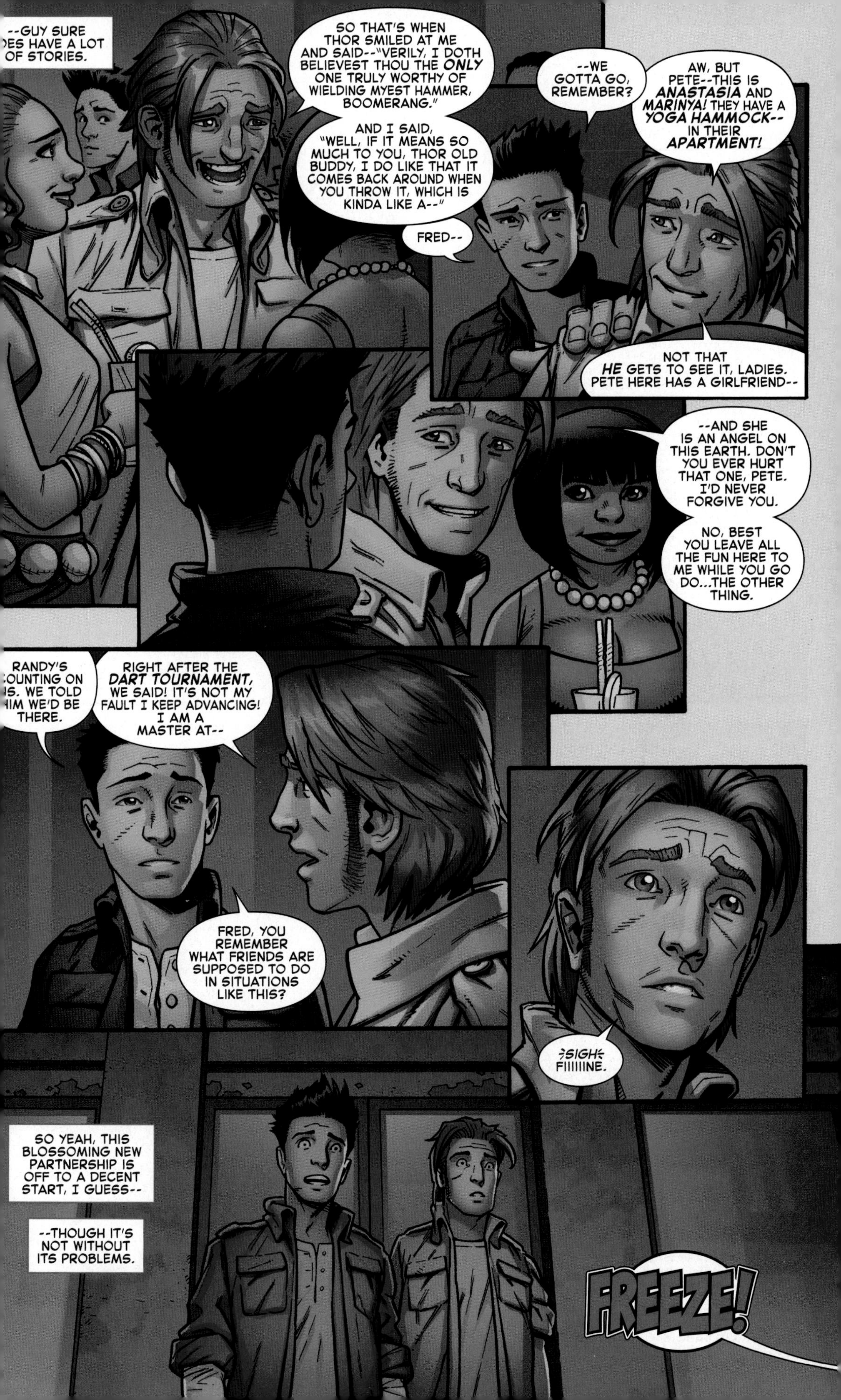
--GUY SURE DES HAVE A LOT OF STORIES.
SO THAT'S WHEN THOR SMILED AT ME AND SAID--"VERILY, I DOTH BELIEVEST THOU THE ONLY ONE TRULY WORTHY OF WIELDING MYEST HAMMER, BOOMERANG."
AND I SAID, "WELL, IF IT MEANS SO MUCH TO YOU, THOR OLD BUDDY, I DO LIKE THAT IT COMES BACK AROUND WHEN YOU THROW IT, WHICH IS KINDA LIKE A--"
FRED--
--WE GOTTA GO, REMEMBER?
AW, BUT PETE--THIS IS ANASTASIA AND MARINYA! THEY HAVE A YOGA HAMMOCK-- IN THEIR APARTMENT!
NOT THAT HE GETS TO SEE IT, LADIES. PETE HERE HAS A GIRLFRIEND--
--AND SHE IS AN ANGEL ON THIS EARTH. DON'T YOU EVER HURT THAT ONE, PETE. I'D NEVER FORGIVE YOU.
NO, BEST YOU LEAVE ALL THE FUN HERE TO ME WHILE YOU GO DO...THE OTHER THING.
RANDY'S COUNTING ON US. WE TOLD HIM WE'D BE THERE.
RIGHT AFTER THE DART TOURNAMENT, WE SAID! IT'S NOT MY FAULT I KEEP ADVANCING! I AM A MASTER AT--
FRED, YOU REMEMBER WHAT FRIENDS ARE SUPPOSED TO DO IN SITUATIONS LIKE THIS?
SIGH FIIIIINE.
SO YEAH, THIS BLOSSOMING NEW PARTNERSHIP IS OFF TO A DECENT START, I GUESS--
--THOUGH IT'S NOT WITHOUT ITS PROBLEMS.
FREEZE!

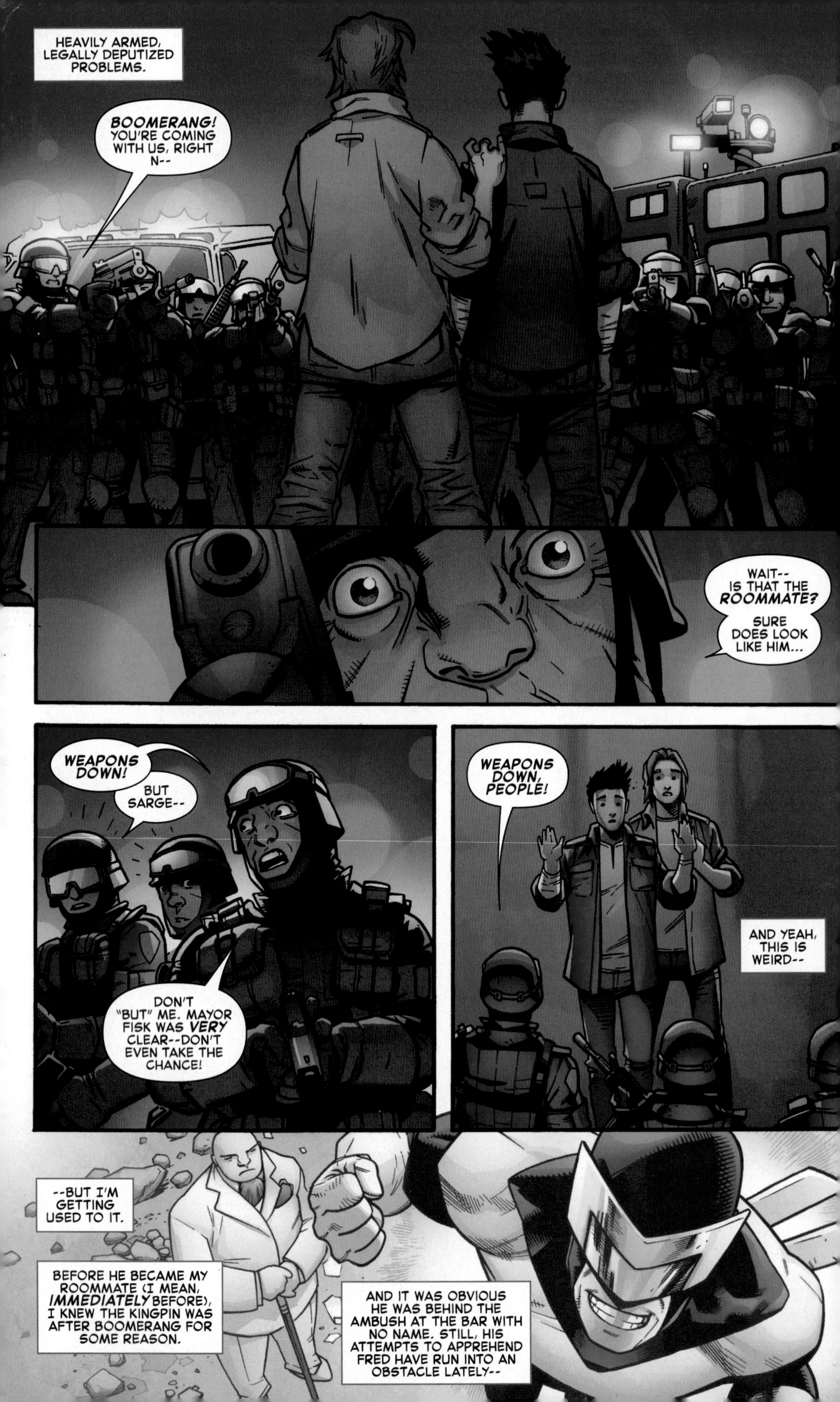

HEAVILY ARMED, LEGALLY DEPUTIZED PROBLEMS.
BOOMERANG! YOU'RE COMING WITH US, RIGHT N--
WAIT-- IS THAT THE ROOMMATE?
SURE DOES LOOK LIKE HIM...
WEAPONS DOWN!
BUT SARGE--
DON'T "BUT" ME. MAYOR FISK WAS VERY CLEAR--DON'T EVEN TAKE THE CHANCE!
WEAPONS DOWN, PEOPLE!
AND YEAH, THIS IS WEIRD--
--BUT I'M GETTING USED TO IT.
BEFORE HE BECAME MY ROOMMATE (I MEAN, IMMEDIATELY BEFORE), I KNEW THE KINGPIN WAS AFTER BOOMERANG FOR SOME REASON.
AND IT WAS OBVIOUS HE WAS BEHIND THE AMBUSH AT THE BAR WITH NO NAME. STILL, HIS ATTEMPTS TO APPREHEND FRED HAVE RUN INTO AN OBSTACLE LATELY--

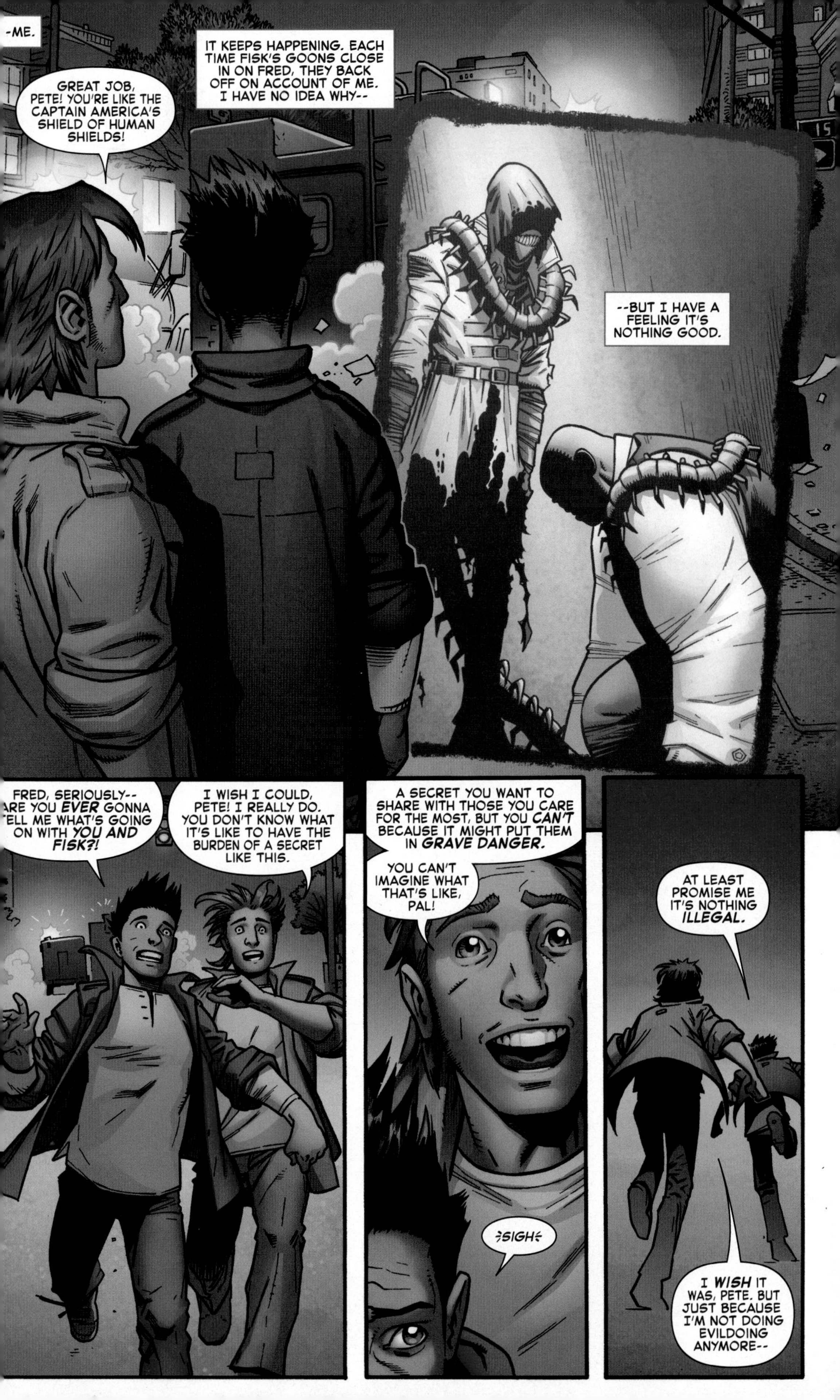

-ME.
IT KEEPS HAPPENING. EACH TIME FISK'S GOONS CLOSE IN ON FRED, THEY BACK OFF ON ACCOUNT OF ME. I HAVE NO IDEA WHY--
GREAT JOB, PETE! YOU'RE LIKE THE CAPTAIN AMERICA'S SHIELD OF HUMAN SHIELDS!
--BUT I HAVE A FEELING IT'S NOTHING GOOD.
FRED, SERIOUSLY-- ARE YOU EVER GONNA TELL ME WHAT'S GOING ON WITH YOU AND FISK?!
I WISH I COULD, PETE! I REALLY DO. YOU DON'T KNOW WHAT IT'S LIKE TO HAVE THE BURDEN OF A SECRET LIKE THIS.
A SECRET YOU WANT TO SHARE WITH THOSE YOU CARE FOR THE MOST, BUT YOU CAN'T BECAUSE IT MIGHT PUT THEM IN GRAVE DANGER.
YOU CAN'T IMAGINE WHAT THAT'S LIKE, PAL!
SIGH
AT LEAST PROMISE ME IT'S NOTHING ILLEGAL.
I WISH IT WAS, PETE. BUT JUST BECAUSE I'M NOT DOING EVILDOING ANYMORE--

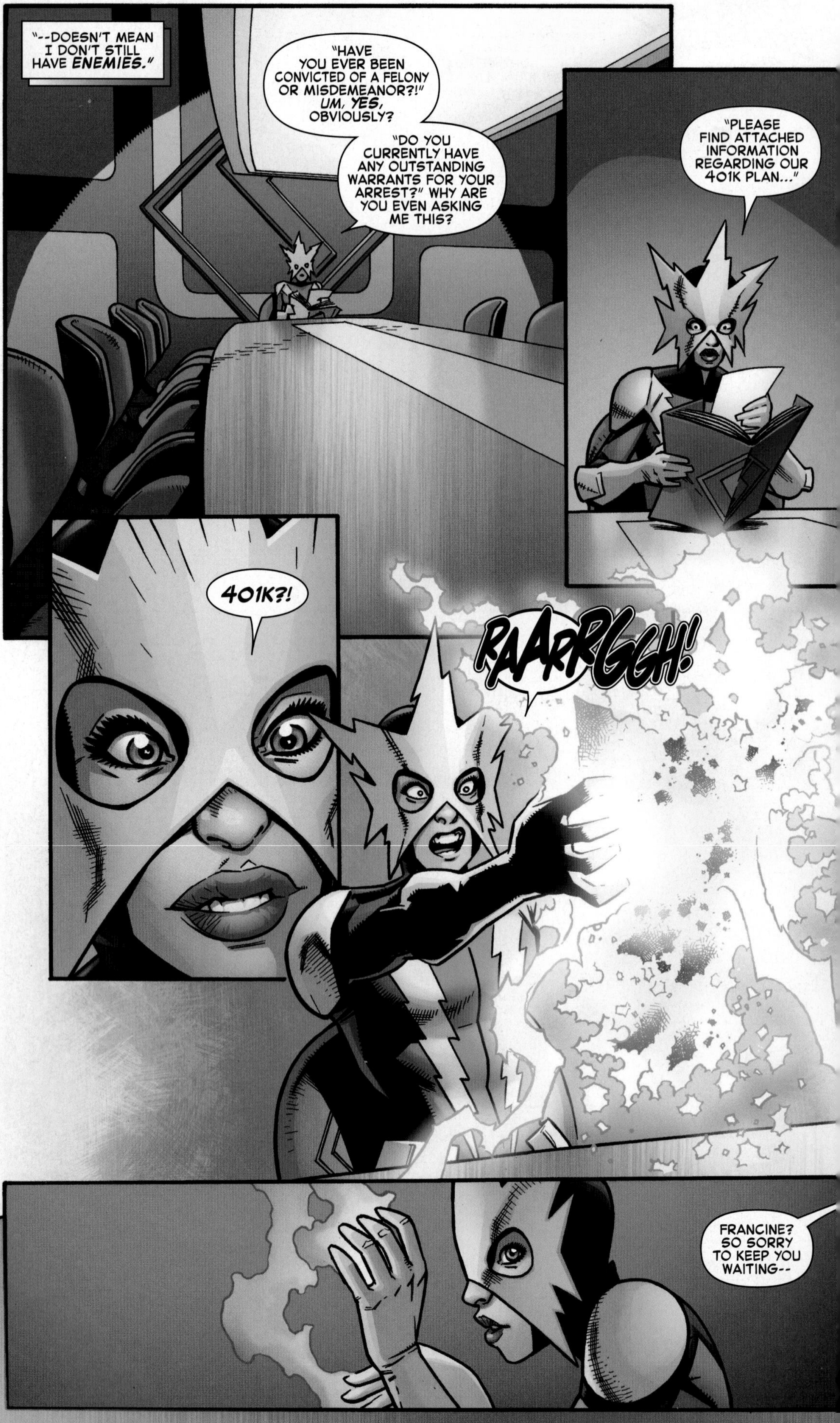
"--DOESN'T MEAN I DON'T STILL HAVE ENEMIES."
"HAVE YOU EVER BEEN CONVICTED OF A FELONY OR MISDEMEANOR?!" UM, YES, OBVIOUSLY?
"DO YOU CURRENTLY HAVE ANY OUTSTANDING WARRANTS FOR YOUR ARREST?" WHY ARE YOU EVEN ASKING ME THIS?
"PLEASE FIND ATTACHED INFORMATION REGARDING OUR 401K PLAN..."
401K?!
RAARRGGH!
FRANCINE? SO SORRY TO KEEP YOU WAITING--

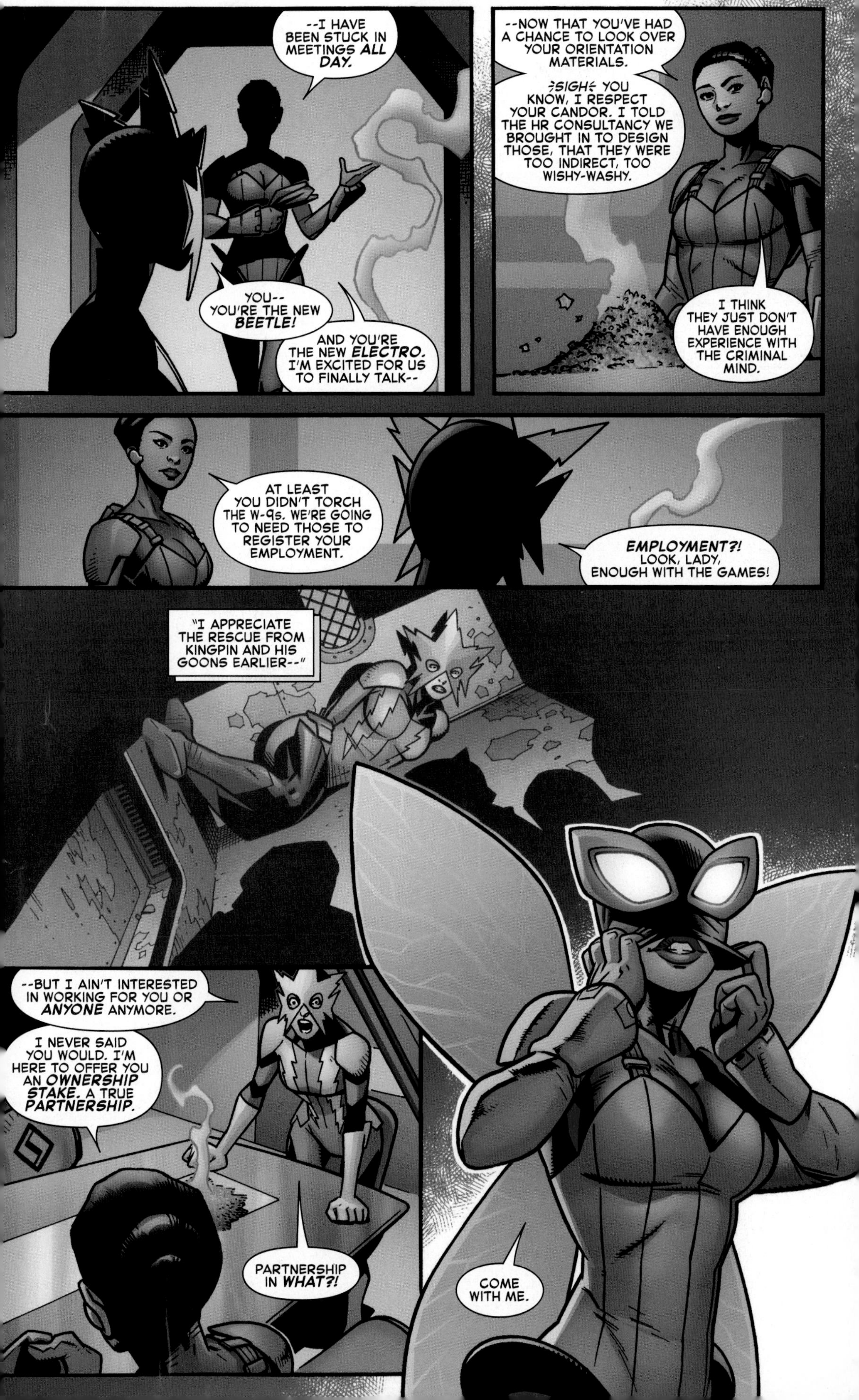

--I HAVE BEEN STUCK IN MEETINGS ALL DAY.
YOU-- YOU'RE THE NEW BEETLE!
AND YOU'RE THE NEW ELECTRO. I'M EXCITED FOR US TO FINALLY TALK--
--NOW THAT YOU'VE HAD A CHANCE TO LOOK OVER YOUR ORIENTATION MATERIALS.
⸗SIGH⸗ YOU KNOW, I RESPECT YOUR CANDOR. I TOLD THE HR CONSULTANCY WE BROUGHT IN TO DESIGN THOSE, THAT THEY WERE TOO INDIRECT, TOO WISHY-WASHY.
I THINK THEY JUST DON'T HAVE ENOUGH EXPERIENCE WITH THE CRIMINAL MIND.
AT LEAST YOU DIDN'T TORCH THE W-9s. WE'RE GOING TO NEED THOSE TO REGISTER YOUR EMPLOYMENT.
EMPLOYMENT?! LOOK, LADY, ENOUGH WITH THE GAMES!
"I APPRECIATE THE RESCUE FROM KINGPIN AND HIS GOONS EARLIER--"
--BUT I AIN'T INTERESTED IN WORKING FOR YOU OR ANYONE ANYMORE.
I NEVER SAID YOU WOULD. I'M HERE TO OFFER YOU AN OWNERSHIP STAKE. A TRUE PARTNERSHIP.
PARTNERSHIP IN WHAT?!
COME WITH ME.

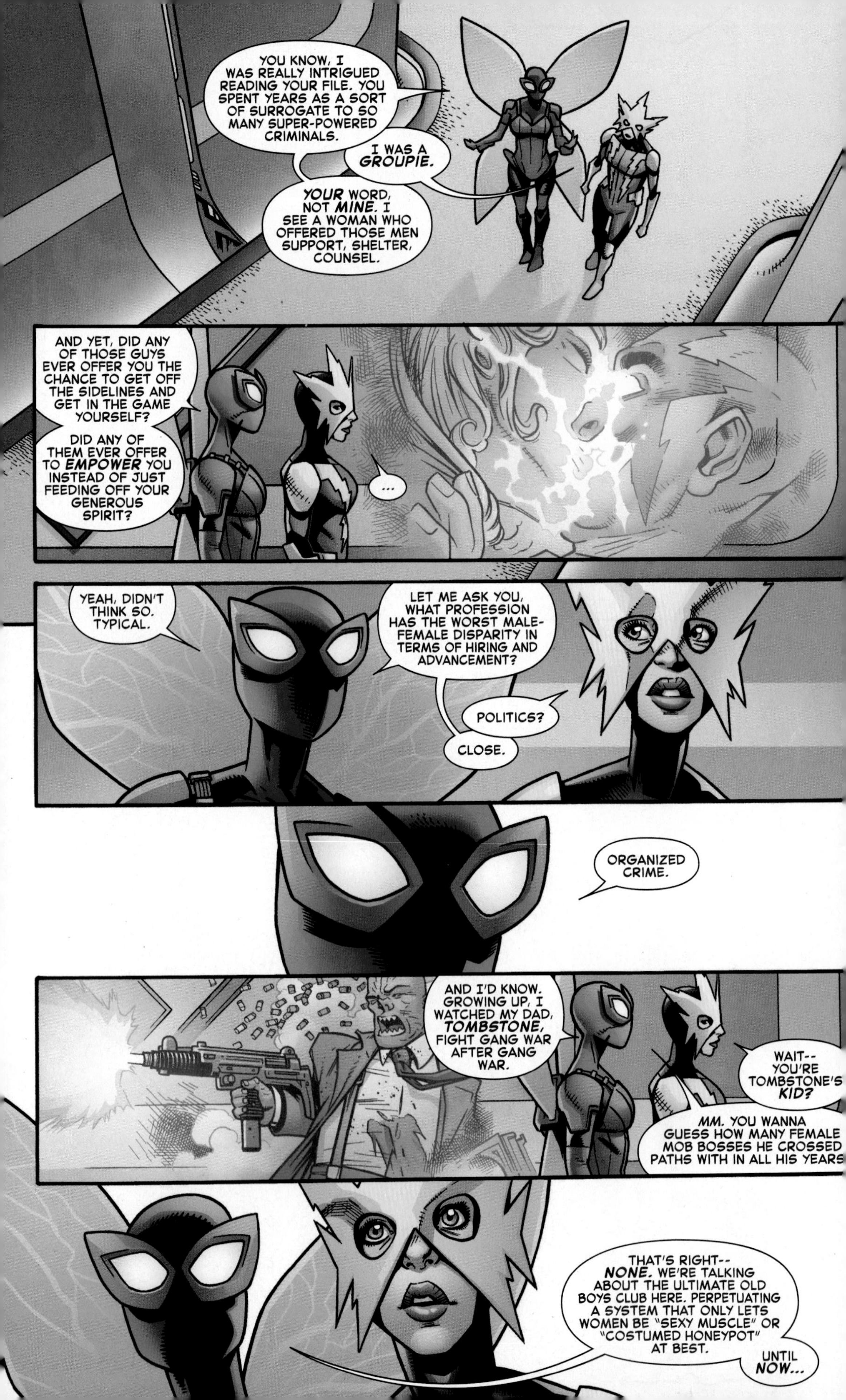
YOU KNOW, I WAS REALLY INTRIGUED READING YOUR FILE. YOU SPENT YEARS AS A SORT OF SURROGATE TO SO MANY SUPER-POWERED CRIMINALS.
I WAS A *GROUPIE.*
YOUR WORD, NOT *MINE.* I SEE A WOMAN WHO OFFERED THOSE MEN SUPPORT, SHELTER, COUNSEL.
AND YET, DID ANY OF THOSE GUYS EVER OFFER YOU THE CHANCE TO GET OFF THE SIDELINES AND GET IN THE GAME YOURSELF?
DID ANY OF THEM EVER OFFER TO *EMPOWER* YOU INSTEAD OF JUST FEEDING OFF YOUR GENEROUS SPIRIT?
...
YEAH, DIDN'T THINK SO. TYPICAL.
LET ME ASK YOU, WHAT PROFESSION HAS THE WORST MALE-FEMALE DISPARITY IN TERMS OF HIRING AND ADVANCEMENT?
POLITICS?
CLOSE.
ORGANIZED CRIME.
AND I'D KNOW. GROWING UP, I WATCHED MY DAD, *TOMBSTONE,* FIGHT GANG WAR AFTER GANG WAR.
WAIT-- YOU'RE TOMBSTONE'S *KID?*
MM. YOU WANNA GUESS HOW MANY FEMALE MOB BOSSES HE CROSSED PATHS WITH IN ALL HIS YEARS
THAT'S RIGHT-- *NONE.* WE'RE TALKING ABOUT THE ULTIMATE OLD BOYS CLUB HERE. PERPETUATING A SYSTEM THAT ONLY LETS WOMEN BE "SEXY MUSCLE" OR "COSTUMED HONEYPOT" AT BEST.
UNTIL *NOW...*

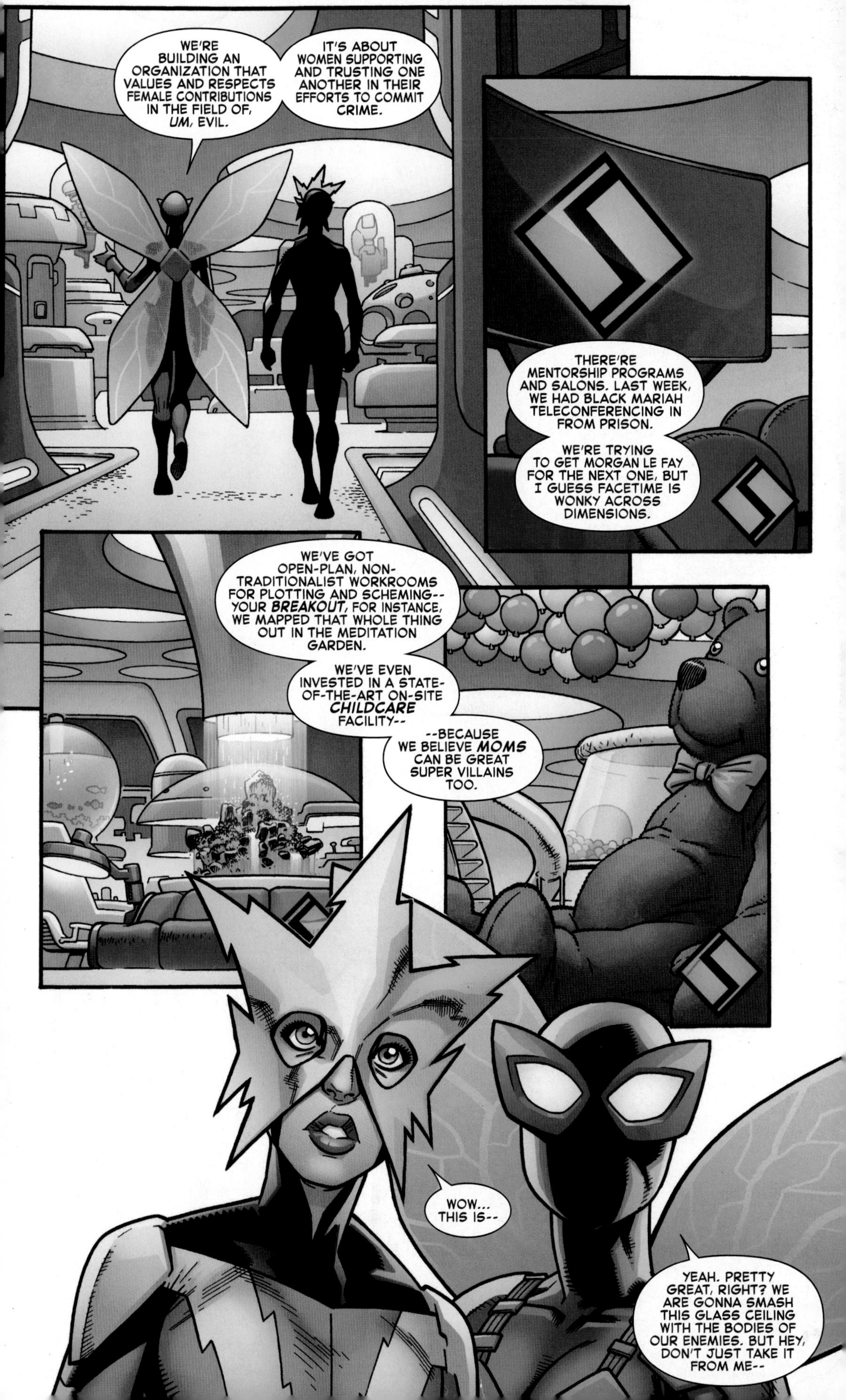
WE'RE BUILDING AN ORGANIZATION THAT VALUES AND RESPECTS FEMALE CONTRIBUTIONS IN THE FIELD OF, *UM*, EVIL.
IT'S ABOUT WOMEN SUPPORTING AND TRUSTING ONE ANOTHER IN THEIR EFFORTS TO COMMIT CRIME.
THERE'RE MENTORSHIP PROGRAMS AND SALONS. LAST WEEK, WE HAD BLACK MARIAH TELECONFERENCING IN FROM PRISON.
WE'RE TRYING TO GET MORGAN LE FAY FOR THE NEXT ONE, BUT I GUESS FACETIME IS WONKY ACROSS DIMENSIONS.
WE'VE GOT OPEN-PLAN, NON-TRADITIONALIST WORKROOMS FOR PLOTTING AND SCHEMING-- YOUR *BREAKOUT*, FOR INSTANCE, WE MAPPED THAT WHOLE THING OUT IN THE MEDITATION GARDEN.
WE'VE EVEN INVESTED IN A STATE-OF-THE-ART ON-SITE *CHILDCARE* FACILITY--
--BECAUSE WE BELIEVE *MOMS* CAN BE GREAT SUPER VILLAINS TOO.
WOW... THIS IS--
YEAH. PRETTY GREAT, RIGHT? WE ARE GONNA SMASH THIS GLASS CEILING WITH THE BODIES OF OUR ENEMIES. BUT HEY, DON'T JUST TAKE IT FROM ME--

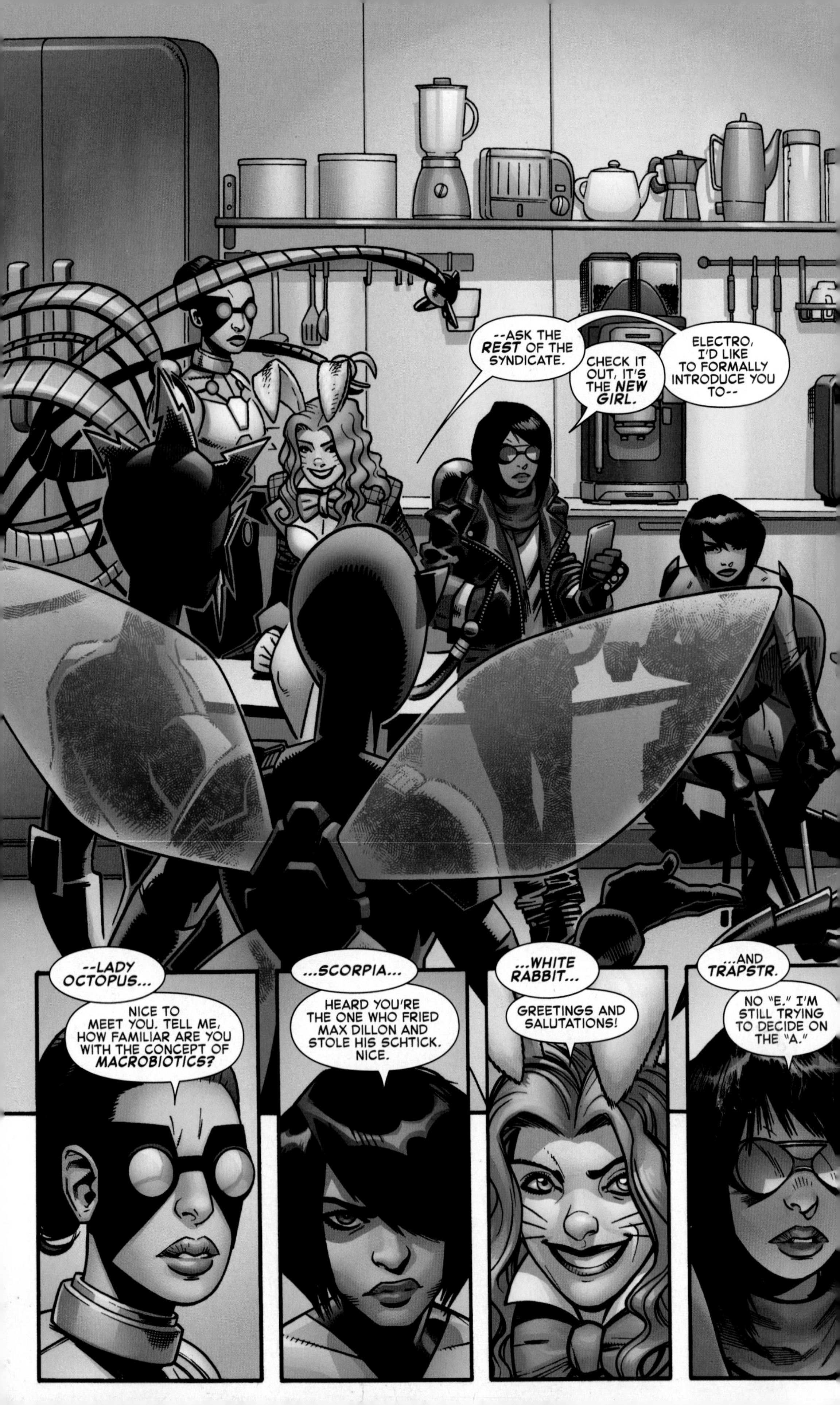
--ASK THE REST OF THE SYNDICATE.
ELECTRO, I'D LIKE TO FORMALLY INTRODUCE YOU TO--
CHECK IT OUT, IT'S THE NEW GIRL.
--LADY OCTOPUS...
NICE TO MEET YOU. TELL ME, HOW FAMILIAR ARE YOU WITH THE CONCEPT OF MACROBIOTICS?
...SCORPIA...
HEARD YOU'RE THE ONE WHO FRIED MAX DILLON AND STOLE HIS SCHTICK. NICE.
...WHITE RABBIT...
GREETINGS AND SALUTATIONS!
...AND TRAPSTR.
NO "E." I'M STILL TRYING TO DECIDE ON THE "A."

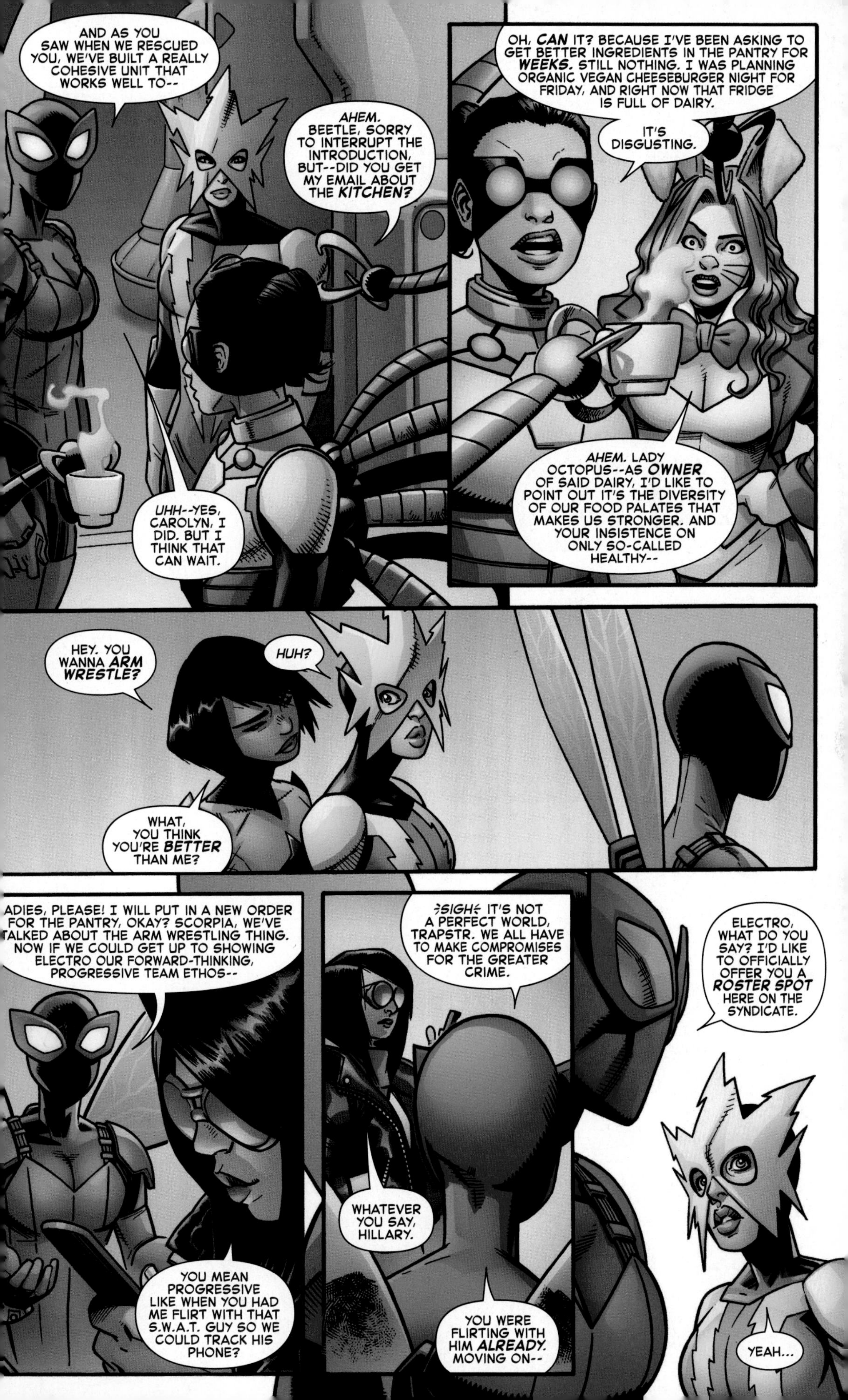
AND AS YOU SAW WHEN WE RESCUED YOU, WE'VE BUILT A REALLY COHESIVE UNIT THAT WORKS WELL TO--
AHEM. BEETLE, SORRY TO INTERRUPT THE INTRODUCTION, BUT--DID YOU GET MY EMAIL ABOUT THE KITCHEN?
UHH--YES, CAROLYN, I DID. BUT I THINK THAT CAN WAIT.
OH, CAN IT? BECAUSE I'VE BEEN ASKING TO GET BETTER INGREDIENTS IN THE PANTRY FOR WEEKS. STILL NOTHING. I WAS PLANNING ORGANIC VEGAN CHEESEBURGER NIGHT FOR FRIDAY, AND RIGHT NOW THAT FRIDGE IS FULL OF DAIRY.
IT'S DISGUSTING.
AHEM. LADY OCTOPUS--AS OWNER OF SAID DAIRY, I'D LIKE TO POINT OUT IT'S THE DIVERSITY OF OUR FOOD PALATES THAT MAKES US STRONGER. AND YOUR INSISTENCE ON ONLY SO-CALLED HEALTHY--
HEY. YOU WANNA ARM WRESTLE?
HUH?
WHAT, YOU THINK YOU'RE BETTER THAN ME?
ADIES, PLEASE! I WILL PUT IN A NEW ORDER FOR THE PANTRY, OKAY? SCORPIA, WE'VE TALKED ABOUT THE ARM WRESTLING THING. NOW IF WE COULD GET UP TO SHOWING ELECTRO OUR FORWARD-THINKING, PROGRESSIVE TEAM ETHOS--
YOU MEAN PROGRESSIVE LIKE WHEN YOU HAD ME FLIRT WITH THAT S.W.A.T. GUY SO WE COULD TRACK HIS PHONE?
SIGH IT'S NOT A PERFECT WORLD, TRAPSTR. WE ALL HAVE TO MAKE COMPROMISES FOR THE GREATER CRIME.
WHATEVER YOU SAY, HILLARY.
YOU WERE FLIRTING WITH HIM ALREADY. MOVING ON--
ELECTRO, WHAT DO YOU SAY? I'D LIKE TO OFFICIALLY OFFER YOU A ROSTER SPOT HERE ON THE SYNDICATE.
YEAH...

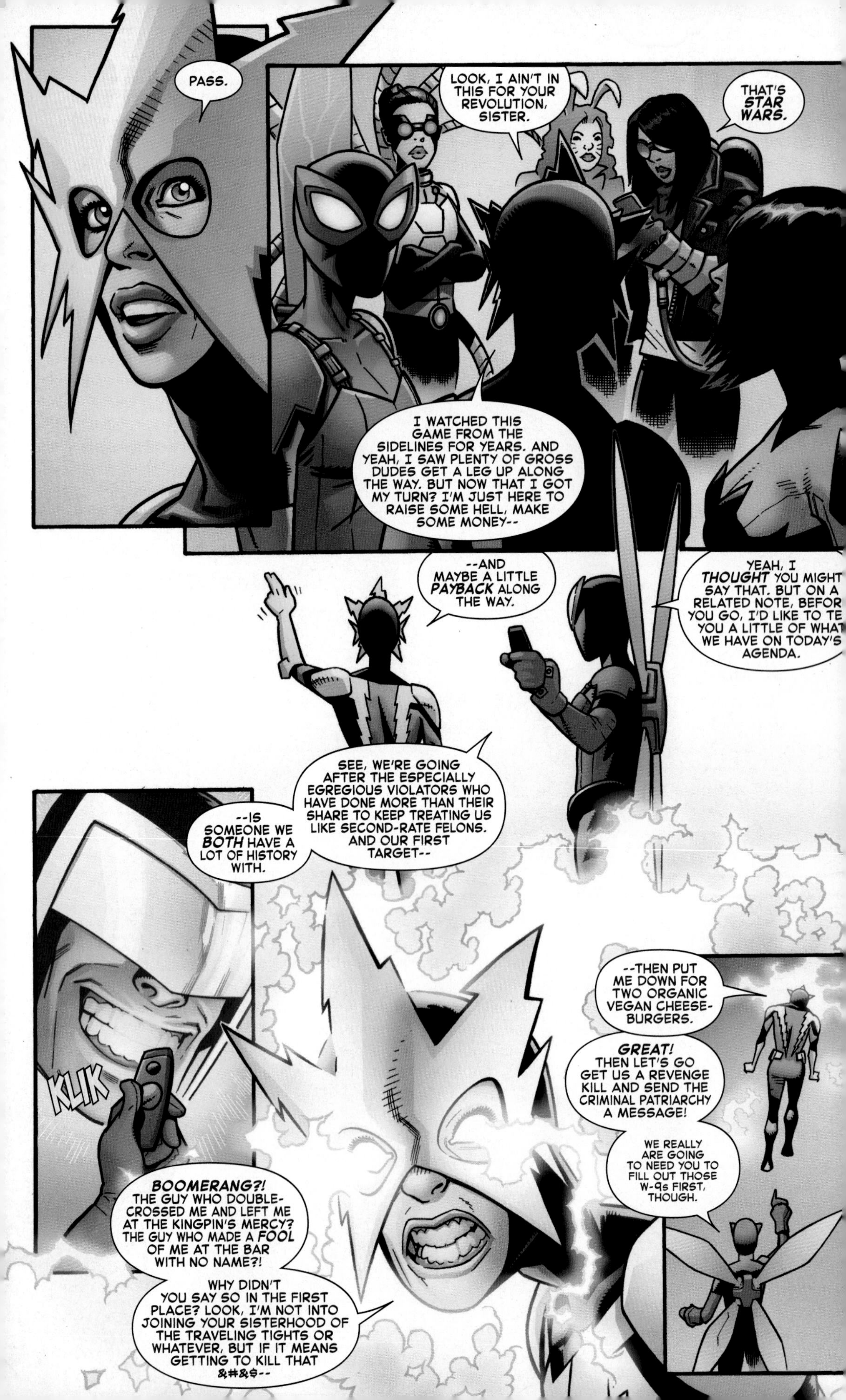

PASS.
LOOK, I AIN'T IN THIS FOR YOUR REVOLUTION, SISTER.
THAT'S STAR WARS.
I WATCHED THIS GAME FROM THE SIDELINES FOR YEARS. AND YEAH, I SAW PLENTY OF GROSS DUDES GET A LEG UP ALONG THE WAY. BUT NOW THAT I GOT MY TURN? I'M JUST HERE TO RAISE SOME HELL, MAKE SOME MONEY--
--AND MAYBE A LITTLE PAYBACK ALONG THE WAY.
YEAH, I THOUGHT YOU MIGHT SAY THAT. BUT ON A RELATED NOTE, BEFOR YOU GO, I'D LIKE TO TE YOU A LITTLE OF WHAT WE HAVE ON TODAY'S AGENDA.
SEE, WE'RE GOING AFTER THE ESPECIALLY EGREGIOUS VIOLATORS WHO HAVE DONE MORE THAN THEIR SHARE TO KEEP TREATING US LIKE SECOND-RATE FELONS. AND OUR FIRST TARGET--
--IS SOMEONE WE BOTH HAVE A LOT OF HISTORY WITH.
KLIK
BOOMERANG?! THE GUY WHO DOUBLE-CROSSED ME AND LEFT ME AT THE KINGPIN'S MERCY? THE GUY WHO MADE A FOOL OF ME AT THE BAR WITH NO NAME?!
WHY DIDN'T YOU SAY SO IN THE FIRST PLACE? LOOK, I'M NOT INTO JOINING YOUR SISTERHOOD OF THE TRAVELING TIGHTS OR WHATEVER, BUT IF IT MEANS GETTING TO KILL THAT &#&$--
--THEN PUT ME DOWN FOR TWO ORGANIC VEGAN CHEESE-BURGERS.
GREAT! THEN LET'S GO GET US A REVENGE KILL AND SEND THE CRIMINAL PATRIARCHY A MESSAGE!
WE REALLY ARE GOING TO NEED YOU TO FILL OUT THOSE W-9s FIRST, THOUGH.

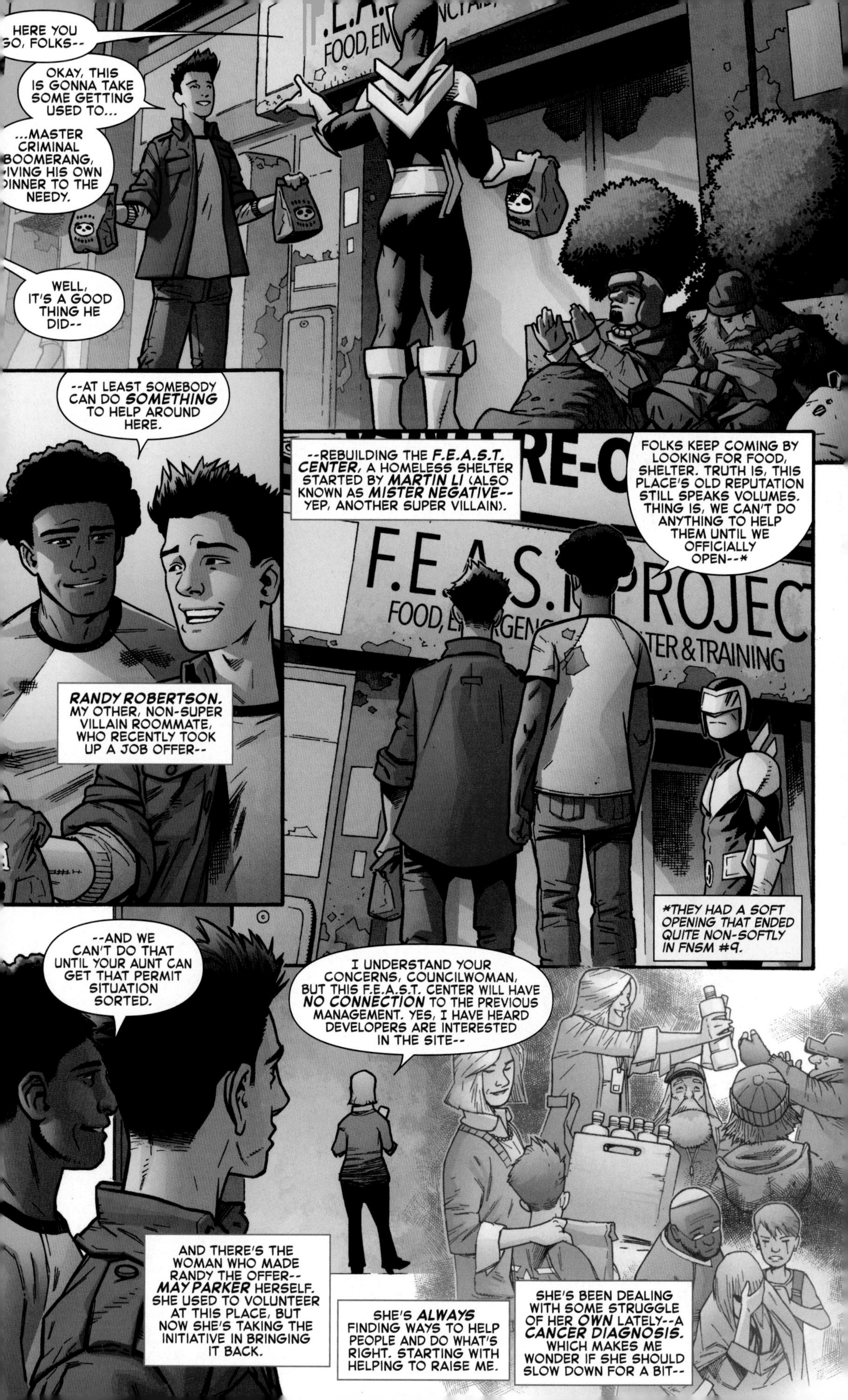

HERE YOU GO, FOLKS--
OKAY, THIS IS GONNA TAKE SOME GETTING USED TO...
...MASTER CRIMINAL BOOMERANG, GIVING HIS OWN DINNER TO THE NEEDY.
WELL, IT'S A GOOD THING HE DID--
--AT LEAST SOMEBODY CAN DO SOMETHING TO HELP AROUND HERE.
RANDY ROBERTSON. MY OTHER, NON-SUPER VILLAIN ROOMMATE, WHO RECENTLY TOOK UP A JOB OFFER--
--REBUILDING THE F.E.A.S.T. CENTER, A HOMELESS SHELTER STARTED BY MARTIN LI (ALSO KNOWN AS MISTER NEGATIVE--YEP, ANOTHER SUPER VILLAIN).
FOLKS KEEP COMING BY LOOKING FOR FOOD, SHELTER. TRUTH IS, THIS PLACE'S OLD REPUTATION STILL SPEAKS VOLUMES. THING IS, WE CAN'T DO ANYTHING TO HELP THEM UNTIL WE OFFICIALLY OPEN--*
F.E.A.S.T. PROJECT
FOOD, EMERGENCY SHELTER & TRAINING
*THEY HAD A SOFT OPENING THAT ENDED QUITE NON-SOFTLY IN FNSM #9.
--AND WE CAN'T DO THAT UNTIL YOUR AUNT CAN GET THAT PERMIT SITUATION SORTED.
I UNDERSTAND YOUR CONCERNS, COUNCILWOMAN, BUT THIS F.E.A.S.T. CENTER WILL HAVE NO CONNECTION TO THE PREVIOUS MANAGEMENT. YES, I HAVE HEARD DEVELOPERS ARE INTERESTED IN THE SITE--
AND THERE'S THE WOMAN WHO MADE RANDY THE OFFER--MAY PARKER HERSELF. SHE USED TO VOLUNTEER AT THIS PLACE, BUT NOW SHE'S TAKING THE INITIATIVE IN BRINGING IT BACK.
SHE'S ALWAYS FINDING WAYS TO HELP PEOPLE AND DO WHAT'S RIGHT. STARTING WITH HELPING TO RAISE ME.
SHE'S BEEN DEALING WITH SOME STRUGGLE OF HER OWN LATELY--A CANCER DIAGNOSIS. WHICH MAKES ME WONDER IF SHE SHOULD SLOW DOWN FOR A BIT--

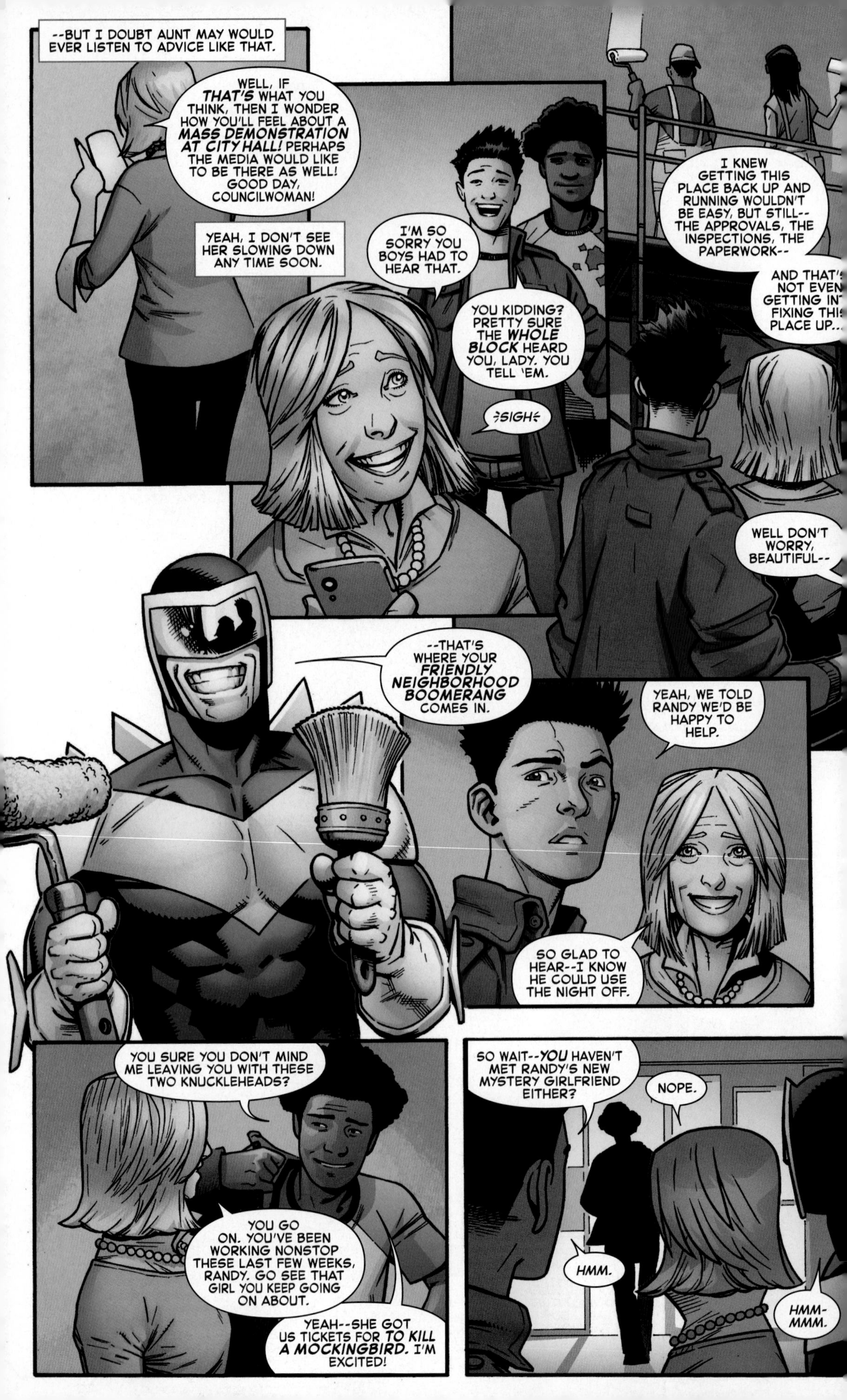
--BUT I DOUBT AUNT MAY WOULD EVER LISTEN TO ADVICE LIKE THAT.
WELL, IF THAT'S WHAT YOU THINK, THEN I WONDER HOW YOU'LL FEEL ABOUT A MASS DEMONSTRATION AT CITY HALL! PERHAPS THE MEDIA WOULD LIKE TO BE THERE AS WELL! GOOD DAY, COUNCILWOMAN!
YEAH, I DON'T SEE HER SLOWING DOWN ANY TIME SOON.
I'M SO SORRY YOU BOYS HAD TO HEAR THAT.
YOU KIDDING? PRETTY SURE THE WHOLE BLOCK HEARD YOU, LADY. YOU TELL 'EM.
SIGH
I KNEW GETTING THIS PLACE BACK UP AND RUNNING WOULDN'T BE EASY, BUT STILL-- THE APPROVALS, THE INSPECTIONS, THE PAPERWORK--
AND THAT'S NOT EVEN GETTING INT FIXING THIS PLACE UP...
WELL DON'T WORRY, BEAUTIFUL--
--THAT'S WHERE YOUR FRIENDLY NEIGHBORHOOD BOOMERANG COMES IN.
YEAH, WE TOLD RANDY WE'D BE HAPPY TO HELP.
SO GLAD TO HEAR--I KNOW HE COULD USE THE NIGHT OFF.
YOU SURE YOU DON'T MIND ME LEAVING YOU WITH THESE TWO KNUCKLEHEADS?
YOU GO ON. YOU'VE BEEN WORKING NONSTOP THESE LAST FEW WEEKS, RANDY. GO SEE THAT GIRL YOU KEEP GOING ON ABOUT.
YEAH--SHE GOT US TICKETS FOR TO KILL A MOCKINGBIRD. I'M EXCITED!
SO WAIT--YOU HAVEN'T MET RANDY'S NEW MYSTERY GIRLFRIEND EITHER?
NOPE.
HMM.
HMM-MMM.

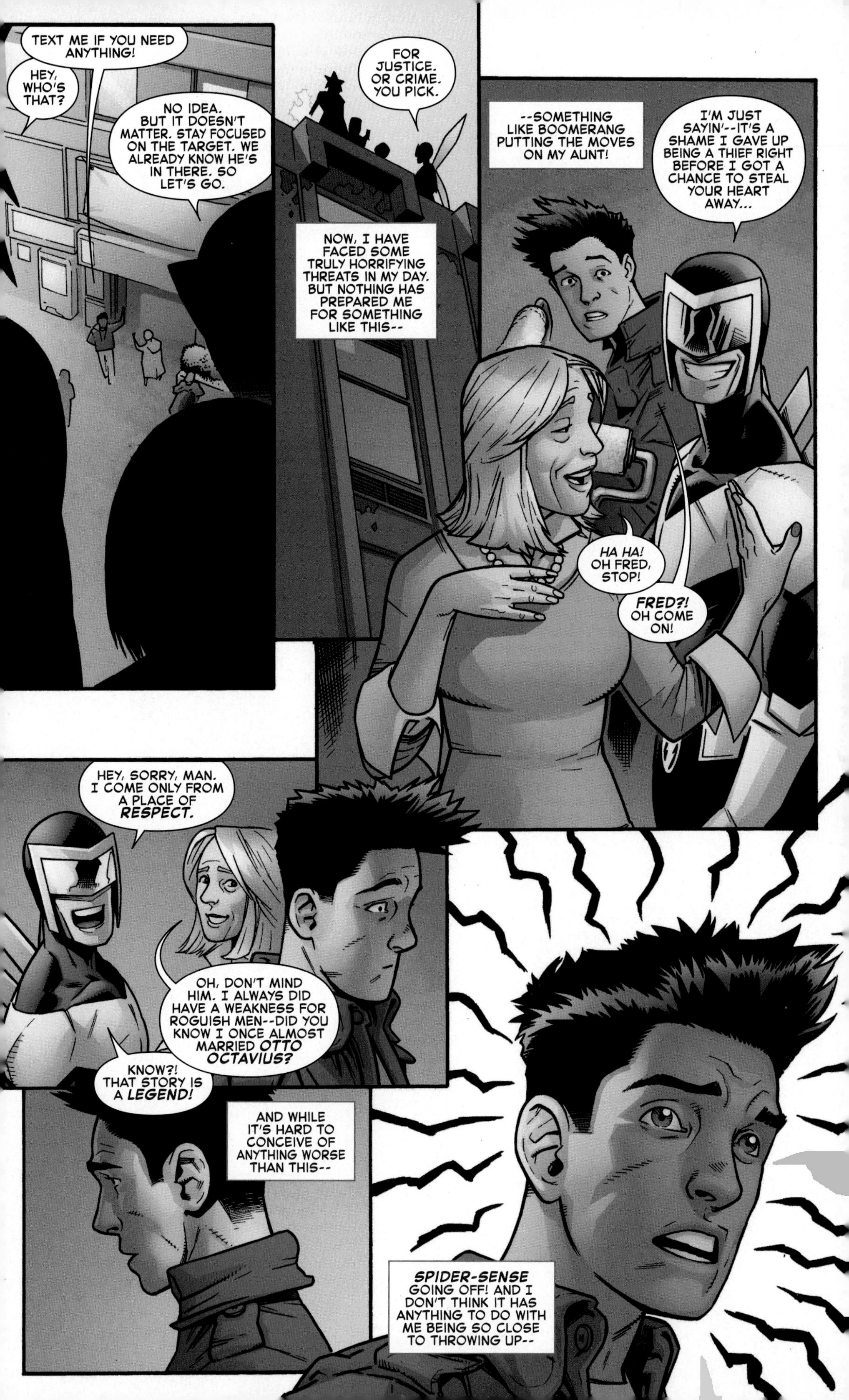

TEXT ME IF YOU NEED ANYTHING!
HEY, WHO'S THAT?
NO IDEA. BUT IT DOESN'T MATTER. STAY FOCUSED ON THE TARGET. WE ALREADY KNOW HE'S IN THERE. SO LET'S GO.
FOR JUSTICE. OR CRIME. YOU PICK.
NOW, I HAVE FACED SOME TRULY HORRIFYING THREATS IN MY DAY. BUT NOTHING HAS PREPARED ME FOR SOMETHING LIKE THIS--
--SOMETHING LIKE BOOMERANG PUTTING THE MOVES ON MY AUNT!
I'M JUST SAYIN'--IT'S A SHAME I GAVE UP BEING A THIEF RIGHT BEFORE I GOT A CHANCE TO STEAL YOUR HEART AWAY...
HA HA! OH FRED, STOP!
FRED?! OH COME ON!
HEY, SORRY, MAN. I COME ONLY FROM A PLACE OF RESPECT.
OH, DON'T MIND HIM. I ALWAYS DID HAVE A WEAKNESS FOR ROGUISH MEN--DID YOU KNOW I ONCE ALMOST MARRIED OTTO OCTAVIUS?
KNOW?! THAT STORY IS A LEGEND!
AND WHILE IT'S HARD TO CONCEIVE OF ANYTHING WORSE THAN THIS--
SPIDER-SENSE GOING OFF! AND I DON'T THINK IT HAS ANYTHING TO DO WITH ME BEING SO CLOSE TO THROWING UP--

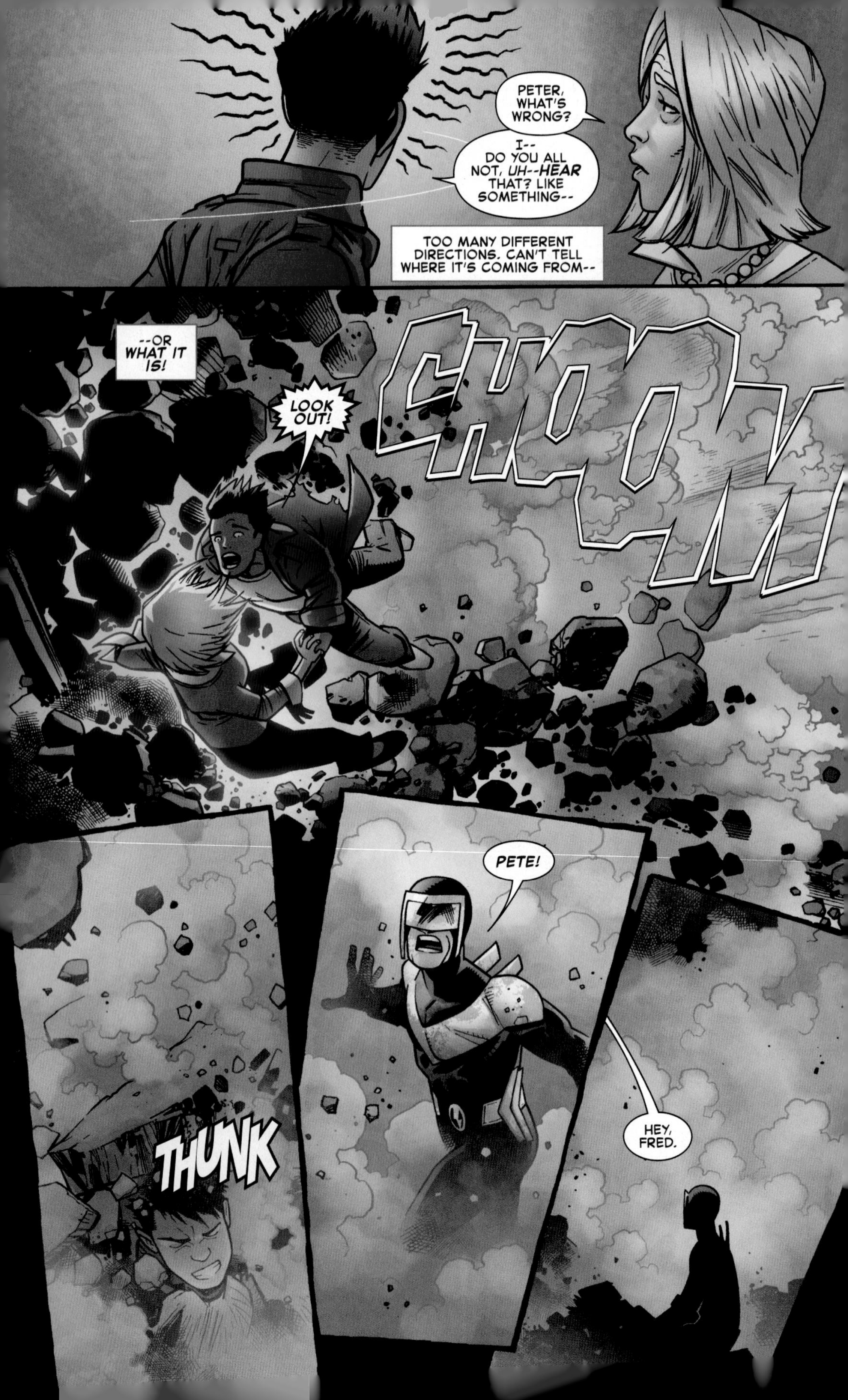
PETER, WHAT'S WRONG?
I-- DO YOU ALL NOT, *UH--HEAR* THAT? LIKE SOMETHING--
TOO MANY DIFFERENT DIRECTIONS. CAN'T TELL WHERE IT'S COMING FROM--
--OR *WHAT* IT *IS!*
LOOK OUT!
CHOOOM
THUNK
PETE!
HEY, FRED.

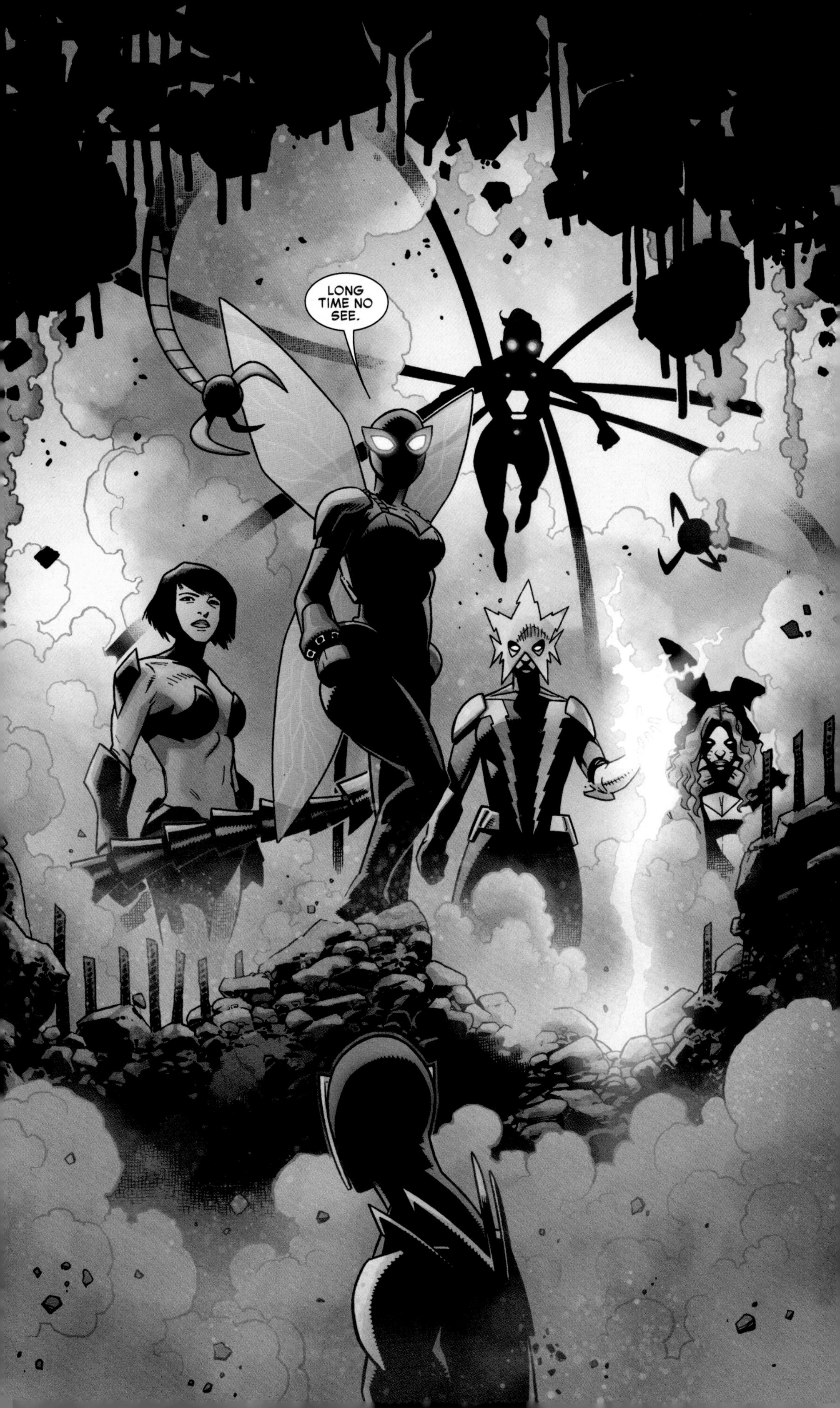
LONG TIME NO SEE.

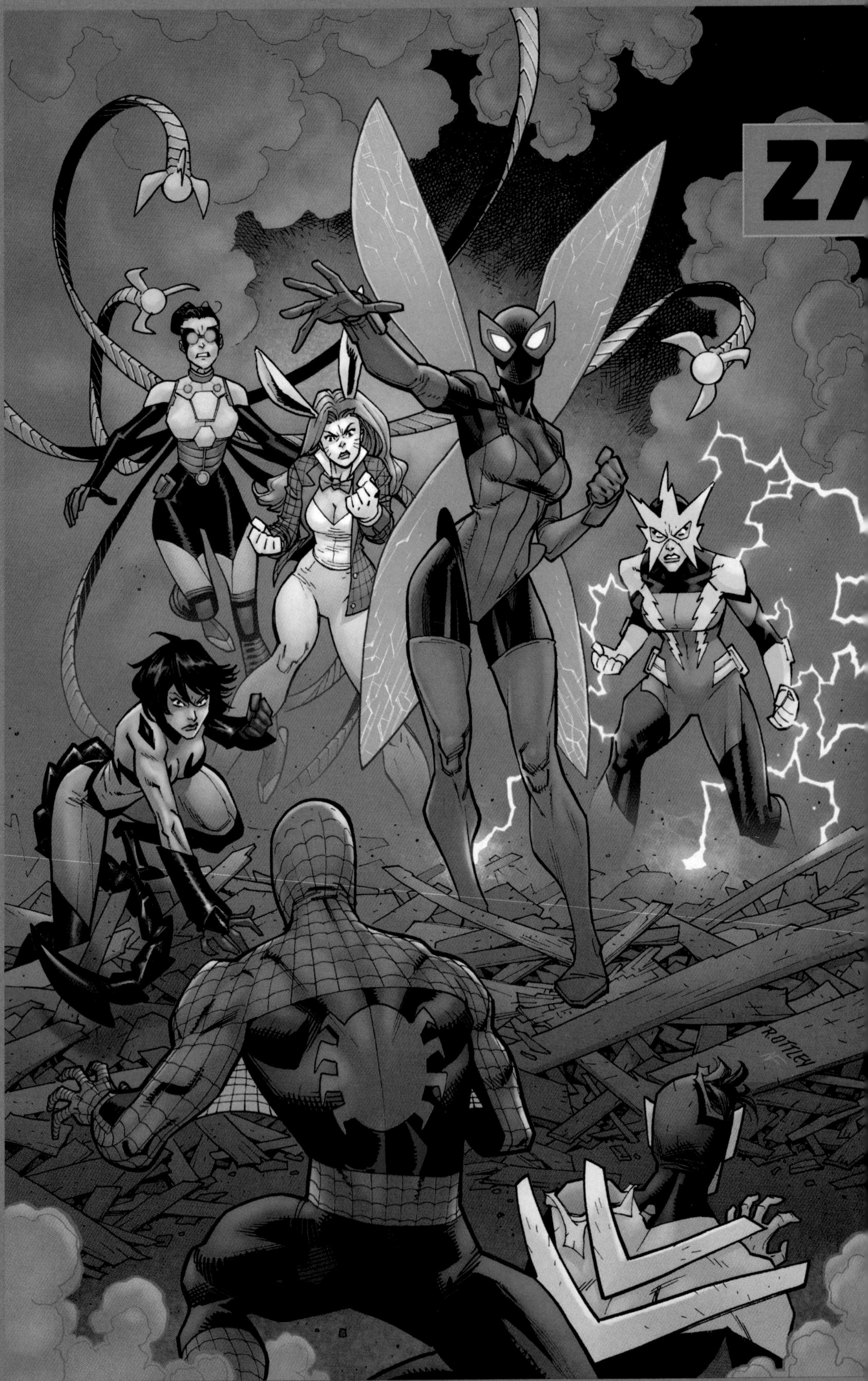
27
R. OTTLEY

WHO RUN THE WORLD? PART 2

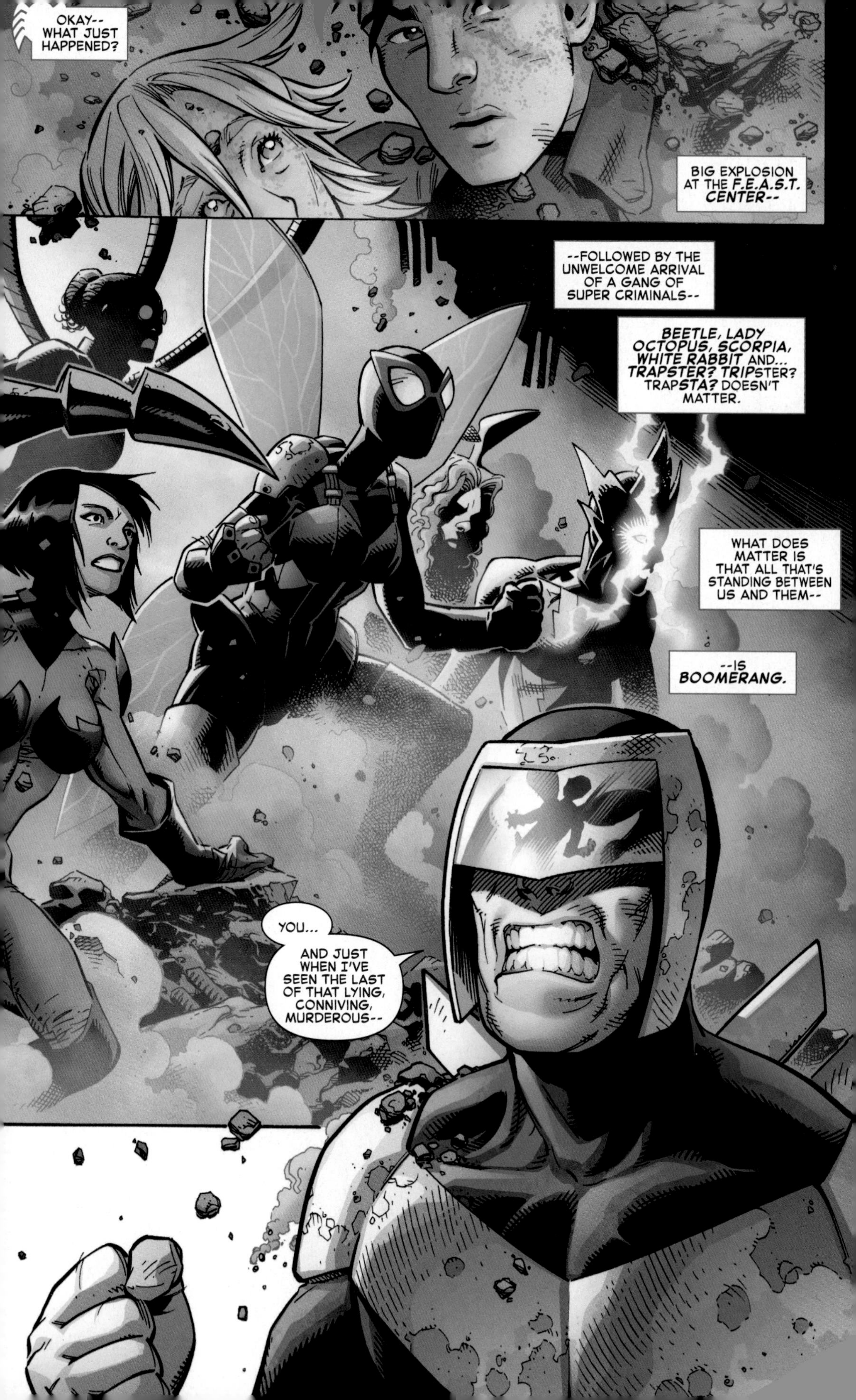
OKAY-- WHAT JUST HAPPENED?
BIG EXPLOSION AT THE F.E.A.S.T. CENTER--
--FOLLOWED BY THE UNWELCOME ARRIVAL OF A GANG OF SUPER CRIMINALS--
BEETLE, LADY OCTOPUS, SCORPIA, WHITE RABBIT AND... TRAPSTER? TRIPSTER? TRAPSTA? DOESN'T MATTER.
WHAT DOES MATTER IS THAT ALL THAT'S STANDING BETWEEN US AND THEM--
--IS BOOMERANG.
YOU...
AND JUST WHEN I'VE SEEN THE LAST OF THAT LYING, CONNIVING, MURDEROUS--

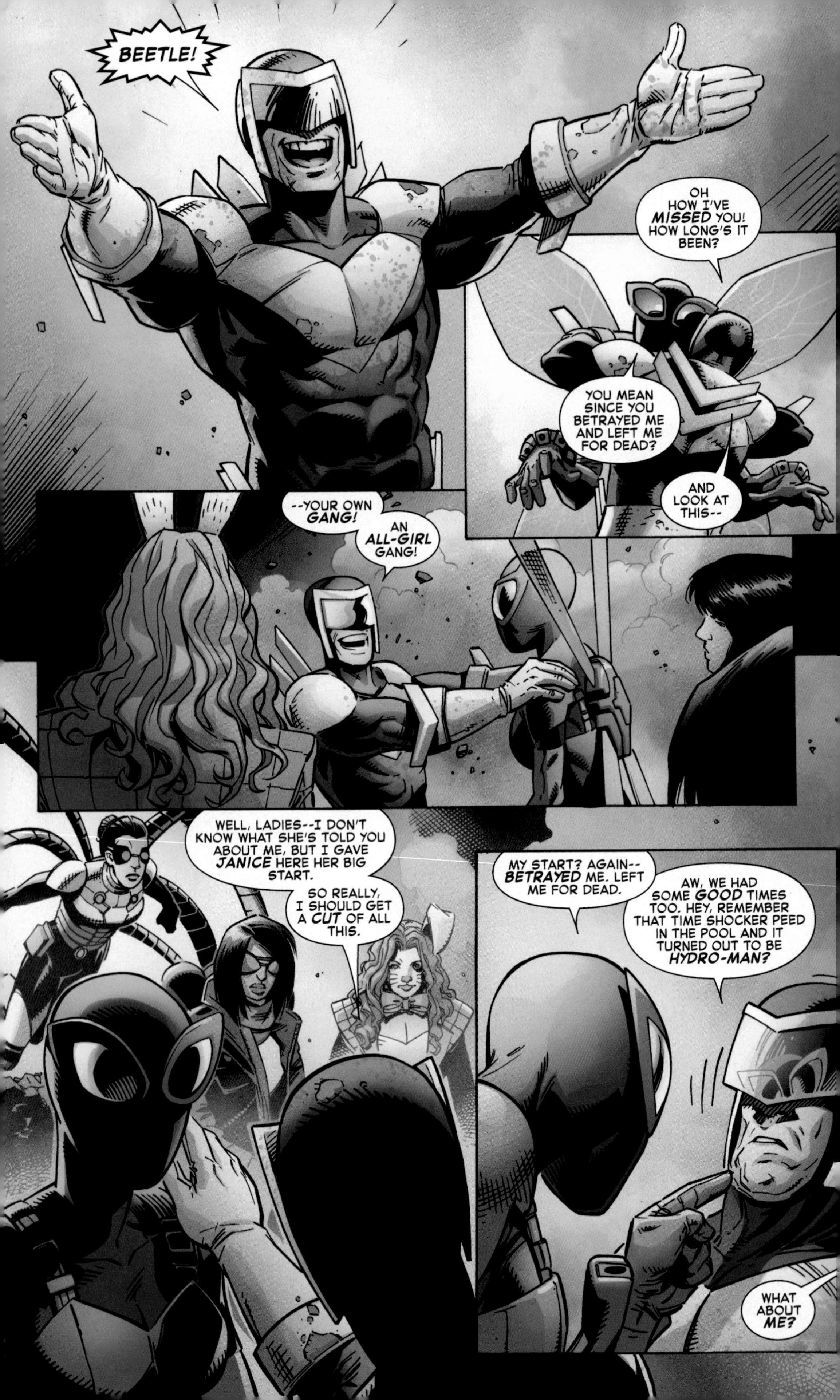
BEETLE!
OH HOW I'VE MISSED YOU! HOW LONG'S IT BEEN?
YOU MEAN SINCE YOU BETRAYED ME AND LEFT ME FOR DEAD?
AND LOOK AT THIS--
--YOUR OWN GANG!
AN ALL-GIRL GANG!
WELL, LADIES--I DON'T KNOW WHAT SHE'S TOLD YOU ABOUT ME, BUT I GAVE JANICE HERE HER BIG START.
SO REALLY, I SHOULD GET A CUT OF ALL THIS.
MY START? AGAIN--BETRAYED ME. LEFT ME FOR DEAD.
AW, WE HAD SOME GOOD TIMES TOO. HEY, REMEMBER THAT TIME SHOCKER PEED IN THE POOL AND IT TURNED OUT TO BE HYDRO-MAN?
WHAT ABOUT ME?

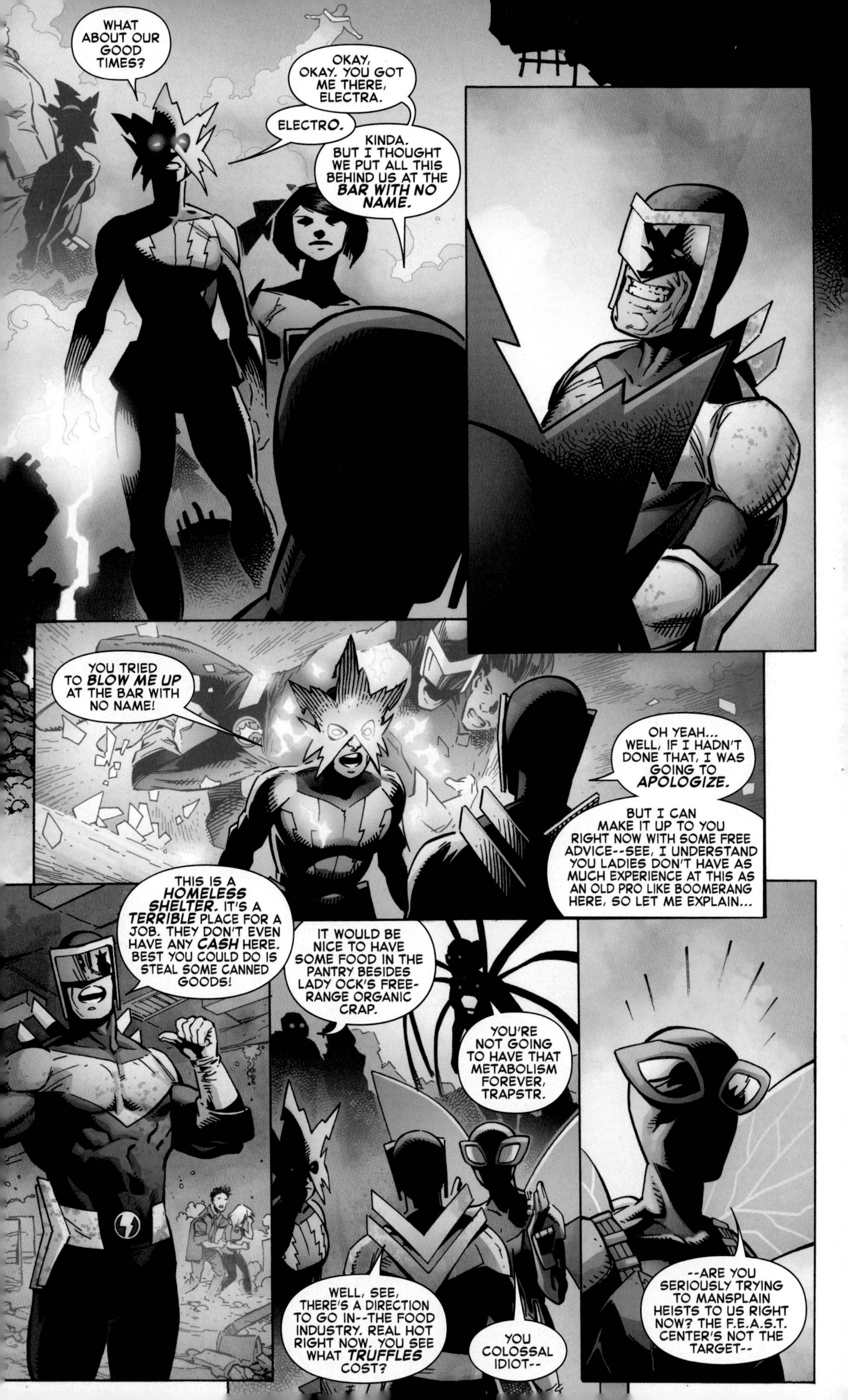
WHAT ABOUT OUR GOOD TIMES?
OKAY, OKAY. YOU GOT ME THERE, ELECTRA.
ELECTRO.
KINDA. BUT I THOUGHT WE PUT ALL THIS BEHIND US AT THE BAR WITH NO NAME.
YOU TRIED TO BLOW ME UP AT THE BAR WITH NO NAME!
OH YEAH... WELL, IF I HADN'T DONE THAT, I WAS GOING TO APOLOGIZE.
BUT I CAN MAKE IT UP TO YOU RIGHT NOW WITH SOME FREE ADVICE--SEE, I UNDERSTAND YOU LADIES DON'T HAVE AS MUCH EXPERIENCE AT THIS AS AN OLD PRO LIKE BOOMERANG HERE, SO LET ME EXPLAIN...
THIS IS A HOMELESS SHELTER. IT'S A TERRIBLE PLACE FOR A JOB. THEY DON'T EVEN HAVE ANY CASH HERE. BEST YOU COULD DO IS STEAL SOME CANNED GOODS!
IT WOULD BE NICE TO HAVE SOME FOOD IN THE PANTRY BESIDES LADY OCK'S FREE-RANGE ORGANIC CRAP.
YOU'RE NOT GOING TO HAVE THAT METABOLISM FOREVER, TRAPSTR.
WELL, SEE, THERE'S A DIRECTION TO GO IN--THE FOOD INDUSTRY. REAL HOT RIGHT NOW. YOU SEE WHAT TRUFFLES COST?
YOU COLOSSAL IDIOT--
--ARE YOU SERIOUSLY TRYING TO MANSPLAIN HEISTS TO US RIGHT NOW? THE F.E.A.S.T. CENTER'S NOT THE TARGET--

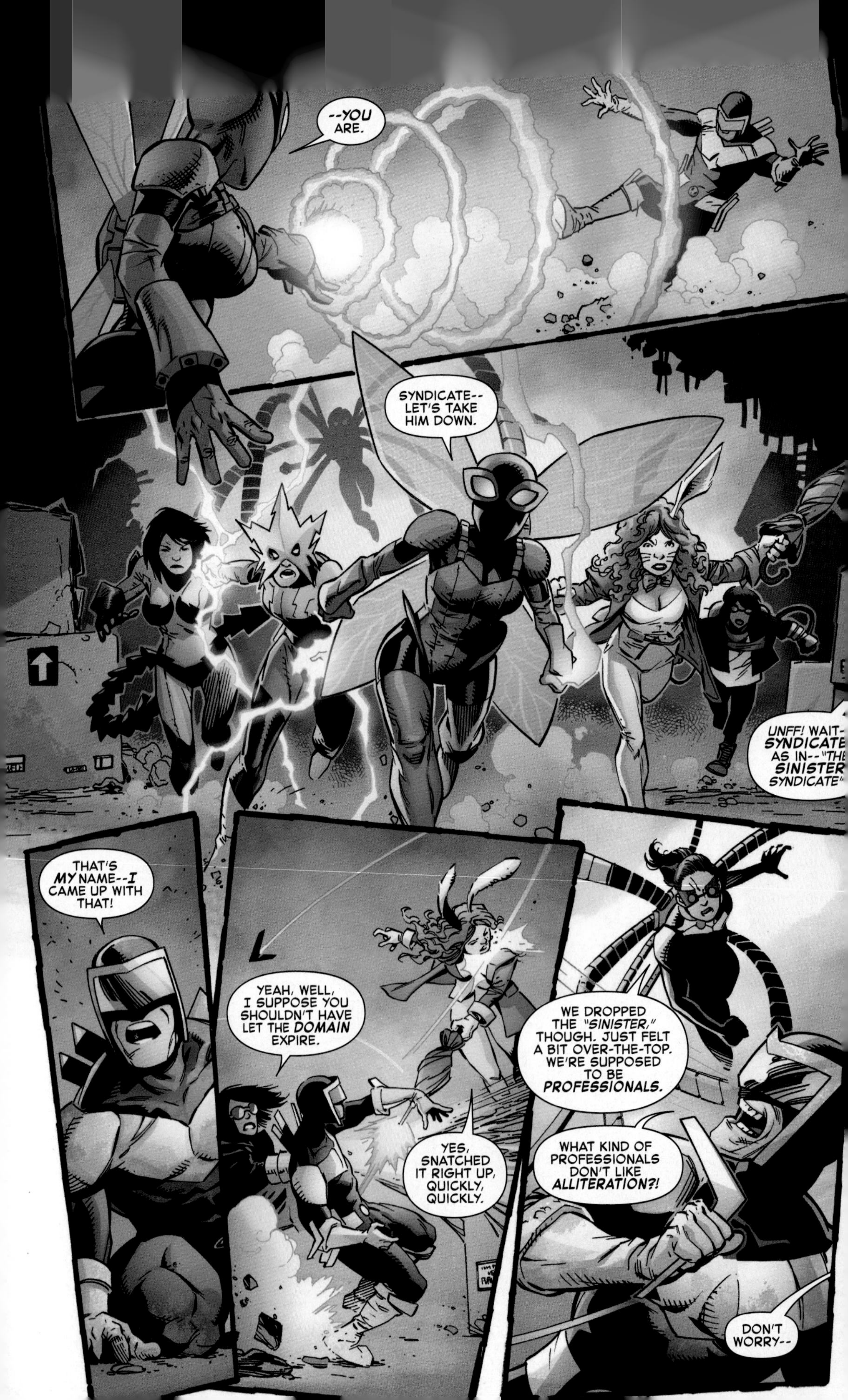

--YOU ARE.
SYNDICATE-- LET'S TAKE HIM DOWN.
UNFF! WAIT-- SYNDICATE AS IN--"THE SINISTER SYNDICATE"
THAT'S MY NAME--I CAME UP WITH THAT!
YEAH, WELL, I SUPPOSE YOU SHOULDN'T HAVE LET THE DOMAIN EXPIRE.
YES, SNATCHED IT RIGHT UP, QUICKLY, QUICKLY.
WE DROPPED THE "SINISTER," THOUGH. JUST FELT A BIT OVER-THE-TOP. WE'RE SUPPOSED TO BE PROFESSIONALS.
WHAT KIND OF PROFESSIONALS DON'T LIKE ALLITERATION?!
DON'T WORRY--

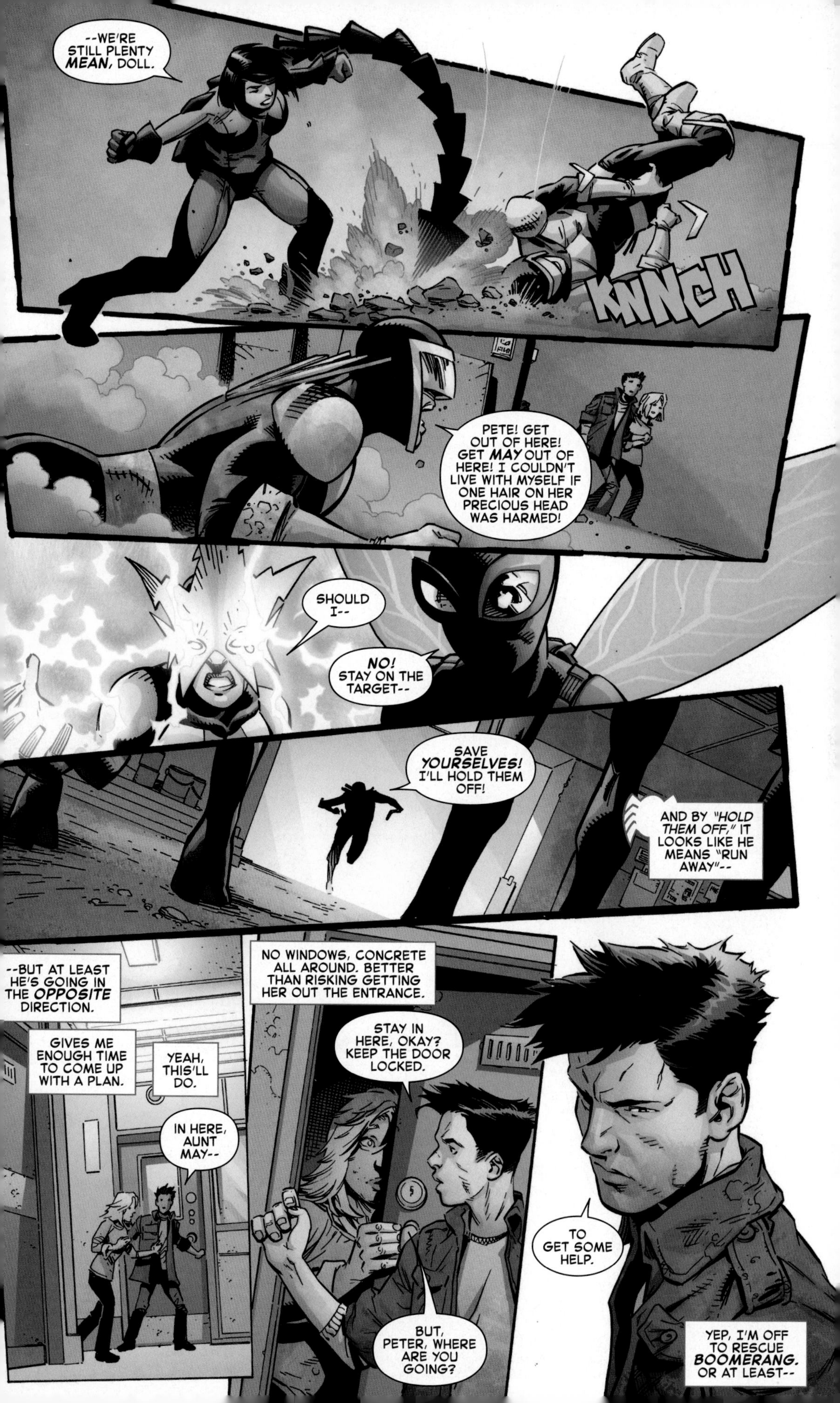
--WE'RE STILL PLENTY MEAN, DOLL.
KNNCH
PETE! GET OUT OF HERE! GET MAY OUT OF HERE! I COULDN'T LIVE WITH MYSELF IF ONE HAIR ON HER PRECIOUS HEAD WAS HARMED!
SHOULD I--
NO! STAY ON THE TARGET--
SAVE YOURSELVES! I'LL HOLD THEM OFF!
AND BY "HOLD THEM OFF," IT LOOKS LIKE HE MEANS "RUN AWAY"--
--BUT AT LEAST HE'S GOING IN THE OPPOSITE DIRECTION.
GIVES ME ENOUGH TIME TO COME UP WITH A PLAN.
YEAH, THIS'LL DO.
IN HERE, AUNT MAY--
NO WINDOWS, CONCRETE ALL AROUND. BETTER THAN RISKING GETTING HER OUT THE ENTRANCE.
STAY IN HERE, OKAY? KEEP THE DOOR LOCKED.
BUT, PETER, WHERE ARE YOU GOING?
TO GET SOME HELP.
YEP, I'M OFF TO RESCUE BOOMERANG. OR AT LEAST--

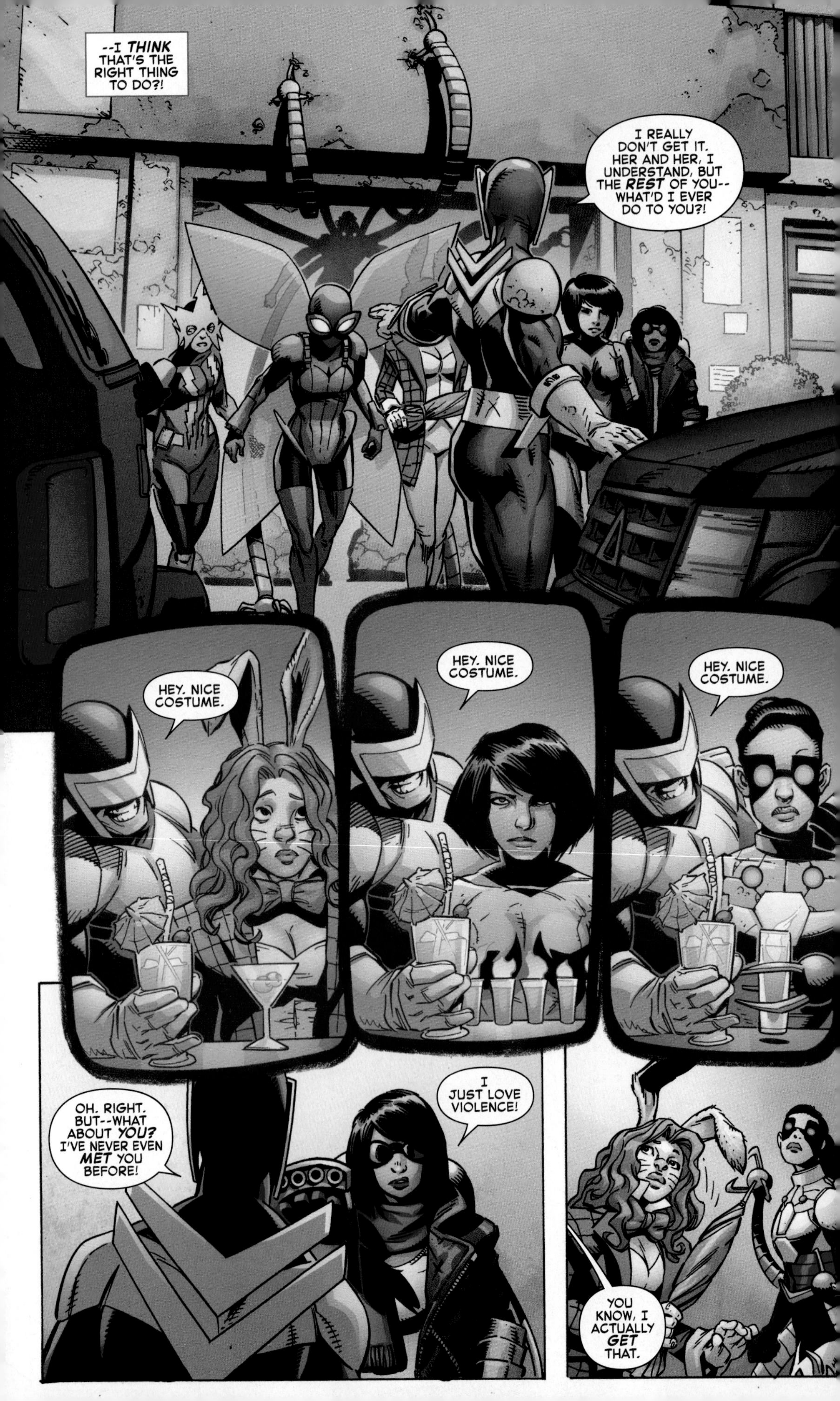

--I THINK THAT'S THE RIGHT THING TO DO?!
I REALLY DON'T GET IT. HER AND HER, I UNDERSTAND, BUT THE REST OF YOU-- WHAT'D I EVER DO TO YOU?!
HEY. NICE COSTUME.
HEY. NICE COSTUME.
HEY. NICE COSTUME.
OH. RIGHT. BUT--WHAT ABOUT YOU? I'VE NEVER EVEN MET YOU BEFORE!
I JUST LOVE VIOLENCE!
YOU KNOW, I ACTUALLY GET THAT.

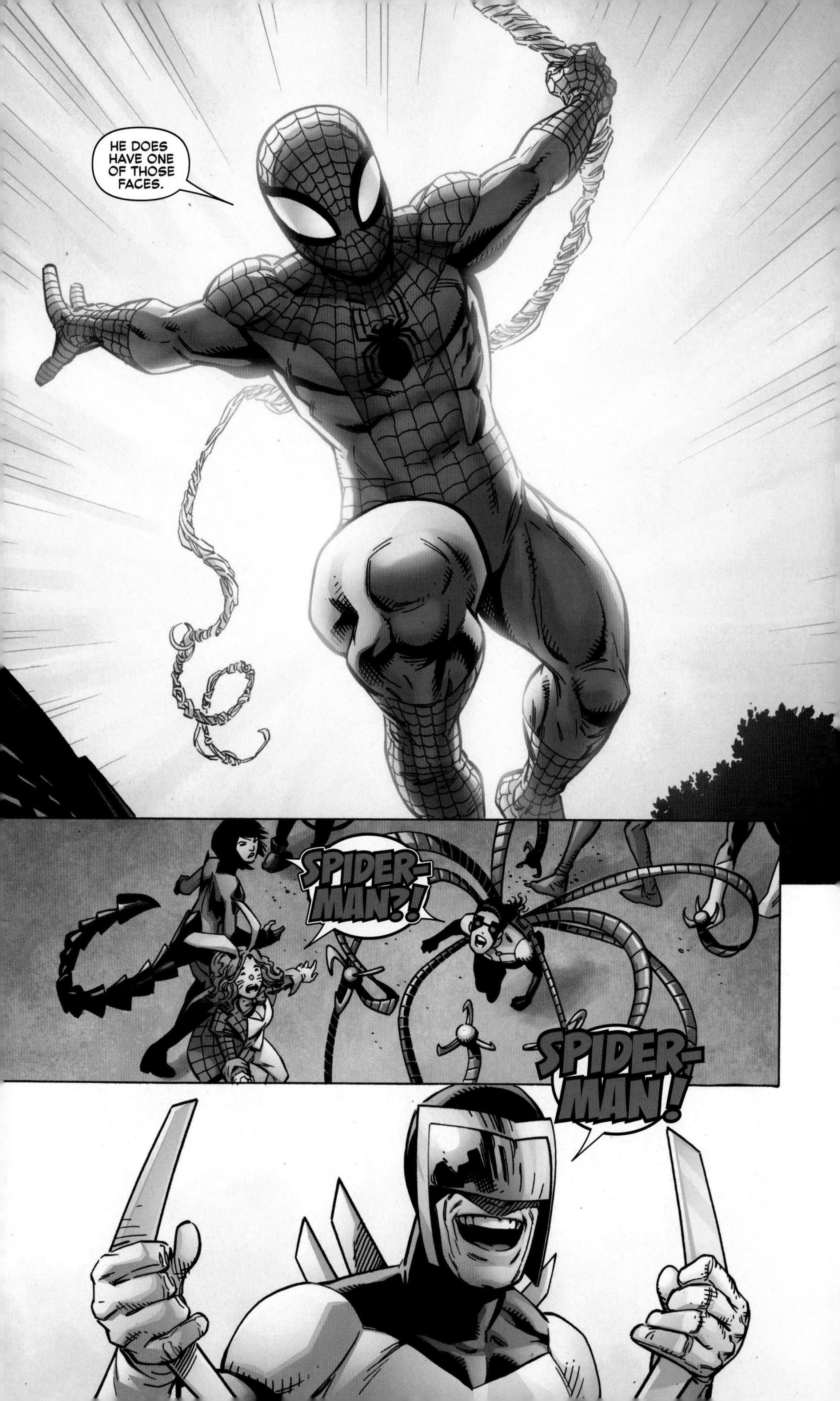

HE DOES HAVE ONE OF THOSE FACES.
SPIDER-MAN?!
SPIDER-MAN!

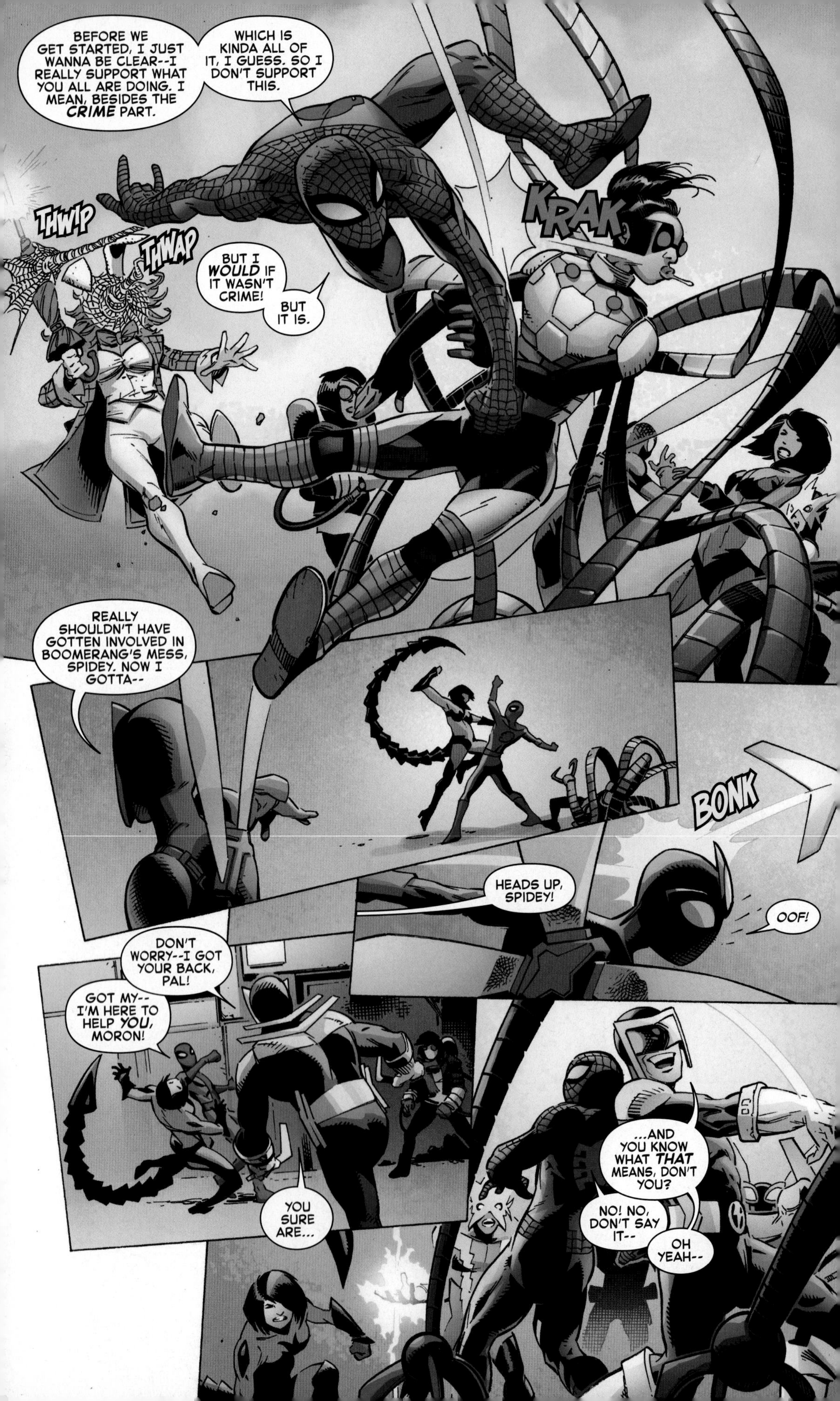

BEFORE WE GET STARTED, I JUST WANNA BE CLEAR--I REALLY SUPPORT WHAT YOU ALL ARE DOING. I MEAN, BESIDES THE CRIME PART.
WHICH IS KINDA ALL OF IT, I GUESS. SO I DON'T SUPPORT THIS.
THWIP
THWAP
KRAK
BUT I WOULD IF IT WASN'T CRIME!
BUT IT IS.
REALLY SHOULDN'T HAVE GOTTEN INVOLVED IN BOOMERANG'S MESS, SPIDEY. NOW I GOTTA--
BONK
HEADS UP, SPIDEY!
OOF!
DON'T WORRY--I GOT YOUR BACK, PAL!
GOT MY-- I'M HERE TO HELP YOU, MORON!
YOU SURE ARE...
...AND YOU KNOW WHAT THAT MEANS, DON'T YOU?
NO! NO, DON'T SAY IT--
OH YEAH--

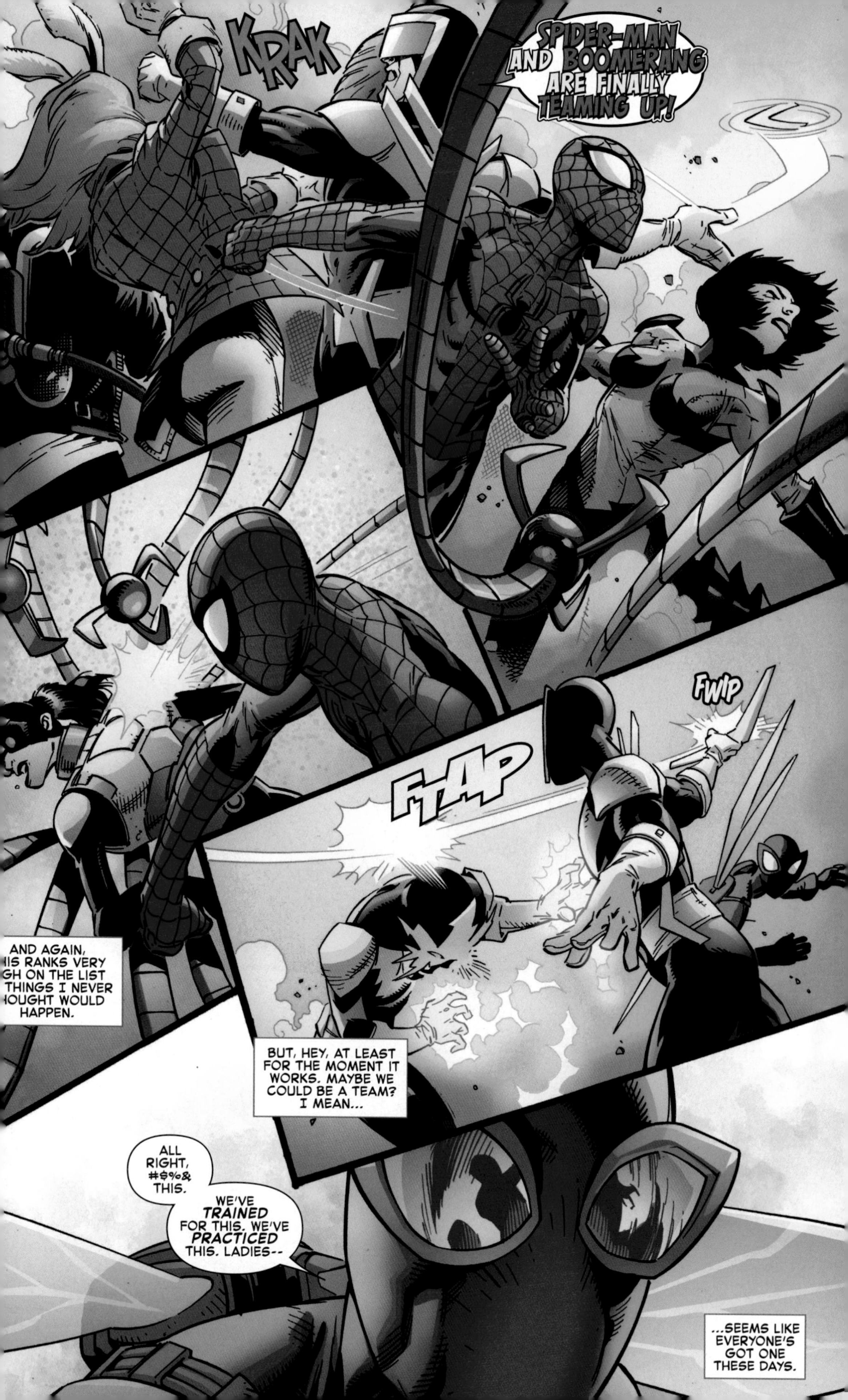
KRAK
SPIDER-MAN AND BOOMERANG ARE FINALLY TEAMING UP!
AND AGAIN, HIS RANKS VERY GH ON THE LIST THINGS I NEVER HOUGHT WOULD HAPPEN.
FWIP
FTAP
BUT, HEY, AT LEAST FOR THE MOMENT IT WORKS. MAYBE WE COULD BE A TEAM? I MEAN...
ALL RIGHT, #$%& THIS.
WE'VE TRAINED FOR THIS. WE'VE PRACTICED THIS. LADIES--
...SEEMS LIKE EVERYONE'S GOT ONE THESE DAYS.

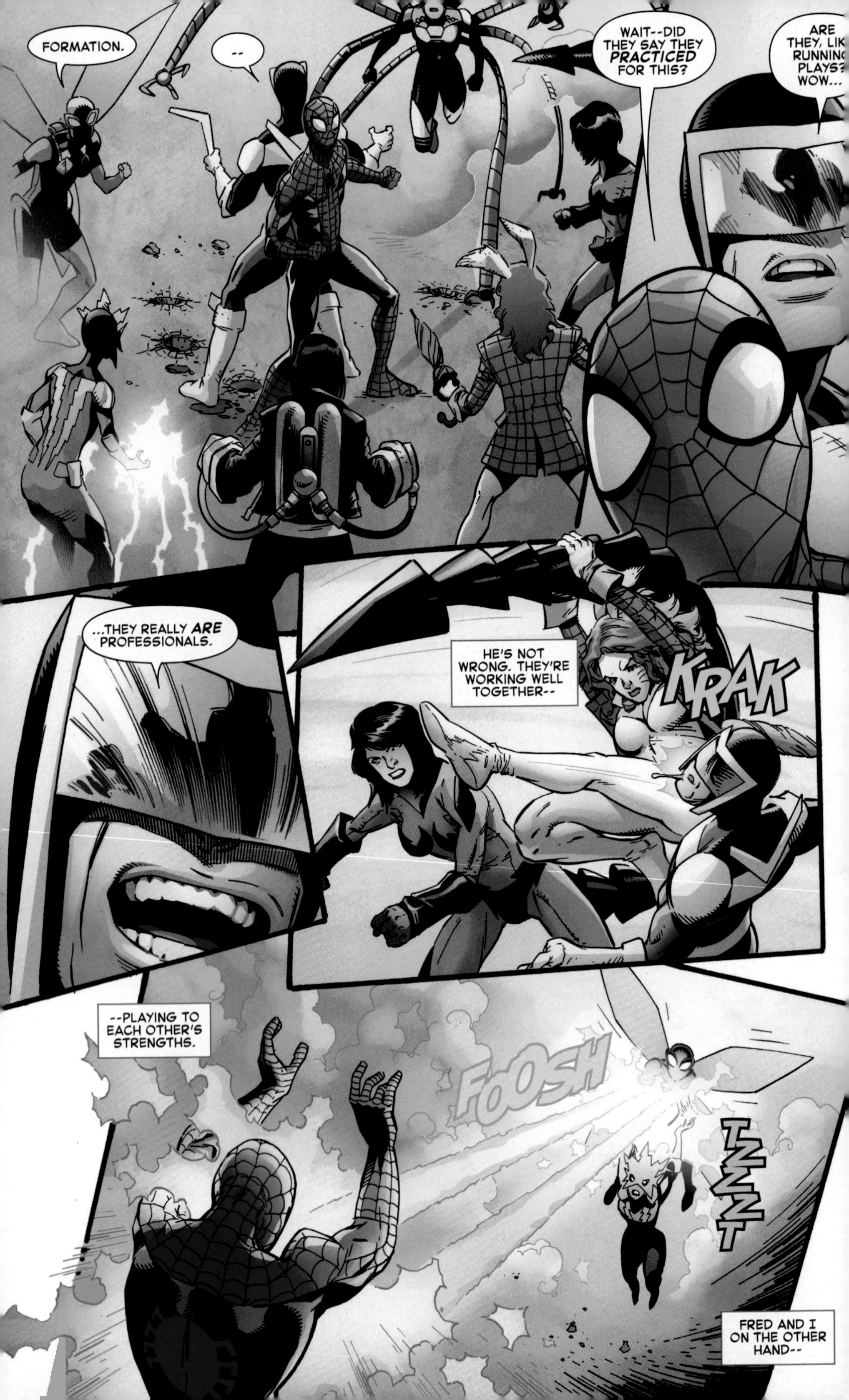
FORMATION.
--
WAIT--DID THEY SAY THEY PRACTICED FOR THIS?
ARE THEY, LIK RUNNING PLAYS? WOW...
...THEY REALLY ARE PROFESSIONALS.
HE'S NOT WRONG. THEY'RE WORKING WELL TOGETHER--
KRAK
--PLAYING TO EACH OTHER'S STRENGTHS.
FOOSH
TZZZT
FRED AND I ON THE OTHER HAND--

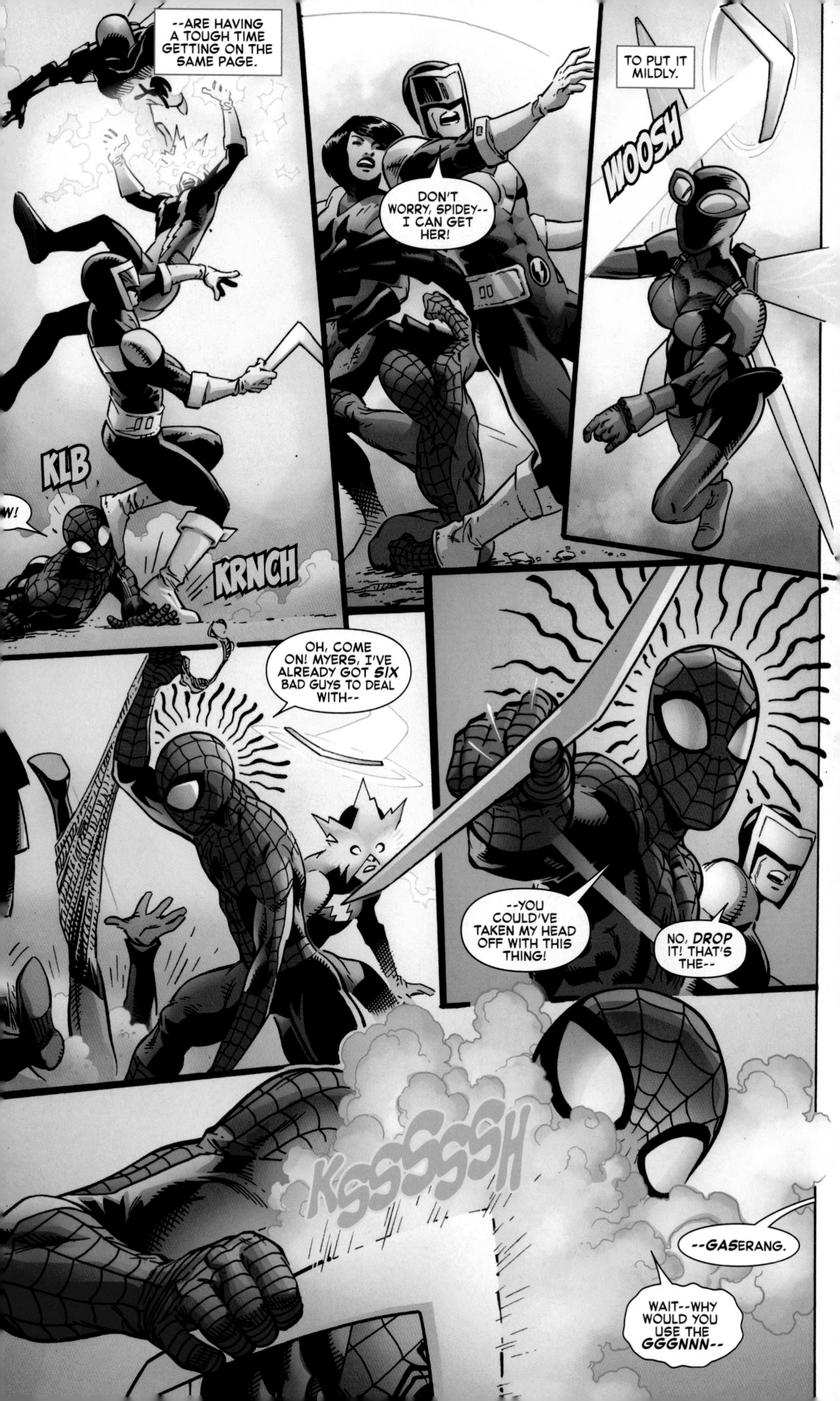
--ARE HAVING A TOUGH TIME GETTING ON THE SAME PAGE.
KLB
KRNCH
DON'T WORRY, SPIDEY-- I CAN GET HER!
TO PUT IT MILDLY.
WOOSH
OH, COME ON! MYERS, I'VE ALREADY GOT SIX BAD GUYS TO DEAL WITH--
--YOU COULD'VE TAKEN MY HEAD OFF WITH THIS THING!
NO, DROP IT! THAT'S THE--
KSSSSSH
--GASERANG.
WAIT--WHY WOULD YOU USE THE GGGNNN--

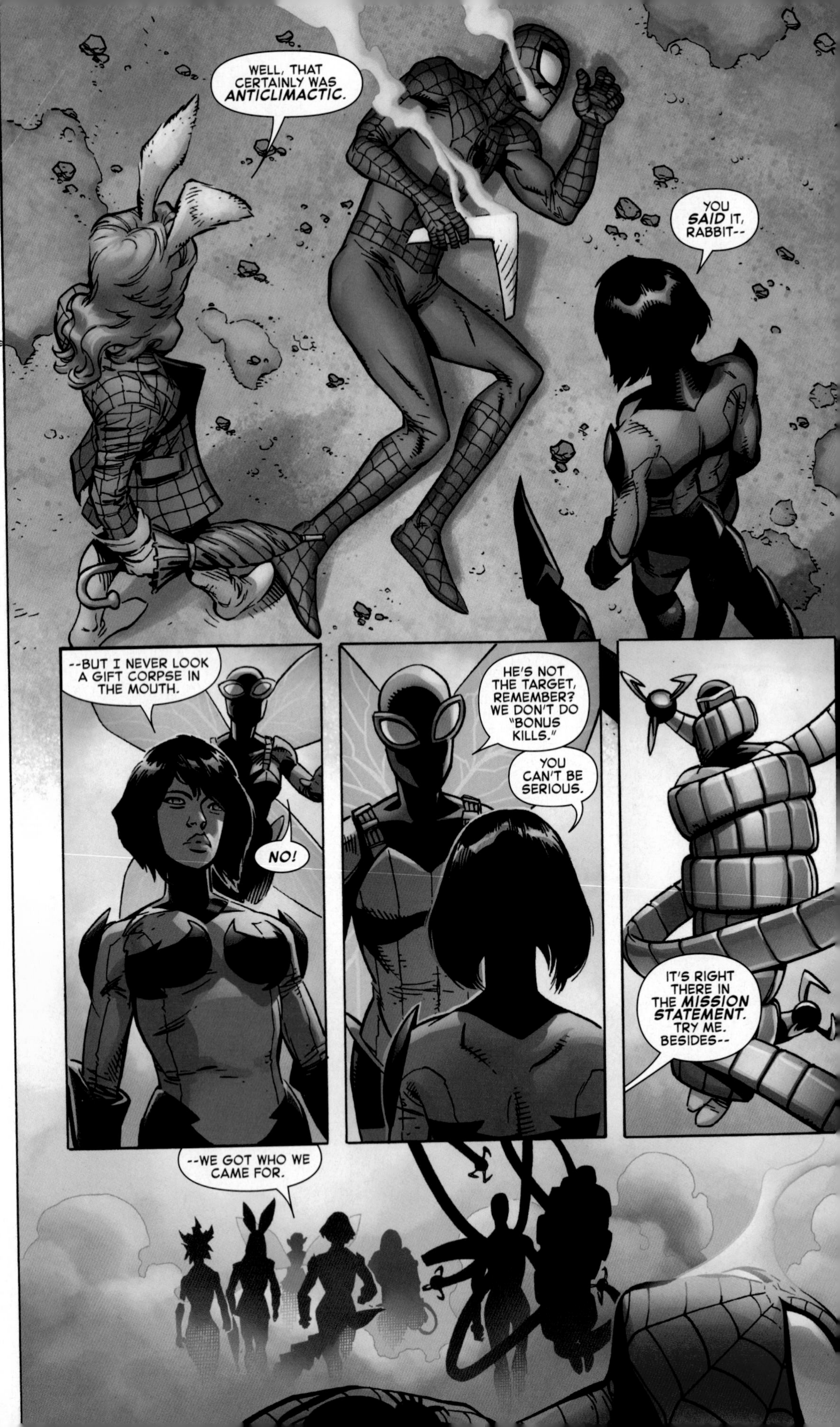
WELL, THAT CERTAINLY WAS ANTICLIMACTIC.
YOU SAID IT, RABBIT--
--BUT I NEVER LOOK A GIFT CORPSE IN THE MOUTH.
NO!
HE'S NOT THE TARGET, REMEMBER? WE DON'T DO "BONUS KILLS."
YOU CAN'T BE SERIOUS.
IT'S RIGHT THERE IN THE MISSION STATEMENT. TRY ME. BESIDES--
--WE GOT WHO WE CAME FOR.

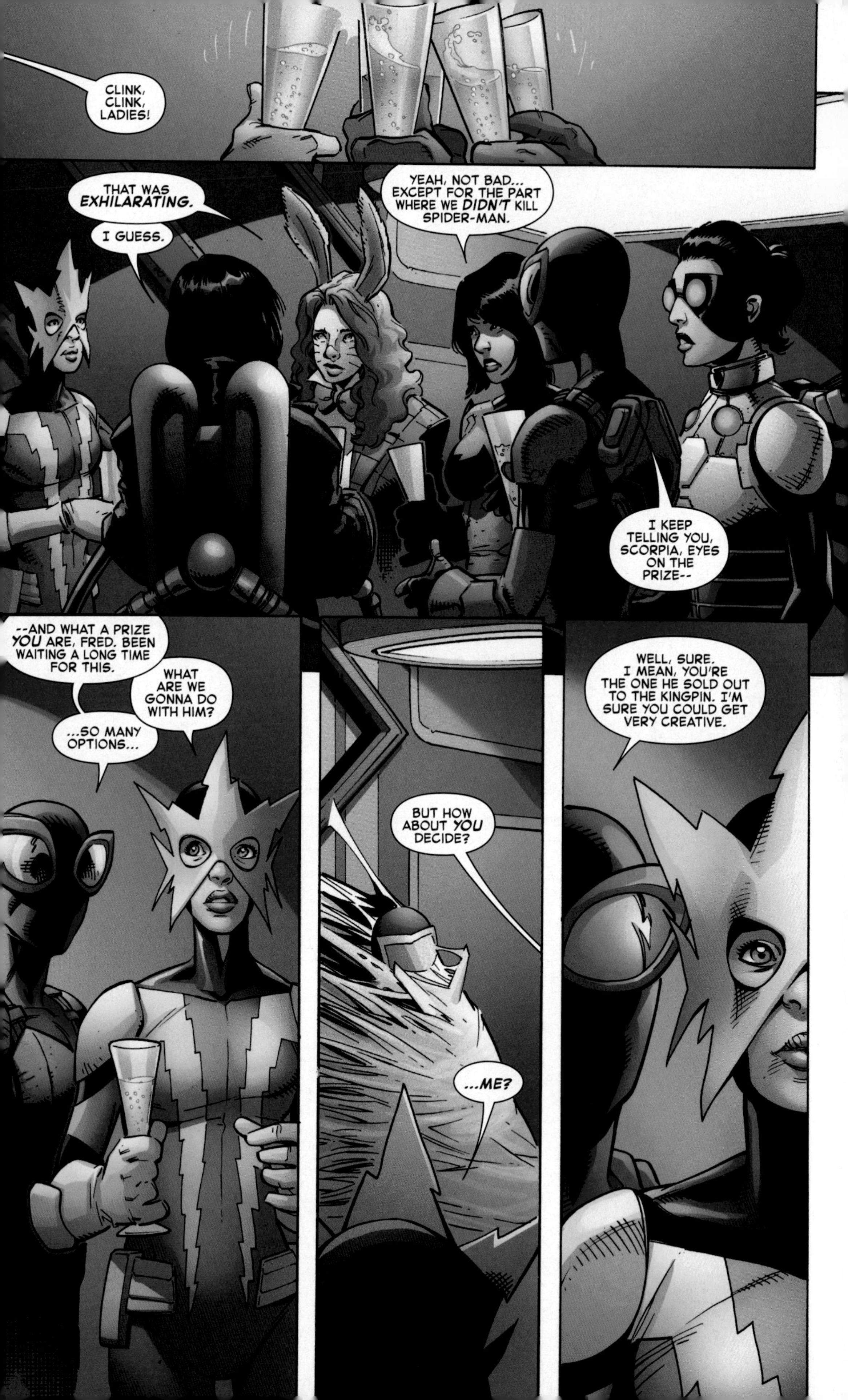
CLINK, CLINK, LADIES!
THAT WAS *EXHILARATING.*
I GUESS.
YEAH, NOT BAD... EXCEPT FOR THE PART WHERE WE *DIDN'T* KILL SPIDER-MAN.
I KEEP TELLING YOU, SCORPIA, EYES ON THE PRIZE--
--AND WHAT A PRIZE *YOU* ARE, FRED. BEEN WAITING A LONG TIME FOR THIS.
...SO MANY OPTIONS...
WHAT ARE WE GONNA DO WITH HIM?
BUT HOW ABOUT *YOU* DECIDE?
...ME?
WELL, SURE. I MEAN, YOU'RE THE ONE HE SOLD OUT TO THE KINGPIN. I'M SURE YOU COULD GET VERY CREATIVE.

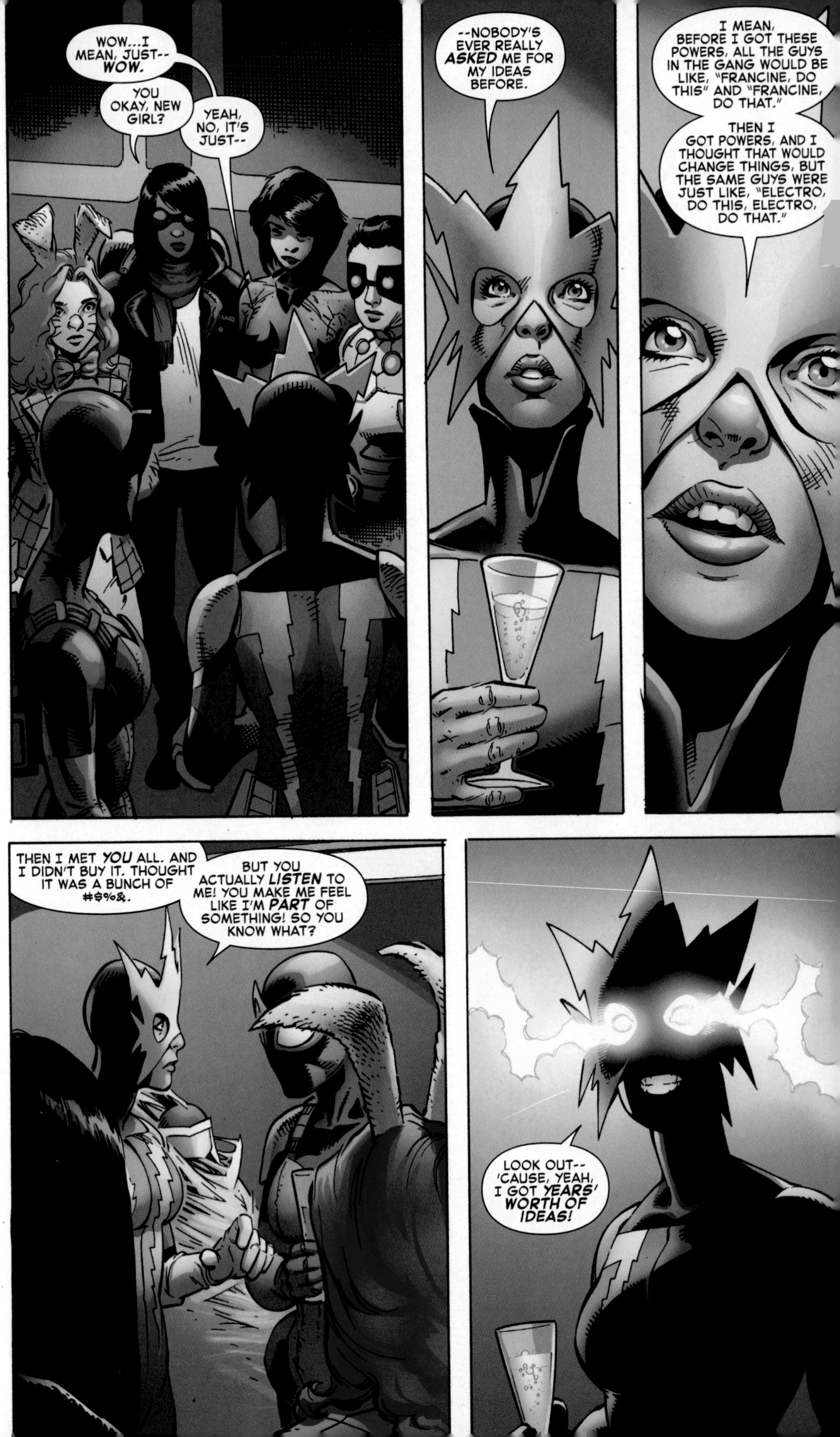
WOW...I MEAN, JUST-- WOW.
YOU OKAY, NEW GIRL?
YEAH, NO, IT'S JUST--
--NOBODY'S EVER REALLY ASKED ME FOR MY IDEAS BEFORE.
I MEAN, BEFORE I GOT THESE POWERS, ALL THE GUYS IN THE GANG WOULD BE LIKE, "FRANCINE, DO THIS" AND "FRANCINE, DO THAT."
THEN I GOT POWERS, AND I THOUGHT THAT WOULD CHANGE THINGS, BUT THE SAME GUYS WERE JUST LIKE, "ELECTRO, DO THIS, ELECTRO, DO THAT."
THEN I MET YOU ALL. AND I DIDN'T BUY IT. THOUGHT IT WAS A BUNCH OF #$%&.
BUT YOU ACTUALLY LISTEN TO ME! YOU MAKE ME FEEL LIKE I'M PART OF SOMETHING! SO YOU KNOW WHAT?
LOOK OUT-- 'CAUSE, YEAH, I GOT YEARS' WORTH OF IDEAS!

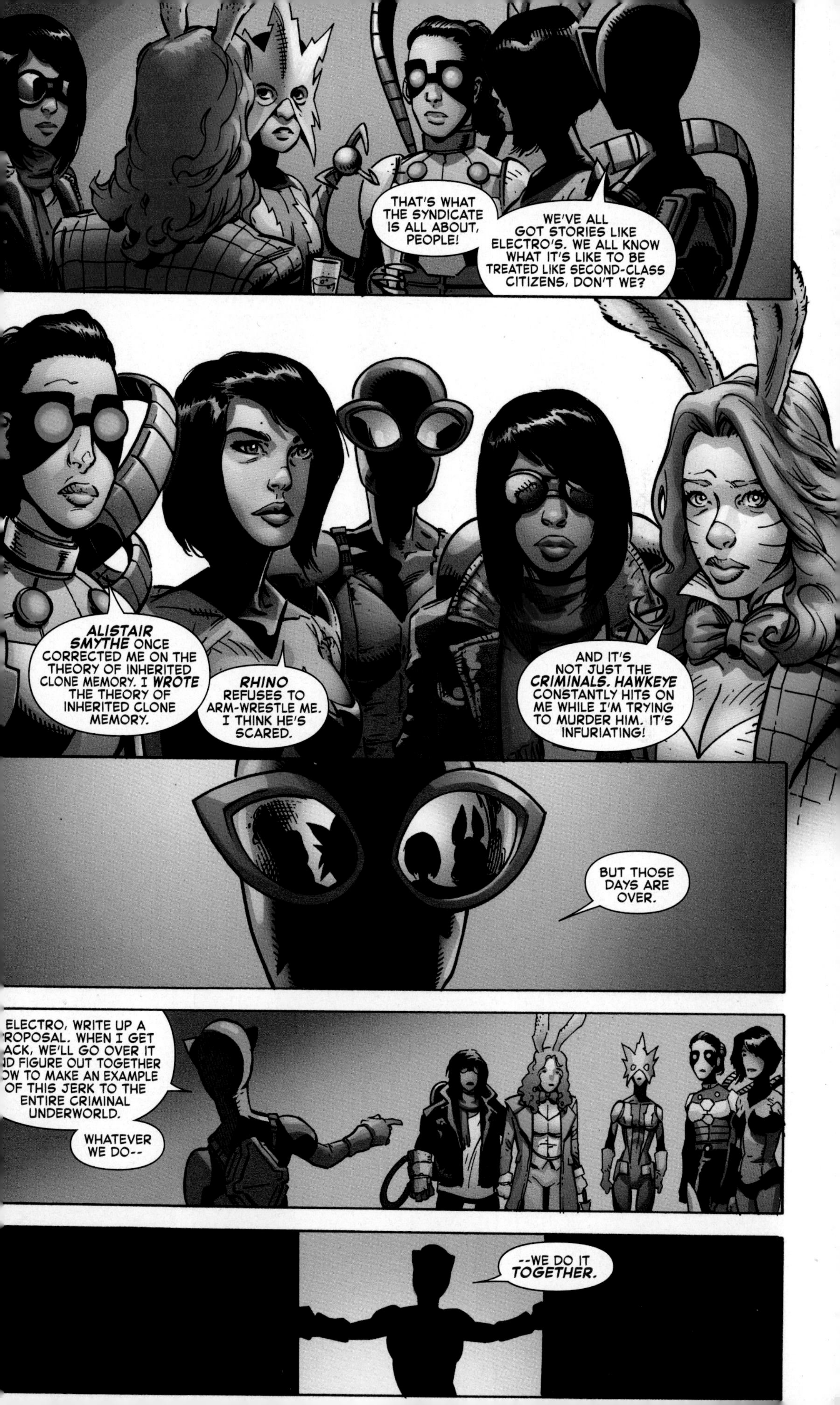
THAT'S WHAT THE SYNDICATE IS ALL ABOUT, PEOPLE!
WE'VE ALL GOT STORIES LIKE ELECTRO'S. WE ALL KNOW WHAT IT'S LIKE TO BE TREATED LIKE SECOND-CLASS CITIZENS, DON'T WE?
ALISTAIR SMYTHE ONCE CORRECTED ME ON THE THEORY OF INHERITED CLONE MEMORY. I WROTE THE THEORY OF INHERITED CLONE MEMORY.
RHINO REFUSES TO ARM-WRESTLE ME. I THINK HE'S SCARED.
AND IT'S NOT JUST THE CRIMINALS. HAWKEYE CONSTANTLY HITS ON ME WHILE I'M TRYING TO MURDER HIM. IT'S INFURIATING!
BUT THOSE DAYS ARE OVER.
ELECTRO, WRITE UP A ROPOSAL. WHEN I GET ACK, WE'LL GO OVER IT ND FIGURE OUT TOGETHER OW TO MAKE AN EXAMPLE OF THIS JERK TO THE ENTIRE CRIMINAL UNDERWORLD.
WHATEVER WE DO--
--WE DO IT TOGETHER.

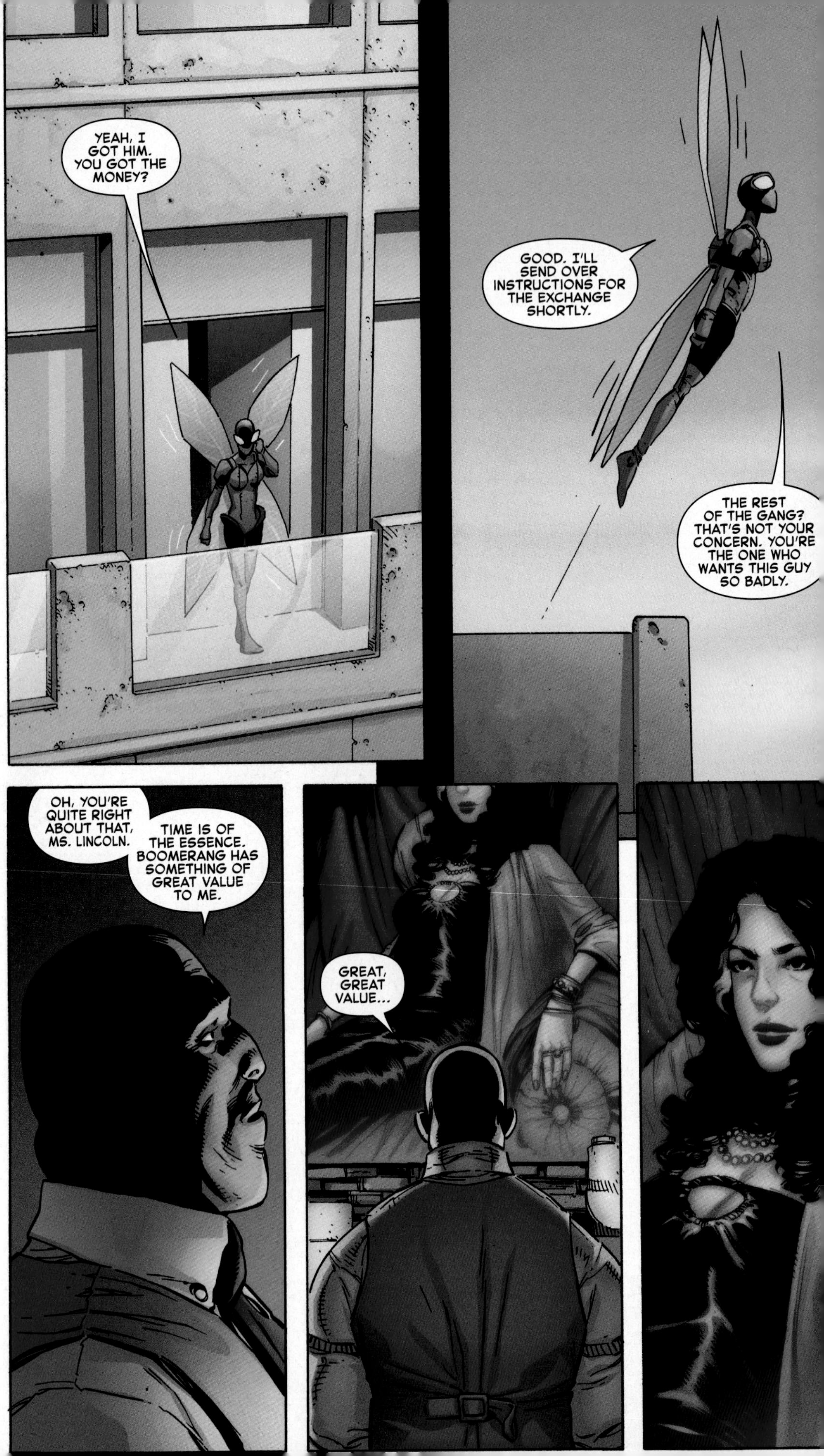
YEAH, I GOT HIM. YOU GOT THE MONEY?
GOOD. I'LL SEND OVER INSTRUCTIONS FOR THE EXCHANGE SHORTLY.
THE REST OF THE GANG? THAT'S NOT YOUR CONCERN. YOU'RE THE ONE WHO WANTS THIS GUY SO BADLY.
OH, YOU'RE QUITE RIGHT ABOUT THAT, MS. LINCOLN.
TIME IS OF THE ESSENCE. BOOMERANG HAS SOMETHING OF GREAT VALUE TO ME.
GREAT, GREAT VALUE...

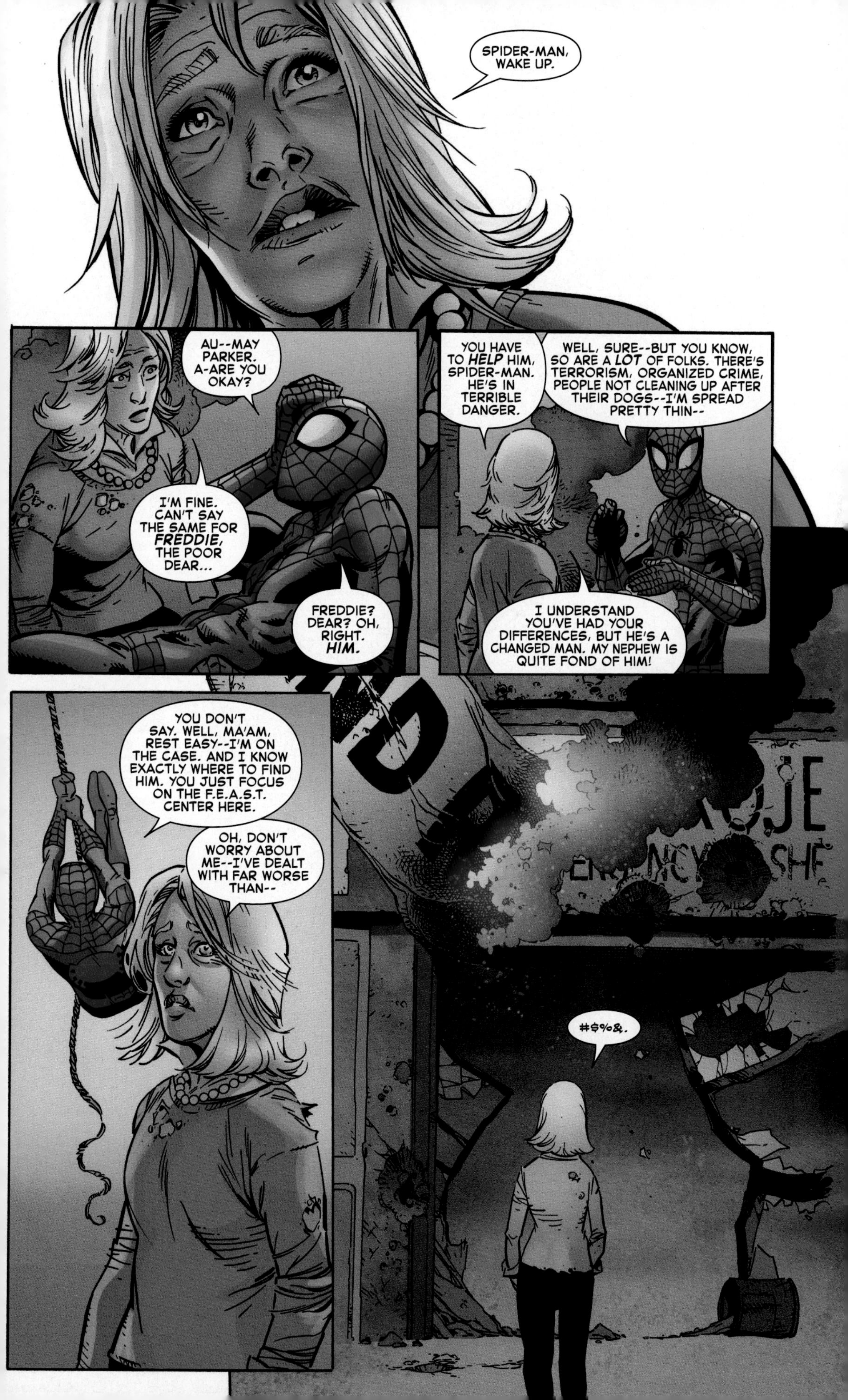
SPIDER-MAN, WAKE UP.
AU--MAY PARKER. A-ARE YOU OKAY?
I'M FINE. CAN'T SAY THE SAME FOR FREDDIE, THE POOR DEAR...
FREDDIE? DEAR? OH, RIGHT. HIM.
YOU HAVE TO HELP HIM, SPIDER-MAN. HE'S IN TERRIBLE DANGER.
WELL, SURE--BUT YOU KNOW, SO ARE A LOT OF FOLKS. THERE'S TERRORISM, ORGANIZED CRIME, PEOPLE NOT CLEANING UP AFTER THEIR DOGS--I'M SPREAD PRETTY THIN--
I UNDERSTAND YOU'VE HAD YOUR DIFFERENCES, BUT HE'S A CHANGED MAN. MY NEPHEW IS QUITE FOND OF HIM!
YOU DON'T SAY. WELL, MA'AM, REST EASY--I'M ON THE CASE. AND I KNOW EXACTLY WHERE TO FIND HIM. YOU JUST FOCUS ON THE F.E.A.S.T. CENTER HERE.
OH, DON'T WORRY ABOUT ME--I'VE DEALT WITH FAR WORSE THAN--
#$%&.

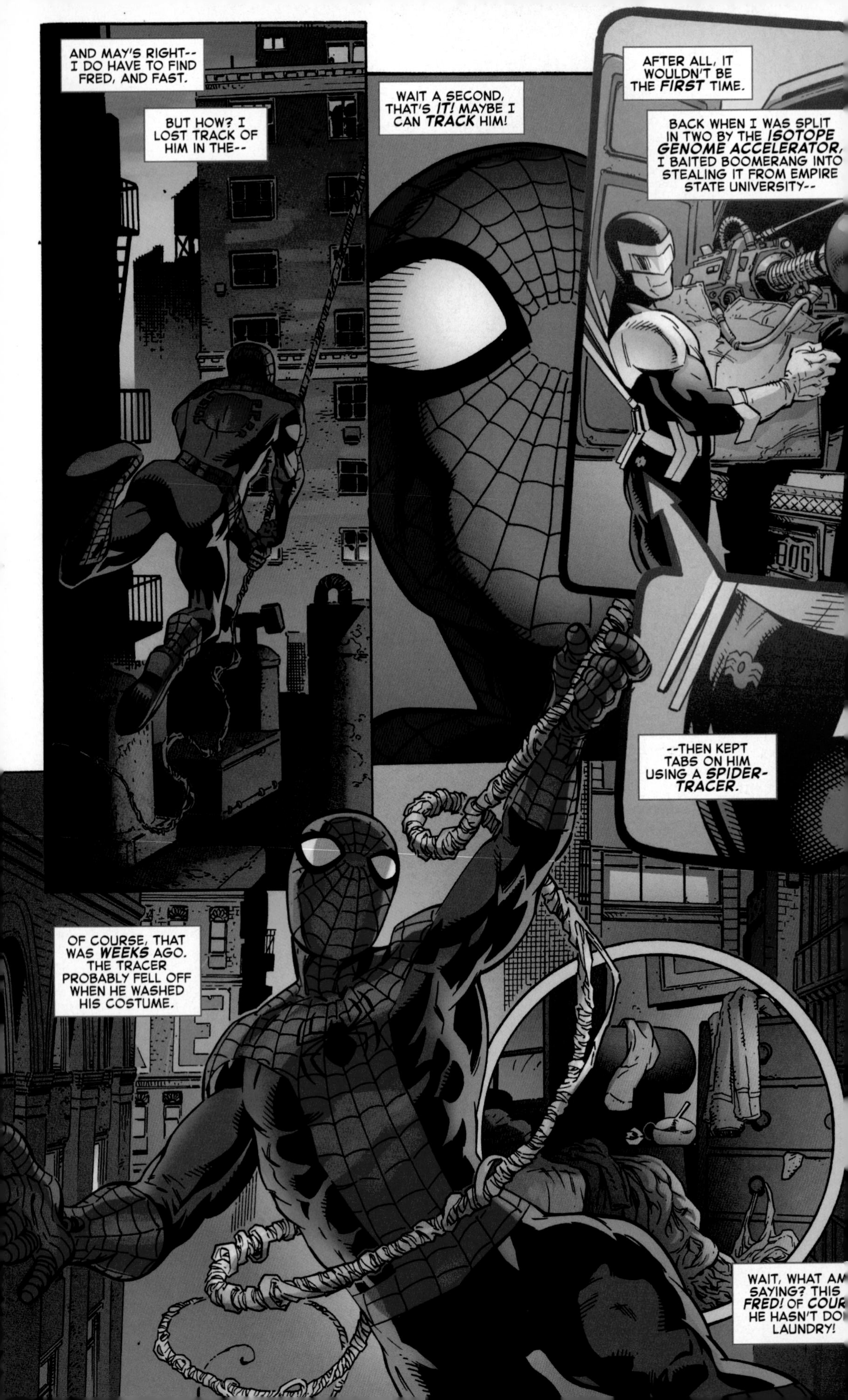
AND MAY'S RIGHT-- I DO HAVE TO FIND FRED, AND FAST.
BUT HOW? I LOST TRACK OF HIM IN THE--
WAIT A SECOND, THAT'S IT! MAYBE I CAN TRACK HIM!
AFTER ALL, IT WOULDN'T BE THE FIRST TIME.
BACK WHEN I WAS SPLIT IN TWO BY THE ISOTOPE GENOME ACCELERATOR, I BAITED BOOMERANG INTO STEALING IT FROM EMPIRE STATE UNIVERSITY--
--THEN KEPT TABS ON HIM USING A SPIDER-TRACER.
OF COURSE, THAT WAS WEEKS AGO. THE TRACER PROBABLY FELL OFF WHEN HE WASHED HIS COSTUME.
WAIT, WHAT AM SAYING? THIS FRED! OF COUR HE HASN'T DO LAUNDRY!

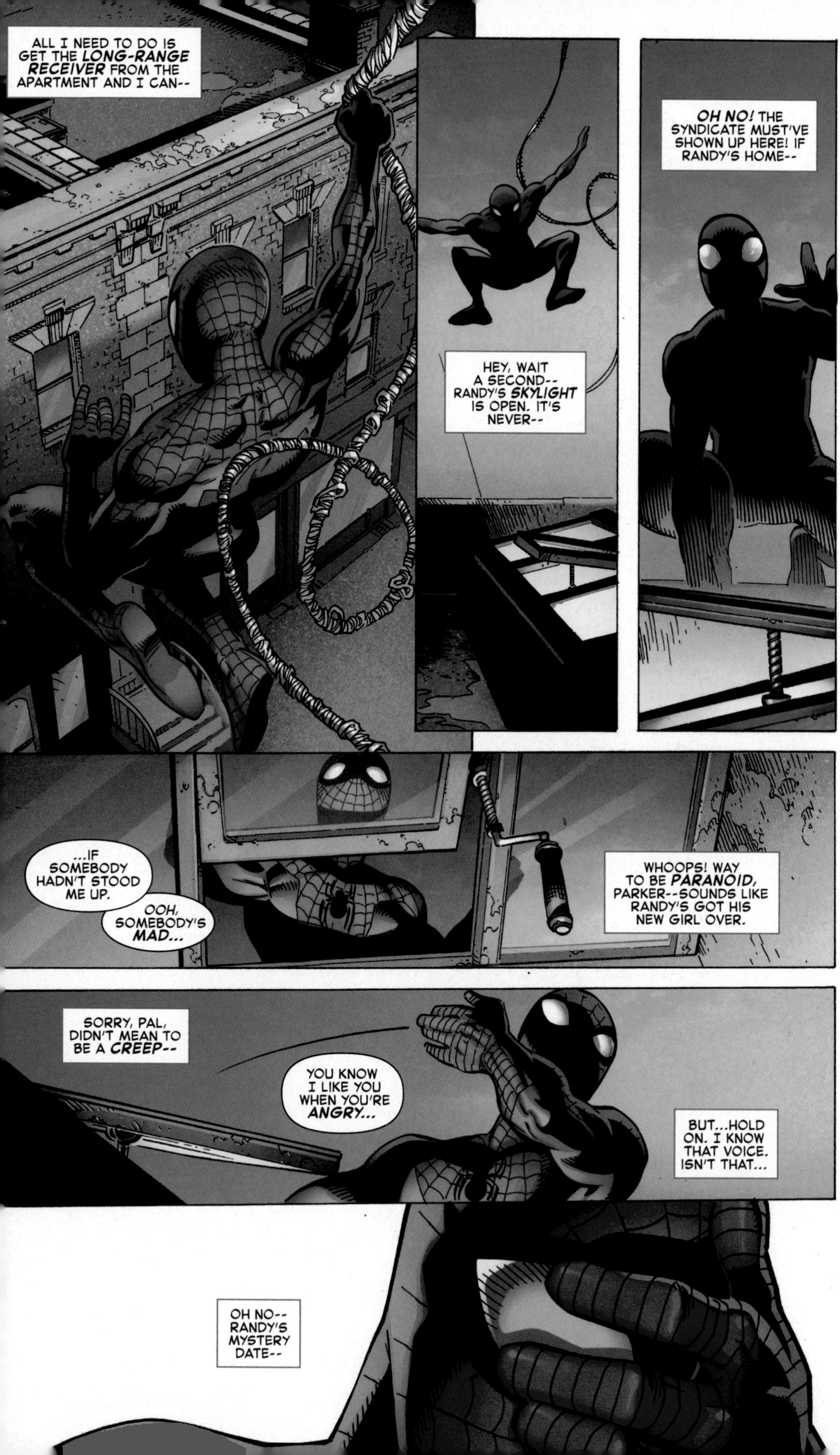
ALL I NEED TO DO IS GET THE LONG-RANGE RECEIVER FROM THE APARTMENT AND I CAN--
HEY, WAIT A SECOND-- RANDY'S SKYLIGHT IS OPEN. IT'S NEVER--
OH NO! THE SYNDICATE MUST'VE SHOWN UP HERE! IF RANDY'S HOME--
...IF SOMEBODY HADN'T STOOD ME UP.
OOH, SOMEBODY'S MAD...
WHOOPS! WAY TO BE PARANOID, PARKER--SOUNDS LIKE RANDY'S GOT HIS NEW GIRL OVER.
SORRY, PAL, DIDN'T MEAN TO BE A CREEP--
YOU KNOW I LIKE YOU WHEN YOU'RE ANGRY...
BUT...HOLD ON. I KNOW THAT VOICE. ISN'T THAT...
OH NO-- RANDY'S MYSTERY DATE--

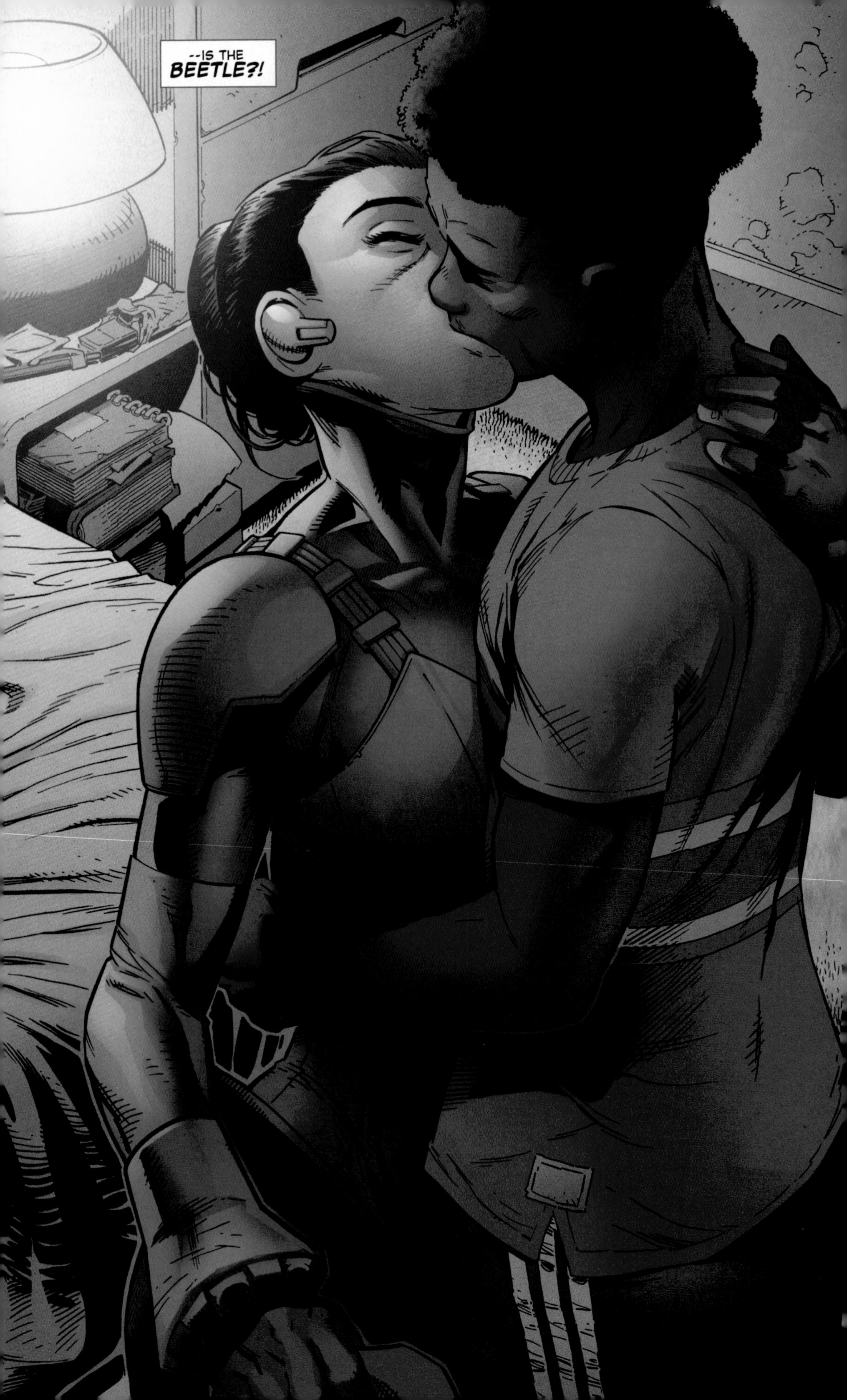
--IS THE BEETLE?!

28

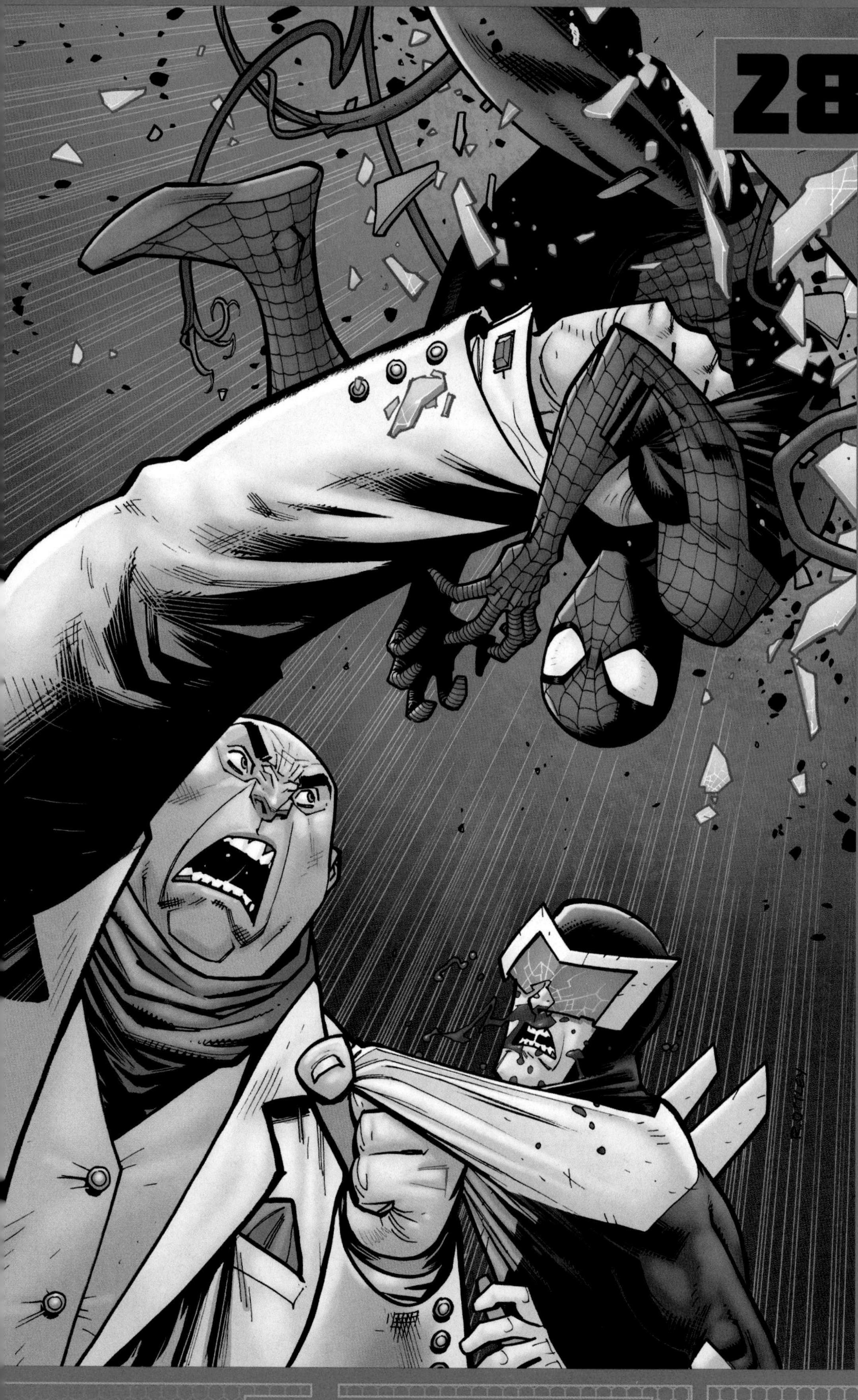

WHO RUN THE WORLD? PART 3

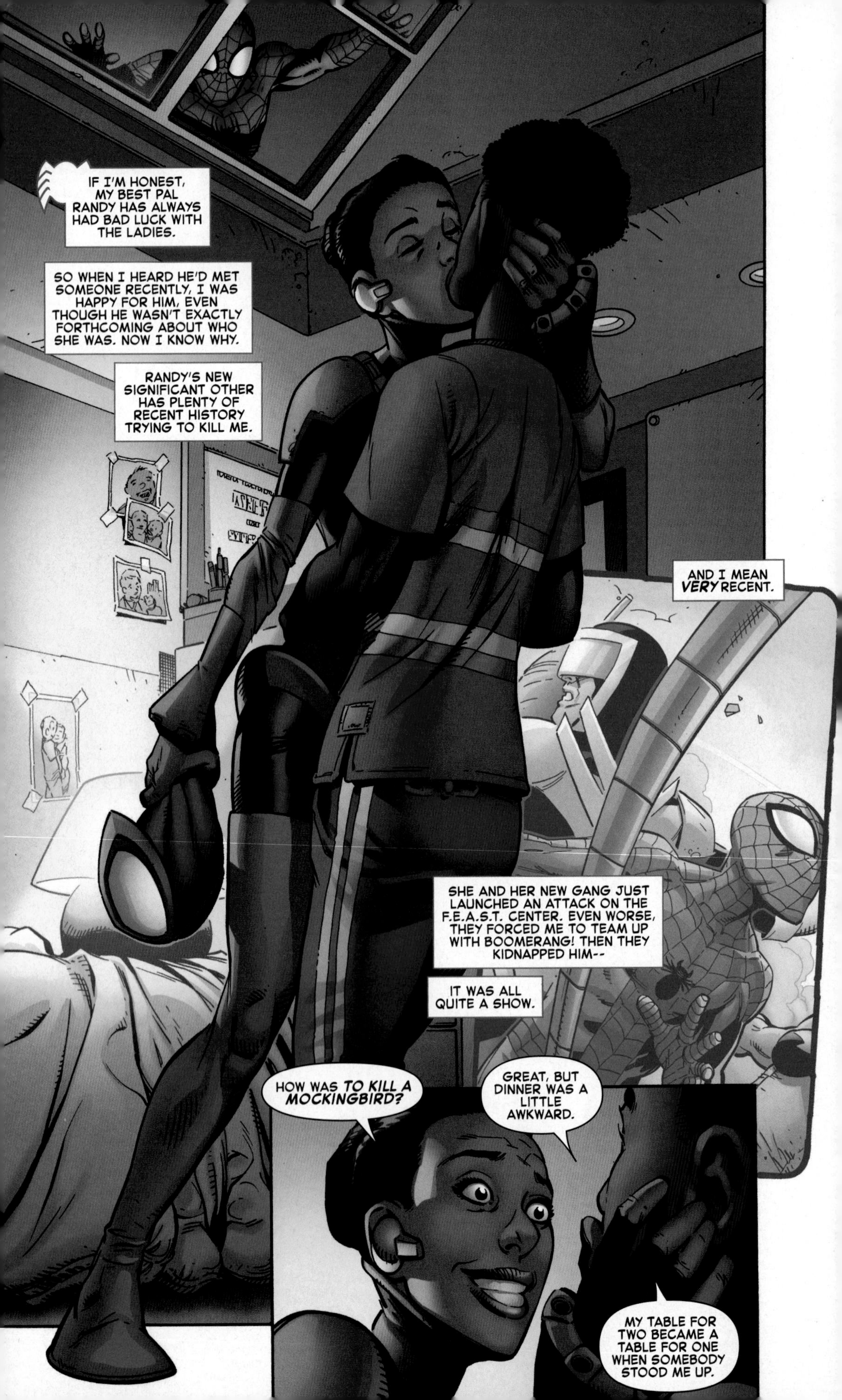

IF I'M HONEST, MY BEST PAL RANDY HAS ALWAYS HAD BAD LUCK WITH THE LADIES.
SO WHEN I HEARD HE'D MET SOMEONE RECENTLY, I WAS HAPPY FOR HIM, EVEN THOUGH HE WASN'T EXACTLY FORTHCOMING ABOUT WHO SHE WAS. NOW I KNOW WHY.
RANDY'S NEW SIGNIFICANT OTHER HAS PLENTY OF RECENT HISTORY TRYING TO KILL ME.
AND I MEAN VERY RECENT.
SHE AND HER NEW GANG JUST LAUNCHED AN ATTACK ON THE F.E.A.S.T. CENTER. EVEN WORSE, THEY FORCED ME TO TEAM UP WITH BOOMERANG! THEN THEY KIDNAPPED HIM--
IT WAS ALL QUITE A SHOW.
HOW WAS TO KILL A MOCKINGBIRD?
GREAT, BUT DINNER WAS A LITTLE AWKWARD.
MY TABLE FOR TWO BECAME A TABLE FOR ONE WHEN SOMEBODY STOOD ME UP.

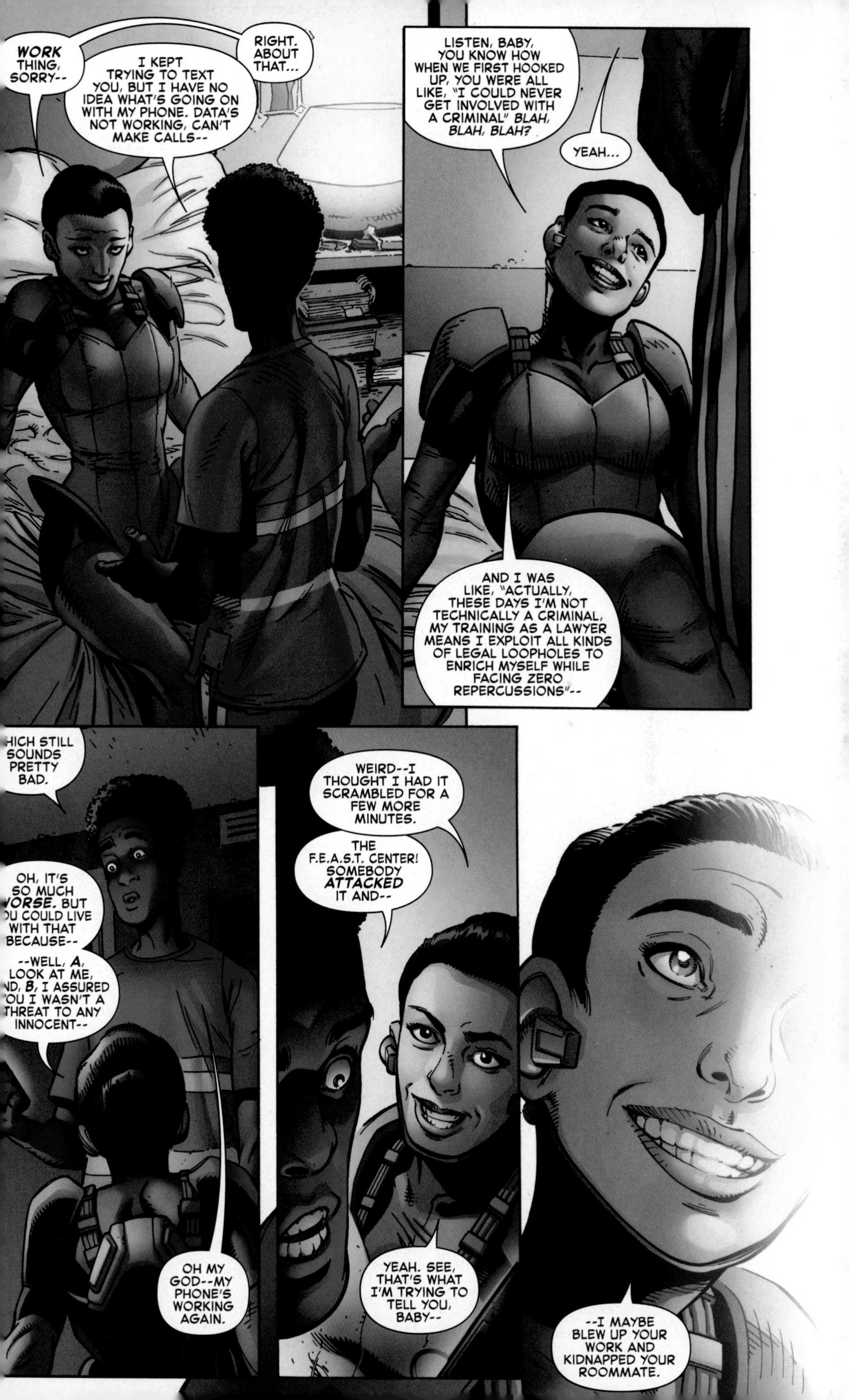
WORK THING, SORRY--
I KEPT TRYING TO TEXT YOU, BUT I HAVE NO IDEA WHAT'S GOING ON WITH MY PHONE. DATA'S NOT WORKING, CAN'T MAKE CALLS--
RIGHT. ABOUT THAT...
LISTEN, BABY, YOU KNOW HOW WHEN WE FIRST HOOKED UP, YOU WERE ALL LIKE, "I COULD NEVER GET INVOLVED WITH A CRIMINAL" BLAH, BLAH, BLAH?
YEAH...
AND I WAS LIKE, "ACTUALLY, THESE DAYS I'M NOT TECHNICALLY A CRIMINAL, MY TRAINING AS A LAWYER MEANS I EXPLOIT ALL KINDS OF LEGAL LOOPHOLES TO ENRICH MYSELF WHILE FACING ZERO REPERCUSSIONS"--
HICH STILL SOUNDS PRETTY BAD.
OH, IT'S SO MUCH ORSE. BUT U COULD LIVE WITH THAT BECAUSE--
--WELL, A, LOOK AT ME, D, B, I ASSURED OU I WASN'T A THREAT TO ANY INNOCENT--
OH MY GOD--MY PHONE'S WORKING AGAIN.
WEIRD--I THOUGHT I HAD IT SCRAMBLED FOR A FEW MORE MINUTES.
THE F.E.A.S.T. CENTER! SOMEBODY ATTACKED IT AND--
YEAH. SEE, THAT'S WHAT I'M TRYING TO TELL YOU, BABY--
--I MAYBE BLEW UP YOUR WORK AND KIDNAPPED YOUR ROOMMATE.

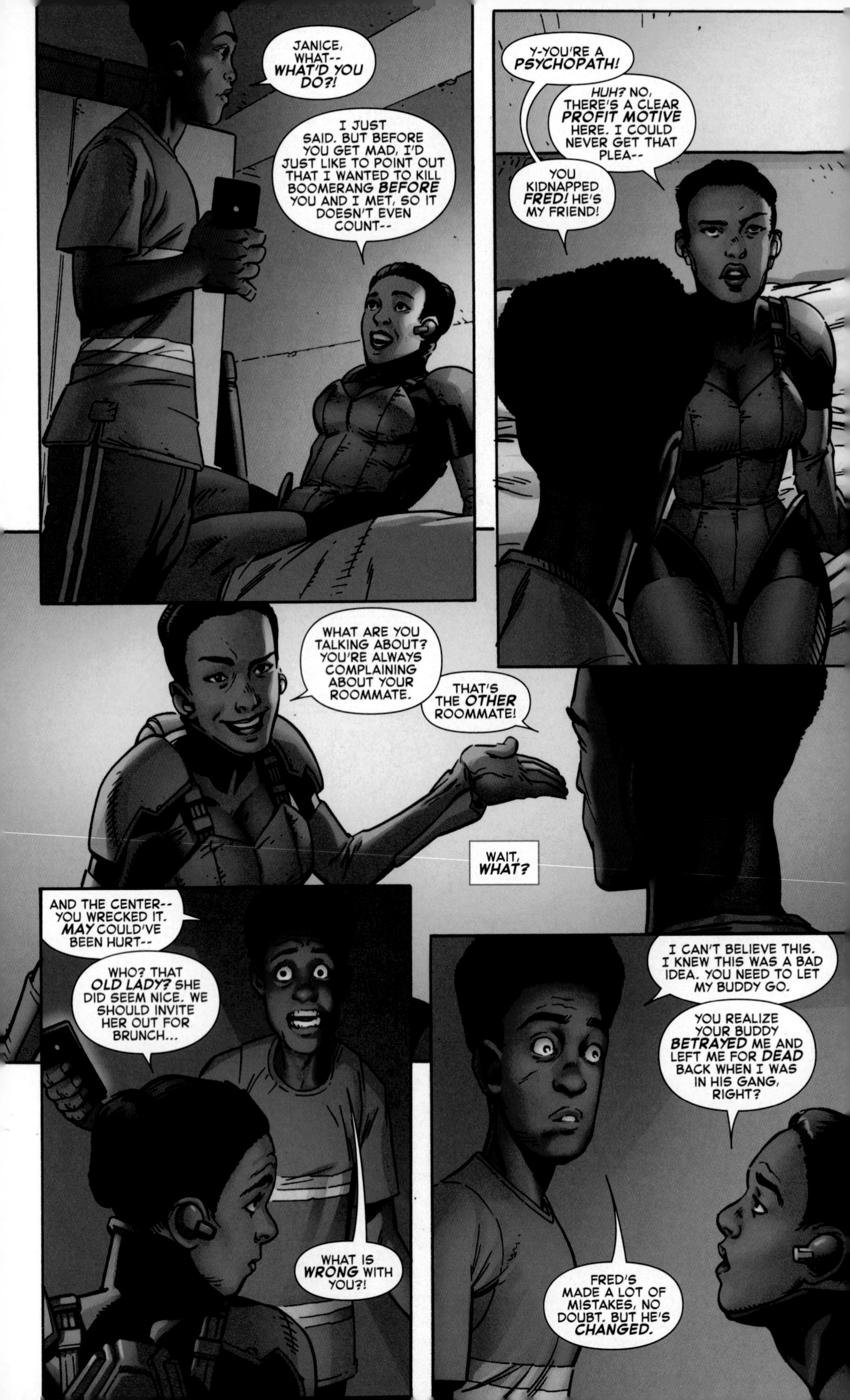

JANICE, WHAT-- WHAT'D YOU DO?!
I JUST SAID. BUT BEFORE YOU GET MAD, I'D JUST LIKE TO POINT OUT THAT I WANTED TO KILL BOOMERANG BEFORE YOU AND I MET, SO IT DOESN'T EVEN COUNT--
Y-YOU'RE A PSYCHOPATH!
HUH? NO, THERE'S A CLEAR PROFIT MOTIVE HERE. I COULD NEVER GET THAT PLEA--
YOU KIDNAPPED FRED! HE'S MY FRIEND!
WHAT ARE YOU TALKING ABOUT? YOU'RE ALWAYS COMPLAINING ABOUT YOUR ROOMMATE.
THAT'S THE OTHER ROOMMATE!
WAIT, WHAT?
AND THE CENTER-- YOU WRECKED IT. MAY COULD'VE BEEN HURT--
WHO? THAT OLD LADY? SHE DID SEEM NICE. WE SHOULD INVITE HER OUT FOR BRUNCH...
WHAT IS WRONG WITH YOU?!
I CAN'T BELIEVE THIS. I KNEW THIS WAS A BAD IDEA. YOU NEED TO LET MY BUDDY GO.
YOU REALIZE YOUR BUDDY BETRAYED ME AND LEFT ME FOR DEAD BACK WHEN I WAS IN HIS GANG, RIGHT?
FRED'S MADE A LOT OF MISTAKES, NO DOUBT. BUT HE'S CHANGED.

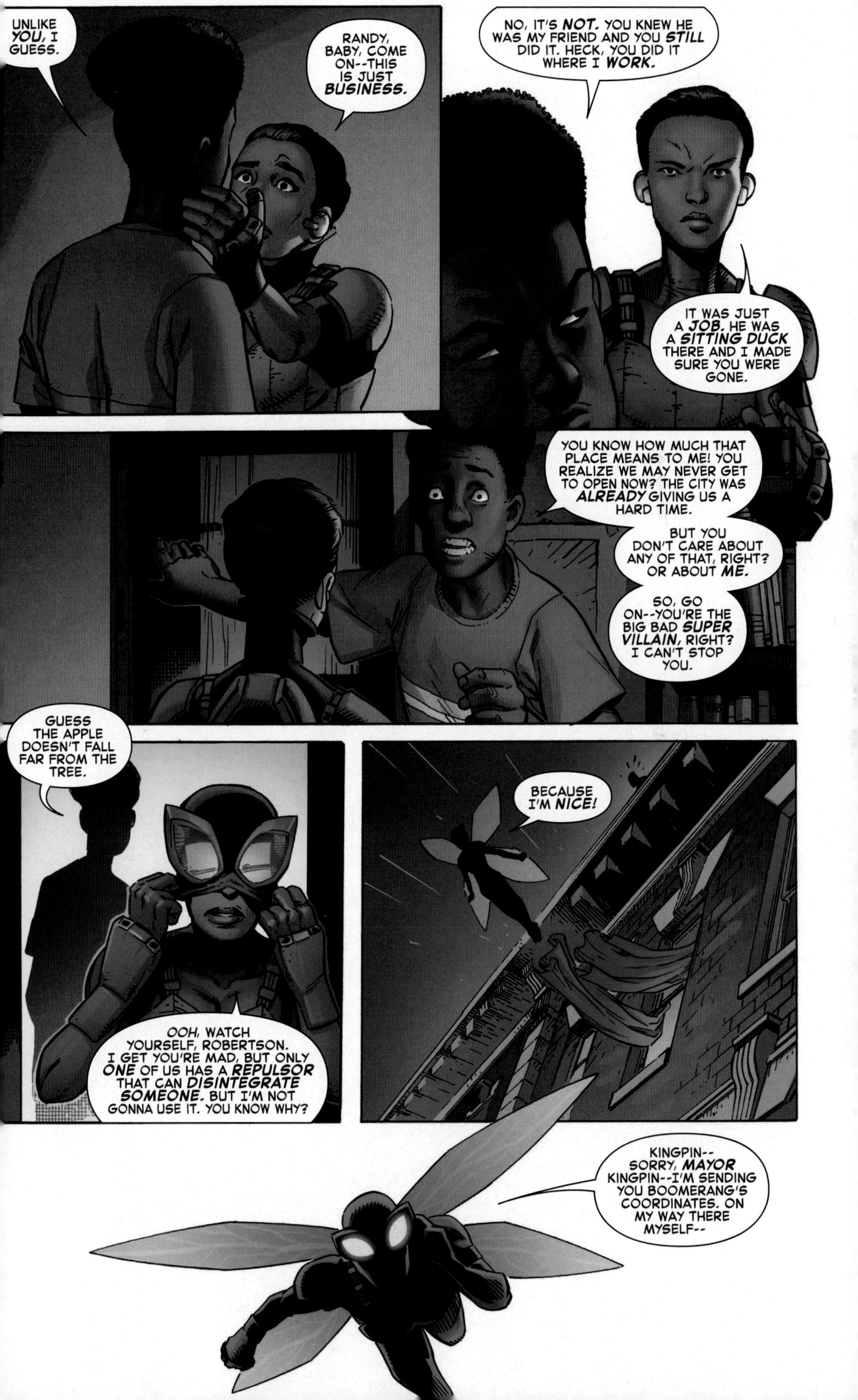

UNLIKE YOU, I GUESS.
RANDY, BABY, COME ON--THIS IS JUST BUSINESS.
NO, IT'S NOT. YOU KNEW HE WAS MY FRIEND AND YOU STILL DID IT. HECK, YOU DID IT WHERE I WORK.
IT WAS JUST A JOB. HE WAS A SITTING DUCK THERE AND I MADE SURE YOU WERE GONE.
YOU KNOW HOW MUCH THAT PLACE MEANS TO ME! YOU REALIZE WE MAY NEVER GET TO OPEN NOW? THE CITY WAS ALREADY GIVING US A HARD TIME.
BUT YOU DON'T CARE ABOUT ANY OF THAT, RIGHT? OR ABOUT ME.
SO, GO ON--YOU'RE THE BIG BAD SUPER VILLAIN, RIGHT? I CAN'T STOP YOU.
GUESS THE APPLE DOESN'T FALL FAR FROM THE TREE.
OOH, WATCH YOURSELF, ROBERTSON. I GET YOU'RE MAD, BUT ONLY ONE OF US HAS A REPULSOR THAT CAN DISINTEGRATE SOMEONE. BUT I'M NOT GONNA USE IT. YOU KNOW WHY?
BECAUSE I'M NICE!
KINGPIN--SORRY, MAYOR KINGPIN--I'M SENDING YOU BOOMERANG'S COORDINATES. ON MY WAY THERE MYSELF--

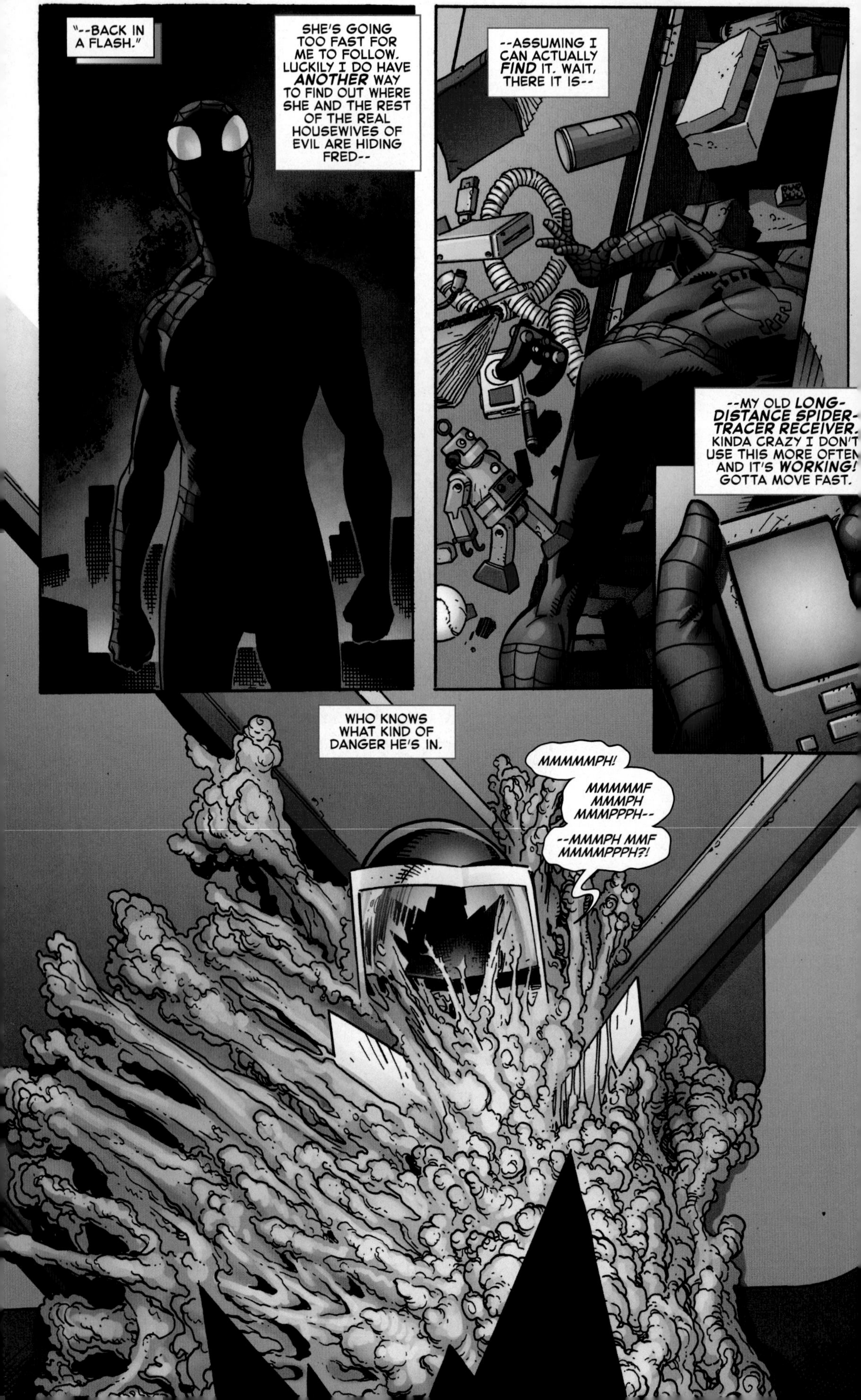
"--BACK IN A FLASH."
SHE'S GOING TOO FAST FOR ME TO FOLLOW. LUCKILY I DO HAVE ANOTHER WAY TO FIND OUT WHERE SHE AND THE REST OF THE REAL HOUSEWIVES OF EVIL ARE HIDING FRED--
--ASSUMING I CAN ACTUALLY FIND IT. WAIT, THERE IT IS--
--MY OLD LONG-DISTANCE SPIDER-TRACER RECEIVER. KINDA CRAZY I DON'T USE THIS MORE OFTEN AND IT'S WORKING! GOTTA MOVE FAST.
WHO KNOWS WHAT KIND OF DANGER HE'S IN.
MMMMMPH!
MMMMMF MMMPH MMMPPPH--
--MMMPH MMF MMMMPPPH?!

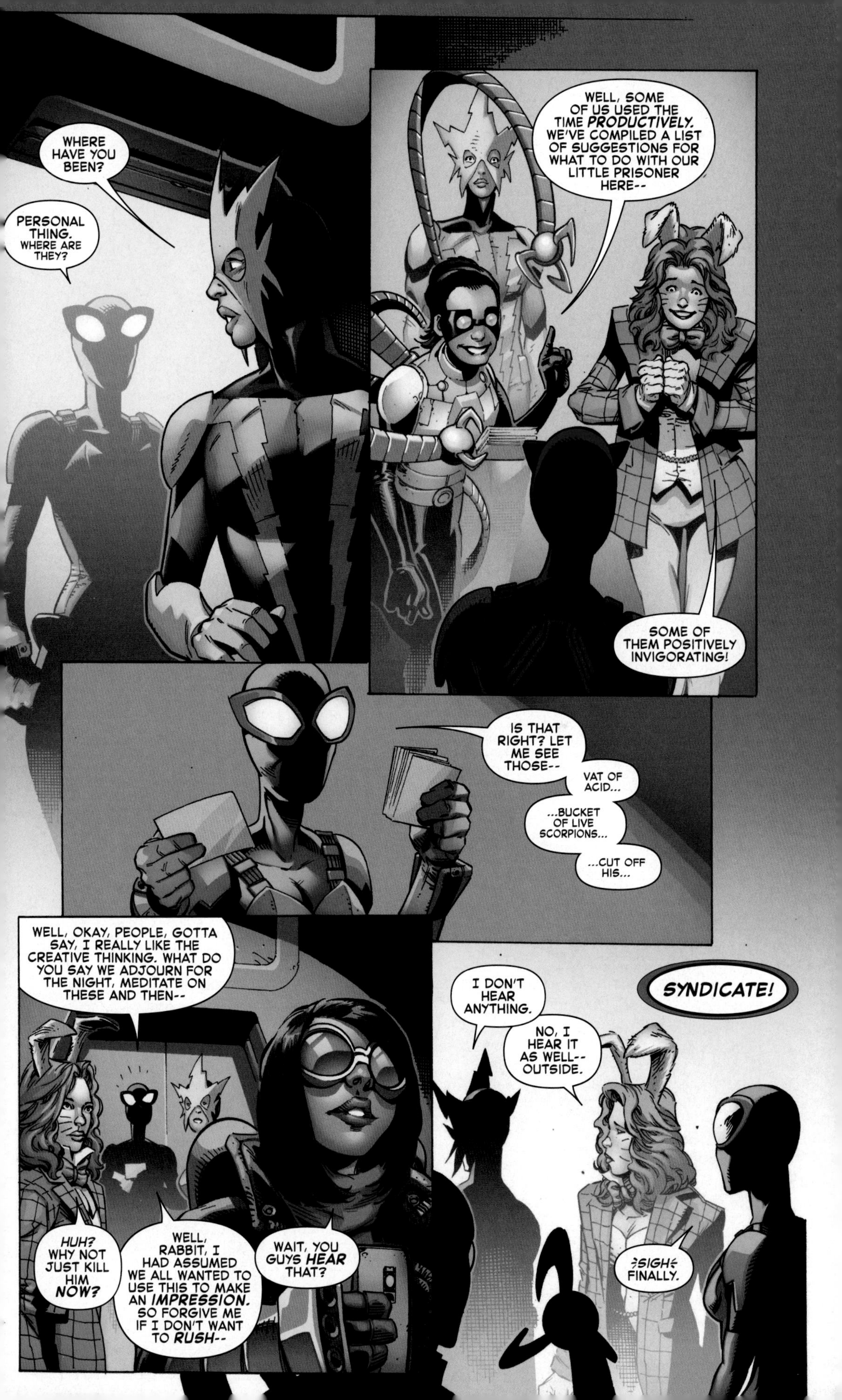
WHERE HAVE YOU BEEN?
PERSONAL THING. WHERE ARE THEY?
WELL, SOME OF US USED THE TIME PRODUCTIVELY. WE'VE COMPILED A LIST OF SUGGESTIONS FOR WHAT TO DO WITH OUR LITTLE PRISONER HERE--
SOME OF THEM POSITIVELY INVIGORATING!
IS THAT RIGHT? LET ME SEE THOSE--
VAT OF ACID...
...BUCKET OF LIVE SCORPIONS...
...CUT OFF HIS...
WELL, OKAY, PEOPLE, GOTTA SAY, I REALLY LIKE THE CREATIVE THINKING. WHAT DO YOU SAY WE ADJOURN FOR THE NIGHT, MEDITATE ON THESE AND THEN--
HUH? WHY NOT JUST KILL HIM NOW?
WELL, RABBIT, I HAD ASSUMED WE ALL WANTED TO USE THIS TO MAKE AN IMPRESSION. SO FORGIVE ME IF I DON'T WANT TO RUSH--
WAIT, YOU GUYS HEAR THAT?
SYNDICATE!
I DON'T HEAR ANYTHING.
NO, I HEAR IT AS WELL-- OUTSIDE.
SIGH FINALLY.

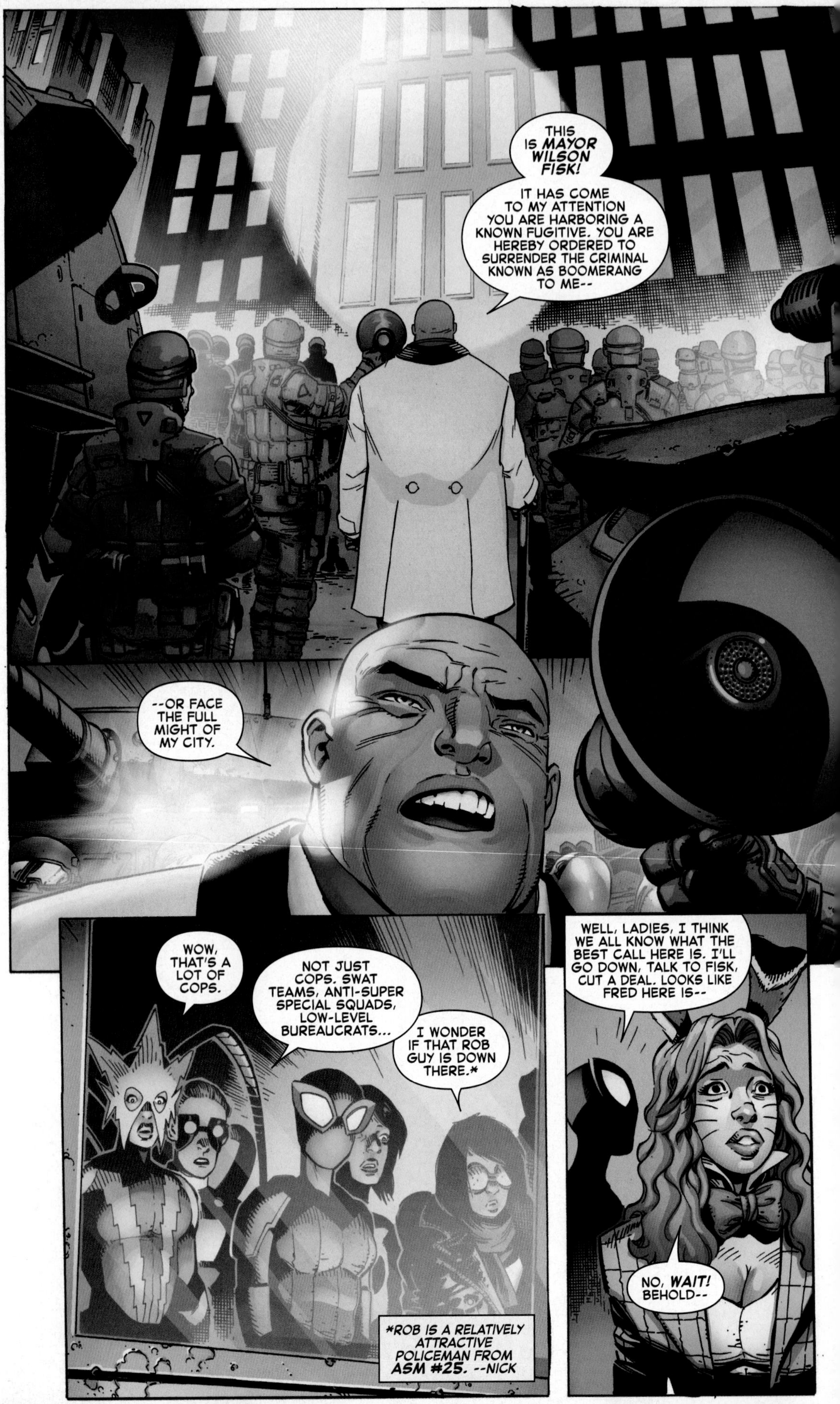
THIS IS MAYOR WILSON FISK!
IT HAS COME TO MY ATTENTION YOU ARE HARBORING A KNOWN FUGITIVE. YOU ARE HEREBY ORDERED TO SURRENDER THE CRIMINAL KNOWN AS BOOMERANG TO ME--
--OR FACE THE FULL MIGHT OF MY CITY.
WOW, THAT'S A LOT OF COPS.
NOT JUST COPS. SWAT TEAMS, ANTI-SUPER SPECIAL SQUADS, LOW-LEVEL BUREAUCRATS...
I WONDER IF THAT ROB GUY IS DOWN THERE.*
*ROB IS A RELATIVELY ATTRACTIVE POLICEMAN FROM ASM #25. --NICK
WELL, LADIES, I THINK WE ALL KNOW WHAT THE BEST CALL HERE IS. I'LL GO DOWN, TALK TO FISK, CUT A DEAL. LOOKS LIKE FRED HERE IS--
NO, WAIT! BEHOLD--

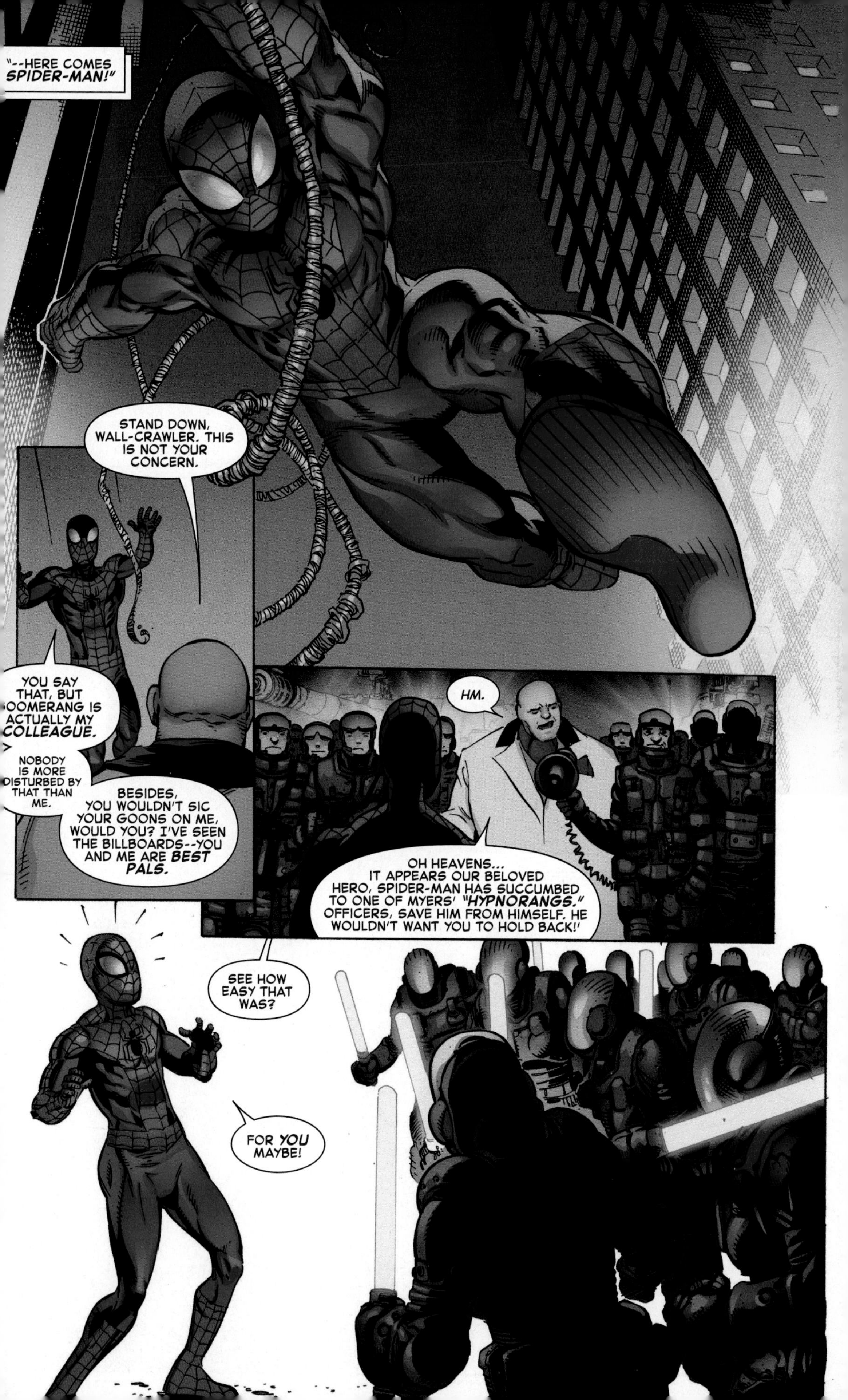
"--HERE COMES SPIDER-MAN!"
STAND DOWN, WALL-CRAWLER. THIS IS NOT YOUR CONCERN.
YOU SAY THAT, BUT OOMERANG IS ACTUALLY MY COLLEAGUE.
NOBODY IS MORE DISTURBED BY THAT THAN ME.
BESIDES, YOU WOULDN'T SIC YOUR GOONS ON ME, WOULD YOU? I'VE SEEN THE BILLBOARDS--YOU AND ME ARE BEST PALS.
HM.
OH HEAVENS... IT APPEARS OUR BELOVED HERO, SPIDER-MAN HAS SUCCUMBED TO ONE OF MYERS' "HYPNORANGS." OFFICERS, SAVE HIM FROM HIMSELF. HE WOULDN'T WANT YOU TO HOLD BACK!
SEE HOW EASY THAT WAS?
FOR YOU MAYBE!

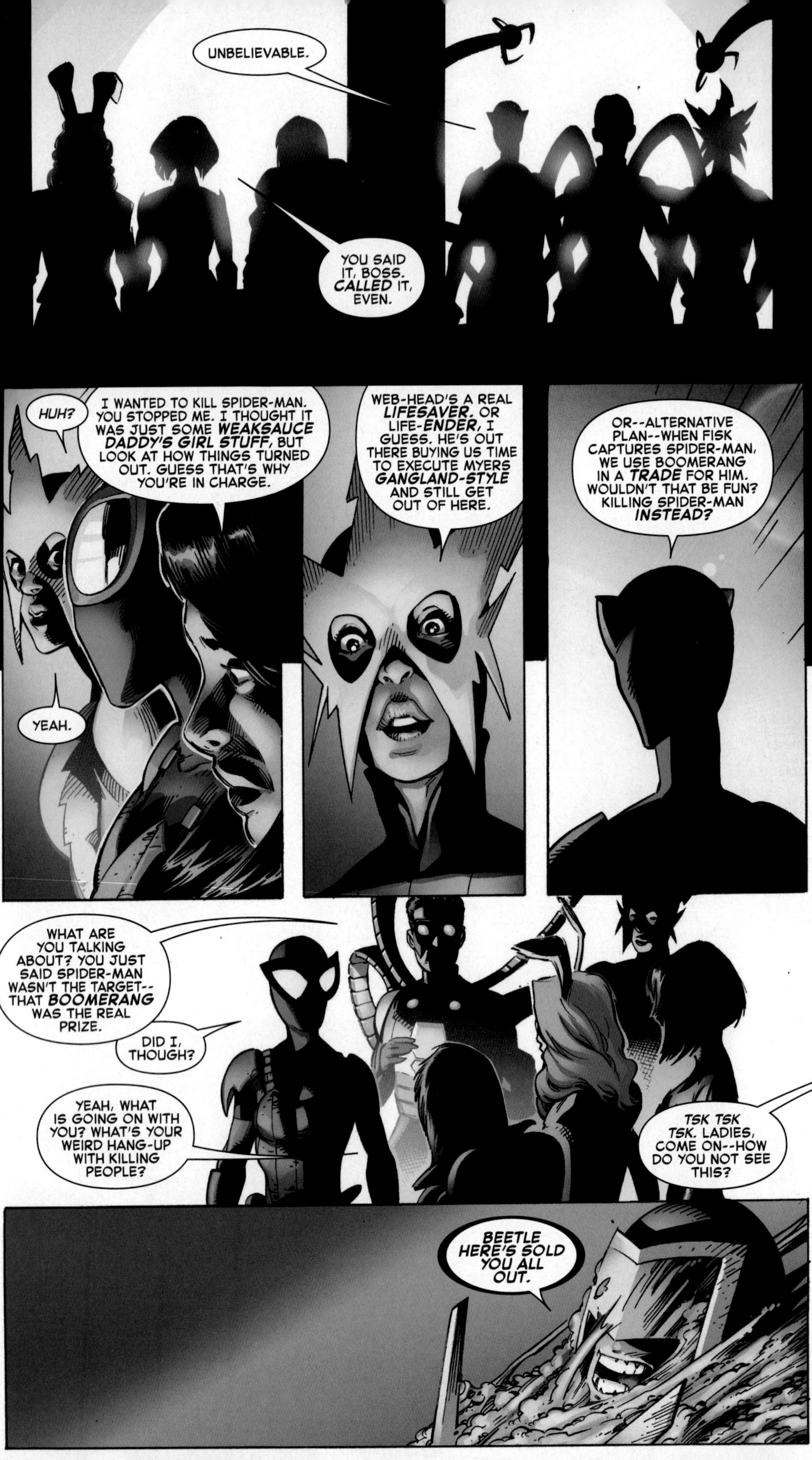
UNBELIEVABLE.
YOU SAID IT, BOSS. CALLED IT, EVEN.
HUH?
I WANTED TO KILL SPIDER-MAN. YOU STOPPED ME. I THOUGHT IT WAS JUST SOME WEAKSAUCE DADDY'S GIRL STUFF, BUT LOOK AT HOW THINGS TURNED OUT. GUESS THAT'S WHY YOU'RE IN CHARGE.
YEAH.
WEB-HEAD'S A REAL LIFESAVER. OR LIFE-ENDER, I GUESS. HE'S OUT THERE BUYING US TIME TO EXECUTE MYERS GANGLAND-STYLE AND STILL GET OUT OF HERE.
OR--ALTERNATIVE PLAN--WHEN FISK CAPTURES SPIDER-MAN, WE USE BOOMERANG IN A TRADE FOR HIM. WOULDN'T THAT BE FUN? KILLING SPIDER-MAN INSTEAD?
WHAT ARE YOU TALKING ABOUT? YOU JUST SAID SPIDER-MAN WASN'T THE TARGET--THAT BOOMERANG WAS THE REAL PRIZE.
DID I, THOUGH?
YEAH, WHAT IS GOING ON WITH YOU? WHAT'S YOUR WEIRD HANG-UP WITH KILLING PEOPLE?
TSK TSK TSK. LADIES, COME ON--HOW DO YOU NOT SEE THIS?
BEETLE HERE'S SOLD YOU ALL OUT.

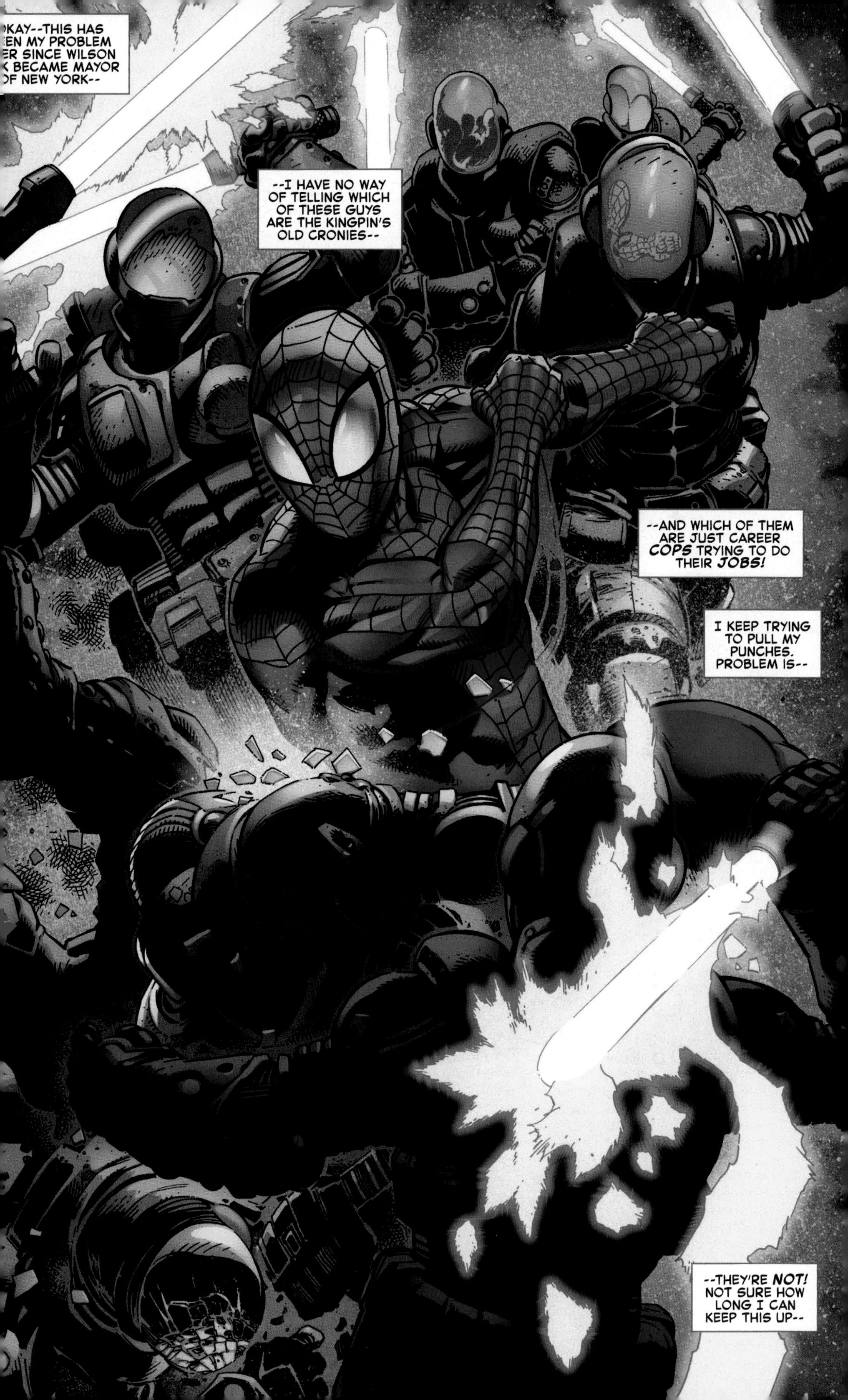
OKAY--THIS HAS BEEN MY PROBLEM EVER SINCE WILSON FISK BECAME MAYOR OF NEW YORK--
--I HAVE NO WAY OF TELLING WHICH OF THESE GUYS ARE THE KINGPIN'S OLD CRONIES--
--AND WHICH OF THEM ARE JUST CAREER *COPS* TRYING TO DO THEIR *JOBS!*
I KEEP TRYING TO PULL MY PUNCHES. PROBLEM IS--
--THEY'RE *NOT!* NOT SURE HOW LONG I CAN KEEP THIS UP--

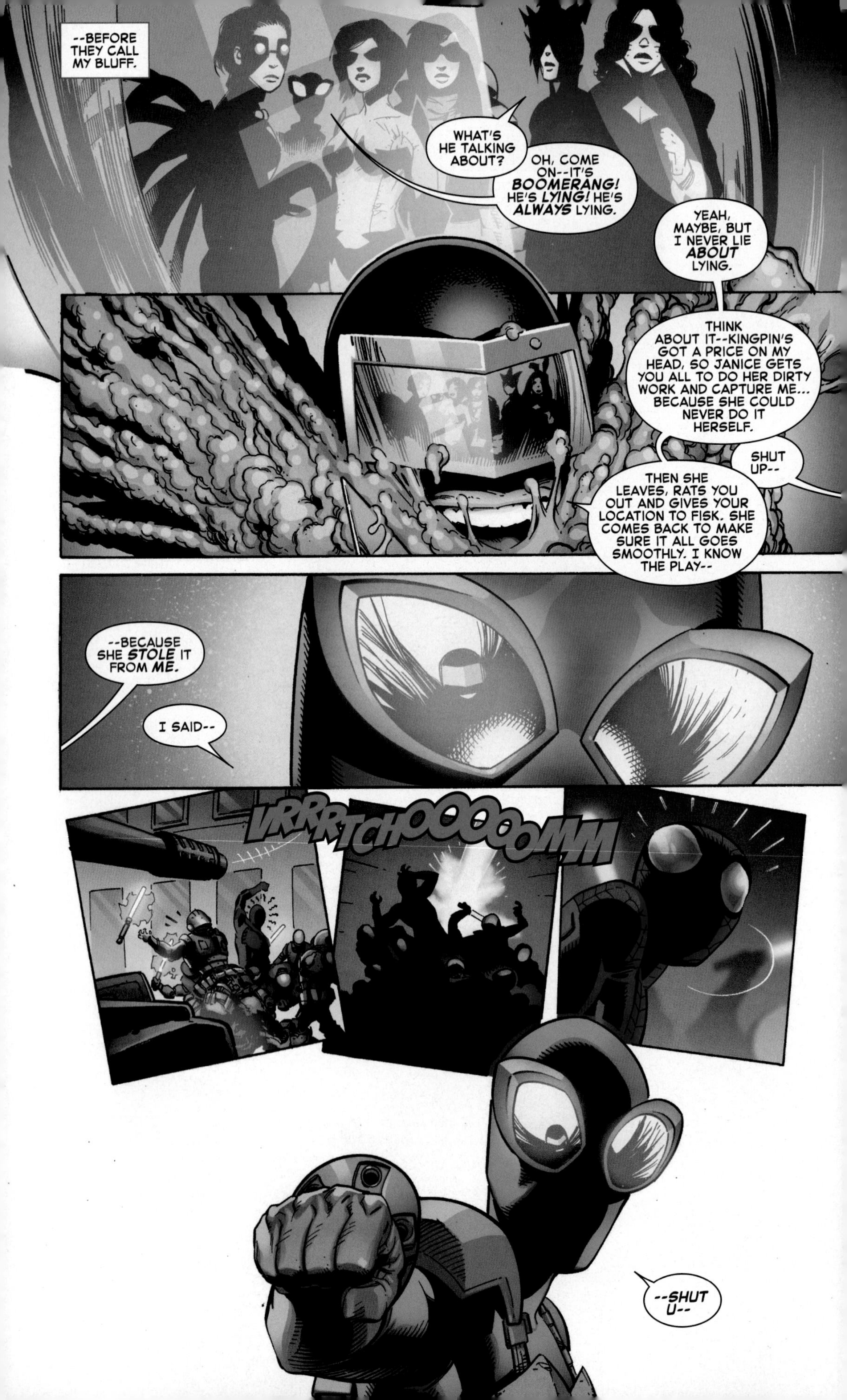

--BEFORE THEY CALL MY BLUFF.
WHAT'S HE TALKING ABOUT?
OH, COME ON--IT'S BOOMERANG! HE'S LYING! HE'S ALWAYS LYING.
YEAH, MAYBE, BUT I NEVER LIE ABOUT LYING.
THINK ABOUT IT--KINGPIN'S GOT A PRICE ON MY HEAD, SO JANICE GETS YOU ALL TO DO HER DIRTY WORK AND CAPTURE ME... BECAUSE SHE COULD NEVER DO IT HERSELF.
SHUT UP--
THEN SHE LEAVES, RATS YOU OUT AND GIVES YOUR LOCATION TO FISK. SHE COMES BACK TO MAKE SURE IT ALL GOES SMOOTHLY. I KNOW THE PLAY--
--BECAUSE SHE STOLE IT FROM ME.
I SAID--
VRRRRTCHOOOOOOMM
--SHUT U--

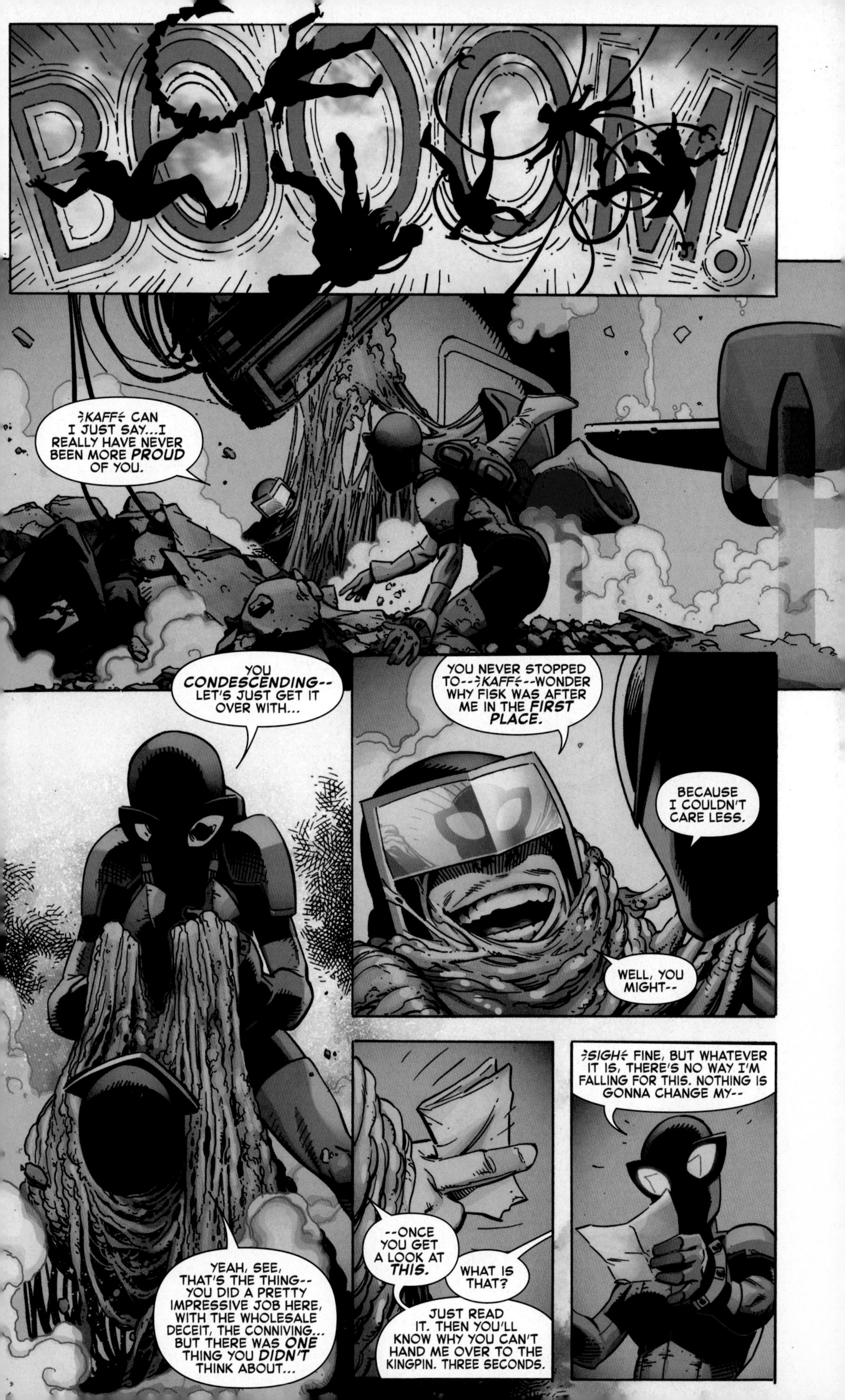
BOOOM!!
≠KAFF≠ CAN I JUST SAY...I REALLY HAVE NEVER BEEN MORE PROUD OF YOU.
YOU CONDESCENDING-- LET'S JUST GET IT OVER WITH...
YOU NEVER STOPPED TO--≠KAFF≠--WONDER WHY FISK WAS AFTER ME IN THE FIRST PLACE.
BECAUSE I COULDN'T CARE LESS.
WELL, YOU MIGHT--
YEAH, SEE, THAT'S THE THING-- YOU DID A PRETTY IMPRESSIVE JOB HERE, WITH THE WHOLESALE DECEIT, THE CONNIVING... BUT THERE WAS ONE THING YOU DIDN'T THINK ABOUT...
--ONCE YOU GET A LOOK AT THIS.
WHAT IS THAT?
JUST READ IT. THEN YOU'LL KNOW WHY YOU CAN'T HAND ME OVER TO THE KINGPIN. THREE SECONDS.
≠SIGH≠ FINE, BUT WHATEVER IT IS, THERE'S NO WAY I'M FALLING FOR THIS. NOTHING IS GONNA CHANGE MY--

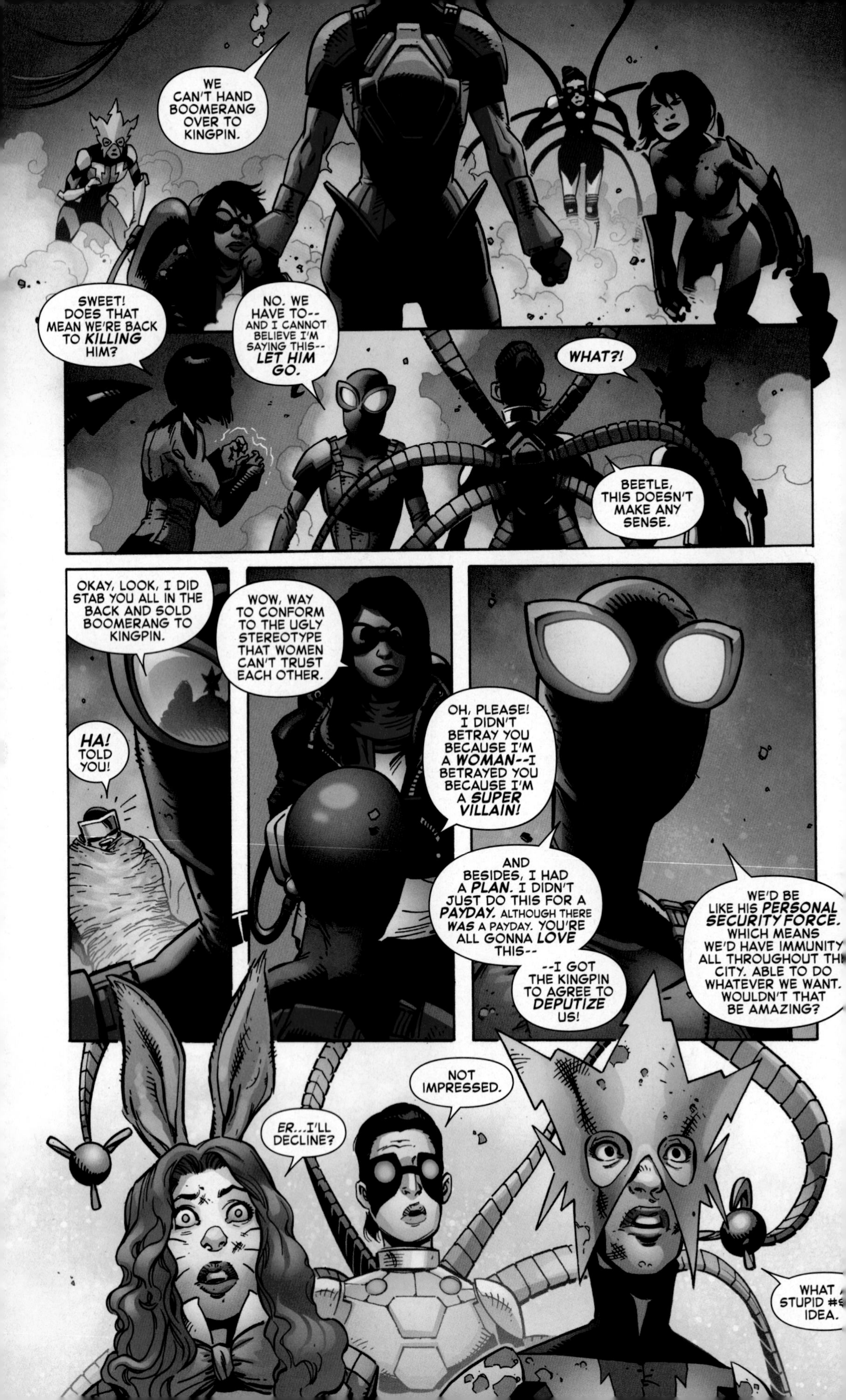
WE CAN'T HAND BOOMERANG OVER TO KINGPIN.
SWEET! DOES THAT MEAN WE'RE BACK TO KILLING HIM?
NO. WE HAVE TO-- AND I CANNOT BELIEVE I'M SAYING THIS-- LET HIM GO.
WHAT?!
BEETLE, THIS DOESN'T MAKE ANY SENSE.
OKAY, LOOK, I DID STAB YOU ALL IN THE BACK AND SOLD BOOMERANG TO KINGPIN.
HA! TOLD YOU!
WOW, WAY TO CONFORM TO THE UGLY STEREOTYPE THAT WOMEN CAN'T TRUST EACH OTHER.
OH, PLEASE! I DIDN'T BETRAY YOU BECAUSE I'M A WOMAN--I BETRAYED YOU BECAUSE I'M A SUPER VILLAIN!
AND BESIDES, I HAD A PLAN. I DIDN'T JUST DO THIS FOR A PAYDAY. ALTHOUGH THERE WAS A PAYDAY. YOU'RE ALL GONNA LOVE THIS--
--I GOT THE KINGPIN TO AGREE TO DEPUTIZE US!
WE'D BE LIKE HIS PERSONAL SECURITY FORCE. WHICH MEANS WE'D HAVE IMMUNITY ALL THROUGHOUT THE CITY. ABLE TO DO WHATEVER WE WANT. WOULDN'T THAT BE AMAZING?
NOT IMPRESSED.
ER...I'LL DECLINE?
WHAT A STUPID #$ IDEA.

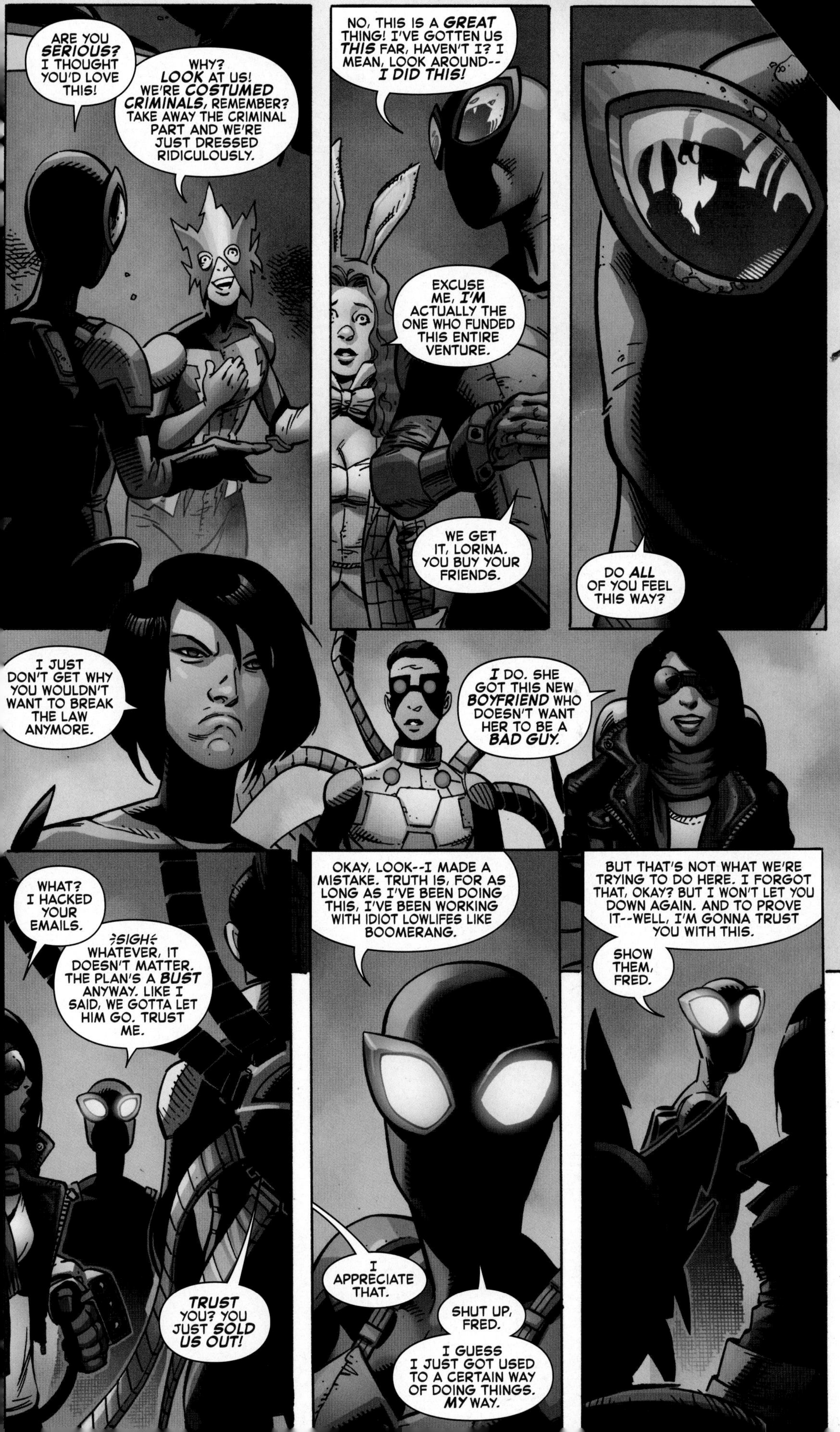

ARE YOU SERIOUS? I THOUGHT YOU'D LOVE THIS!
WHY? LOOK AT US! WE'RE COSTUMED CRIMINALS, REMEMBER? TAKE AWAY THE CRIMINAL PART AND WE'RE JUST DRESSED RIDICULOUSLY.
NO, THIS IS A GREAT THING! I'VE GOTTEN US THIS FAR, HAVEN'T I? I MEAN, LOOK AROUND-- I DID THIS!
EXCUSE ME, I'M ACTUALLY THE ONE WHO FUNDED THIS ENTIRE VENTURE.
WE GET IT, LORINA. YOU BUY YOUR FRIENDS.
DO ALL OF YOU FEEL THIS WAY?
I JUST DON'T GET WHY YOU WOULDN'T WANT TO BREAK THE LAW ANYMORE.
I DO. SHE GOT THIS NEW BOYFRIEND WHO DOESN'T WANT HER TO BE A BAD GUY.
WHAT? I HACKED YOUR EMAILS.
SIGH WHATEVER, IT DOESN'T MATTER. THE PLAN'S A BUST ANYWAY. LIKE I SAID, WE GOTTA LET HIM GO. TRUST ME.
TRUST YOU? YOU JUST SOLD US OUT!
OKAY, LOOK--I MADE A MISTAKE. TRUTH IS, FOR AS LONG AS I'VE BEEN DOING THIS, I'VE BEEN WORKING WITH IDIOT LOWLIFES LIKE BOOMERANG.
I APPRECIATE THAT.
SHUT UP, FRED.
I GUESS I JUST GOT USED TO A CERTAIN WAY OF DOING THINGS. MY WAY.
BUT THAT'S NOT WHAT WE'RE TRYING TO DO HERE. I FORGOT THAT, OKAY? BUT I WON'T LET YOU DOWN AGAIN. AND TO PROVE IT--WELL, I'M GONNA TRUST YOU WITH THIS.
SHOW THEM, FRED.

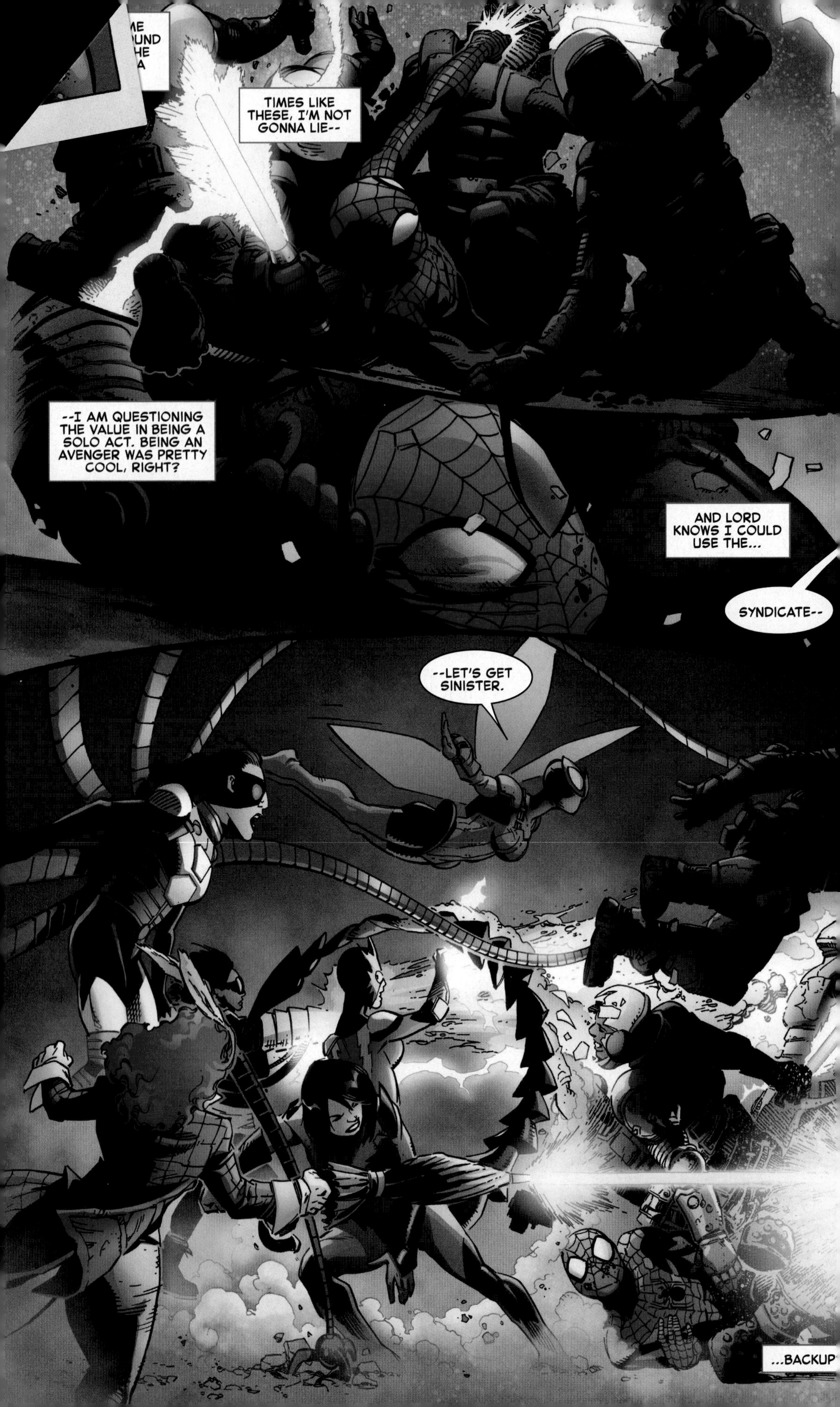

TIMES LIKE THESE, I'M NOT GONNA LIE--
--I AM QUESTIONING THE VALUE IN BEING A SOLO ACT. BEING AN AVENGER WAS PRETTY COOL, RIGHT?
AND LORD KNOWS I COULD USE THE...
SYNDICATE--
--LET'S GET SINISTER.
...BACKUP

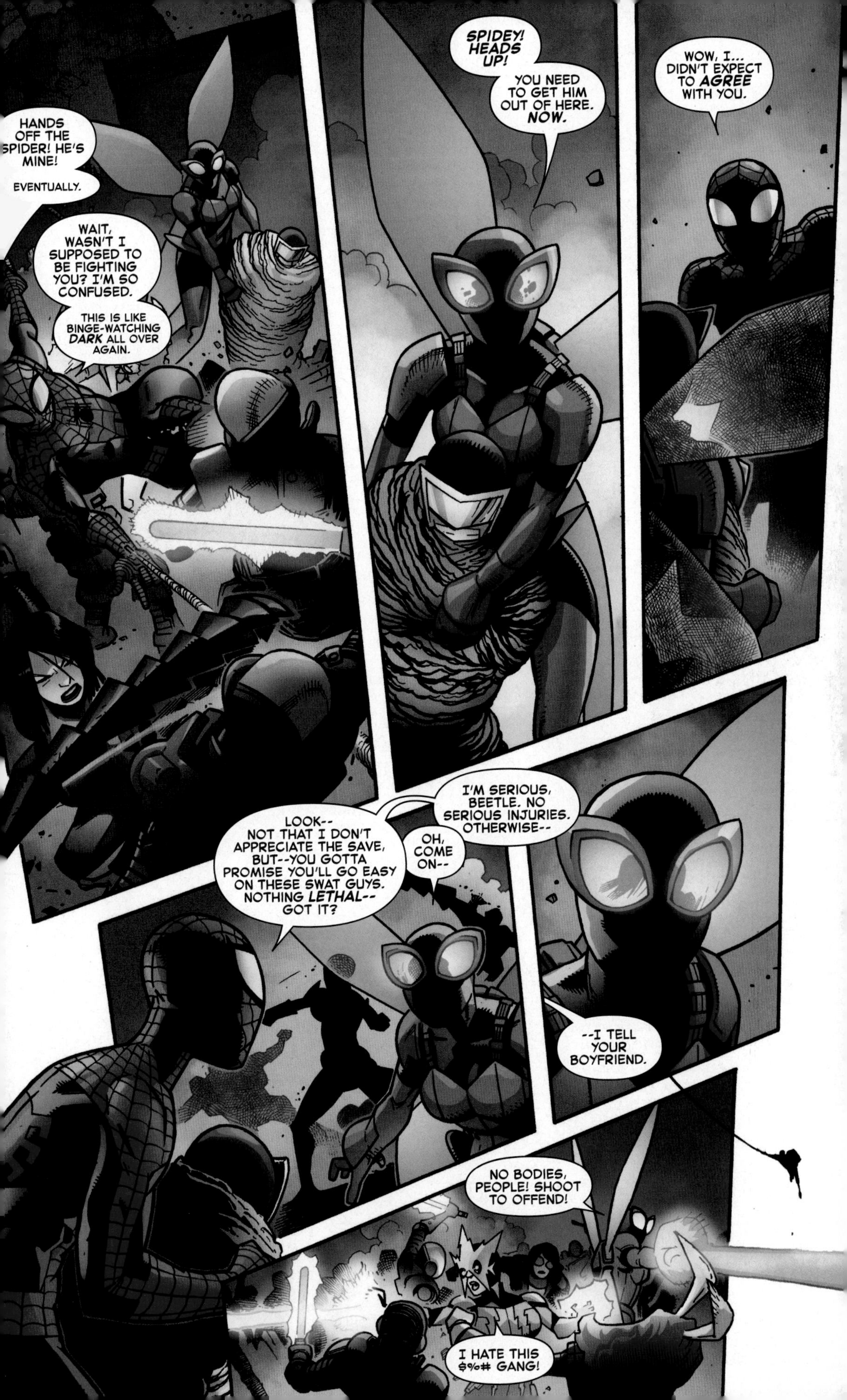

HANDS OFF THE SPIDER! HE'S MINE!
EVENTUALLY.
WAIT, WASN'T I SUPPOSED TO BE FIGHTING YOU? I'M SO CONFUSED.
THIS IS LIKE BINGE-WATCHING DARK ALL OVER AGAIN.
SPIDEY! HEADS UP!
YOU NEED TO GET HIM OUT OF HERE. NOW.
WOW, I... DIDN'T EXPECT TO AGREE WITH YOU.
LOOK-- NOT THAT I DON'T APPRECIATE THE SAVE, BUT--YOU GOTTA PROMISE YOU'LL GO EASY ON THESE SWAT GUYS. NOTHING LETHAL-- GOT IT?
OH, COME ON--
I'M SERIOUS, BEETLE. NO SERIOUS INJURIES. OTHERWISE--
--I TELL YOUR BOYFRIEND.
NO BODIES, PEOPLE! SHOOT TO OFFEND!
I HATE THIS $%# GANG!

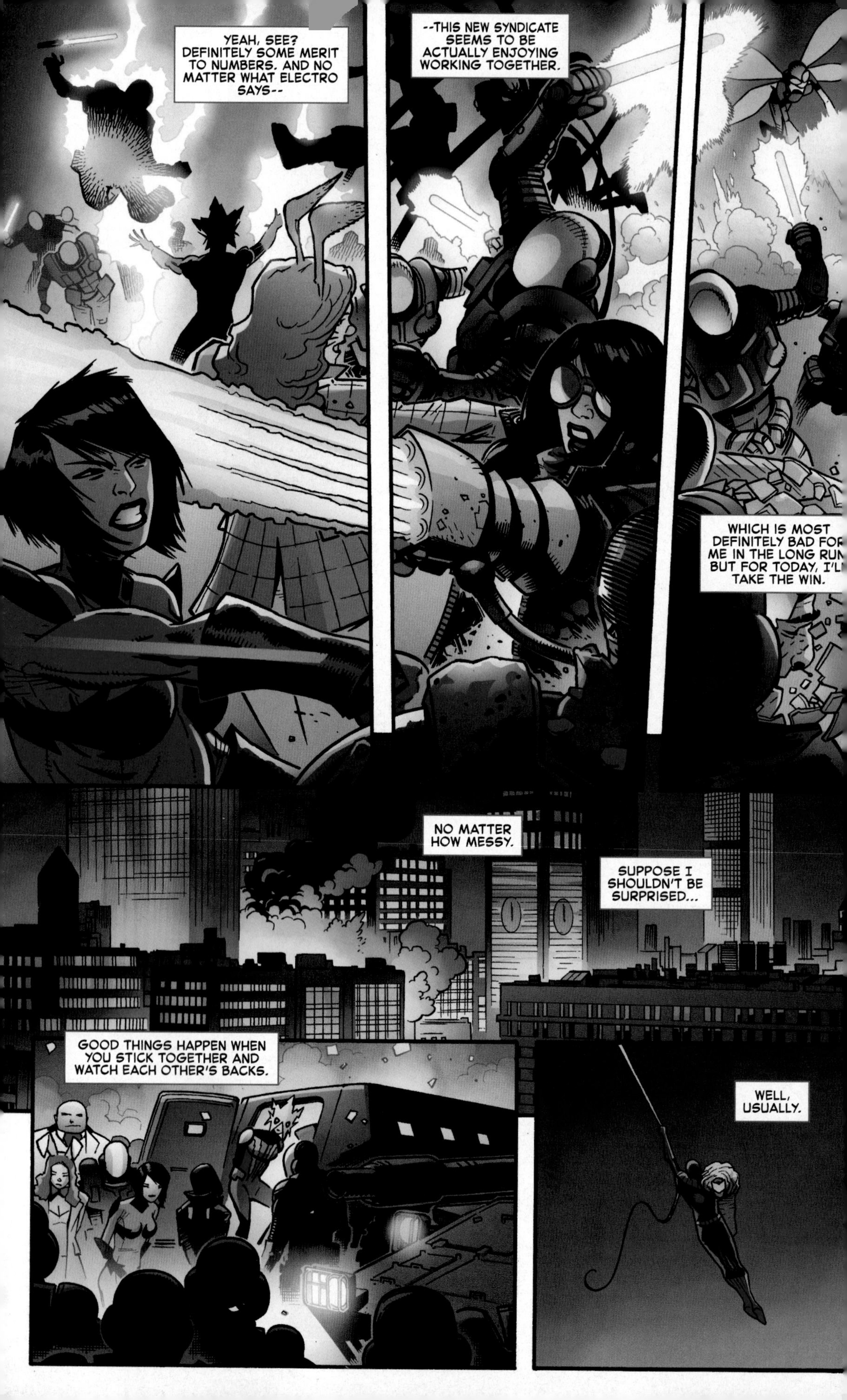
YEAH, SEE? DEFINITELY SOME MERIT TO NUMBERS. AND NO MATTER WHAT ELECTRO SAYS--
--THIS NEW SYNDICATE SEEMS TO BE ACTUALLY ENJOYING WORKING TOGETHER.
WHICH IS MOST DEFINITELY BAD FOR ME IN THE LONG RUN BUT FOR TODAY, I'LL TAKE THE WIN.
NO MATTER HOW MESSY.
SUPPOSE I SHOULDN'T BE SURPRISED...
GOOD THINGS HAPPEN WHEN YOU STICK TOGETHER AND WATCH EACH OTHER'S BACKS.
WELL, USUALLY.

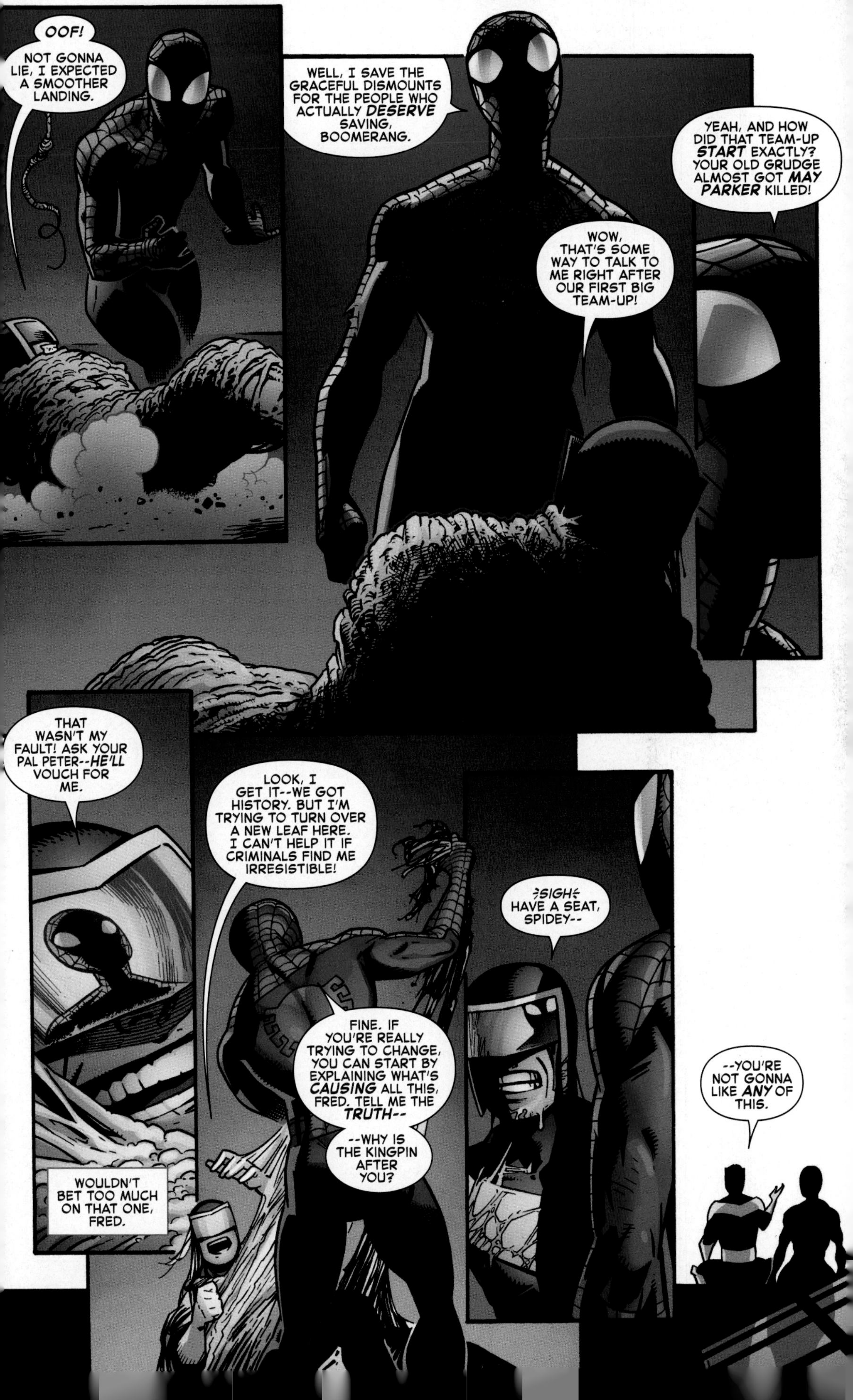
OOF!
NOT GONNA LIE, I EXPECTED A SMOOTHER LANDING.
WELL, I SAVE THE GRACEFUL DISMOUNTS FOR THE PEOPLE WHO ACTUALLY DESERVE SAVING, BOOMERANG.
WOW, THAT'S SOME WAY TO TALK TO ME RIGHT AFTER OUR FIRST BIG TEAM-UP!
YEAH, AND HOW DID THAT TEAM-UP START EXACTLY? YOUR OLD GRUDGE ALMOST GOT MAY PARKER KILLED!
THAT WASN'T MY FAULT! ASK YOUR PAL PETER--HE'LL VOUCH FOR ME.
WOULDN'T BET TOO MUCH ON THAT ONE, FRED.
LOOK, I GET IT--WE GOT HISTORY. BUT I'M TRYING TO TURN OVER A NEW LEAF HERE. I CAN'T HELP IT IF CRIMINALS FIND ME IRRESISTIBLE!
FINE. IF YOU'RE REALLY TRYING TO CHANGE, YOU CAN START BY EXPLAINING WHAT'S CAUSING ALL THIS, FRED. TELL ME THE TRUTH--
--WHY IS THE KINGPIN AFTER YOU?
SIGH HAVE A SEAT, SPIDEY--
--YOU'RE NOT GONNA LIKE ANY OF THIS.

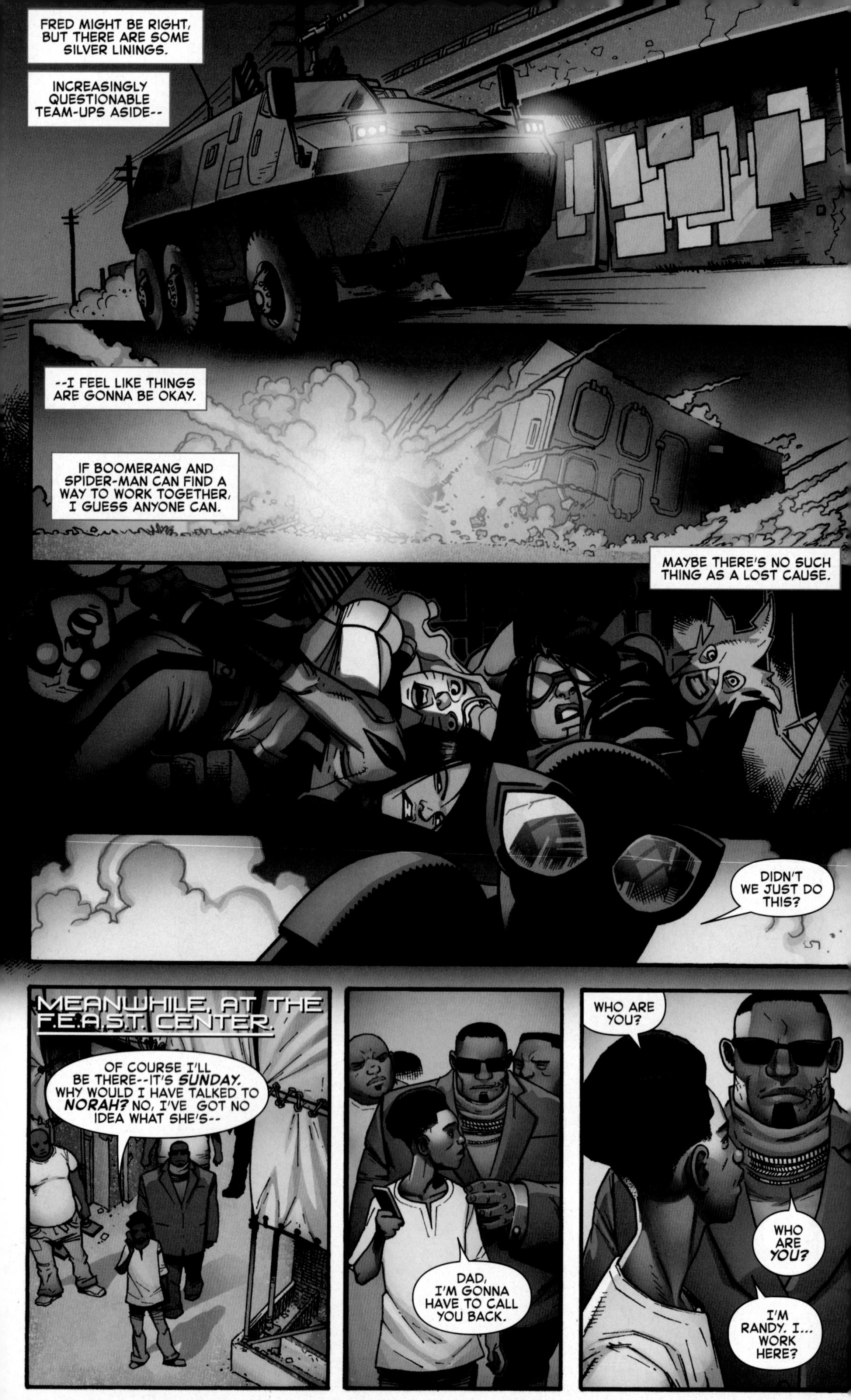

FRED MIGHT BE RIGHT, BUT THERE ARE SOME SILVER LININGS.
INCREASINGLY QUESTIONABLE TEAM-UPS ASIDE--
--I FEEL LIKE THINGS ARE GONNA BE OKAY.
IF BOOMERANG AND SPIDER-MAN CAN FIND A WAY TO WORK TOGETHER, I GUESS ANYONE CAN.
MAYBE THERE'S NO SUCH THING AS A LOST CAUSE.
DIDN'T WE JUST DO THIS?
MEANWHILE, AT THE F.E.A.S.T. CENTER.
OF COURSE I'LL BE THERE--IT'S SUNDAY. WHY WOULD I HAVE TALKED TO NORAH? NO, I'VE GOT NO IDEA WHAT SHE'S--
DAD, I'M GONNA HAVE TO CALL YOU BACK.
WHO ARE YOU?
WHO ARE YOU?
I'M RANDY. I... WORK HERE?

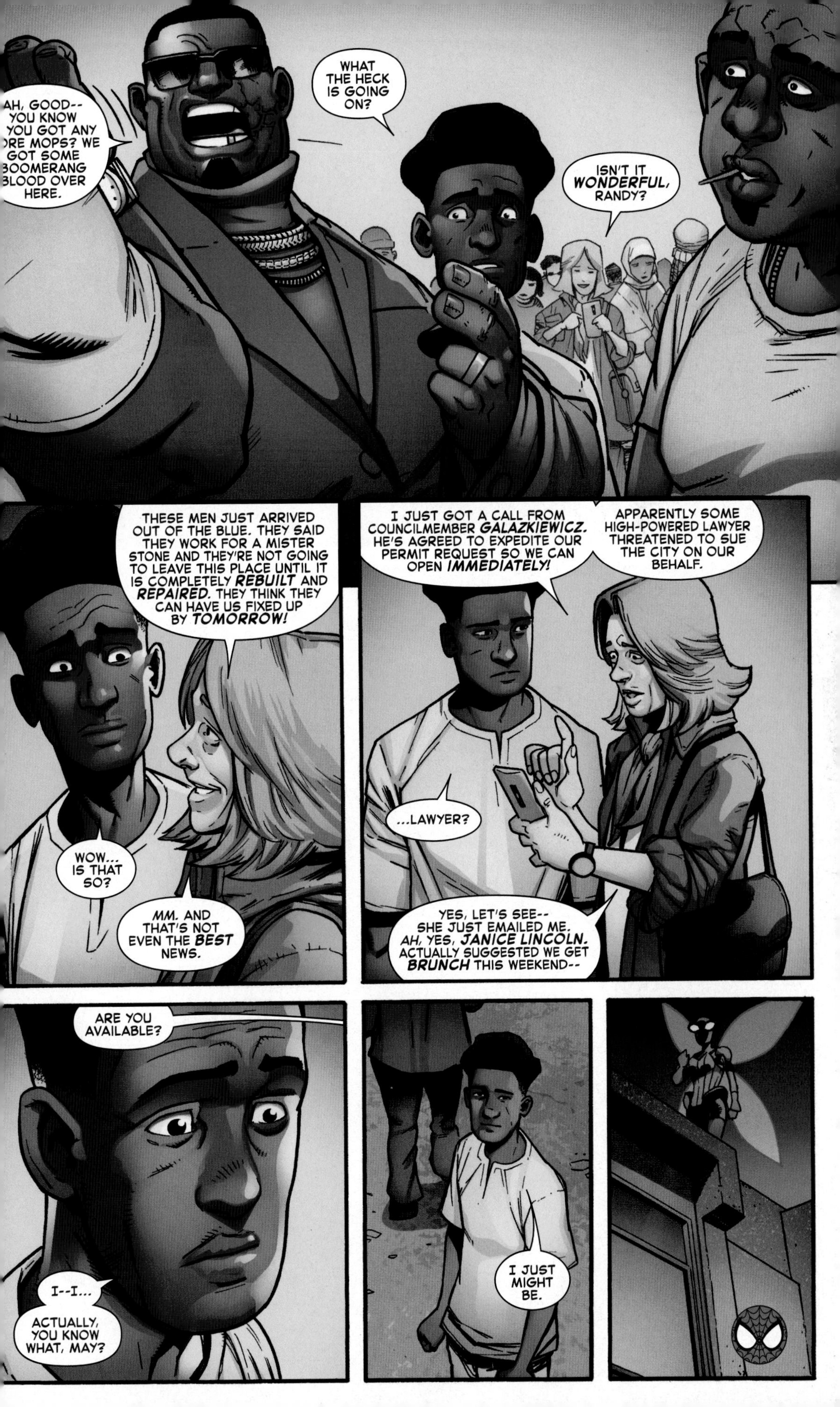
AH, GOOD-- YOU KNOW YOU GOT ANY ORE MOPS? WE GOT SOME BOOMERANG BLOOD OVER HERE.
WHAT THE HECK IS GOING ON?
ISN'T IT WONDERFUL, RANDY?
THESE MEN JUST ARRIVED OUT OF THE BLUE. THEY SAID THEY WORK FOR A MISTER STONE AND THEY'RE NOT GOING TO LEAVE THIS PLACE UNTIL IT IS COMPLETELY REBUILT AND REPAIRED. THEY THINK THEY CAN HAVE US FIXED UP BY TOMORROW!
WOW... IS THAT SO?
MM. AND THAT'S NOT EVEN THE BEST NEWS.
I JUST GOT A CALL FROM COUNCILMEMBER GALAZKIEWICZ. HE'S AGREED TO EXPEDITE OUR PERMIT REQUEST SO WE CAN OPEN IMMEDIATELY!
APPARENTLY SOME HIGH-POWERED LAWYER THREATENED TO SUE THE CITY ON OUR BEHALF.
...LAWYER?
YES, LET'S SEE-- SHE JUST EMAILED ME. AH, YES, JANICE LINCOLN. ACTUALLY SUGGESTED WE GET BRUNCH THIS WEEKEND--
ARE YOU AVAILABLE?
I--I...
ACTUALLY, YOU KNOW WHAT, MAY?
I JUST MIGHT BE.

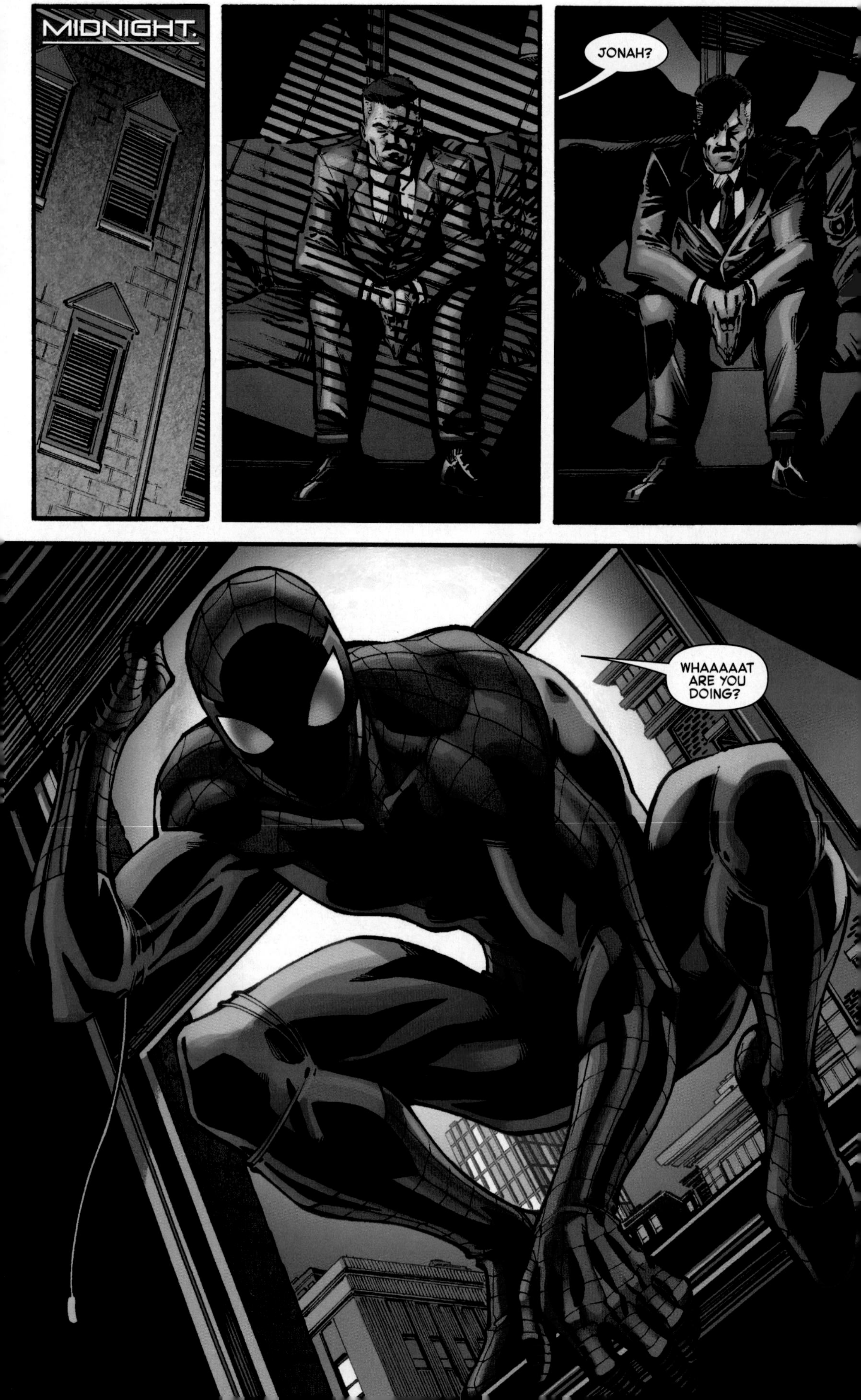
MIDNIGHT.
JONAH?
WHAAAAAT ARE YOU DOING?

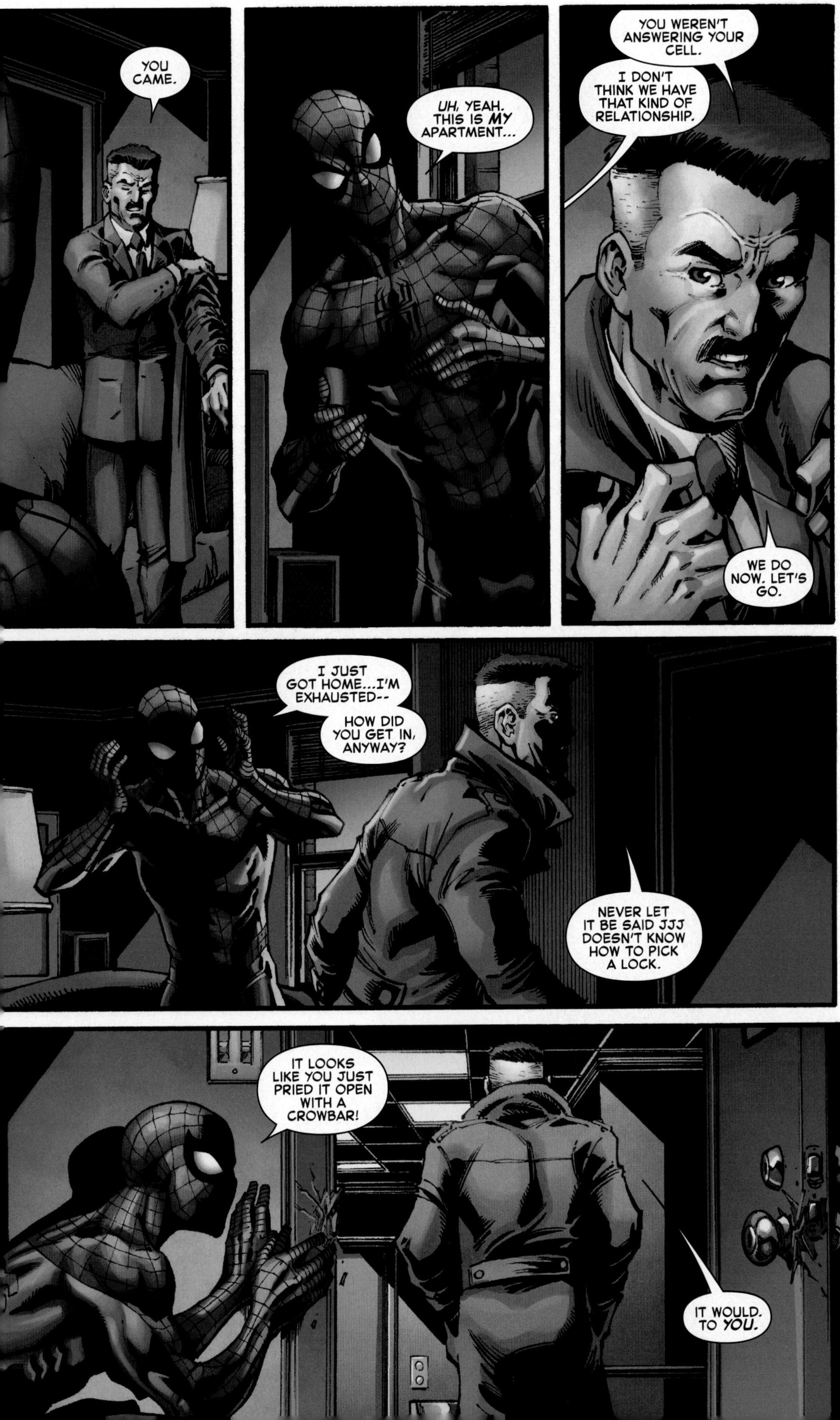
YOU CAME.
UH, YEAH. THIS IS MY APARTMENT...
YOU WEREN'T ANSWERING YOUR CELL.
I DON'T THINK WE HAVE THAT KIND OF RELATIONSHIP.
WE DO NOW. LET'S GO.
I JUST GOT HOME...I'M EXHAUSTED--
HOW DID YOU GET IN, ANYWAY?
NEVER LET IT BE SAID JJJ DOESN'T KNOW HOW TO PICK A LOCK.
IT LOOKS LIKE YOU JUST PRIED IT OPEN WITH A CROWBAR!
IT WOULD. TO YOU.

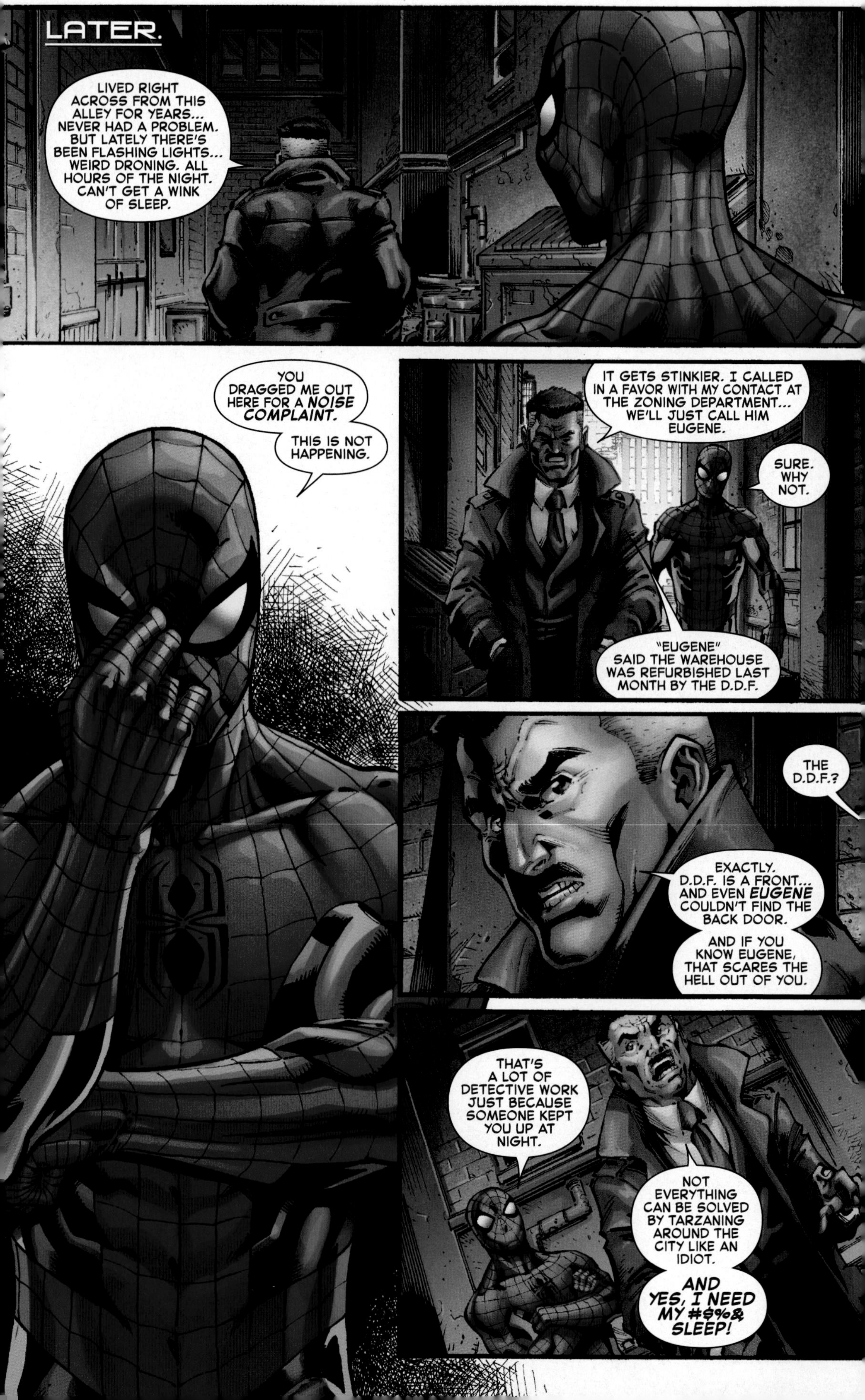
LATER.
LIVED RIGHT ACROSS FROM THIS ALLEY FOR YEARS... NEVER HAD A PROBLEM. BUT LATELY THERE'S BEEN FLASHING LIGHTS... WEIRD DRONING. ALL HOURS OF THE NIGHT. CAN'T GET A WINK OF SLEEP.
YOU DRAGGED ME OUT HERE FOR A NOISE COMPLAINT.
THIS IS NOT HAPPENING.
IT GETS STINKIER. I CALLED IN A FAVOR WITH MY CONTACT AT THE ZONING DEPARTMENT... WE'LL JUST CALL HIM EUGENE.
SURE. WHY NOT.
"EUGENE" SAID THE WAREHOUSE WAS REFURBISHED LAST MONTH BY THE D.D.F.
THE D.D.F.?
EXACTLY. D.D.F. IS A FRONT... AND EVEN EUGENE COULDN'T FIND THE BACK DOOR.
AND IF YOU KNOW EUGENE, THAT SCARES THE HELL OUT OF YOU.
THAT'S A LOT OF DETECTIVE WORK JUST BECAUSE SOMEONE KEPT YOU UP AT NIGHT.
NOT EVERYTHING CAN BE SOLVED BY TARZANING AROUND THE CITY LIKE AN IDIOT.
AND YES, I NEED MY #$%& SLEEP!

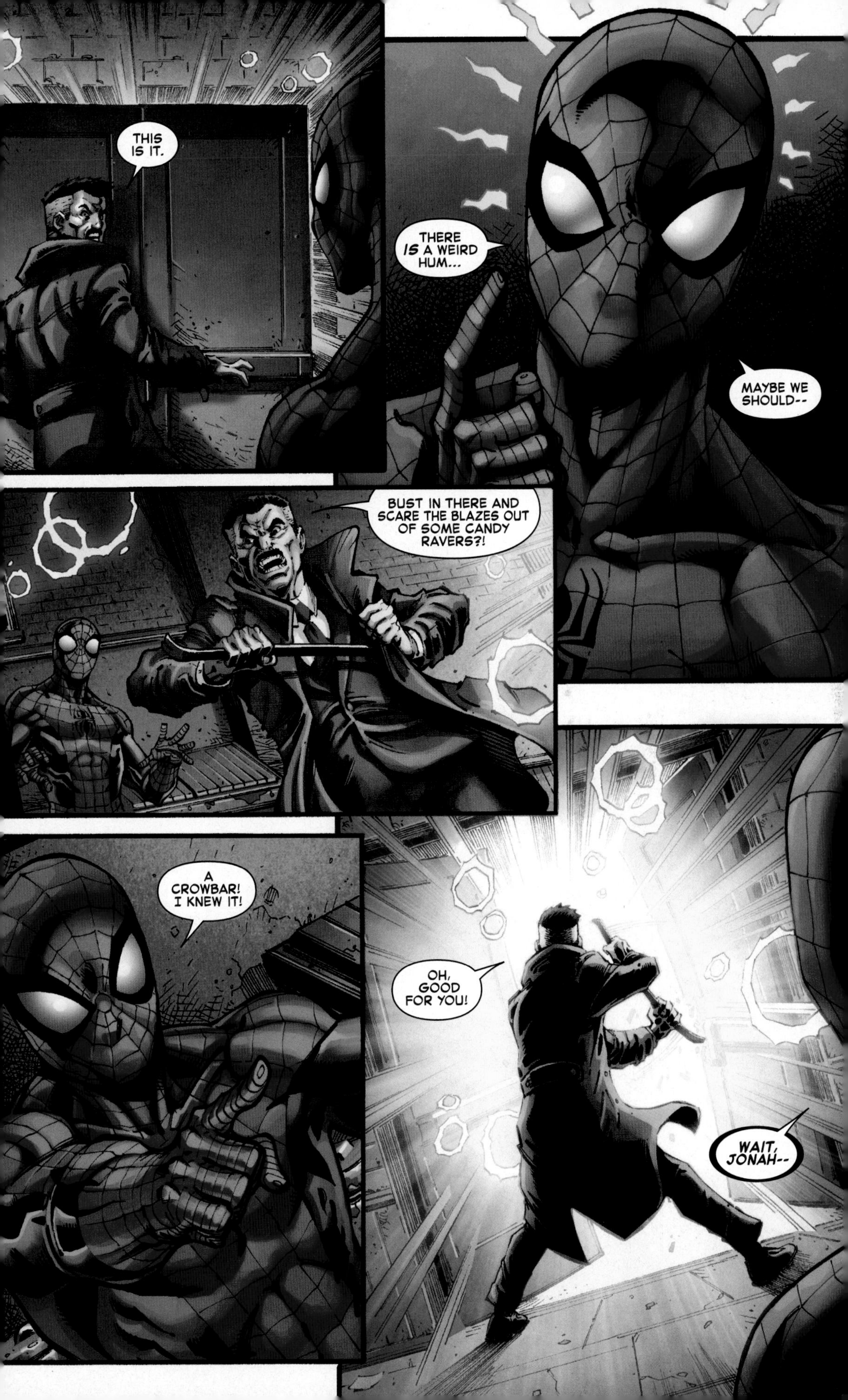
THIS IS IT.
THERE *IS* A WEIRD HUM...
MAYBE WE SHOULD--
BUST IN THERE AND SCARE THE BLAZES OUT OF SOME CANDY RAVERS?!
A CROWBAR! I KNEW IT!
OH, GOOD FOR YOU!
WAIT, JONAH--

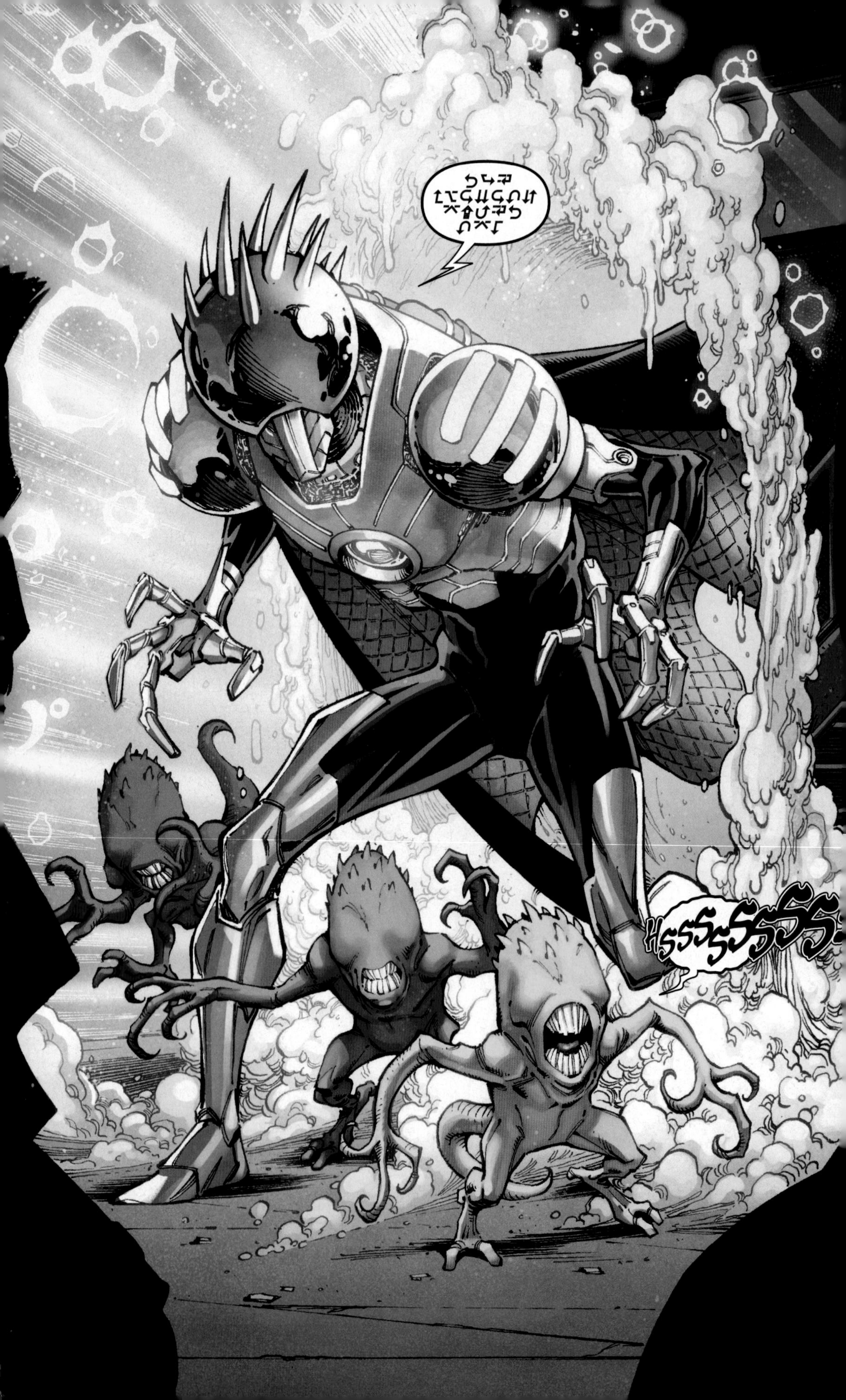
HSSSSSSSS

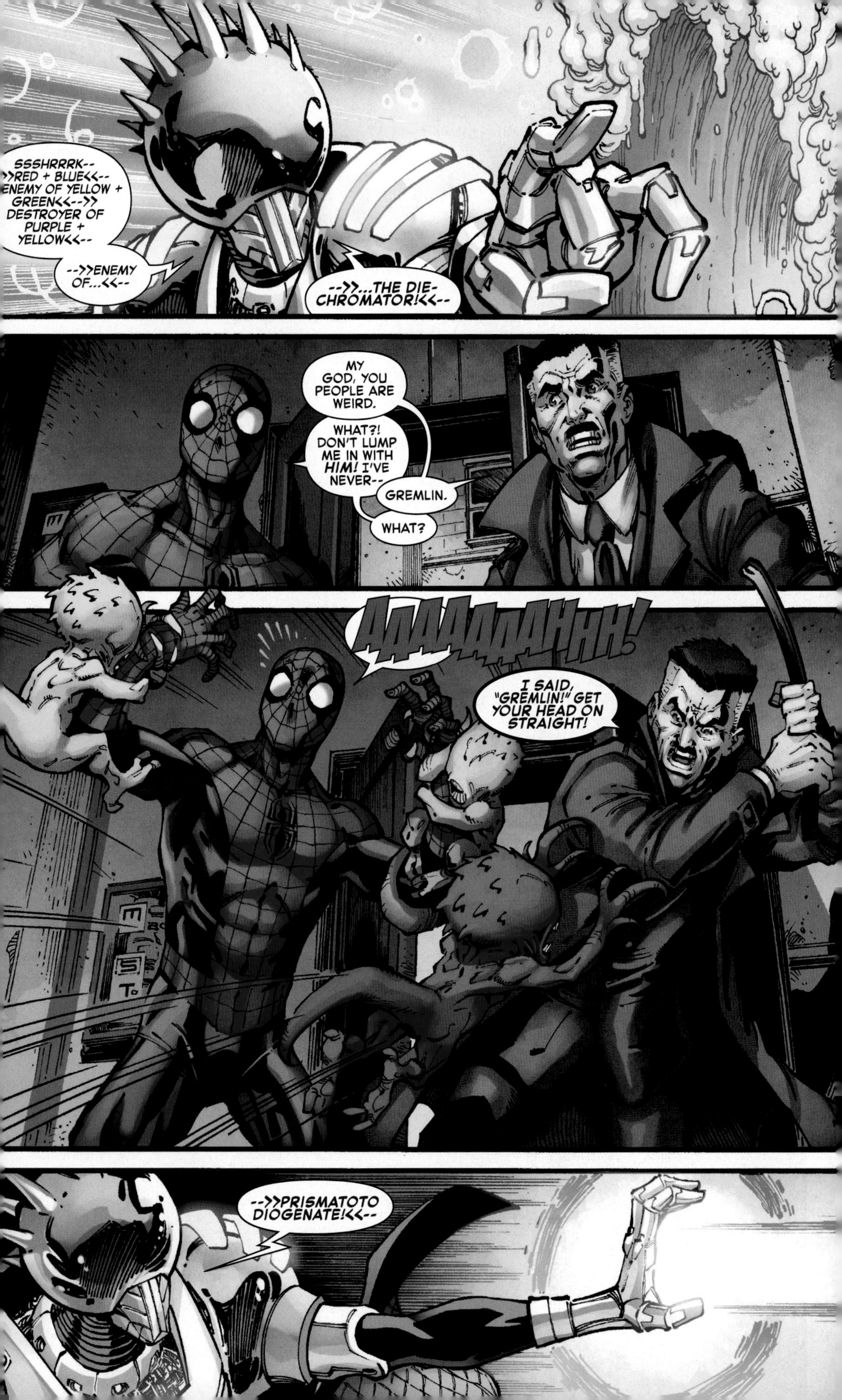

SSSHRRRK-- >>RED + BLUE<<-- ENEMY OF YELLOW + GREEN<<-->> DESTROYER OF PURPLE + YELLOW<<--
-->>ENEMY OF...<<--
-->>...THE DIE-CHROMATOR!<<--
MY GOD, YOU PEOPLE ARE WEIRD.
WHAT?! DON'T LUMP ME IN WITH *HIM!* I'VE NEVER--
GREMLIN.
WHAT?
AAAAAAAHHH!
I SAID, "GREMLIN!" GET YOUR HEAD ON STRAIGHT!
-->>PRISMATOTO DIOGENATE!<<--

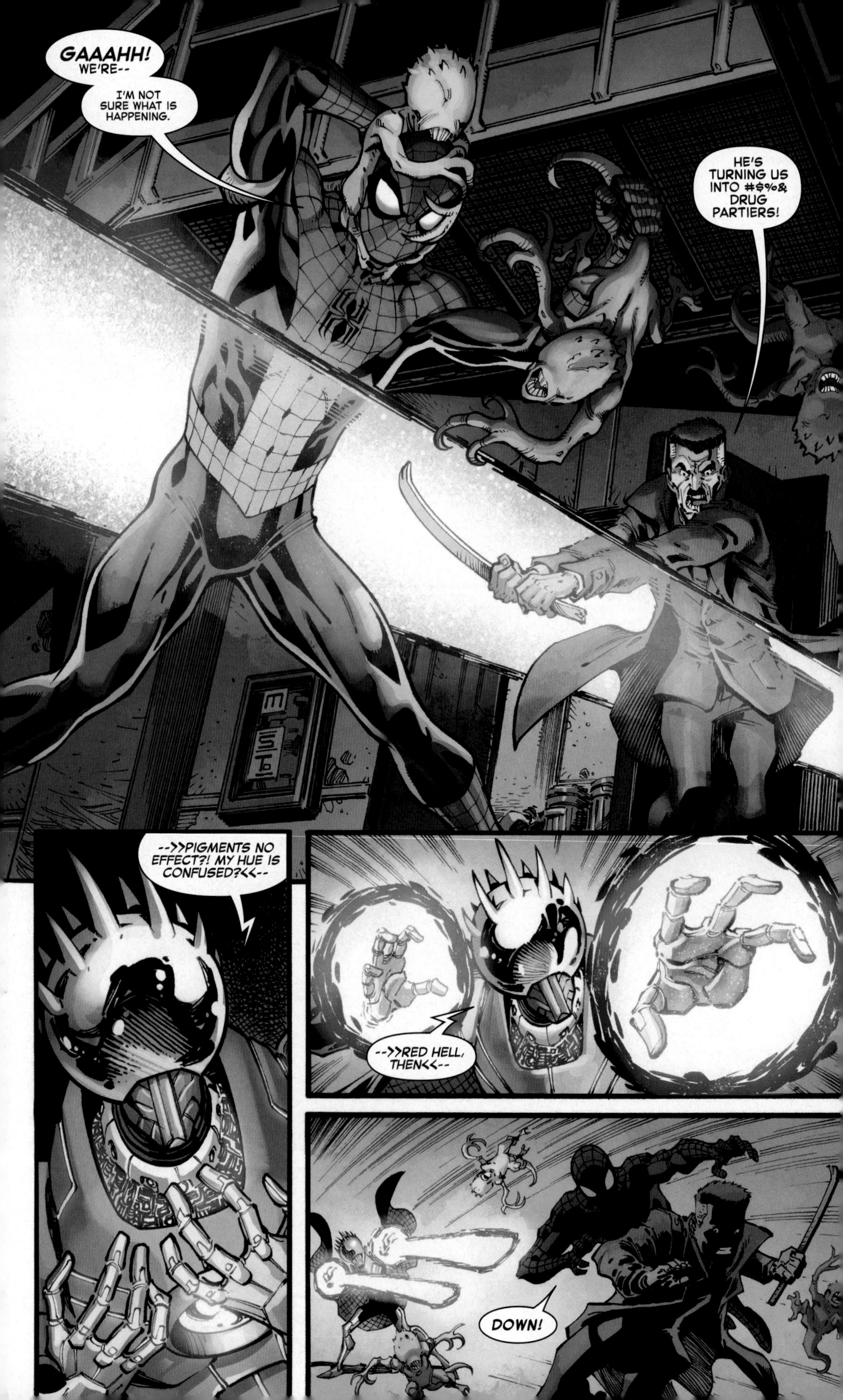
GAAAHH! WE'RE--
I'M NOT SURE WHAT IS HAPPENING.
HE'S TURNING US INTO #$%& DRUG PARTIERS!
-->>PIGMENTS NO EFFECT?! MY HUE IS CONFUSED?<<--
-->>RED HELL, THEN<<--
DOWN!

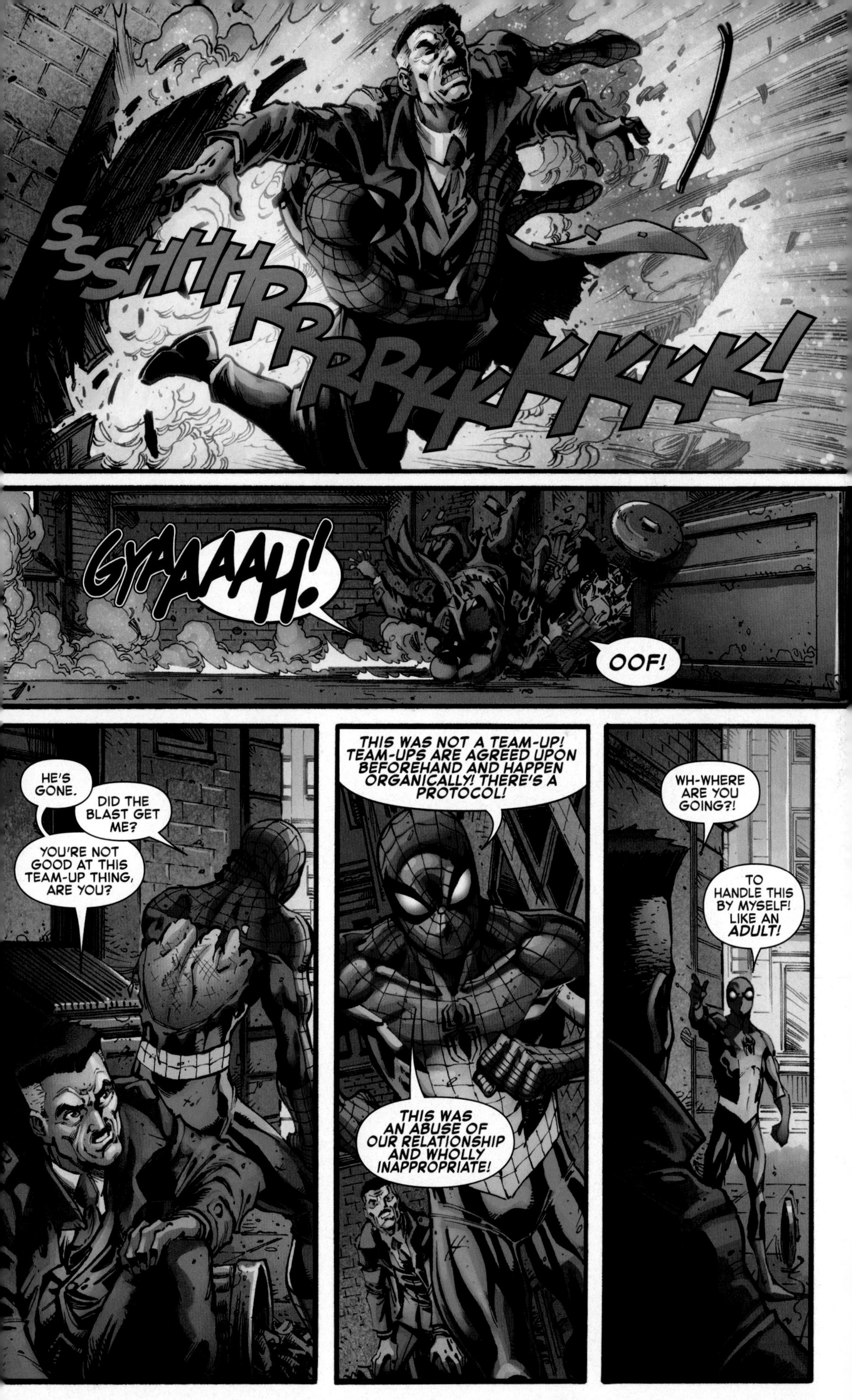
SSSHHHRRRKKKKKKK!
GYAAAAH!
OOF!
HE'S GONE.
DID THE BLAST GET ME?
YOU'RE NOT GOOD AT THIS TEAM-UP THING, ARE YOU?
THIS WAS NOT A TEAM-UP! TEAM-UPS ARE AGREED UPON BEFOREHAND AND HAPPEN ORGANICALLY! THERE'S A PROTOCOL!
THIS WAS AN ABUSE OF OUR RELATIONSHIP AND WHOLLY INAPPROPRIATE!
WH-WHERE ARE YOU GOING?!
TO HANDLE THIS BY MYSELF! LIKE AN ADULT!

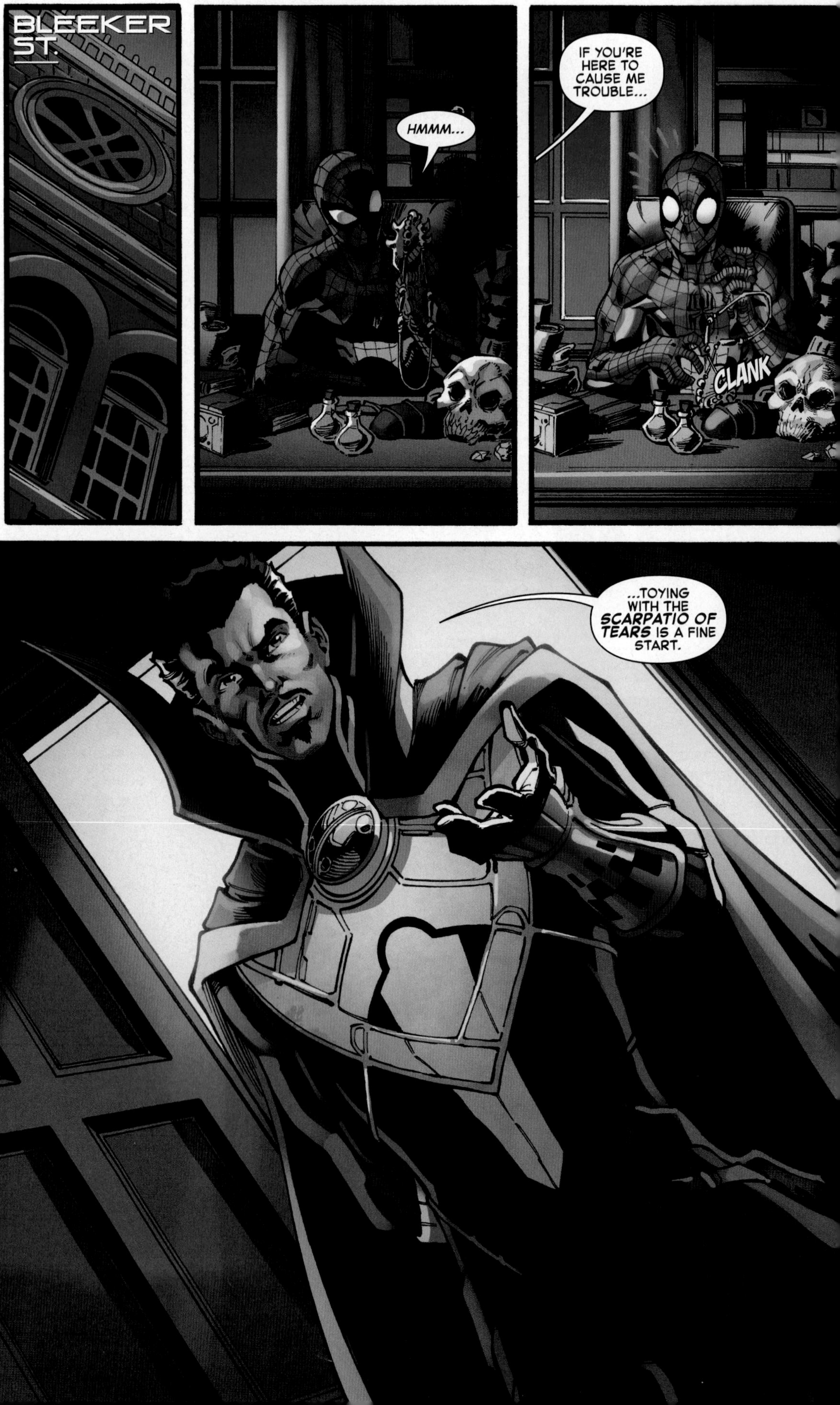
BLEEKER ST.
HMMM...
IF YOU'RE HERE TO CAUSE ME TROUBLE...
CLANK
...TOYING WITH THE SCARPATIO OF TEARS IS A FINE START.

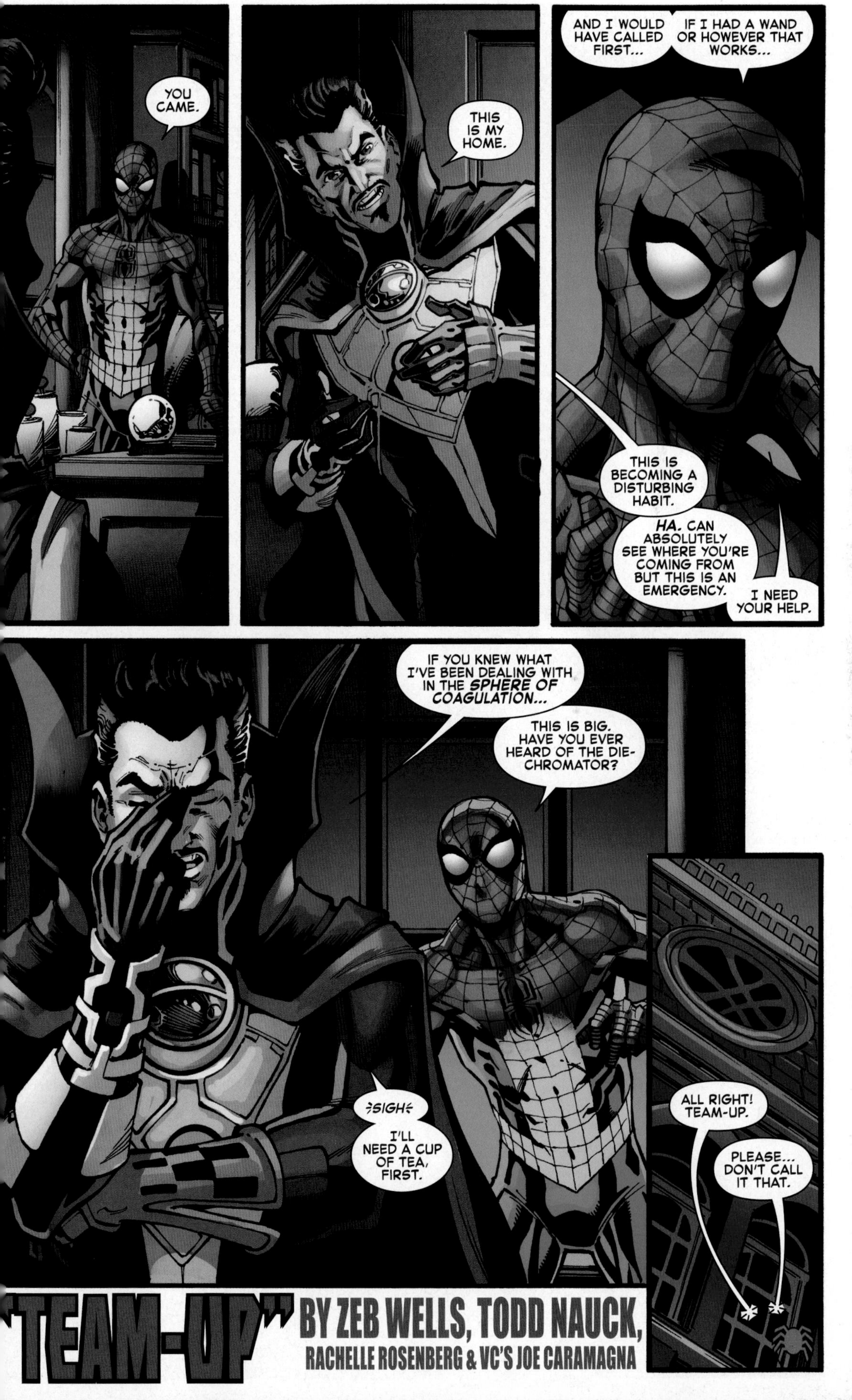

YOU CAME.
THIS IS MY HOME.
AND I WOULD HAVE CALLED FIRST...
IF I HAD A WAND OR HOWEVER THAT WORKS...
THIS IS BECOMING A DISTURBING HABIT.
HA. CAN ABSOLUTELY SEE WHERE YOU'RE COMING FROM BUT THIS IS AN EMERGENCY.
I NEED YOUR HELP.
IF YOU KNEW WHAT I'VE BEEN DEALING WITH IN THE SPHERE OF COAGULATION...
THIS IS BIG. HAVE YOU EVER HEARD OF THE DIE-CHROMATOR?
SIGH
I'LL NEED A CUP OF TEA, FIRST.
ALL RIGHT! TEAM-UP.
PLEASE... DON'T CALL IT THAT.
"TEAM-UP"
BY ZEB WELLS, TODD NAUCK,
RACHELLE ROSENBERG & VC'S JOE CARAMAGNA

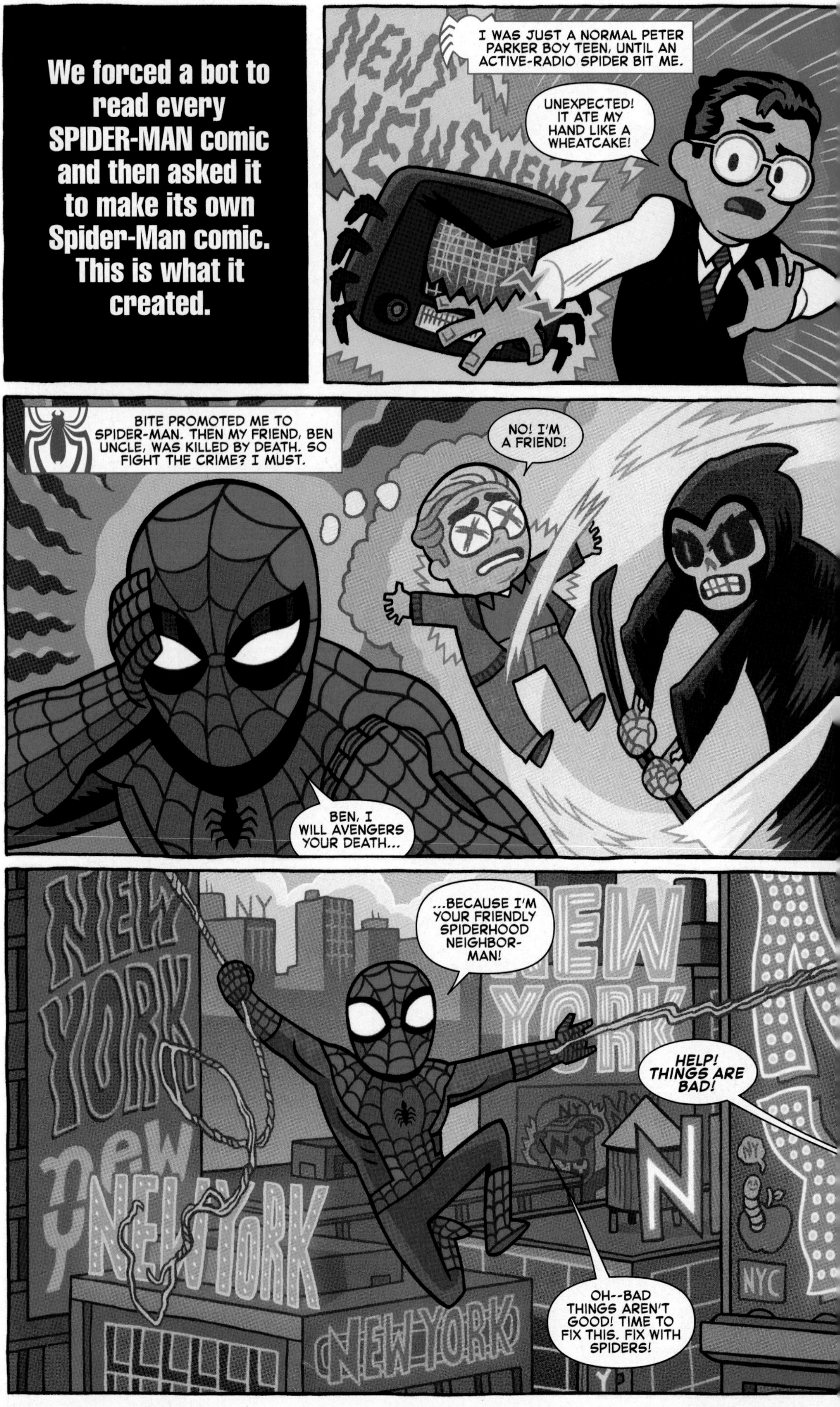
We forced a bot to read every SPIDER-MAN comic and then asked it to make its own Spider-Man comic. This is what it created.
I WAS JUST A NORMAL PETER PARKER BOY TEEN, UNTIL AN ACTIVE-RADIO SPIDER BIT ME.
UNEXPECTED! IT ATE MY HAND LIKE A WHEATCAKE!
BITE PROMOTED ME TO SPIDER-MAN. THEN MY FRIEND, BEN UNCLE, WAS KILLED BY DEATH. SO FIGHT THE CRIME? I MUST.
NO! I'M A FRIEND!
BEN, I WILL AVENGERS YOUR DEATH...
...BECAUSE I'M YOUR FRIENDLY SPIDERHOOD NEIGHBOR-MAN!
HELP! THINGS ARE BAD!
OH--BAD THINGS AREN'T GOOD! TIME TO FIX THIS. FIX WITH SPIDERS!
NEW YORK
NEW YORK
NYC

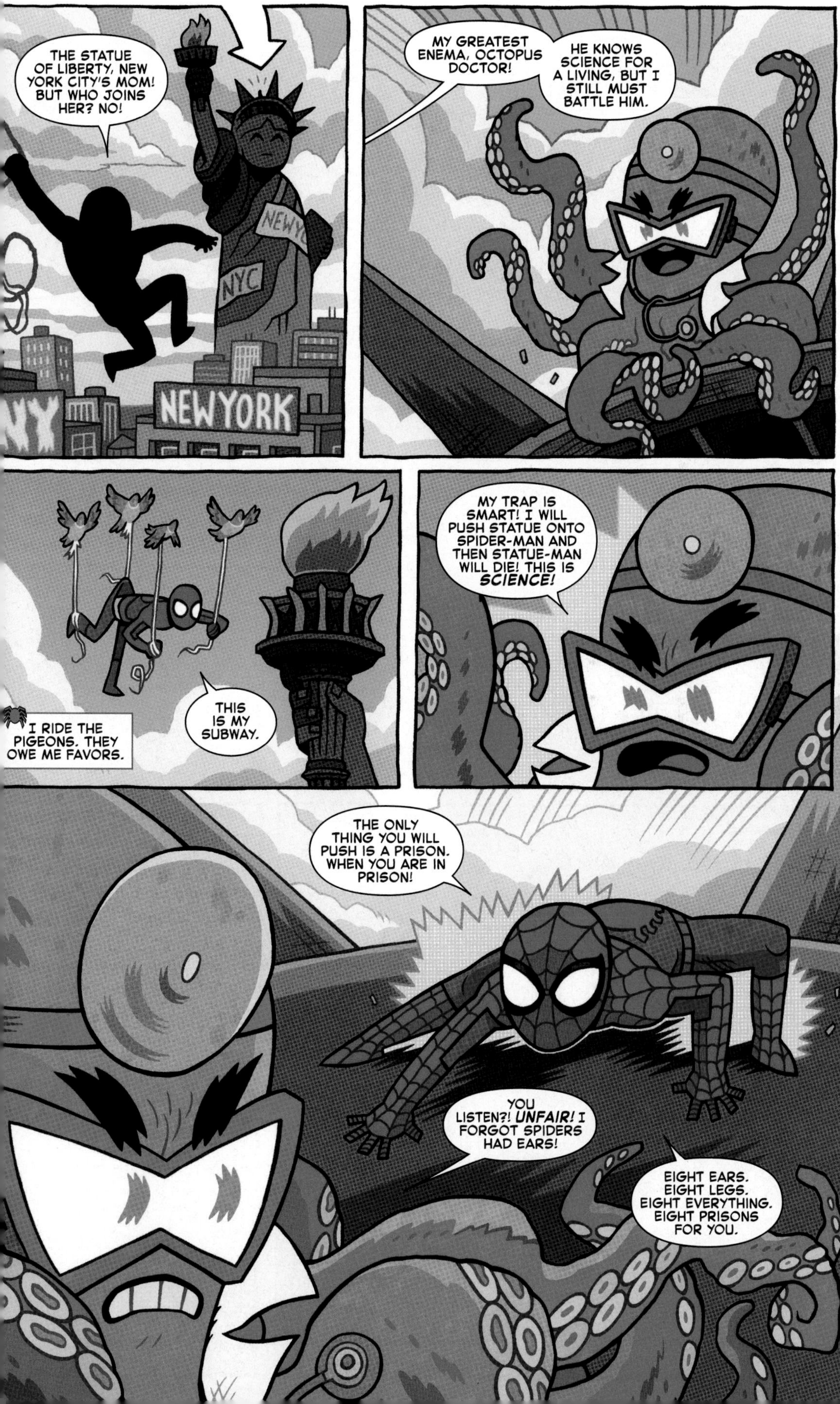
THE STATUE OF LIBERTY, NEW YORK CITY'S MOM! BUT WHO JOINS HER? NO!
NEW YORK
NYC
NEW YORK
MY GREATEST ENEMA, OCTOPUS DOCTOR!
HE KNOWS SCIENCE FOR A LIVING, BUT I STILL MUST BATTLE HIM.
I RIDE THE PIGEONS. THEY OWE ME FAVORS.
THIS IS MY SUBWAY.
MY TRAP IS SMART! I WILL PUSH STATUE ONTO SPIDER-MAN AND THEN STATUE-MAN WILL DIE! THIS IS *SCIENCE!*
THE ONLY THING YOU WILL PUSH IS A PRISON. WHEN YOU ARE IN PRISON!
YOU LISTEN?! *UNFAIR!* I FORGOT SPIDERS HAD EARS!
EIGHT EARS. EIGHT LEGS. EIGHT EVERYTHING. EIGHT PRISONS FOR YOU.

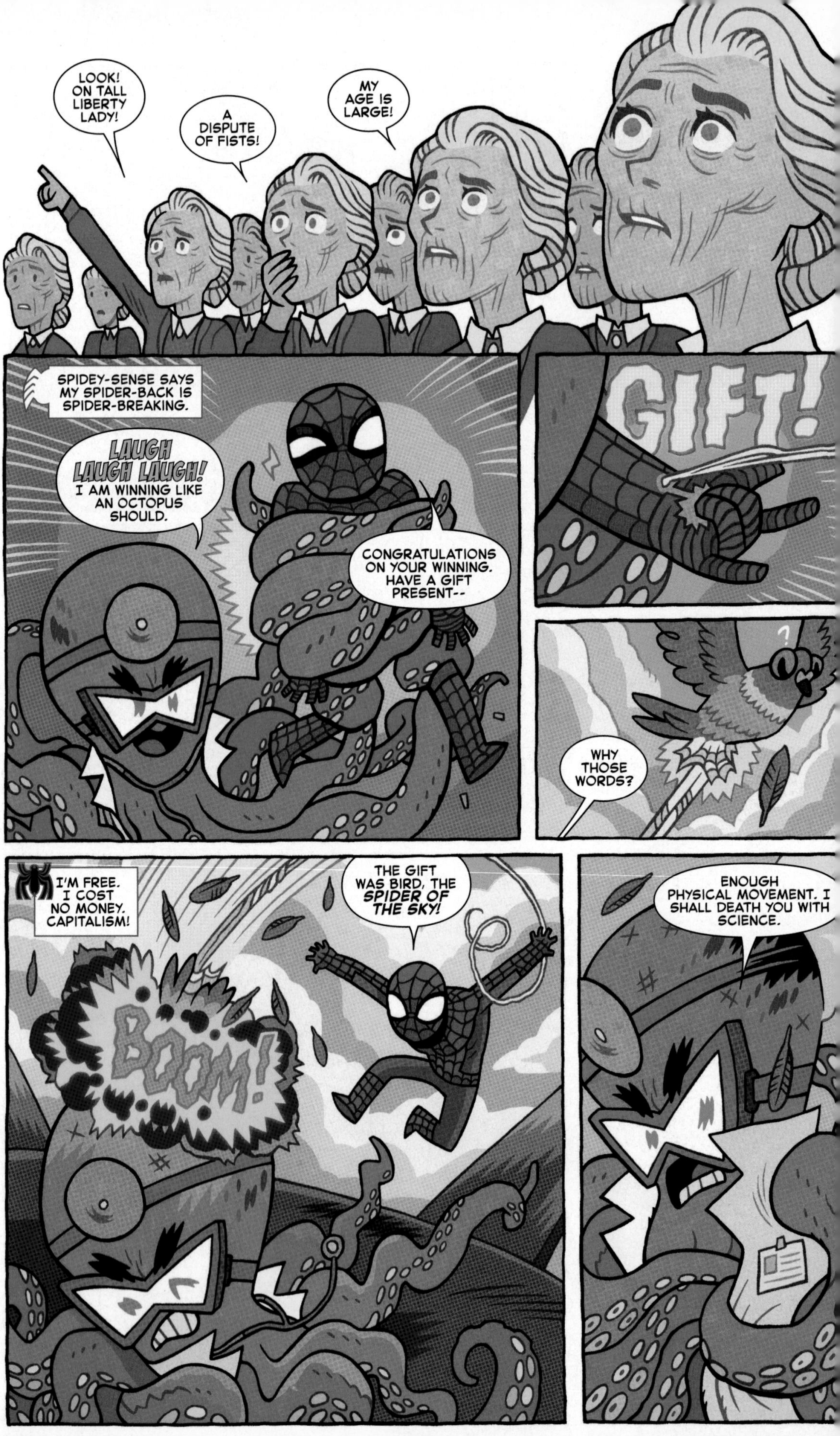
LOOK! ON TALL LIBERTY LADY!
A DISPUTE OF FISTS!
MY AGE IS LARGE!
SPIDEY-SENSE SAYS MY SPIDER-BACK IS SPIDER-BREAKING.
LAUGH LAUGH LAUGH! I AM WINNING LIKE AN OCTOPUS SHOULD.
CONGRATULATIONS ON YOUR WINNING. HAVE A GIFT PRESENT--
GIFT!
?
WHY THOSE WORDS?
I'M FREE. I COST NO MONEY. CAPITALISM!
THE GIFT WAS BIRD, THE SPIDER OF THE SKY!
BOOM!
ENOUGH PHYSICAL MOVEMENT. I SHALL DEATH YOU WITH SCIENCE.

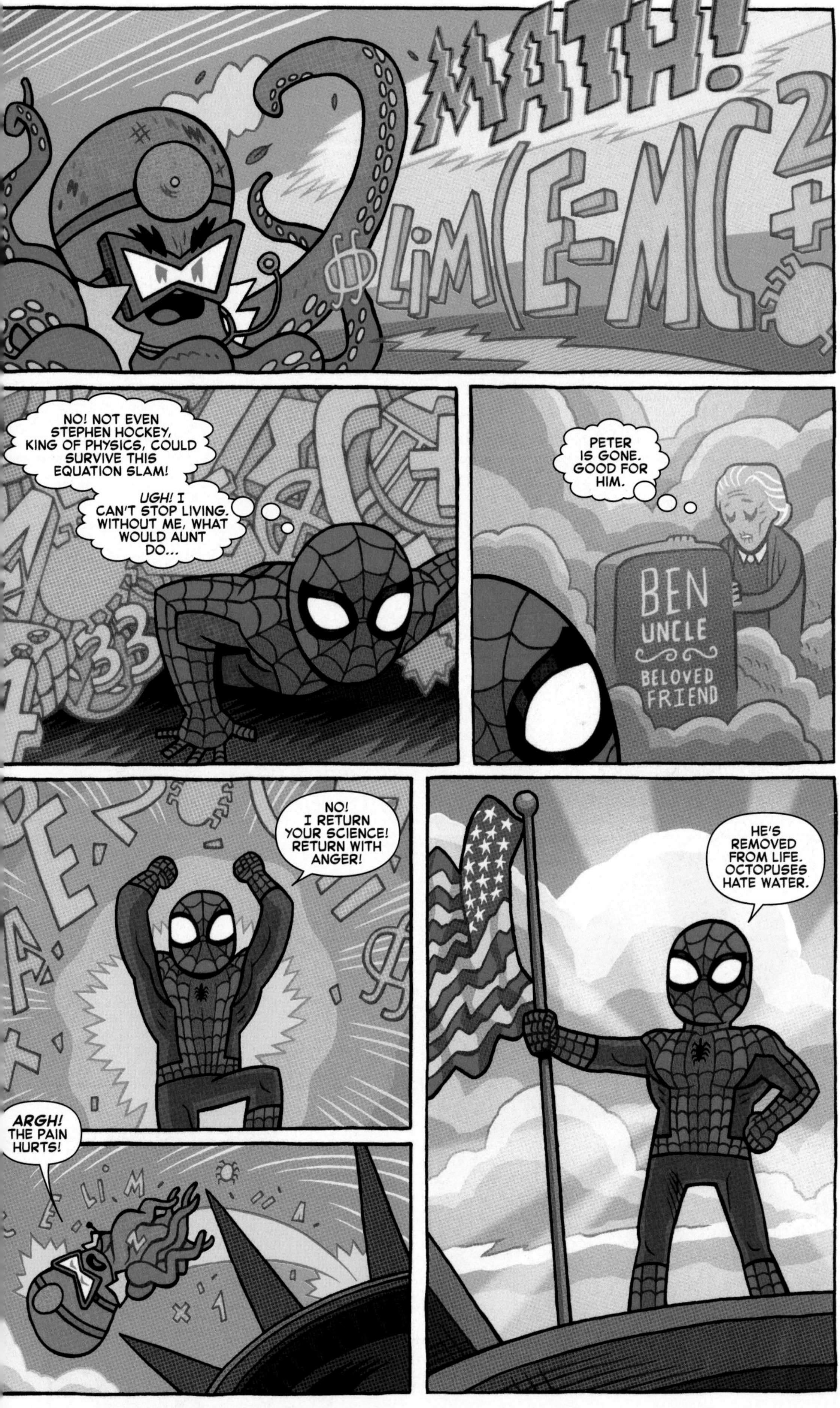
MATH!
LIM(E-MC2+
NO! NOT EVEN STEPHEN HOCKEY, KING OF PHYSICS, COULD SURVIVE THIS EQUATION SLAM!
UGH! I CAN'T STOP LIVING. WITHOUT ME, WHAT WOULD AUNT DO...
PETER IS GONE. GOOD FOR HIM.
BEN UNCLE BELOVED FRIEND
NO! I RETURN YOUR SCIENCE! RETURN WITH ANGER!
ARGH! THE PAIN HURTS!
HE'S REMOVED FROM LIFE. OCTOPUSES HATE WATER.

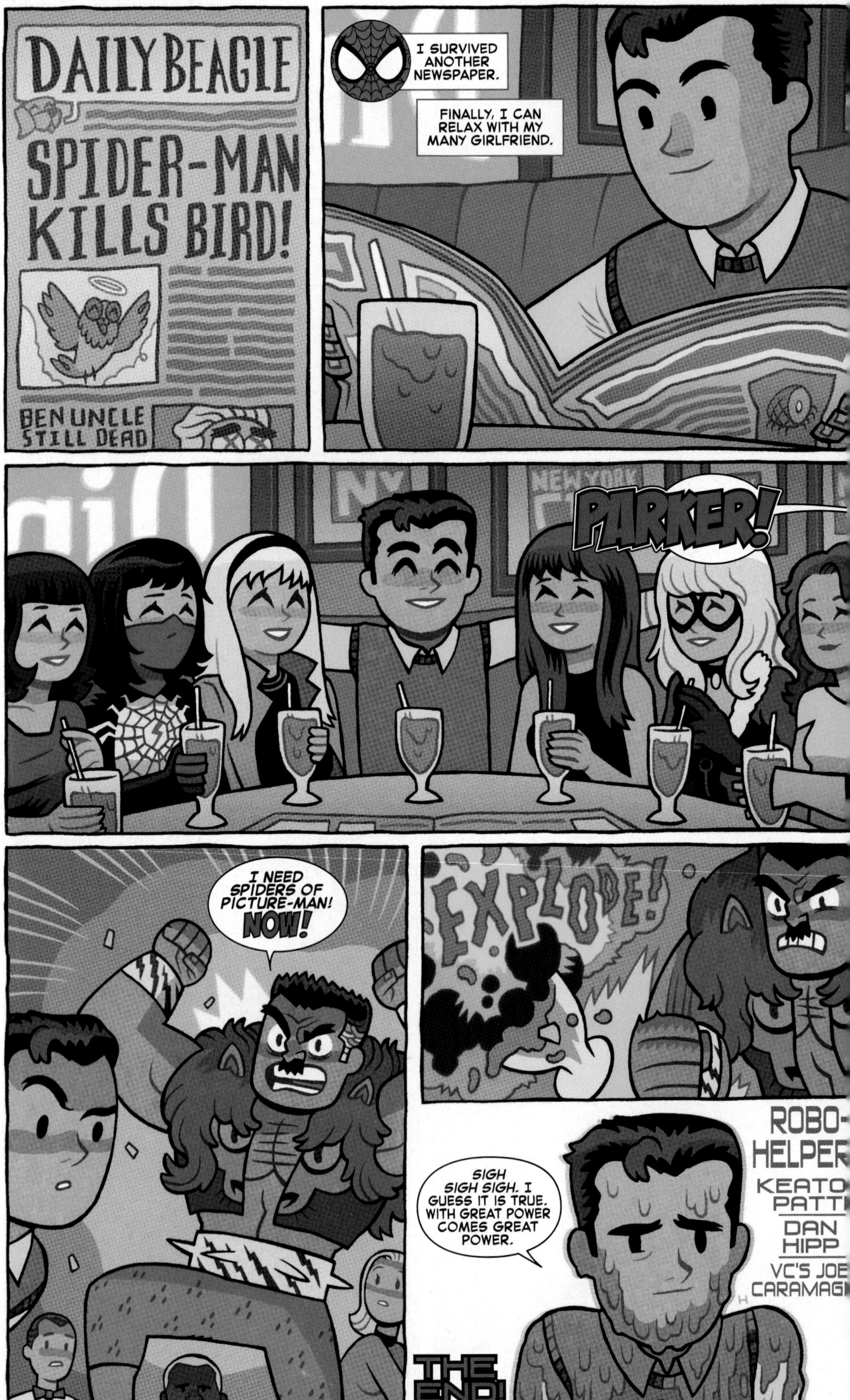
DAILY BEAGLE
SPIDER-MAN KILLS BIRD!
BEN UNCLE STILL DEAD
I SURVIVED ANOTHER NEWSPAPER.
FINALLY, I CAN RELAX WITH MY MANY GIRLFRIEND.
PARKER!
I NEED SPIDERS OF PICTURE-MAN! NOW!
EXPLODE!
SIGH SIGH SIGH. I GUESS IT IS TRUE. WITH GREAT POWER COMES GREAT POWER.
THE END!
ROBO-
HELPER
KEATO
PATTI
DAN
HIPP
VC'S JOE
CARAMAG

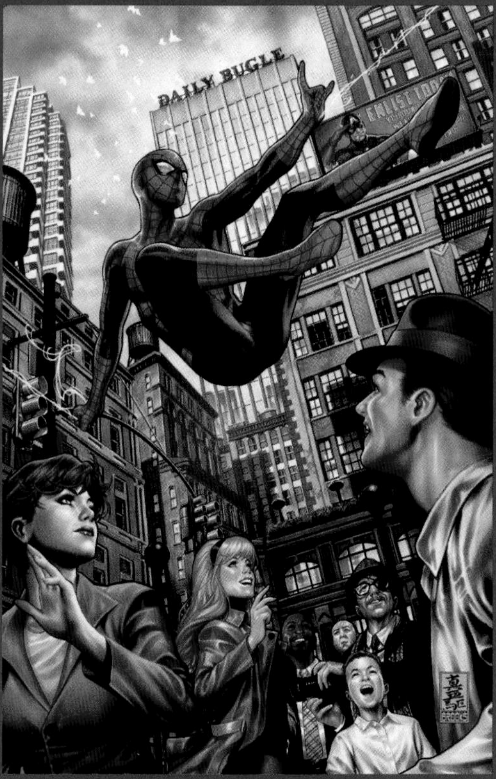
DAILY BUGLE

#24 *MARVELS* 25TH TRIBUTE
VARIANT COVER BY MARK BROOKS

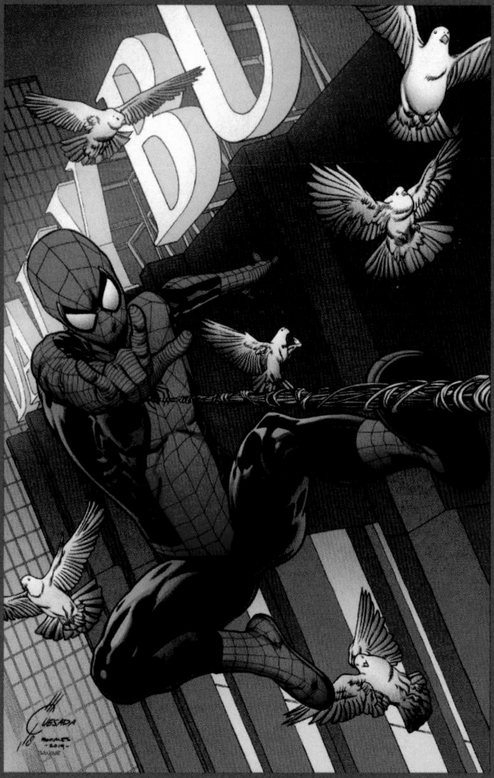

#24 VARIANT COVER BY JOE QUESADA,
MARK MORALES & RICHARD ISANOVE

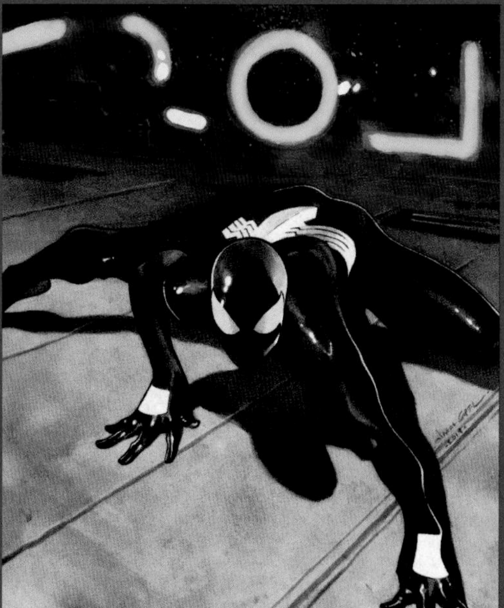

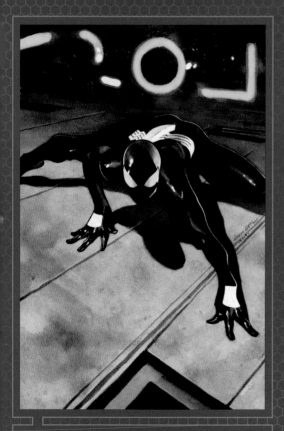

#24 SPIDER-MAN SYMBIOTE SUIT
VARIANT COVER BY OLIVIER COIPEL

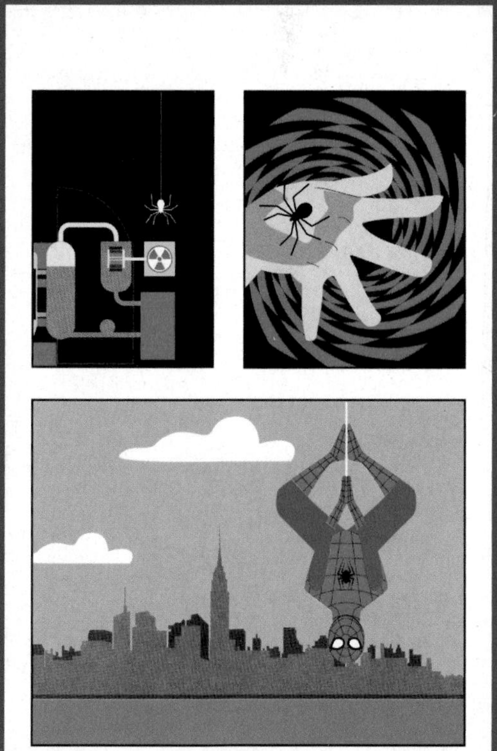

#25 POP CHART VARIANT

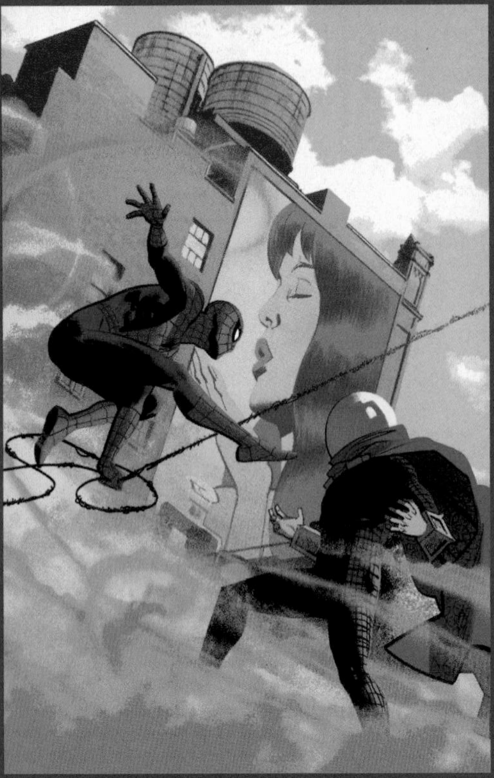

#25 VARIANT BY GREG SMALLWOOD

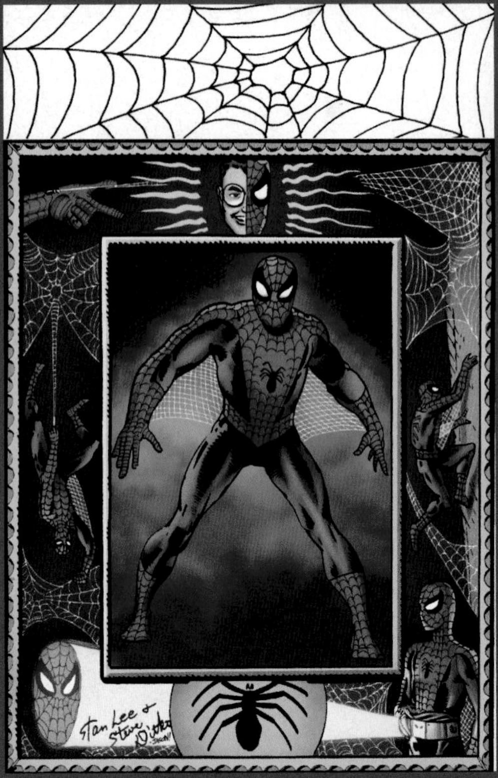

#25 HIDDEN GEM VARIANT
BY STEVE DITKO & JASON KEITH

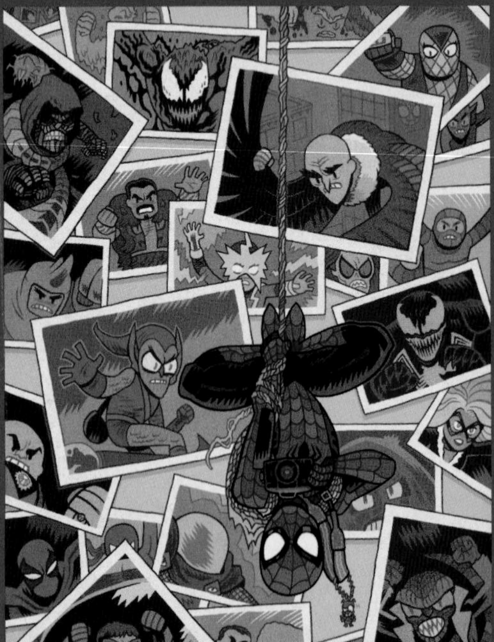

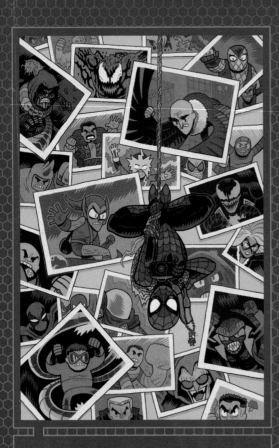

#25 VARIANT BY DAN HIPP

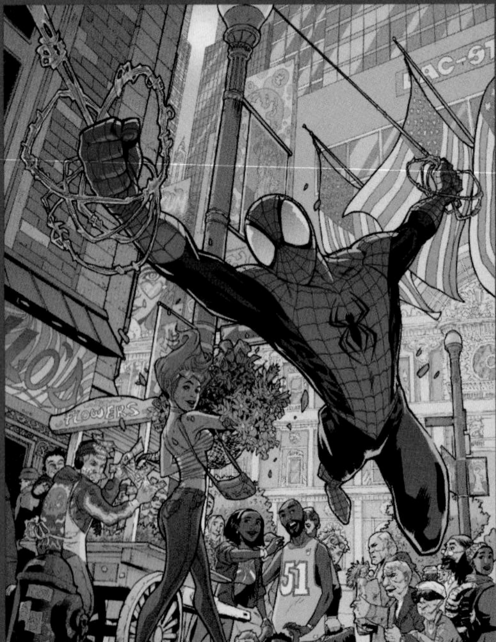
FLOWERS
51

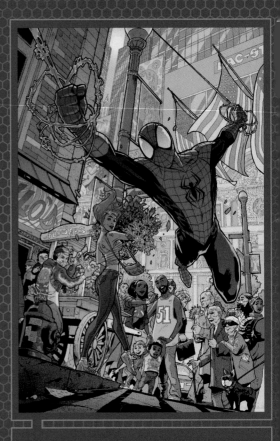

#25 VARIANT BY PAT GLEASON & DAVE STEWART

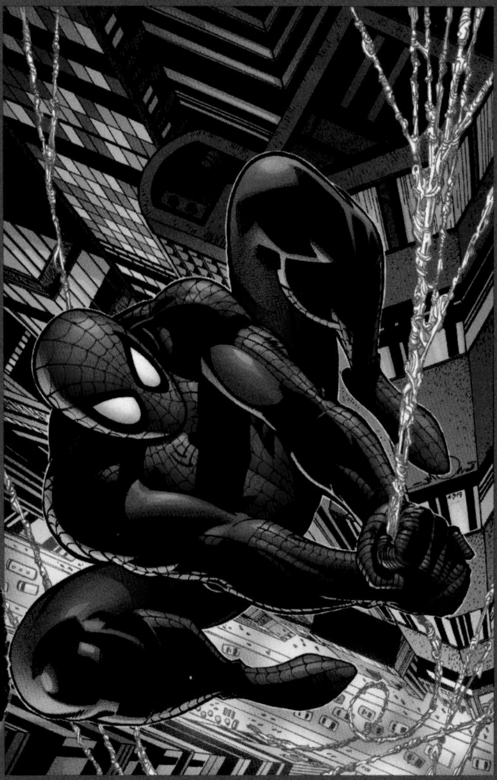

#25 VARIANT BY WALTER SIMONSON & LAURA MARTIN

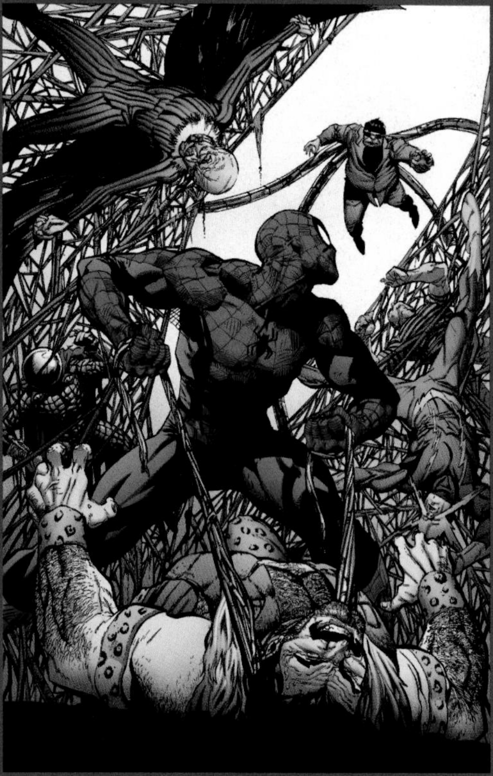

#25 VARIANT BY RYAN STEGMAN & RICHARD ISANOVE

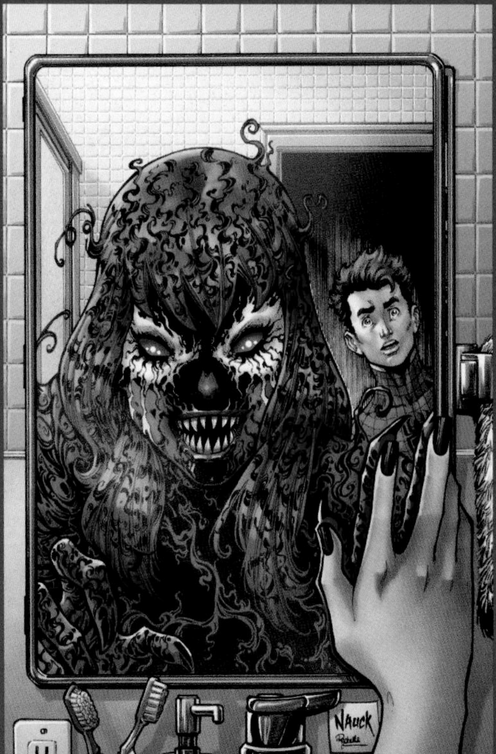

#25 CARNAGE-IZED VARIANT BY
TODD NAUCK & RACHELLE ROSENBERG

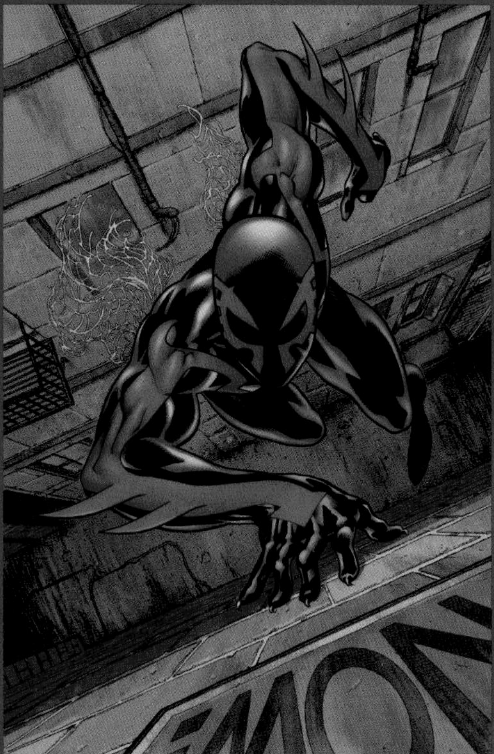

#25 2ND PRINTING VARIANT
BY ED McGUINNESS & DAVE STEART

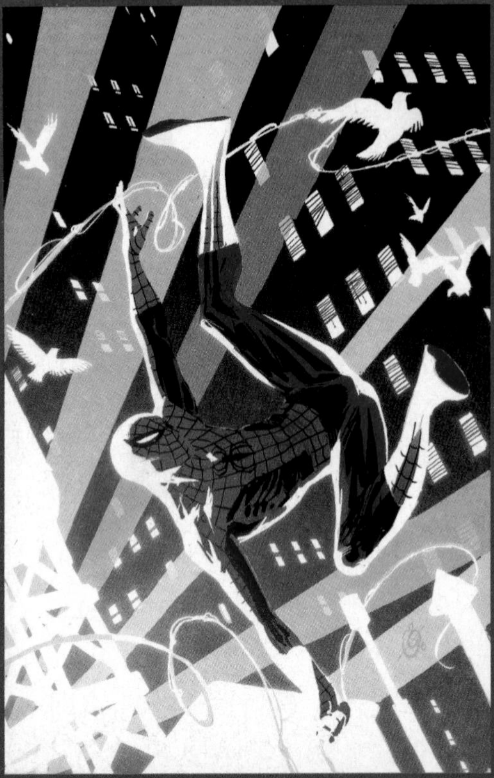

#26 VARIANT BY
RON GARNEY & MATTHEW WILSON

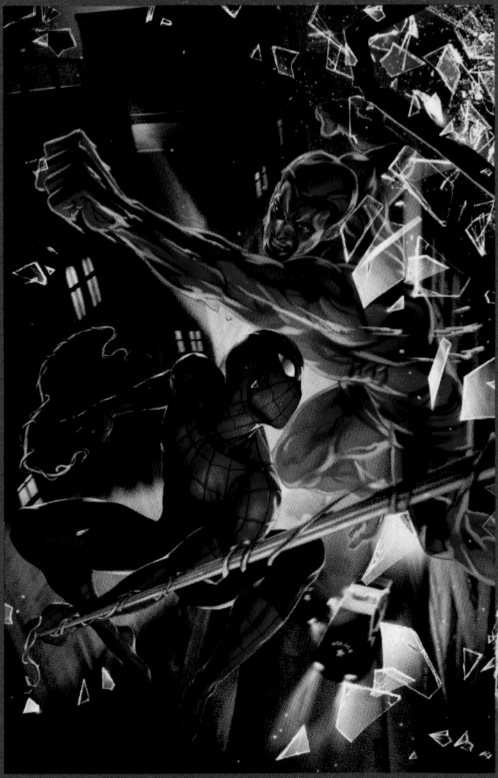

#27 BRING ON THE BAD GUYS VARIANT
BY WOO-CHUL LEE

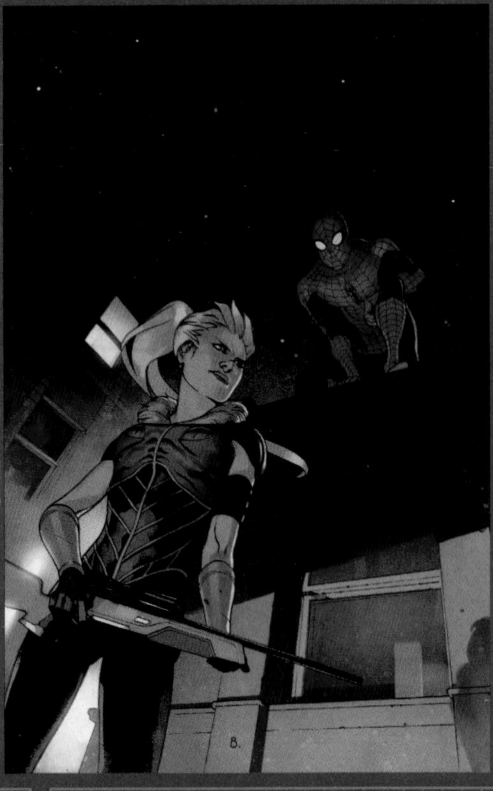

#28 BRING ON THE BAD GUYS VARIANT BY BENGAL

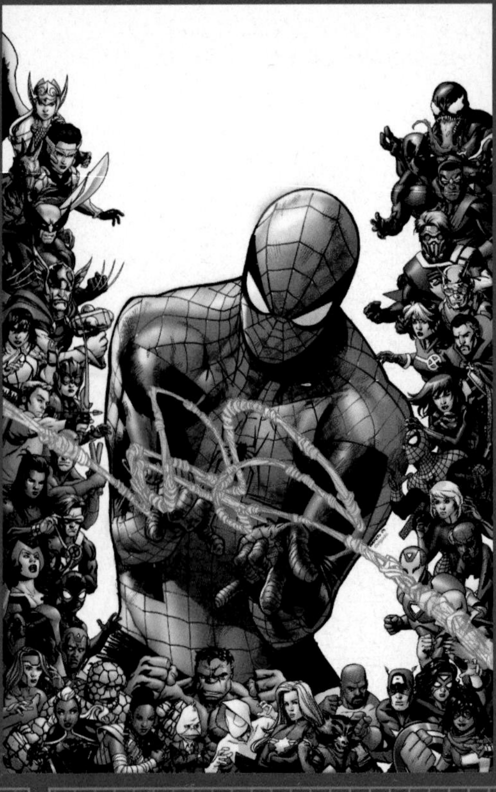

#28 MARVEL 80TH FRAME VARIANT BY
HUMBERTO RAMOS & EDGAR DELGADO